MW00666872

Pg 127
GEORGETOWN

PAGE 1?
VICTORIO
JUH
GERONIMO

PAGE 115
GUNMAN
DAN TUCKER
1879

Pg 97
SECESSION OF
Ag CITY - ~1876

Pg 115
NMT
GOVERNOR
AXTELL

Pg 39
1868

Pg 41
PEOPLE

Pg 104
APACHE
RELOCATION

Pg 65
1871
MASSACRE

RALSTON = SHAKESPEARE

Page 73
1872
GEN HOWARD
&
JEFFORDS

Six-Guns and Single-Jacks

A History of Silver City and Southwest New Mexico

Bob Alexander

GILA
BOOKS
www.gilabooks.com

Gila Books
PO Box 191
Silver City, NM 88062
(505) 538-4374
fax (505) 534-4134
sales@gilabooks.com
www.gilabooks.com

Castaway Media

A Division of Castaway Media

Manufactured in the United States of America

Library of Congress Control Number: 2005925314

Paperback edition ISBN: 0-9765728-0-X
Limited-edition (400 copies) hardcover edition ISBN: 0-9765728-1-8

Contents

Introduction by Robert G. McCubbin v

Preface and Acknowledgments vii

Chapter 1:
"I am an Apache, a Warm Springs Apache" 1

Chapter 2:
"These Indians Must Be Well-Flogged" 14

Chapter 3:
"Hell, Boys!...There's Plenty of It!" 35

Chapter 4:
"From Hell to Breakfast" 50

Chapter 5:
"That Go-Ahead Town" 68

Chapter 6:
"Jack Has Skinned Out" 84

Chapter 7:
"A Dead Game Hombre" 102

Chapter 8:
"Popped Him and Killed Him Right There" 123

Chapter 9:
"$100 for Every Head of Any Indian" 139

Chapter 10:
"A Man's Life Goes for Naught" 158

Chapter 11:
"Well Mounted and Armed to the Teeth" 176

Chapter 12:
"I Fired One Shot... as They Passed the Corner of the Corral" 196

Chapter 13:
"New Mexico... Produces the Champion Breed of Liars" 211

Chapter 14:
"Notoriety for Shooting and Shooting Scrapes" 230

Chapter 15:
"A Dirty Deuce in a New Deck" 247

Notes 267

Bibliography 299

Index 307

Introduction

By Robert G. McCubbin

Nestled in the foothills of the wild Mogollon Mountains of southwestern New Mexico, Silver City remains today, as it has been throughout history, a destination rather than a stop-along-the-way. Isolated by inhospitable mountains and desert, the area has nonetheless seen a parade of remarkable people and events in its long history. It has a story that has been crying to be told. Now, at long last, Bob Alexander has once again done meticulous research and given us the fascinating and thoroughly documented account of Silver City and Grant County that we have long awaited.

From the time Spanish soldiers first traveled to the unexplored region in the early 1700s, seeking to punish the troublesome Apaches, to the days of the outlaws and gunfighters at the close of the 19th century, here is a story rarely equaled in the history of the Old West.

A hunting ground of the Apaches for centuries, the area saw its first permanent settlers in the Spanish, attracted by the extensive copper deposits. American trappers came for the beaver in the mountain streams. The discovery of silver in 1870 brought a rush of American miners, and the sleepy village of San Vicente became the boom town of Silver City. Later, cattlemen from Texas found good ranges for their longhorns nearby. All along, the Apaches contested these intruders, making it a tough and dangerous country in which to survive. It was therefore peopled by tough adventurous individuals ... and that is a big part of why its history is so interesting.

The reader will recognize familiar names in the history of Silver City, one of which is none other than "Billy the Kid." It was here that a very young "kid" named Henry Antrim was first jailed for a minor "crime," and thus began an adventurous, lawless life that has propelled him into one of the most famous people in American history. The silver boom town of Tombstone, just across the border in Arizona Territory, shared many of its notorious desperadoes with Silver City during the 1880s. All in all, the area had more than its share of genuine outlaws and gunfighters, interestingly brought to life by the author.

Although dominated by the violence and the lawlessness, there is much more to the Silver City story. The author gives us just enough of everything so we get a complete picture of the people and events that have brought Silver City and Grant County to where they are today. Still an isolated area, its beautiful setting and excellent climate today attract people to live and retire there. The violence is gone but there is still evidence everywhere of its exciting history and it is always worth a visit.

As a long-time enthusiast of Western history, I can assure the reader he will find new and interesting facts in this well-told and thoroughly documented chronological account of a previously neglected area of the Old West. This book will join the other important works of Bob Alexander, all of which the reader will want to add to his library. Bob, in a few short years, has joined the ranks of the foremost writers in the field of Southwestern history. We are grateful for his untiring efforts to ferret out much of the little-known history that has been buried away in old newspapers and dusty archives awaiting someone such as he.

Robert G. McCubbin
True West Magazine

Preface and Acknowledgments

Mentioning the names "Tombstone" or "Dodge City" or "Deadwood" straight away conjures up Old West images. "Silver City, New Mexico," does not. It should! For a time—50 years or so—Silver City was the stage for Wild West drama of the first order, with a cast of colorful players numbering in the hundreds. They were not actors, though, and the set was not a sham. There was nothing counterfeit about the people or the place.

Although their concept of historical accuracy may or may not be somewhat askew, there are very few people who have not heard of the mythically romanticized Earps; the nattily dressed Bat Masterson; "Wild Bill" Hickok and his ivory-handled pair of fire-belching Colt's sixguns; or that baffling little icon of badmen, Henry Antrim, aka "Billy the Kid." For that demographic segment fortunate enough to have grown up with Westerns on the silver screen and television, the visual experience proved formative—much more than just an enjoyable way to pass time. The Western was America's morality play. Whether a clean-shaven hero was based on an actual historical character, or was wholly artificial, he inevitably sported a white hat, straddled a dandy horse, wore starched shirts, carried an engraved and limitlessly loaded six-shooter, and got the girl. He did no wrong. Comparatively, the badman could do not right. And he was easy to recognize: Aside from his abhorrent acts of unadulterated devilment such as actually shooting adversaries in the back or orchestrating a cowardly bushwhacking, he never smiled, but always sneered. The obligatory sweeping dark mustache was as conspicuous as his absence of a soul. The villain's hat was black. His horse and saddle were black. Often he carried a blacksnake bullwhip to accentuate his meanness. Needless to say, he never got the girl. The message was not subliminal; it was deliberately clear.

Those dashing cavaliers wearing the pristine Stetsons were a paradigm for virtue, worthy of emulation: flawless characters blessed with honesty, integrity and, perhaps above all else, unwavering courage. One and all they were kind to little children, compassionate to the less fortunate, and always perfect gentlemen in the company of dainty ladies. Many smoked hand-rolled cigarettes, but none ever drank whiskey to excess, if they took a drink at all. With certainty it was understood they never swore. Those Old West heroes were how fathers vicariously imagined themselves, and what they wanted sons to grow into. Conquering evil was relatively simple: Do right, live right, and everything would turn out right.

Of course, measuring "right" was subjective. Murder and stealing, cattle rustling and cheating at stud poker, whoring and wastefulness were universally acknowledged as objectionable behavior. Subjugating a Native American population during the self-ordained quest for a "Manifest Destiny" presented more thorns than answers, but for our Western morality play the solution was, once again, quite simple. In the end, the good guys won, and the good guys weren't Apache, Comanche, Cheyenne or Sioux. Indisputably, by no means were all of the Mexicans living in Old Mexico bandits, nor were their relations who were born north of that troublesome international line, but that proved a hard truth for profit-mined movie producers and/or scriptwriters to corral, much less to effectively market.

The oft-used phrase that "history is written by the winners" is not bogus. Neither is a declaration that America's avid fascination with the Western was generally a 20th-century phenomenon. The fact that 19th-century literature sometimes focused on the frontier West is not arguable. Yes, there were skillfully written books, sensational dime-novels, over-the-top theatrical productions and breathtaking Wild West shows, but it would be during an age of modern communications [radio, movies, television] when the West's allure was wholesaled and carried to virtually every household. So, then, the realm of fabricating champions and the compulsory chore of fashioning convincing scoundrels—their personal antagonists—was left to moneyed entertainment moguls. They passed out the halos and the pitchforks. Likewise, it was they who ordered up the backdrop, be it extraordinarily vivid panoramas for a thrilling "on location" Indian War epic, or an Old West town's dirt Main Street laid over asphalt in a Hollywood backlot. It was an illusion. But, maybe, leading up to World War II and just afterward, it was what most American folks needed. Decency winning out over decadence, despotism and deceitfulness is not necessarily a bad theme, especially when it's mixed with stirring action scenes absent the shedding of any real blood. Fidelity to historic truthfulness? Well, that bothersome little ingredient was many times inconvenient and, besides, who really wanted to accept as fact that many of the authentic cutting-edge Westerners wore gray hats? Sometimes they drank hard liquor to the point of foolishness, were occasionally racially bigoted, sneaked around on their wives, were shrewdly opportunistic, and were adept at twisting truthfulness to fit their needs. Fair play was relative. For those times a barking Colt's sixgun was brought into play, it was usually already in someone's trembling hand before the shooter even issued the obligatory warning, "Go for your gun, you son-of-a-bitch!" Almost within that same breath the revolver bucked in thunderous recoil. It was a grand plus, to fire first! The legendary storybook "Code of the West" was, in fact, fairly malleable.

Sadly, noteworthy Old West personalities and locales were overlooked during that mad dash to the pay window, the cashing in on fiction rather than factuality. Silver City, New Mexico Territory, is but one sterling example, but she's a good one. For whatever reason, Silver City got short shrift in the Western annals devoted to frontier hot spots. Silver City and her outlying suburbs were a quintessential model for all that a first-class Western had to offer—good and bad. Many Western towns are but ghostly reminders of the past, and others seem to limp along selling outdated postcards and cheap knick-knacks, while a few—a very few—proudly and profitably proclaim the intrinsic, aesthetic and historical worth of their rightful inheritance of an Old West heritage. Plainly it may be seen now that Silver City has simply outlasted many of her municipal rivals. Longevity speaks well. The road to permanency, however, has been rough and rocky. For a chronicle based on a Western premise, it may be rightly tendered that during Silver City's palmy days there wasn't a town anywhere in the American Southwest that could surpass her as a wild and woolly neighborhood. Due to geographical juxtaposition, Silver City lay in mining country, cattle country, cowboy country, Indian country and outlaw country. She was, if any town was, emblematically positioned perfectly for Old West high drama.

Renowned explorers and boundary commissioners had crisscrossed the area and left their mark before the town even had a beginning—or a name. Silver City was grown atop the very southwestern ground tramped by well-known Apache combatants such as Cochise, Mangas Coloradas, Victorio and Geronimo. Each and every one played a not-insignificant role in Silver City's bold and bloody historic legacy. Celebrated United States Army men like General George Crook, Edward Hatch, Henry Carroll and Albert P. Morrow knew her hospitality—and her hubris. Renowned ranchers imported, exported and valiantly guarded their vast Grant County herds from natural and some not-so-natural shrinkage.

Names now inscribed on the roster of infamous outlaws and lawmen walked her dusty streets and warped boardwalks. Silver City was the site for Billy the Kid's first quantifiable brush with the law. Wyatt Earp and Doc Holliday rode into town, too, sporting false names and a fear of being arrested for crimes committed in the Arizona Territory. Curly Bill, John Peters Ringo and John Kinney, "the King of the Rustlers," were no strangers to Silver City's barrooms and bordellos and blustery past. Skipped over by 20th-century pastime promoters were some of the so-called "lesser lights" of southwestern New Mexico. These hard men had every much real regional name recognition as those speciously puffed-up scalawags: James W. "Six-Shooter" Smith, Jimmy McDaniels, "Wild Bill" Martin, Bob "Nelson of the Gila" Nelson, Robert "Bob" Martin, George "Buffalo Bill" Spawn, Charley Small, "Dutch Joe" Hubert, John W. Gilmo, "Three-Fingered" Jack Dunlap, Hugh Martin Childress, Jr., Joel Fowler, Anthony "One-Arm" Price, Tom Bowe, Carson "Kit" Joy and that ever-deadly frontier gambler, Frank Thurmond. They form part of the Silver City area's iniquitous list of ne'er-do-wells and killers and robbers—but barely begin the tally. Totaling the town's and county's scorecard for genuine gunfights, whodunit murders, senseless stabbings and head-thumpin' happenings is well-nigh an unworkable exercise, due to their near-everyday frequency.

Strolling Silver City's avenues with a town marshal's badge pinned to his vest was one of the Old West's toughest lawmen, Dan Tucker. Though today his name is known only to aficionados of serious outlaw-lawman history, during the time he lived and gunned men down on Silver City's streets Tucker was a living legend. Many others not of his stature subsequently sought greedy biographers and publicity agents during their twilight years. During the time they lived and fought, however, the figurative cuts on Dan Tucker's notch stick—balanced against blowhards' and braggarts' fallacious claims—makes them look like weak-kneed stepsisters. For bona fide and authenticated Western shoot-

'em-up theater, Silver City was the "real McCoy!"

But the frontier town was much more than an amphitheater for meaningless and gratuitous early deaths, or battles with renegade Apache. Silver City, illustrative of the rootin' and tootin' variety of Old West towns, was likewise a superb pattern for how resilient and hardy pioneers—men and women alike—could cut from near nothingness a city of noteworthy import, one that boomed then and, despite harsh conditions and hard times, flourishes today. Silver City was a player. Unquestionably, the town should have its name near the top billing on any marquee. To not tell her neat story—at least the Old West part—is historically impolite. She is deserving of that much, settling a debt long laying in arrears.

Novelists have a distinct advantage over nonfiction writers. The former let their work stand as an expression of what naturally flows from within. They may take the full measure of credit, and rightfully so. The nonfiction folks have to stick to the truth. And finding those truths obligates the scholars, biographers and grassroots historians to seek courteous help from others. Expressing a heartfelt "thank you" is not laborious, nor is it difficult; realizing the very real possibility for an innocent omission is. In this instance, if it's happened no lame excuse is sufficient, and none will be proffered. Simply, it was unintentional and for someone thus slighted, I stand before you—hat in hand—and humbly ask forgiveness. The others, thankfully, have not been overlooked and will be mentioned by name.

Several years ago, during research for *Dangerous Dan Tucker: New Mexico's Deadly Lawman*, I made the acquaintance of a lifelong resident of Southwestern New Mexico. The helping hand he extended was gladly accepted, and because his reservoir of historical knowledge about Silver City and old Grant County is bottomless, the underpinnings for a book-length story were set. In subsequent historical projects, his rallying around research tasks has proven invaluable and indispensable. Much more important than the contribution to my journalistic stabs at giving certain Old West characters and places their due is his camaraderie. I am proud to call Terry Humble of Bayard, NM, a friend. My life is better for knowing him. To not single him out for proper adulatory remarks depreciates his gift to this, Silver City's tale of vibrancy, heartaches and triumph. Regionally he is widely known for his expertise. Now, after his publication of a dynamite story in the National Outlaw/Lawman Historical Association *Quarterly*, Terry's innate talents will be recognized outside the local area. Good luck, my friend!

Certainly the name Robert G. "Bob" McCubbin requires no introduction to Western devotees. Bob is co-publisher of *True West* magazine. Perhaps, however, Bob is more universally recognized as *the* authority on Old West photography. Bob McCubbin's personal knowledge about those old-time photos does not border on the legendary—it *is* legendary! Bob is known throughout the world for his outstanding collection of photographs, books and primary documents. Writers, historians, documentary film makers and quizzical novices turn to him for a myriad of problem-solving answers. When broached with the request to review this manuscript and, perhaps, write an introduction, Bob nonchalantly replied in the gentlemanly demeanor he is so very well known for: "I'd be honored." The reader will be the beneficiary of his comments—as well as for the many photographs Bob furnished for this volume. Likewise, thank you, my friend.

Other Old West nonfiction authors [and a book dealer] play a role in all I do writing-wise, and they, too, are esteemed personal friends. Frequent, indeed, are the telephone calls, letters and electronic communications when specific answers are sought, or when an idea simply needs a bouncing around. Continually I am in historical debt to: Robert K. DeArment, Sylvania, Ohio; Chuck Parsons, Luling, Texas; Leon Claire Metz, El Paso, Texas; Harold L. Edwards, Bakersfield, Calif.; John and Karen Tanner, Fallbrook, Calif.; Michael Hickey of Talei Publishers, Inc., Honolulu, Hawaii; Mark Boardman, Lafayette, Ind.; Paul Cool, Eldersburg, Md.; Bill O'Neal, Carthage, Texas; Don Bullis, Rio Rancho, NM; Sharon Cunningham, Union City, Tenn.; Donaly Brice [as a writer], Lockhart, Texas; Paula Mitchell Marks, Austin, Texas; Sunny and Dakota Livesay, *Chronicle of the Old West*, Show Low, Ariz.; Roy B. Young, Apache, Okla.; Bob Pugh, The Trail To Yesterday Book Niche, Tucson, Ariz.; and that consummate researchin' and writin' expert on those plucky Hoo Doo War boys who started six-shooter careers during a Texas feud, but ended up in turbulent southwestern New Mexico and southeastern Arizona, Dave Johnson of Zionsville, Ind.

More particularly in Silver City, assistance for this undertaking was wholly dependent on the highly competent cooperation from four individuals. They, not surprisingly but characteristically, stepped up and squared off with the challenges. Susan Berry, director of the Silver City Museum, as always, shared her time and knowledge in highlighting several ancillary topics that are normally not the bailiwick of Old West writers zeroing in on the more violent aspects of frontier societies. Susan's well-reasoned perspectives added that balance so necessary to make Silver City's saga round, as it should be. Working in conjunction with Susan at the marvelous museum is Jim Carlson, curator of collections. Ever amicable and a highly proficient authority on the comprehensive assemblage of early-day Silver City and Grant County photographs catalogued in the institution's archives, Jim displays a collegial dedication that is not undervalued or unappreciated. The reader will at once recognize his touch while thumbing the pages and enjoying the delightful old-time photographs contained herein. The Miller Library in Silver City's Western New Mexico University is the working home for Cookie Stolpe. She is a first-rate professional, a friend and one of the linchpin researchers for tellin' Silver City's captivating story. Cookie, never, not once, shied from hunting down the most obscure historic tidbit. And she did it with a smile. Another library employee played well his part, too. Peter "Piñon" Crum, reference librarian at Silver City's Public Library, is a friend who knows not indifference, not when it comes to historical sleuthing. As with other projects Pete has helped out on in the past, he never winced when that very "last request" was made—time and time again! He wanted to see the town's story told, and he did his part, above and beyond the call of an overworked research librarian's everyday duty. He, like Cookie, Susan and Jim, is an asset to Silver City. They, one and all, are tenaciously dedicated to preserving the town's more than illustrious history.

So very many others added their individual help. They are deserving specific mention by name: Sibel Melik, archivist, New Mexico Commission of Public Records, State Records Center and Archives, Santa Fe; Nancy Brown, Zimmerman Library, Center for Southwest Research, University of New Mexico, Albuquerque; Amy Verheide, Museum of New Mexico, Santa Fe; Heather Dominick, Arizona Historical Society, Tucson; Linda Offney, Yuma Territorial Prison State Park, Yuma, Ariz.; Robert Richardson, National Archives, College Park, Md.; Alisha Mauldin, United States Military Academy, West Point, NY; Donaly Brice [as an archivist], Texas State Library and Archives Commission, Austin; Dean Holloway, secretary, Silver City Lodge No. 8, AF&AM, Silver City; Gail Hall, Lordsburg-Hidalgo Library, Lordsburg, NM; Sylvia Ligocky and Art Roman, archivists, Deming Luna Mimbres Museum, Deming, NM; Dick Staley, El Paso Public Library, El Paso; Jim Bradshaw, Nita Stewart Haley Memorial Library and History Center, Midland, Texas; William M. Bishop, Jr., Murrieta, Calif.; John Keibel, historian, Wells Fargo Historical Service,

San Francisco; Wayne B. Humphrey, Deming; Amos and LaDorna Chenowth, McNeal, Ariz.; Roy B. Sinclair, Jr., El Paso; and sketch artist H. C. Stinson, Maypearl, Texas.

Lastly, an especially warm thanks must be extended to Jan Devereaux, a fellow writer of Old West stuff, but more important, the person I share my life with. To enumerate all of the positively helpful suggestions and recommendations she made concerning this, the Silver City story, would comprise an ad infinitum list. So, too, would be the reasons I admire and respect Jan, professionally and personally, publicly and privately.

Bob Alexander
Maypearl, Texas
2005

Six-Guns and Single-Jacks

Chapter 1

"I am an Apache, a Warm Springs Apache"

With a fervently revealing shout—"Hell, boys! If that's silver, I know where there's plenty of it!"—an Old West story of extraordinary meaning began. Those exclamatory remarks were bedrock dialogue for a grandly exhilarating yarn about the future town of Silver City, New Mexico Territory. By corollary extension, then, the words too were harbinger for telling frontier Grant County's thrilling story.

The riveting chronicle of Silver City is a legitimate example of everything a wild and woolly West had to provide. There is no need for fiction. Fabrication is not necessary. Journalistically creative melodrama would—in light of the truth—prove comic. That in the tawdry beginnings she was a raw, blustery and lascivious mining camp is not arguable. That she was a borderland town absent barrooms and bordellos would be naive misnomer. That from time to time steely-eyed shootists, desperadoes, cardsharps, cowboys, hardscrabble miners and sinfully painted ladies walked her delightfully shaded streets is indisputable. Sporadically, they fought and gouged, bit and clawed, and sometimes even shot each other. Demonstrably the whole scorching section was "the gunfighter proving ground of the Southwest...the blistering cauldron where so many Wild West gunmen made their reputations." Even the beleaguered territorial governor at vibrant Santa Fe cynically admitted that southern New Mexico was "a catch basin for rogues."

During those early years, there were several legal hangings—and a few not so legal. Moreover, the era and area were the ghastly scenes of seemingly incessant and scary Indian forays. Feted US Cavalry officers chased after warrior chiefs for fame and flattery; renowned Apache fighters raided and ravished for respect and revenge. From both camps, legends were born. As she steadily matured, however, unlike so many of her short-lived sisters, those cutting-edge mining and cow camp towns, Silver City came of age with an aura of eternalness. Her founding fathers had been atypical. From the outset they had demonstrated surprising farsightedness, and, as it has so skillfully been described, Silver City was indeed "built to last." The picturesque community would endure despite hardship and hazard, in large part due to the resilient spirit of her pioneering folks. They were single-minded and they weren't quitters. In an abbreviated structure, this simple try is her story—and theirs.[1]

It may seem somewhat shabby, historically, but highlighting the Old West is genesis for the theme of this narrative. There will not be too many words expended explaining geographical fault patterns, archeologically excavating ancient cliff dwellings or anthropologically classifying fragmentary shards of prehistoric pottery. Plainly, it may be rightly said that southwestern New Mexico was—millions of years ago—underwater. After the seas had receded, geological upheavals violently fashioned the imposing mountains and yawning canyons, and starkly unforgiving desert floors were uncovered. In her wake Mother Nature gladly or grudgingly left behind precious deposits of copper, gold and silver. The very first human inhabitants of the region, however, were not seeking mineral wealth; they were primitive hunters and gatherers, collectively known as the Mogollon culture. They traipsed about perhaps 5,000 years ago. Gradually settling in, they became an evolving identifiable subgroup and showed themselves to be first-rate architects. Their defensible homes high in the cliffs and hidden chasms appeared impenetrable and permanent. Slowly perfecting rudimentary farming techniques and, over time, honing skills as superb craftsmen in the art of basket and pottery making, this cutoff culture was seemingly destined for everlastingness. It was not to be![2]

Lamentably, there cannot be a pinpointing with exactitude of when, why or where the Mogollon people went. Theories cannot yet rise above the level of mere speculation, no matter how logical or well-intentioned the ideas may be. What is certain is that by 1300 AD a living Mogollon culture had vanished from the Southwest. Whether the disappearance was rooted in meteorological pressures such as prolonged and devastating draughts, or etched ecologically with the transgressions of overindulgent mismanagement and the depletion of natural resources is immaterial for the story at hand. The Mogollon people evaporated into the abyss of prehistoric murkiness.[3]

Next came the Apache. Anthropologists and historians are not unanimous about the time period or the impetus for the Apache first appearing in New Mexico. One hypothesis credits changing demographic patterns elsewhere during several centuries after the Mogollons' disappearance: To the northeast—on the Southern Plains—because of sheer numbers, keen trading acumen, the unparalleled adaptation to an energetic horse culture and a mastery of mounted warfare, fierce Comanche fighters displaced the nomadic Apache. Always a wandering people, the Apache moved on, this time to the south and southwest.[4] In the vastness of West Texas, New Mexico, Arizona and Old Mexico, the various Apache subdivisions over generations marked territorial boundaries and made what others would later record as their history. That normally is the saga and historic epoch so familiar to readers captivated by nonfiction Westerns. Realistically, sans any stab at requisite political correctness, the Apache left a bold and brave record—but, justly or not, it was also a bloody legacy. Pithily, a truth of the times was spoken: "Until I was about 10 years old I did not know that people died except by violence. That is because I am an Apache, a Warm Springs Apache."[5] And it was the Warm Springs Apache that swarmed at will throughout southwest New Mexico Territory, the focal point for this true-life Old West tale.

Unfortunately, early Apache history was anchored solely by storytelling and tradition rather than by any written record.[6] Other wanderers would serve as historians for the time period. Of course—and understandably so—their voluminous handwritten manuscripts, reports and proclamations were shaded by ethnocentric beliefs, viewpoints and value systems. Their abundant writings were penned in the language of their homeland, Spanish. Their expectant bronzed faces were covered with flawlessly trimmed beards black as the devil's heart. Their breasts were protectively encased in glittering armor. Their fantasy-filled heads sported polished helmets festooned with flashy plumes. They sat astride fiery mounts dancing with barely restrained eagerness, in spite of the fact that horses, too, were weighted by a buffer of chain mail. They had boldly ridden into the Southwest for gold and for God. They were the *Conquistadors*.[7]

Audaciously during that summer of 1540, the Spaniards had marched into a mysterious new world. In the caravan's vanguard rode the vigorous commander, Francisco Vásquez de Coronado, 32 years old and governor of Nueva Galicia, Mexico's northernmost settlement. The trailblazing explorer was supported by 300 likewise willing blue-blooded adventurers and more than a thousand Indians doggedly laboring as "scouts, sappers, servants, herdsmen, horse wranglers, camp cooks or in other occupations." Lumbering in the "drag" were some 1,500 animals burdened with packs, "the baggage, arms, provisions, munitions and other things necessary for the journey." Straggling and sprawling even farther behind were generous numbers of cattle and sheep, the "walking commissary." Guaranteeing a workable rationale of righteousness for the extravagant export of Christianity and the manifest geographical expansionism of New Spain was the contingent of clergy. Four friars meandered along with the cavalcade, imparting divine wisdom and standing at the ready to convert the soul of any "savage," by force if need be. Topography that 300 years later would become New Mexico Territory was changed forevermore during that first 16th-century *entrada*—as were her indigenous people.[8]

Coronado's probing arc had bypassed southwestern New Mexico. Over the ensuing decades, Spain's New Mexican awareness had been raptly concentrated on coveting, conquering and converting. Pueblo Indians living along the life-giving Rio Grande River were the recipients, rightly or wrongly. The commerce and traffic and Spanish settlements that grew over time from the embryonic exploratory incursions were fixed along a north-south corridor, next to the river. Dawdling travel between the Taos/Santa Fe section and Chihuahua City and Mexico City, although an exhaustively slow trudge, was a myopic pathway between poverty and possibility. Slogging passage on *El Camino Real*—The Royal Road—mushroomed.[9] After the stubborn elapse of nearly a full century, yearning Spanish eyes at last were cast toward the heretofore neglected southwestern expanse of New Mexican colonization.[10] The inquisitive glimpse was not aimed at acquiring worldly treasure, but was calculated for Christianizing the heathen and pagan Apache.

Fray Alonso de Benavides, irrevocably convinced that Satan had possession of the Apaches' spirits, determined it was his mandate to drive the demon from their bodies and consciousness by converting the natives to Catholicism. Missions had been founded since the very beginnings of the Spanish incursion into *Nuevo Mexico*. In his desire to "undertake nothing less than the spiritual conquest of all of North America," Benavides broadened Mexico's religious frontier.[11] Meeting western Apache, those not formerly blessed by unwavering missionaries or touched by the Cross, enlivened the vow of Fray Alonso. Sanaba, a leader of what were then referred to as the *Gileño* Apache, frequently left his headquarters on the headwaters of the Gila River [north of present day Silver City] to visit the Piro Pueblos in the temperately agreeable Rio Grande Valley—to gamble.[12] Purportedly, Sanaba listened intently as Benavides preached of righteousness and the coming of Christ. Just how much Sanaba truly understood may be debatable but, temporarily, this was the gateway event for his affably entertaining a friar in the Upper Gila country. The anticipated mass conversions failed to take place, however. After availing themselves of the padre's knowledge about planting crops, the *Gileño* Apache nudged him back to the more settled vales—intact. Other clerics during New Mexico's turbulent infancy had not been so well-treated. Many were martyred.[13] Apache were warriors, not worshipers, as the Spanish interlopers would soon surmise.[14] Before the close of the 18th century, in 1796, a lieutenant colonel in New Spain's army would characterize Apache males: "The man knows no other obligation than that of the hunt and of war...The Apache is proud of nothing, except of being brave, this attitude reaching such a degree, that he despises the man of whom no bold deed is known...the *Gileños* and *Mimbreños* actually are the boldest."[15]

All through the 18th century, the Spaniards persisted in their struggle to salvage savage souls and widen their exploratory acquaintance with the Southwest. Prying into remote southwestern reaches of New Mexico as early as 1712, an embattled Gov. Ignacio Flores Mogollon ineffectively tried to chastise Apaches who had been pillaging villages along the lower Rio Grande. During the century's last quarter the Spanish sponsored at least four strategic tours throughout an area that would in due course wrap scenic Silver City.[16] Tabulating figures of New Mexicans killed by Indians during lightning-strike raids, it may be accurately and sorrowfully registered that the decade of the 1770s would prove the century's bloodiest.[17] Any attempt to precisely tally deaths of Apaches killed in retribution swiftly runs up against the apathetic vagueness of their adversaries.

On New Spain's northern frontier, Apache marauding and mayhem were the plague of failed policies and jaded judgments, on top of already unpromising inherent cultural dissimilarities. "Raiding, which brought prestige as well as economic benefits to Apaches" portended a thorny ethnic cross-current the Indians were loathe to discard.[18] The wily Apache fought and fled. The Crown's loyal soldiers stalked and skirmished—such as, notably for this Old West story, the 1785 Apache-chasing expedition of Don Antonio Cordero. The triumph of this military campaign was not closing with an ever-elusive enemy, but rather the discovery of extensive deposits of uncorrupted copper extruding to the surface: "In New Mexico we know of copper mines of rare purity, where not even a fifth of the ore is lost as dross."[19]

Lieutenant Colonel José Manuel Carrasco served under Cordero during that 1785 soldiery campaign nosing southwestern New Mexico. Perhaps on that jaunt he made this fateful finding utterly independently, but local oral tradition suggests otherwise, crediting a friendly *Gileño* Apache with first showing Carrasco the earth's treasure. That assertion is backed up by a primary source.[20] In any case, as the 19th century beckoned, Carrasco retired his military commission at Janos and, assuming the role of a budding entrepreneur, outfitted an expedition for ferreting out underground riches. In the sacred shadows of a New Mexican landmark, the Kneeling Nun, Carrasco made his noteworthy mark:[21] The ex-soldier and hopeful capitalist established one of the American

Don Francisco Manuel Elguea's triangular walled fortification near the *Santa Rita del Cobre* copper mine. Later, after American acquisition of New Mexico, it was designated Fort Webster. *Courtesy National Archives.*

Southwest's legendary and enduring excavations, the *Santa Rita del Cobre* copper mine. Two centuries later, she is still surrendering her wealth—financially and historically.

It would be another Spaniard, however, who had the monetary wherewithal and no-nonsense forethought to began tapping *Santa Rita del Cobre*'s far-reaching potential. The unexploited reservoir of raw high-grade copper was immense, but the pulling-out process was labor-intensive—much, much too costly for middleman José Manuel Carrasco. Stepping into the vacuum with a near-bursting purse was Don Francisco Manuel Elguea, a prosperous and politically connected merchant from the city of Chihuahua, the heart of New Spain's trading link with the northernmost provinces. By 1804, ownership of the copper mine had transferred to Don Francisco.

Imaginatively, Elguea soon cracked the shortfall labor nut. En masse, convicts were hustled out of dark and dank Chihuahuan jails and prisons. Guarded by military troops dispatched from Janos, the inmates were promptly conveyed to *Santa Rita del Cobre*. The site was wholly cut off from the rest of the world, bounded by a remorseless and thirsty landscape. It was also a hazardous zone brimming with merciless Apache. Just to get there, as one early voyager reminisced, was like "going through the gates of Hell."[22] Resourcefully, with tenacious labors directed at solving his dual dilemmas—keeping the prisoners in and the Apache out—Elguea built a substantial triangular stronghold, an adobe fort. High walls four feet thick jutted 200 feet in three directions, boldly protruding for juncture with the circular and ported watchtowers at each corner. For a man-made structure, the very first built with adobe brick in what would later become the Silver City vicinity, it looked imposing and muscular.[23] Strategically situated along a canyon leading to the mine, the earth-toned edifice was not only a realistic fortification but also a symbol—an elaborate pictogram that a new people were entrenching themselves. As many as 50 adobe houses, sheds and corrals popped up within protective gunshot range of the citadel. The forward step of progress on a raw northwestern frontier, once more, was at hand for New Spain.[24]

For *Nuevo Mexico*—during the Spanish reign—*Santa Rita del Cobre* would be the only thriving and truly lucrative mining venture.[25] And flourishing it was! Tightly cinched with crossbuck packsaddles and each carrying two 150-pound ingots of costly copper, some 20,000 mule loads would make the friendless march to Chihuahua City. Months later the packtrains managed an exacting reverse route, carrying much-needed provisions for the mine and the men.[26] For 40 years *Santa Rita del Cobre* was a vital component of Mexico's struggling economy. Most of the metal used in minting her coins came from the mine.[27] *Santa Rita del Cobre* was, then, plainly of umbilical importance.

Nearby, sharp-eyed Apache watched the burgeoning hubbub with anticipatory awe. By necessity and profession they were excruciatingly patient and sly opportunists. Stealth and blinding surprise were their trademarks. Incredibly, so it must have seemed, those laughable Spaniards were bringing horses and mules, guns and powder, pots and pans, beads and bauble—and whiskey—to the Apaches' secluded backyard. The forecast for tradin' and takin' was good. Whenever fleeing prisoners, military deserters, muleteers, freighters, woodchoppers, women, or charcoal-burners foolishly miscalculated, their reward was a vigilantly executed Apache ambuscade. Prospects were plentiful—pity in short supply.

But maybe those seemingly ludicrous Spaniards weren't so green after all. Deplorable decades of genocidal warfare with *indios bárbaros* on New Spain's northern frontiers had forced a rethinking of their Indian policy. Out-and-out appeasement was the solution. Deceptively, it was underpinned with a tricky sleight of hand. Adopting a new approach based largely on earlier models of English and French diplomacy, the Spanish opted to alter course, changing from an undoable plan of absolute eradication to a workable stratagem of cultural division, destruction and dependency. Feed 'em rather than fight 'em. Substitute buying 'em for battling 'em. Assimilate 'em versus annihilate 'em. Furnish them meat and wheat! Give them plenty of unwieldy long-barreled guns and gunpowder by the keg, thus weaning Apache warriors from the much more—in skilled hands—operatively efficient and deadly bow.

There was, however, a straightforward caveat: Firearms supplied to restless Apache must be of antiquated vintage and/or of inferior workmanship. Over time, then, the barbed arrow would be replaced by malfunctioning arms compelling the skilled services of duplicitous Spanish gunsmiths. And, too, dole out intoxicants by the barrelful, generating an addictive taste for the fiery liquor and a corresponding pathetic dependence on the Crown's double-dealing whiskey dispensers. Apache not wanting to play the new game were to be searched out and slaughtered. "It was at once a highly sophisticated, brutal and deceptive policy of divide and conquer, of peace by purchase, of studied debilitation of those who accepted peace and of extermination of those who rejected it. However, it was also, at long last, a practical policy and one which offered both races the opportunity for survival."[28]

Admittedly, the Spanish change in Indian philosophy had taken place shortly before the feverish notice of *Santa Rita del Cobre*'s latent copper possibilities. The upending of a timeworn equation for dealing with Apache raiders was at hand. Make not a mistake, though, it was a shaky truce. There were still murderous raids and wholesale livestock thefts. Cutoff mules and miners were simply mouth-watering targets—too good to forgo.[29] Generally there was, however, an air of tenuous tranquillity for a period approximating 25 years. It was not to last!

Much as American colonists had done nearly a half-century earlier, Spaniards and native-born Mexicans living in New Spain stridently clamored for out-and-out independence. They got it in 1821. A free and self-governing Mexico was born. With the sovereignty came the setback. Politically free from the Crown, Mexico unavoidably had to take her eye off the Apache ball and develop a game plan for dealing with real and imagined infringements by cunning European and American expansionists. The practical posture for dealing with Apache in the northern districts—in light of a hemorrhaging national treasury and diplomatic diversions—would drastically shift. The phenomenon was magnified with the materialistic opening of that historic highway, the Santa Fe Trail. The welfare program ran out for the Apache of southwestern New Mexico

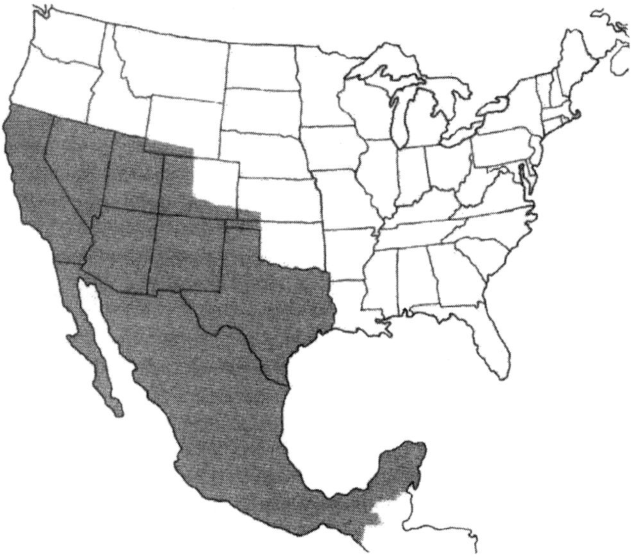

Left: Mexico in 1830, after independence from Spain. From *Border: The US-Mexico Line.* *Courtesy Leon C. Metz.*

and northern Mexico, as American fur trappers and traders rushed in. A very real nuisance was brewing in another of Mexico's northern frontier regions: Texas was a mess. For the spreading-out-minded folks from the United States, zealously getting hold of more land, Manifest Destiny was in full sway. Apache and Mexicans alike would suffer the sting.

In due time, adventurous American fellows made their appearance in southwestern New Mexico, trapping for beaver pelts along the zigzagging Gila River. Characterized as a "reckless breed," the mountain men recurrently made *Santa Rita del Cobre* their seasonal layover point. As a lot, they were all colorful characters. Most are buried in anonymity. Some few earned fame with now familiar names. Several capitalized on jotting down breathtaking and sometimes exaggerated memoirs. Well before Silver City was birthed, men such as Kit Carson, Bill Williams, Hiram Allen, Sylvester S. Pratte, Ewing Young, Sylvester Pattie, his son James Ohio, and an audacious Frenchman, Michel Robidoux, tramped the area laying traps and plans.[30] Varyingly they swapped or scrapped with area Apache.

Christopher "Kit" Carson. As a young man he roamed southwestern New Mexico, and for awhile was a teamster at the *Santa Rita del Cobre* copper mine. *Courtesy the New Mexico History Museum, #7151.*

With an influx of English speakers, it is understandable that Americanized tags were soon used to differentiate between various Apache subgroups. The Apache referred to themselves as *N'de* or *Inde*, the "People." Spaniards, Mexicans and Americans plainly knew them as *Apache*, the Zuni Indian word for "Enemy." For the present story, Apaches of the Chiricahua sorting are spotlighted in the historic lens, as opposed to Mescaleros, Jicarillas, Lipans, Kiowa-Apaches, Western Apaches or Navahos. The Chiricahua Apache were subdivided into four bands, cut along geographical lines: The Nednhis, the "Enemy People" of the northern states of Sonora and Chihuahua, were screened in the nooks and crannies of Mexico's daunting Sirrea Madres; Chokonens, the "Ridge of the Mountainside People," roamed the Peloncillo, Dragoon, Dos Cabezas, Chiricahua and Huachuca mountain ranges of what would later become that perpetually troublesome New Mexico/Arizona/Mexico borderland country; Bedonkohes dwelled in the ominous-looking Mogollon Mountains along the Gila and San Francisco river sections; and the poised but poisonously dangerous Chihennes, the "Red Paint People," roved little-known New Mexico west of the slashing Rio Grande and south of the striking Datil Mountains. Frequently the crafty Chihenne established *rancherías* [Apache camps] in the Black, Mimbres, Piños Altos, Mogollon, Victorio, Florida and Tres Hermanas mountain ranges. Collectively, Southwestern New Mexico's Apache were known as Chiricahuas, or sometimes in bastardized Anglo slang as the "Cherrycows." The farthest southeastern cluster, the Chihennes, to local Americans and Mexicans alike were commonly identified by localized nicknames. They were the Copper Mine Apache, or *Ojo Caliente* Apache, or Warm Springs Apache, or Mimbres Apache, or Red Paint Apache or—among several other labels no doubt—the *Mimbreño* Apache.[31] Together the four bands of Chiricahua Apache would extract a bitter and bleeding toll in exchange for the Anglos' lasting excursion into the American Southwest. The Mexicans paid even more dearly.

So searing had Apache raids become in the Mexican states of Sonora and Chihuahua that desperation rattled reasonableness. On April 22, 1837, 32-year-old John James Johnson, a former hatter from Kentucky but then a trapping and trading denizen at Oposura [Moctezuma], Sonora, Mexico, wrought a workable but dastardly plan. Barely across the southern border in New Mexico's Las Ánimas Mountains, accompanied by 17 Anglo cronies and five Mexican packers, Johnson parleyed with *Mimbreño* Apache boss Juan José Compá and his hard-edged band. When the time was right, James Johnson lit the fuse on a swivel gun loaded with shrapnel that had been hidden under a packsaddle. Death's work not done by the cannon was finished with rifles, six-shooters and Bowie knives. Apache captains Juan José Compá, Juan Diego Compá and Marcelo were killed, as were many other now nameless Apache warriors.[32] "Instead of taking the ears of all 20 of the Apaches killed and presenting them as *piezas*, as required by the Sonoran law of 1835, Johnson took the scalps of the above chiefs."[33] Payback was due!

It wasn't long in coming. "Soon after, the Indians wiped out the [Charles] Kemp party of 22 trappers [near the Gila]."[34] Farther east, the recalcitrant Apache attacked an El Paso del Norte-bound wagon train and massacred 12 teamsters. In Mexico, revenge-minded Chiricahua Apache captured horses and mules, kidnapped children and killed adults—men and women alike, including a local justice of the peace.[35] Mexican towns in their entirety were free-falling into the void of disrepair and desertion. Particularly fitting for Silver City's budding story, however, is the simple methodology brought to bear on *Santa Rita del Cobre*. An outright frontal assault wasn't necessary and, besides, Apache of all stripes were loath to abandon their hit-and-run tactics. Three factors presaged triumph at the copper mine for the assorted Chihenne Apache bands: First, the point of diminishing return had been reached, and financially the celebrated copper mine was in steep decline; production and transportation costs outweighed profits. Second, *Santa Rita del Cobre*'s sheer isolation was untenable; she was wholly reliant on provisions brought up from Chihuahua City, her lifeline. Third, the calculating Chihennes, like other Apache groups, could be uncompromisingly merciless to an enemy, a trait that invoked near panic in many nervous Mexicans' hearts and minds.

The Warm Springs Apache sarcastically boasted that they would allow southbound packtrains from *Santa Rita del Cobre* to proceed unmolested, laughingly declaring they "couldn't eat copper!" Northbound mules loaded with supplies, though, wouldn't be awarded that same exemption. Using the Florida and Tres Hermanas mountains 60 miles south of the mine as a staging platform, the Apache kept their word. Traffic on the well-worn road to *Santa Rita del Cobre* was snappily shut down. Mexican freighters, after just a few harrowing raids, forewent paying the blood-toll with lost cargo and stolen livestock. With an ever-tightening stranglehold, commerce at *Santa Rita del Cobre* was choked to a standstill. During that 1838 summer, the Mexicans deserted the copper mine. Some scribes write that many Mexicans were pitilessly killed during their flight. Others deny this bloody assertion. No matter, they were gone, long gone! The Chihenne Apache were now solitary tenants of Southwestern New Mexico—they had run the hated Mexicans off—and they were emboldened.[36]

Although it is unshakably a gruesome and legitimate chapter in southwestern New Mexico's lively history, this abbreviated backward glance at early Silver City will skip any explaining or justifying or making excuses for the wretchedly deteriorating Apache/Mexican state of affairs.

Correctly casting blame from days so fully removed is impractical and, frankly, impossible. Plainly, it was a different time and a different place. On the bloody ground the Apache raided and the Mexicans retaliated—and vice versa. Examples of personal valor were offset by instances of deliberate treachery and compassionless butchery from both blocs. In newborn Mexico, trading pacts between storming Apache bands and whole Mexican states—as well as smaller municipal subdivisions—were shrewdly and self-servingly accomplished. Many times the expedient trading deals were devastatingly disadvantageous to their own neighbors down the road or to fellow countrymen just across jurisdictional borderlines. Booty forcibly taken in one village was openly bartered for at a settlement nearby. Powerfully exploiting impoverished Mexican towns was par business for warlike Apache tacticians. Crying *niños* were snatched and spirited away to the Chiricahuas' hush-hush *rancherías*. Grisly bounties for Apache scalps were offered and paid. Ambushes and assassinations were commonplace; empathy and sympathy were not.[37]

Chapter 2

"These Indians Must Be Well-Flogged"

Officials of the central government at Mexico City had much more to worry about than bothersome Apache prowling the frontiers of the desolate northern provinces. Those land-grabbing guys working on behalf of the United States were busy again. Already, even before Mexico's independence from Spain, they had acquired that colossal landmass west of the Mississippi River, the Louisiana Purchase, from the French in 1803. At three cents a square mile it had been a real bargain. Just 15 years after shedding the Spanish Crown's yoke, Mexico had been aversely prodded—under force of arms—to yield a whole section from her northern state of Coahuila. Damn those unruly Texans! This time, with the advent of Texas' recent annexation, the 1846 quarrel revolved around which river would be used as the United States' international borderline, the Rio Grande or the Nueces. On April 23, 1846, Mexico's insurgency-installed president, Mariano Paredes y Arrillaga, declared a "defense war." The next day, Mexican cavalry General Anastasico Torrejón's men shot down US Army Captain Seth Thornton's horse and killed 16 American soldiers at the southern tip of Texas. General Zachary "Old Rough and Ready" Taylor then tersely messaged President James K. Polk in Washington: "Hostilities may be considered to have commenced. American blood has been spilled." The US Congress, after acrimonious debate between Whigs who opposed outright declaring war and Democrats who were unfalteringly loyal to the sitting president, on May 13 appropriated $10 million for Polk to call up 50,000 additional troops and bring an already "existing" war to a "speedy and successful termination."[38]

Seventeen months later, at war's end, the whole of *Apachería*, including New Mexico and her people, were re-tailored ad infinitum—squeezed into the mold of a government decreed by an American bureaucracy in

Washington, like it or not! The Mexican War, only the second major conflict the United States fought on foreign soil, had prompted military innovations: widespread use of proficient riflemen as an operationally strategic force and the hard service of an improved Colt's revolving six-shooter, the touted Walker model. Tactically fashioning horse-drawn light-artillery batteries—mobile and quick—were likewise novel devices for the US military. Amphibious landings at enticing Veracruz on Mexico's Gulf Coast and mountaintop combat at the country's breathtaking higher elevations were new chapters for American warfare. Many of America's military men were now first-rate professionals, career soldiers. As graduates of the national military academy at West Point, they were saber-rattling proud and they publicly revered their esprit de corps. Many of these dynamics, when taken in the cumulative, spelled a discernible upgrading of the nation's military strength. She was, in all her manifest

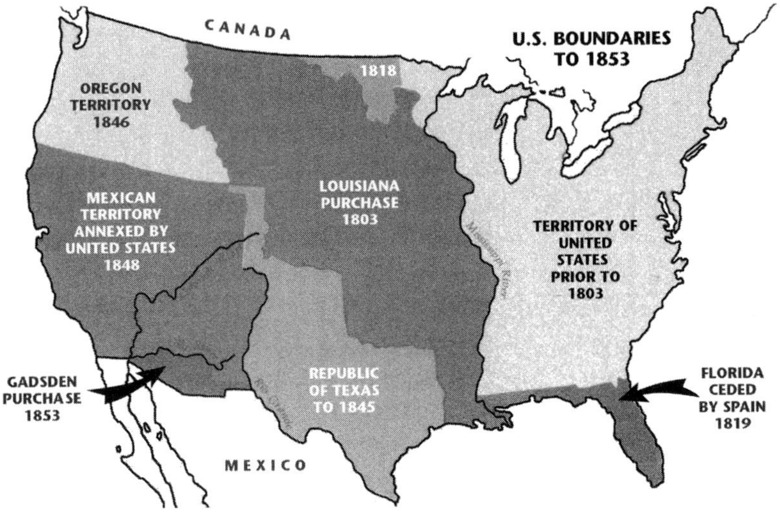

US borders to 1853. New Mexico as a part of the Mexican Territory was annexed to the United States after the War of 1846. From *Border: The US–Mexico Line. Courtesy Leon C. Metz.*

glory, a power to be reckoned with—from sea to shining sea.[39]

The war with Mexico had netted big geographical dividends. No longer was there any argument as to which watercourse defined a border with the Lone Star State. It would be the Rio Grande, all the way from the briny Gulf of Mexico near Brownsville, Texas, to a sandy point slightly north of pleasantly quaint, yet faraway El Paso del Norte. Furthermore, with ratification of the Treaty of Guadalupe Hidalgo and the stroke of a pen, Mexico had surrendered title to fully one-third of her entire country.[40] In the deal, which included a $15 million payment, she halfheartedly forfeited to the United States a fabulous frontier: New Mexico, California and "all the vast wilderness from the Rocky Mountains to the Pacific Ocean."[41] Sizewise it was a prize of a million-plus square miles, a "region nearly equal in size to the United States from the eastern seaboard to the Mississippi."[42] Another less tangible overhaul, too, was blowing in the takeover wind: Forevermore, New Mexico changed "from the easygoing Mexican way to the avaricious, restless, dog-eat-dog Yankee mode."[43]

Part of that American style of governance was bureaucracy building, and so in March 1849 the US Congress created the Department of the Interior. Responsibility for oversight of Indian affairs was placed under its umbrella, and various patronage positions were filled. Germane to this story was the April 11 appointment by Commissioner William Medill of the celebrated John Coffee "Jack" Hays, a former Comanche-fighting Texas Ranger and Mexican War veteran, as Indian Subagent on the Gila River.[44] With Jack Hays' commission came a daunting reality. Medill, somewhat out of character for most government types, freely acknowledged ignorance: "So little is known here of the conditions and situation of the Indians in that [Gila] region, that no specific instructions relative to them can be given at present."[45] Not out of step for a red-tape outfit, however, Hays was told that "the greatest economy shall be observed" and that only a $400 annual salary could be paid to his lone full-time employee, an interpreter, that being deducted from his yearly budget of $2,300. Making preparations for the trip, Hays quickly learned the funds would be insufficient and officially complained: "Its very remote position, and the enormous expense necessarily attending it must be apparent to you...and my own outfit has already far exceeded the allowance your instructions established."[46]

After an arduous trip, Hays landed in the vicinity of El Paso del Norte, making camp on America's side the evening of Sept. 8. For several days he desperately assembled meaningful data concerning the area farther west and its people. Not unexpectedly, the onslaught of brisk traffic to the promising California goldfields by a southern route—through El Paso del Norte—depleted local storehouse inventories and increased the merchants' takings. Prices were sky-high for the would-be millionaires, a fact Hays soon learned while replenishing his supplies. He, too, was made aware that "there was little or no gold along the Gila" and, for his especial attention, that "the Apaches were rising against the emigrants."[47] There, too, Hays bumped into an old comrade in arms, John Joel Glanton. The ex-Texas Ranger was by anyone's yardstick a frontiersman of the first order, but he had shamelessly degenerated into making his living by collecting bounty money from Mexican state governments for Apache scalps.[48] Glanton, recognizing the whopping profits to be made by dumping scruples and hunting for "hairy banknotes," started indiscriminately slaughtering any Indian, friendly or not. Mexican paymasters couldn't tell the difference. Sadly, he made his historic contribution setting aflame the Southwest with an Apache hatred for Americans, at least so says one chronicler.[49] Reportedly, out of admiration for Hays, Glanton the scalp-hunter agreed to temporarily suspend his border killings until Hays' party had an occasion to parley with Gila area Apache.[50] *¿Quien sabe?*

While at El Paso del Norte, the newly appointed subagent had a hush-hush meeting with another of the Southwest's most nefarious personalities, Peter Worthington—though when Jack Hays made his acquaintance, Worthington was known by an alias, Jack "Apache Jack" Gordon. If there ever was a bona fide renegade, this was one. "Gordon" was on the dodge for his part in an area killing, and while a fugitive in the lonesome country was captured by Apache. Almost defying belief, he had successfully integrated himself into their raiding-and-running lifestyle, becoming a local band's foremost war leader.[51] Much like the abhorrent skunk John Joel Glanton, "Apache Jack" Gordon was not hesitant to close with an enemy, be they Apache, Mexican or American.[52] In fact, just two months prior to his clandestine conversation with Hays, Gordon had even skirmished with US forces. Major Enoch Steen, on the first day of August, at the head of Companies D, F and H, 1st Dragoons, had established a small post at the sleepy village of Doña Ana. At the southern edge of the dreaded *Jornada del Murerto*, the 90-mile shortcut veering northeast away from the Rio Grande, the post was juxtaposed just right for its intended mission—Indian taming. Two weeks later, Steen, leading 50 dragoons, was chasing a band of *Mimbreño* Apache marauders who were fast making a getaway. Steen, who was favorably known for "showing much zeal," tracked the fleeing Apache to the environs of *Santa Rita del Cobre*. There, on Aug. 16, Steen engaged the Indians in a fierce fight, himself being wounded during the bloody incident. The man who shot Major Steen out of his saddle was none other than Jack Gordon, a fact later confirmed by both the shooter and the injured.[53]

Gordon slipped into El Paso del Norte, ostensibly to do some needed trading, and was introduced to Jack Hays, who had been forewarned that Gordon "would steal, lie and kill but he would be true to you" once he had given his word.[54] Hays contracted with the outlaw to make contact with Apache, persuade them to meet for a powwow, receive presents and settle into a hunky-dory liaison with the envious Americans scurrying back and forth to California or up and down the Rio Grande's watershed. Failing this, Hays avowed to meet with the Apache in their own country. A future meeting date was set, and Gordon went his way—presumably to do good work.[55]

Several weeks later, Jack Hays rode out of El Paso del Norte, joined by a party of California-bound emigrants. By way of Doña Ana and an informative visit with the wounded Enoch Steen, Hays crossed the Rio Grande at San Diego Crossing, and camped near the 4,954-foot Picacho Peak northwest of Las Cruces. The preset day for Apache Jack's visit was at hand. During a drenching downpour Jack Gordon rode in: "A heavy rifle hung at his saddlebow, and he wore a Colt's revolver on one hip, a long dagger-shaped knife on the other, and an eagle feather in his hat." One band of Apache, after accepting the presents, had refused to come in for a parley, so Gordon said—anyway, he didn't have the gewgaws. Afterward, his claim of riding west and contacting more favorably inclined Apache was tendered. According to Gordon, those Chihennes in *rancherías* along the Gila had willingly assented to the proposed confab, selecting Ben Moore Mountain overlooking the *Santa Rita del Cobre* mine as the camping spot. All seemed well.[56]

Moving to the neighborhood of the upcoming conference after a half-week's ride, Hays bivouacked. Apache were moving, too. And moving about in the same area was a 400-man punitive expedition from south of an as yet ill-defined international borderline. The Mexican soldiers were under the command of General José María Elías, four small brass cannons accentuating the no-nonsense vigor of his steely-eyed regiment. The "unfortunate collision" that resulted was catastrophic from two viewpoints: Nine pair of Apache ears ended up nailed to artillery carriages shortly after four female Mexican hostages were liberated, and Jack Hays' desire for an amicable assembly were hopelessly dashed. Understandably, although it had not been an American-planned clash, the Apache "suspected the proposed conference had been a ruse to entice them within the vicinity of the council ground to be ambushed."[57] Their refusal to treat was unyielding and Hays was forced to continue his westerly course sans any parley. After talking with Americans and Mexicans, pioneers and passers-through, those who had borne Apache ruin and some who had yet to taste the havoc or suffer the hell, Jack Hays was plumb fed up.

When the new year rolled in, Hays' resignation rolled out. To Thomas Ewing, secretary of the Department of the Interior, on Jan. 3, 1850, the disillusioned and disappointed Hays messaged, in part:

> I sought to have an interview, but I failed in every effort to see them. They were shy and hostile, with feeling aroused against the white by an attack recently made on them by some Americans employed by the Gov. of Chihuahua expressly to fight Indians. I went into the country of the Gila Apaches, and sought by every means to establish a friendly intercourse with them without success. At one time a few were preparing to come into our camp, and had actually collected within two or three miles of us, but were unfortunately dispersed by a Mexican force of four hundred men, the day before they were to visit us. Unprovided with any other protection than a few emigrants and without the right to ask for an escort, with a very limited supply of money, I deemed it folly to attempt to effect any good with these Indians. If I remained long in their country it was at the very great risk of life and I accordingly felt myself forced to abandon as an impossible thing the undertaking of treating with [or] conciliating these dangerous and refractory Indians. From all I have seen and known of the Apaches, they are treacherous, warlike and cruel, and need severe chastisement before they can be made to know the policy of observing good faith with white people. Some of my own companions were killed by them at the very time they were intimating an intention to treat with us. It is exceedingly hazardous for any but large parties to pass through their country...I have had no other opportunity of reporting to you before arriving at this place, to which I came for the purpose of tendering my letter of resignation, which will accompany this report.[58]

Disheartened, Hays maintained his meandering path to California, following destiny to an illustrious public career in the limelight. The Southwest he left behind, that Gila River country, was yet dark and desolate, puzzling and perilous. For the short-term, until civilian government could be established—either statehood or territorial status—the US Army was placed in charge of New Mexico, although her precise boundaries were yet to be permanently laid down.[59] The martial buildup had begun after the Mexican War, and by 1850, New Mexico, the 9th Military Department, was transitory home to 21 companies of infantry and dragoons, nearly 1,000 soldiers. Soldiery effort was designed to protect established settlements along the Rio Grande from Indian depredations and ensure safe passage along travel routes.[60] The departmental commander dually functioned as governor and as the area's military strong arm.[61] Territorial status was officially conferred on Sept. 9, 1850, with passage of the Organic Act Establishing the Territory of New Mexico, but it wasn't until March 3, 1851, that her first civilian chief executive, the former Indian agent James S. Calhoun, escorted by a company of artillery and a company of infantry, assumed control.[62] By then, the obligatory boundary survey was well under way.

It had been determined the international borderline would make an abrupt westerly turn from a prescribed point just north of El Paso del Norte, running straight overland to a fixed spot several miles south of the southernmost tip of San Diego harbor. To actually mark the borderline and reach reasonable compromise on any discrepancies, a boundary commissioner and a chief surveyor were appointed—one team from each country. They were to congregate civilian personnel, muster military escorts and camp equipage, and meet within a year, starting the geodesic measurements east from San Diego—straight through *Apachería*. Their mutual agreements would bind both the United States and Mexico. From the get-go it was prickly and perplexing:

> The diplomats did not foresee faulty maps, niggardly politicians, hostile Indians, fluctuating rivers, dry water holes, towering mountains, awesome deserts, hordes of immigrants, impossible supply problems and argumentative, self-important commissioners. Reputations would be destroyed, diplomatic exchanges would irritate the two countries, the civilian and military members of the United States commission would quibble and obstruct

> each other, and partisan politics would lead to sectional strife. The Treaty of Guadalupe Hidalgo was an interesting case of sign now and worry later.[63]

On July 6, 1849, at San Diego, the eastbound survey ranks had kicked off. Similar hordes were, at the same time, trekking west. The California gold rush was on.[64] After marking the borderline to the confluence of the Colorado and Gila rivers, and after no little inter-commission squabbling, a firm decision was reached to move the burdensome quartermaster operations to El Paso del Norte for the next leg of the survey. One crew was to work downriver to the Gulf of Mexico. The other was tasked with marching west through *Apachería* to the previously established marker. The American government, through the hopeful eyes of her boundary commission staff, was about to take her first real hard look at southwestern New Mexico.[65]

Touchy, indeed, had been the wrangle over precisely just where the westerly advance should be calculated from. El Paso del Norte on paper was at a north latitude and west longitude 34 miles north and 100 miles west of El Paso del Norte's actual spot on the ground. Geographical miscalculation based on a slipshod mapmakers' previous errors could prove costly, land-wise and otherwise. Contentious was the confab. An accord was, at last, negotiated with both sides giving and taking, but "completely unforeseen and unexpected by Mexico," the amply lucrative *Santa Rita del Cobre* landed on America's side of the international boundary line.[66] Marshaling a civilian staff exceeding 100, including a surgeon, US Boundary Commissioner John Russell Bartlett made the copper mine his headquarters—for a while—settling in on May 2, 1851, and renaming the spot Cantonment Dawson.[67] The work crew was protectively augmented by 85 well-armed soldiers of the

John Russell Bartlett, United States Boundary Commissioner. *Courtesy Arizona Historical Society, #28103.*

American Army's 3rd Infantry, commanded by the competent Captain Louis S. Craig. Counting teamsters, cooks and laborers, Bartlett's cadre of Americans and Mexicans numbered near "three hundred whites."[68] In but short order, the formerly forsaken flat-roofed adobe dwellings and Don Francisco Elguea's triangular fortress—still in good shape—were reoccupied. Reliable water was nearby. Ample timber was at hand. Pasturage was adequate. Apache were everywhere!

And it was at *Santa Rita del Cobre* that Mangas Coloradas, the Warm Springs Apache—who, perhaps, was years earlier known as Fuerte—and the border surveyors and soldiers good-naturedly interacted, albeit with mutual suspicion and watchfulness. The Apache had a dozen years earlier run the Mexicans out of the area. Now Americans were tramping everywhere, refurbishing dilapidated buildings, and soldiers once more were occupying the fort. Had they, too, come to stay? Assured by John Bartlett that the commission's sojourn in the area was but temporary, Mangas relaxed—a little. Captain Craig's squadrons maintained alertness. Mexicans in the camp were edgy, conceivably rightfully so. Commissioner Bartlett idealistically presented gifts and gab. The first Mangas Coloradas accepted with delight; the latter he unequivocally cast off, replying brusquely that he was too old to settle down and take up farming. Too, it was hopeless to impress upon him that the Treaty of Guadalupe Hidalgo carried stipulations mandating that America's military put a stop to Chiricahua raiding in Mexico and that all prisoners taken by the Apache must be repatriated. Little could Mangas understand the good sense of forgoing the raids into Mexico. Weren't Americans and Mexicans enemies? Why could he not cross the border and kill a few Mexicans—hadn't US soldiers recently done that very thing? Weren't the Americans—right now—taking lands away from the Mexicans? Were there not enslaved Apache serving masters at Mexican mines and *haciendas*? To Mangas Coloradas the boundary commissioners' logic was baffling, even downright silly.

Peacefulness came near being shattered when two naked boys, Mexican captives, made their break from Apache vanquishers, scurrying straight into the tent and lunging for safety under interpreter John Carey Cremony's wood-framed canvas cot. Savero Aredia, 13 years old, had been taken from Bacuachi, Sonora, six months earlier. José Trinfan, two years younger, had been abducted from Fronteras, likewise in the Mexican state of Sonora, six years before. Abruptly the affair turned dicey with the appearance of about 30 Apache intent on recovering what was, from their

John C. Cremony, Boundary Commission Interpreter and rescuer of Apache captives. *Courtesy Arizona Historical Society, #24548.*

outlook, rightly theirs. At this juncture a certain irony bubbles up. In defending one emancipation, Cremony ordered his own subjugated "servant," a 19-year-old Mexican, José, to grab the close-by double-barreled shotgun and Sharp's carbine. Cremony jerked up all four of his Colt's six-shooters, thrusting two into his belt and yanking back the cock on the other two pistols. The plucky duo were now bristling with firepower, but still in a dreadfully tight spot. Standing back to back, Cremony and José then began protectively rotating around and around, inching toward Bartlett's campgrounds, the scared youngsters in tow. After they'd covered 200 yards in this dizzying dance, friends espied their predicament and rushed to the rescue with drawn revolvers and intimidating long guns. The frightened captives were eventually turned over to the Mexican boundary commissioner, General Alejo García Conde, so arrangements could be made for reunification with the boys' parents in Sonora. Shortly thereafter, Mangas Coloradas burst forth on the scene, demanding the terrified brown-eyed boys be promptly returned.[69]

John Bartlett and Mangas, escorted by an Apache delegation, deliberated. Each side was adamantly fused to a diametrically conflicting ideology. Finally, however, a bargain was reached and the boys' freedom was bought with trade goods, $250 worth.

The early warranty of passivity at the boundary commissioner's camp was fast beginning to sour—especially after the July 6, 1851, six-shooter difficulty between Mexican teamster Jesus Lopez and an Apache. Lopez got his bullwhip back. The Apache died. The Mexican was immediately arrested, put in irons, and held for imposition of American civil law to be administered at Santa Fe.[70] Mangas and his followers wanted Lopez's blood—all of it. Ponce, an ever-vocal Apache, spoke his mind:

"If an Apache should take the life of an American, would you not make war on us and take many Apache lives?" Intractably, John Bartlett explained the irreversibility and reasoning behind his legalistic decision. New Mexico was now a land of law. He, too, made clear—somewhat prophetically—what was likely to happen if errant *Mimbreños* chose the wrong course: "War will then follow; thousands of soldiers will take possession of your lands, your grazing valleys, and your watering places. They will destroy every Apache warrior they find, and take your women and children captives." Once again, open hostilities were snuffed out through monetary means. The dead Apache's mother agreed to salve her grief with a monthly annuity while boundary commissioners remained at *Santa Rita del Cobre*.[71] The Chihennes, as a group, were not so easily soothed.

Good-natured interaction was on the downhill slide. The Americans and Mexicans were a well-armed and formidable force, too strong for an outright attack. The Apache, by most accounts, began pilfering and running off US Army mules at just about the same time the joint boundary commission pulled up stakes at *Santa Rita de Cobre*, engaged with extending the borderline survey farther west. Before riding out, the dutiful but irritated Captain Craig, who had been worn to a frazzle chasing after Indian raiders, recognized reality. He made two recommendations, one founded on military logic, one exasperatingly fogged with bitterness. Appreciating that the copper mine was "in the heart of Apache country," he suggested to higher-ups that a long-term military presence be maintained in the area, and that these Apaches "must be well-flogged, and be made to return all the property which they have stolen."[72]

The chain of command listened—and acted. On Jan. 23, 1852, for America's military *Santa Rita del Cobre* became Fort Webster, named after US Senator Daniel Webster from Massachusetts.[73] The new post was garrisoned by two military units, a company of the 3rd US Infantry and a company of the 2nd US Dragoons.[74] From the outset, turmoil bubbled to the surface. Lame excuses or revisionist apologies would not be tendered, for either side. In late January 1852, Captain Israel Bush Richardson, blaming area Apache for depredations and deaths along the Rio Grande during December of the preceding year, opened up with muskets and a howitzer on Chihennes near Fort Webster, wounding several and capturing two women. The Indians counterattacked on Feb. 6. Swooping down on a herd of grazing livestock, the Apache were successful in drawing overconfident soldiers into a trap, killing Sergeants Bernard O'Daugherty and Nicholas Wade and Private John Croty. Sergeant Wade, apparently captured alive, was "horribly mutilated" and, though not a customary Apache ritual, scalped.[75] Busily the adept Apache raided and ran while fatigued soldiers chased and sometimes clashed. The unrelenting cycle was vicious and wearisome. Rightly or wrongly these early and bloody collisions were sad omens for southwestern New Mexico's foreseeable future.

At pulsating Santa Fe, the territorial capital, civilian lawmakers, too, were busy as dam-building beavers. They were gnawing on creating a new local sphere and defining its gargantuan jurisdictional borderlines. The new county, Doña Ana, was birthed during 1852 and it was—size-wise—a hale and hearty delivery. The fledgling political subdivision stretched from the Texas border on the east to the California line on the west. Horizontally, then, Doña Ana County was roughly 800 miles wide, and vertically she stretched well past 100 miles north from the Mexican border.[76] After a bitter dispute between the United States and Mexico, as well as in America's congressional hallways, and the expenditure of $10 million, a new accord was reached—the Gadsden Purchase, signed in the Mesilla Plaza in 1854. With the Gadsden Purchase, Doña Ana County would put on even more weight, adding real estate south of the Gila River, including that distinctly cut Bootheel region.[77] One of the early-day Doña Ana County sheriffs was the powerfully built, Kentucky-born Samuel G. Bean, an older brother of the waggish Roy Bean. Sam had married Petra, a daughter of the infamous Apache scalp-hunter *Santiago Querque* [James Kirker], often referred to as the "King of New Mexico" due to his Indian-killing expeditions.[78] The sheriff conjectured that in his realm there were 10,000 more Indians than "constituents." Furthermore, and history would prove him dead right, he wryly asserted that the untamed Gadsden Purchase section held a particularly special "charm" for outlaws and misfits.[79]

The geographical birthing of Doña Ana County in early summer 1852 had been a legislators' stratagem; quick-witted military thinkers were likewise realignment-minded. Several months later, on Sept. 9, Fort Webster's effectiveness was augmented by the addition of another company of dragoons, but, more important, the fort was moved to a site along the Mimbres River, 14 miles northeast of the celebrated copper mine. Two sparsely populated civilian villages nestled under Fort Webster's protective wing, San Lorenzo and Mimbres, sometimes referred to as Rio Mimbres.[80] Gradually a few Apache settled near the new fortress, too.

Because of the fertile soil and a promise of annuity goods, a few of the Chihennes took up peaceful farming in the clement Mimbres Valley. Depending upon the source, either the US government failed to ratify the treaty and furnish promised subsistence wares to the Chihenne farmers, or cultivation was the work of only old men, women and children in the first place, leaving open to fighting-age men the time-honored option of warfare and raiding.[81] In any case, the simple repositioning of Fort Webster had little if any effect on curtailing the Apache sorties calculated for punishment, praise or plunder. An on-the-ground and up-close personal assessment of New Mexico's military strengths and weaknesses was ordered from the US Army Inspector General's Department. During this 1853 checkup, Colonel Joseph K. F. Mansfield recommended that Fort Webster, since it was a small post, be abandoned. The squadrons, in his estimation, should then be deployed to a brand-new post, Fort Thorn, situated along the Rio Grande's right bank at the Mesilla Valley's upper end, near present-day Hatch, New Mexico.[82] Just a few days before Christmas 1853, Mansfield's proposal was adhered to and Fort Webster became a ghost, a stronghold of the past.[83] Understandably then—but foolishly now in the light of hindsight—the Chihenne Apache thought once more that they had driven bothersome intruders from their mountain and desert domain. Fierce combat with other Indians and Mexicans and sporadic skirmishes with Americans—in one form or another—were a way of life to Chiricahua Apache men in the prime of life.

The second half of the 1850s brought many Americans to friendless southwestern New Mexico Territory. For the most part they came as transients passing through, rather than as settlers intent on staying. Traffic to California via the southern route, especially during winter months, was brisk—so vigorous, in fact, that US Mail contracts were awarded and coaches carrying dry-throated passengers willingly challenged the gauntlet of parched deserts, wretched heat and lurking Chiricahuas. First had been James E. Birch's San Antonio to San Diego run, "the Jackass Mail." Later that route was nearly paralleled by the Butterfield Overland Trail, John Butterfield's brainchild. In relatively short order, stage stops scattered across southern New Mexico were identifiably well-known. Throughout the Southwest, such mule-changing spots and layovers as Mesilla, Rough & Ready, Cooke's Spring, Mimbres River Station, Ojo de Vaca [Cow Springs], Soldier's Farewell, Barney's Station and Stein's Peak Station became household names to self-assured Southwestern trekkers and tourists. For New Mexico Territory's section of *Apachería*, more often than not, the lonely stage stations were built with stone instead of less durable adobe; dreadful Apache attacks and sieges were not just storybook whimsy.[84] The station agents and their employees were instructed to maintain an aloofness and avoidance of excessive personal contacts with area Apache. Those same workers were heavily armed with Sharp's carbines, Colt's six-shooters and wooden crates crammed full of powder, lead and percussion caps furnished by Butterfield. One and all, they were specifically cautioned to be on perpetual guard against Apache assaults or acts of treachery.[85] Several of the locales, predominantly Cooke's Canyon at the base of the prominent Cooke's Peak and Doubtful Canyon close by the Stein's Peak Station, would prove frightful hot spots for Chiricahua hit-and-run atrocities.

James Tevis, early Piños Altos settler and storyteller. *Courtesy Arizona Historical Society, #30165.*

One spot that was taking on specific and grand notice was Mowry City, pleasantly reposed along the Mimbres River's east bank. Reportedly, it was a metropolis not lazily bustling in the shadows thrown by Cooke's Peak. It was an investors' paradise, so it was said. There were, by some accounts, steamboats navigating the shallow Mimbres. Truthfully, it was baloney. Mowry City, though it did actually exist as a tiny settlement, was one of the first Southwest land-sale schemes. "It was a sham and a scam."[86]

Diametrically divergent from the dark days soon to come, for the time being a comparatively peaceful veil shrouded southwestern New Mexico Territory. The Mexican states of Sonora and Chihuahua were not, however, let off the hook. The Apache still made their cross-border incursions—with a vengeance—but on the American side of the line they chose a course of less brazenness, in large part due to the fact that rations were being issued and earnest efforts at assimilation were well under way. Resultantly, there ever so slowly began a trickle of settlement in the fertile Mimbres Valley and a limited revival of mining doings at *Santa Rita del Cobre*. And, par for the course of Western development, with the good came the bad. Fugitives, whiskey peddlers, gamblers, gunmen, horse thieves and other assorted riffraff intermixed with the hardworking frontier folks. Chihennes watched with a jaundiced eye. Pioneering Anglos and Hispanics too were dubious about living in close proximity to a warlike people who would regularly throw down the hoe and pick up the bow for scorching strikes across the international border. Yet still, in southwestern New Mexico Territory there were many more daring Apache than there were plucky palefaces. That was about to change!

Thomas Henry "Three-Fingered" Birch and his avid prospecting companions, Jacob Snively and James Hicks, outfitted at Mesilla and struck out for an adventuresome and, they hoped, profitable trip. After a stop at Apache Tejo south of *Santa Rita del Cobre* and a restocking of necessary supplies at the copper mine, the "last outpost of civilization," the trio moved northwest some 10 or 12 miles into the Piños Altos Mountains.[87] On the morning of May 18, 1860, just above the junction of Cherry and Bear Creeks, Birch knelt to take a drink from the Bear's sparkling waters. Quite by accident he espied an extra glitter in the pebble-dancing current—free-washing gold.[88] Traditionally, reports of prospective mineral wealth are hard-kept secrets. With whirlwind speed, the news was broadcast throughout the Southwest from Texas to California and south into Old Mexico. It was a stampede! Within a few short months, 700 men were hustling and bustling about in the section. Deferentially, the active conclave was christened Birchville, named in honor of its discoverer.[89] By year's end, 1,500 zealous prospectors "were scraping the gulches and streams beds," many earning as much as $10 to $15 a day placer mining, a more than handsome sum for the time.[90] One early-day chronicler, James H. Tevis, claimed he never made less than $25 per day, and sometimes cleared as much as $600.[91] Undoubtedly, the vast majority of miners were flush, enough to pay a head-tax.

After 25-year-old Miss Rhoda Parker arrived from Iowa wearing "a broad-brimmed hat and a tight-fitting dress, with [a] skirt quite short," accompanied by her aging father and an uncle, more than a few bids were proffered for her hand. Purportedly a gaggle of some 300 lonely-hearted gold seekers proposed matrimony, at least so Tevis claimed. Miss Parker spurned their pitches for romance, but did agree to institute a school and teach reading, writing and ciphering to the "seven or eight Mexican" and the "few half-breed children" purposelessly wandering the mountainous town site. Area miners were assessed $2.50 apiece to pay for her salary and school was in session. So, at least for a part of the day, wee folk were kept busy. Beyond a doubt, Birchville was a bustling burg.[92]

The roaring explosion of hungry argonauts brought appetites that yearned to be sated. Not all were connected to the tummy, though. With so many single men in the region, most with bags of gold dust in their pockets, there quite expectedly was no shortage of adult entertainment. "Joe and Sam Shultz set up a whiskey shop between two pine trees, using a plank for a counter nailed up between the trees, charging 50 cents a drink, 50 cents for cigars, or 50 cents for anything they had."[93] Within a short time, gamblers had arrived and "all kinds of games started up. George Harrington built a log house 100 feet long and 20 feet wide, dirt floor and dirt roof, with barroom at one end and pine slab tables for the hall of the room, 15 or 20 tables going all night." A Mexican brass band and "25 fast Mexican women" were soon banging, figuratively and literally.[94] Unfailingly, whiskey and whores ooze toward wealth, no matter where it may be found. Though sometimes prone to overstatement, Tevis amplifies:

> After the town was begun, houses went up thick and fast. Saloons, dance halls, and a tenpin alley were in operation, with gamblers galore. Between them and the Mexican *señoritas,* the miners soon parted with their gold. Sundays were used for dueling, and all difficulties were settled on that day, unless contending persons were full of whiskey, in which case the killing was quickly done.[95]

And some six-shooter handiwork was done pretty damn quick. The hard-boiled and hard-drinking John William "Jack" Swilling plugged a 21-year-old gent named Printer during a drunken row in an area dance hall. Swilling, in his cups at the time of the fireworks, couldn't remember what had taken place, and "no one seemed to know how it happened, or why."[96] There is little doubt no one really cared.[97] The next day, dutiful miners laid Printer "away in the graveyard, just below the dueling ground, where there were many graves of fellows who had died under such circumstances, for not many died a natural death."[98] During another six-shooter dustup, a noted gambler, George Caldwell, and George Harrington got into it. The lights were shot out. "The only light hung behind the bar and everybody crowded to get to light or get out."[99] When all was said and done, Harrington was dead, Caldwell suffered a nasty shot to the shoulder and three Mexican women were wounded, one later dying as a result of the errant gunshots.[100]

In yet another six-gun "difficulty," Ben Diamond cold-bloodedly shot and killed a local butcher, a man named Schwartz.[101] Diamond got a fair trial—miners' style. He was allowed to handpick his own jurymen, but they neatly returned a unanimous verdict of guilty. At sunrise the next day, Diamond was hanged.[102] Collaterally, another personal vendetta deteriorated and detonated. "The shooting became general and for about five minutes it seemed a perfect hell between the screams of women and groans of wounded and dying men."[103] Will Taylor was wounded in the thigh, but Bill Dick and John DeLong were killed outright. They were buried the next day, and "everything went on as usual."[104]

Two colorful characters who also came to the area and did manage natural deaths were the former Doña Ana County Sheriff Sam Bean and his brother Roy.[105] At blooming Birchville, the pugnacious and business-minded siblings opened a store—with a fine stock of "merchandise and liquors" and, imported all the way from the village of Mesilla, a "fine billiard table."[106] Another brotherly set on the full-of-zip scene were James "Jim" and John Bullard from Boone County, Missouri. According to one account, they became "typical borderers, dividing their time between hunting Apaches with like-minded whites, and prospecting for gold or silver."[107] A soldier who was well acquainted with Jim Bullard declared he was hardly civilized and "was about as morose, insolent and foul-mouthed brute" as he had "ever

Judge Roy Bean. Before he made a name for himself as the Law West of the Pecos, Roy and his brother Sam [a former sheriff of Doña Ana County] were early-day saloon operators in Piños Altos. *Courtesy Robert G. McCubbin.*

Henry Clay "Hank" Smith, a true grit Southwest pioneer and early day denizen at remote Piños Altos during the palmy days. For the hard times he remarked that sometimes it was "knick-knocks for breakfast, knock-knicks for dinner, and damn hard knocking for supper." *Courtesy Nita Stewart Haley Memorial Library.*

saw."[108] Another of the spirited players making Birchville home was the Bavarian-born Henry Clay "Hank" Smith, a teamster, livestock herder, professional hunter and gold prospector—an all-around frontiersman, in short.[109] Later came such notable pioneers as Elijah Weeks, a superior judge of quality ore; Joseph T. Yankie; John Swisshelm; Richard Yeamans; Andrew J. Hurlburt, an English-born orphan; Richard "Dick" Hudson; and William Logan Rynerson, a California Column veteran of the Civil War with a no-nonsense temperament.

Throughout the chaotic 1860s, population at Birchville erratically ebbed and flowed—down and up—dependent upon the gravity of Apache depredations, the predictable retaliatory counterattacks and, in certain instances, the unprovoked thrill kills. There were major Indian raids on the hatchling settlement, and many miners forewent their dreams and skedaddled for safer parts. Southwestern New Mexico, the most dangerous section of the territory, was ablaze with reports of one Apache ambush after another.

Thomas Mastin, one of the charter pioneers at remote Birchville, was killed—along with three others—by an extraordinarily large force of angry Chihenne and Chokonen Apache warriors led by Mangas Coloradas and Cochise.[110] Not far to the southeast near Cooke's Peak, the seven-man Freeman "Free" Thomas party was waylaid, again by the allied forces of Cochise and Mangas. After a gruesome fight that lasted two days, all the Anglos were killed. The downright courageousness of the pinned-down travelers is measured by the number of Apache killed—perhaps as many as 25. Both Mangas and Cochise afterward noted the slain men's bravery, Mangas declaring that if his Apache were as brave, he could "whip the world," and Cochise taunting "that with 25 such men he would undertake to whip the whole United States."[111] To the southwest at Stein's Peak, three white men were found dead, hanging upside down from a piñon limb, smoldering fires built directly under their blackened heads, "giving them a ghastly appearance as they swung there perfectly naked."[112] Plainly, it was tough country.

Back at Birchville, however, others hung on for dear life, venturing to the outskirts of town or beyond only if supported by a watchfully armed crowd. For a while, as it alarmingly turned out, Birchville's preliminary pioneers were more prisoners than free men. Historically laying the total blame for this mess at anyone's doorstep is fraudulent. Sometimes the Chihennes seemed justified in their actions, sometimes not. Likewise, the Americans and the Mexicans vacillated between conduct that at one end of the morality scale was idealistically compassionate and, at the other, blatantly brutal and shameful.

Appreciably contributing to the fluctuating population numbers at Birchville was the manpower drain created by the Civil War. Supplies began to shrink as freighters and packtrain captains were caught up in speculation concerning possible confiscation of their stores by Federals coming from the west or the Rebels already in possession of old Mesilla on the Rio Grande. Hank Smith bemoaned: "Chuck was so scarce that people began to suffer. It was knick-knocks for breakfast, knock-knicks for dinner, and damn hard knocking for supper."[113] Many of the gold miners signed on—for the Blue or for the Gray. The split was acrimonious. Naturally, sharp-eyed Apache saw a shrinking pool of Birchville's residents as a strategic advantage, and sensibly—from their standpoint—they capitalized on it.

By the tragic war's end, much had changed. The log-hut military post 15 miles south of *Santa Rita del Cobre* at Apache Tejo, Fort Floyd, was re-christened Fort McLane after US Secretary of War John B. Floyd defected to the Confederacy, and then in July 1861 shut down for keeps. Mangas Coloradas had been deceptively made a lonesome prisoner, tormented and foully murdered by bayonet wielding soldiers; Apache were belligerently buzzing thick as agitated bees throughout the Southwest. Arizona had been lopped off and made a separate territory. Many Union and

Confederate veterans had either remained in or returned to New Mexico Territory because they had been hopelessly awestruck with its intrinsic allure and promise. And Birchville's name had reverted to an earlier Spanish appellation, *Piños Altos*, named for the towering Ponderosa pines nearby.

Other changes, too, had taken place—militarily. US Army brass had established two posts in the area. During the fall of 1863, Fort Cummings was set up in an effort to protect emigrants traveling west to California, notably those who by the sheer want of potable water were funneled into Cooke's Canyon and to its reliably surging and refreshing namesake spring. Uncharacteristically for US military bastions on America's elastically stretching western frontiers, Fort Cummings was of a stockade blueprint. Fully enclosed by 10-foot-high adobe walls running 320 feet east to west and 366 feet north to south, Fort Cummings looked daunting and impregnable. Behind those imposing walls were the enlisted men's and officers' quarters, a hospital, bakery, guardhouse, powder magazine and an inventory of provisions—two years' worth—for 100 Apache-chasing soldiers. Three years later, just a short hop from Piños Altos, Fort Bayard was founded. It was of more traditional design—a nakedly exposed plan—with barracks, officers' duplexes and other requisite structures separated, as if voyeuristically staring at each other across open ground and around the amply erect flagpole. It, like its neighbor to the south, Fort Cummings, was in the very heart of *Apachería*. The Chihenne, at this point in time, were not friendly. Hardly had Fort Bayard been birthed before hostile Apache let loose with a searing raid straight across the parade ground.[114]

Despite the dangerousness of southwestern New Mexico Territory, the overpowering lure of nature's buried treasures and Americans' ever-itching feet for settling just over the next horizon meant the vast region, step by step, began to fill up with raring-to-go dreamers. For the growing population floundering about in the western extremity of Doña Ana County, travel to the county seat at Mesilla for routine courthouse business and the filing of mining claims proved a burdensome and time-consuming outing. Plus, it was an out-and-out hazardous trip. Equally, Doña Ana County officialdom was plainly hamstrung from doing its job at such faraway hinterlands. Effectual law enforcement, serving the civil and criminal courts' process, and collecting taxes were well neigh unworkable chores. The Feb. 20, 1863, chunking off of Arizona Territory helped. Even with that, though, Doña Ana County sprawled from well past the Rio

Grande on the east to New Mexico Territory's borderline on the west, still a county of colossal proportion. Chiricahua Apache didn't do courthouse business. Fugitives on the dodge and horse-stealing and murdering desperadoes, if given their choice, could straightforwardly shun courthouses and sheriffs. The US Army, while a vital spoke in the wheel of any nearby community's local economy, had little business at the local courthouse. Other frontier folk, however, moaned—shrilly and seriously! Politicos listened.

Chapter 3

"Hell, Boys!...There's Plenty of It!"

Apache trouble throughout New Mexico Territory was not fresh news; politicians on the warpath at Santa Fe was. In one corner was early Piños Altos arrival William Logan Rynerson, who, after importing a quartz mill from California to work his five gold claims, earned a seat as a territorial representative.[115] Rynerson was not a man inclined to accept insults. In the other corner was New Mexico Territorial Supreme Court Justice John P. Slough, who could dish them out; it was written he "had an exceptional command of abusive language, which he used masterfully and willingly against any opponent.[116] On Dec. 14, 1867, Slough harangued that Rynerson was "a thief in the army, a thief out of the army, a coward and a SOB."[117] The next day, the two antagonists collided at Santa Fe's Exchange Hotel. Rynerson coolly demanded an apology, telling the chief justice he "must" retract his spiteful slur. Judge Slough demurred from making amends and instead taunted Rynerson, "What are you going to do about it?" Both men reached for their pockets, Slough yelling, "Shoot, damn you!" Rynerson unhesitatingly obeyed the judge's command. Slough collapsed to the floor,

Willian Logan Rynerson, New Mexico Territory powerhouse politician and early-day mining speculator in Piños Altos. He killed Supreme Court Justice John P. Slough at a Santa Fe hotel. *Courtesy Robert G. McCubbin.*

sledgehammer dead. Rynerson pocketed his smoking six-shooter and calmly waited for the law to take its due course. He was acquitted after a jury trial. Of the verdict, the Santa Fe *New Mexican* pithily reflected public sentiment: "Thus ends this case, and we congratulate Colonel Rynerson upon this issue."[118] Elected officials went back to work. William L. Rynerson and others had an agenda.

On Jan. 30, 1868, territorial legislators at Santa Fe whacked off another section of Doña Ana County's enormous landscape. Reflecting Union sympathies, the new county was named in honor of General Ulysses S. Grant, who was atop the pinnacle of popularity for winning the Civil War.[119] Lawmakers at Santa Fe could ill-afford taking a compassionate look at any ex-Confederates with an aim toward veneration. It would have simply been political suicide—plain foolishness! Dubbing the new county after a popular Army man, one with presidential aspirations, was not an unwise career tactic, especially for those who might themselves someday seek patronage positions from Washington. The recalcitrant South had yet to be "reconstructed," at least in the self-satisfied eyes of many Yankees.

Picking a county seat was less taxing. The small village of *Santa Clara*, which sprang to life catering to Fort Bayard's civilian needs, was renamed Central City and made Grant County's new shiretown due to its central geographical location.[120]

Newly surveyed Grant County was, by any stretch of the imagination, whopping in size: 9,000 square miles. The new geographical swath butted against historic Socorro County on the north side, Doña Ana County to the east, Arizona Territory on the west, and the troublesomely communal border with Old Mexico on the south. Grant County was still in *Apachería's* heartland, too! She was, as far as a county was concerned, one of the most dangerous places to live or pass through in the whole Southwest. At the very same time she was harsh yet beautiful, inviting yet inhospitable, sustaining yet unforgiving. A nest-egg builder for some frontier homemakers, a callous widow-maker for others. County residents, if they were so inclined, could boast of being juxtaposed in "a transition zone between the cool/wet Rockies and the warm/dry Chihuahuan Desert and Sierra Madre Mountains."[121] The jagged-toothed southern spur of North America's Continental Divide cuts right through Grant County, as does the ever-twisting Gila River and the sneakily vanishing Mimbres River.[122] Depending on the individual traveler's viewpoint and physical condition at the time interrogated, old Grant County was lovingly

Map of Grant County from Railroad and Township Map of New Mexico by Walter V. Hayt, ca. 1885. *Courtesy Silver City Museum collection.*

blessed or hatefully cursed with "sharply defined precipices, mountain hogbacks, lofty ridges and expansive desert floors."[123] The topography, with its varying elevations, was ideally suited to support a wide variety of wildlife and, in turn, human life. Even the novice hunter could count on getting a fair shot at an antelope, turkey, deer, elk, mountain lion, black bear or, yes, even a grizzly.[124]

A frontline Silver City pioneer and the first sheriff of Grant County, Richard "Dick" Husdon. Later he owned the renowned Hudson's Hot Springs between Deming and Silver City. *Courtesy Silver City Public Library.*

It was, indeed, wild country. Grant County was outdoor country with plenty of elbow room. She was, too, as with any brand-new county, destined to limp along for awhile, mired by an embryonic system of local government. The first term of District Court was held at Central City under the shade of a spreading juniper tree. Apparently there was a shortage of sufficient space for Grant County's first sheriff, Dick Hudson, to rent for that initial July 1868 district court session. A New Yorker and ex-Santa Fe trader "lacking legal training," Judge Joab Houghton, presided. The ceaselessly controversial Thomas B. Catron acted as prosecuting attorney for New Mexico's Third Judicial District.[125]

Adding to a territorial sheriff's nightmarish job description, in addition to serving as an officer of the court and as a keeper of the peace and the prisoners, was the thankless job of tax collecting. In New Mexico Territory, the assessment of taxes fell within the county clerk's realm. It was, however, the sheriff's duty to ensure prompt payment of tax monies, and for this he got a fair piece of the revenue—usually five percent for his time, trouble and expenses.[126] Donning the hat of a tax collector could prove both profitable and problematic. Handling public money was delicate business, especially in a politically partisan environment, which New Mexico Territory was. Charges of public corruption were commonplace. Insinuations were easy to manufacture, more difficult to sustain. A few county residents failed to make any tax settlement at all, primarily during Grant County's infancy. One early resident, justifying tax avoidance, distills the truth: "As far as taxes and other business of the county were concerned, these were lost in the 'shuffle' by the press of each individual looking out for his own 'bacon and beans.'"[127]

On another issue, though, everybody's fat was in the same fire. Grant County's early-day denizens and the Army's fatigued cavalry and mounted infantrymen were more concerned with bringing to bay a mutual prey, and it wasn't the defiant tax dodger. Captain Alexander Moore, stationed at Fort Cummings, was more than thoroughly convinced that unscrupulous Mexicans across the international line were encouraging Apache to raid and steal livestock in southwestern New Mexico Territory. Then, he theorized, they hurriedly sprinted the booty into Old Mexico for devious moonlight disposal. Captain Moore wasn't off the mark. Leaving his post on Aug. 23, 1868, Moore led a "scout" intent on patrolling the ominous-looking Florida and Hatchet Mountains just north of the US-Mexico border and, once and for all, putting an end to the illicit traffic. During the 23-day campaign, Moore's command traveled well over 400 miles, and twice closed in on shrewdly hidden *rancherías* in the neighborhood of Ojo Alamo, just four miles from the border. Three Apache were killed, others wounded, and three Indian children "captured." The Apaches' commissary, including some horses, was destroyed. Moore jubilantly returned to Fort Cummings on Sept. 14, reporting that his men were "in excellent health and spirits." Other "sizable scouts" were dispatched from Fort Bayard.[128] In spite of such sporadic setbacks, however, haggard Apache still controlled the tenor of battle—surprise, hit, run and vanish!

Establishment of two military posts in forlorn southwestern New Mexico Territory assuaged some fears but—realistically—made little, if any, real adjustment in corralling the Apache or mollifying the valid concerns of pioneers and prospectors. The region's non-Indian population was for all practical purposes buckled down snugly. Earlier, in the southern stretch of Grant County, east-west stagecoach service to California or El Paso had been hurriedly suspended. Ever so slowly after the Big War, traffic had resumed. With that lifeline, although desperately thin, another civilian conclave began to develop around Mexican Spring south of the Burro Mountains and but 15 dehydrated miles from the New Mexico-Arizona borderline. The Kerns and Mitchell Stage Line operating over the old Butterfield Trail for the National Mail and Transportation Company hired a gutsy station keeper, 53-year-old Norwegian-born John N. "Uncle Johnny" Evensen, and the stage stop at Mexican Spring was semi-officially designated as Grant—again, presumably in honor of a president to be.[129] The incredulous Apache leaders took note; Mexican Spring had for years been their watering layover before moving farther south and raiding into Old Mexico. For newly mapped Grant County, then, anxious travelers either hurried straight through, tethered themselves to the far-flung stage stations, erected housing near military citadels or tentatively settled at pretty but perilous Piños Altos. Early stalwarts who opted to stay and whittle out lasting prospects for their future unquestionably were carved from sturdy stock.

For such a cutoff gold mining town, Piños Altos was continuing to draw her fair share of consideration, not only from scruffy miners full of expectation but from commonsense politicians as well. On Jan. 8, 1869, Central City was stripped of her short-lived county seat status and the prize was awarded to Piños Altos.[130] The little hamlet agreeably nestled in the tall pines was just the place for a 30-year-old New Yorker, Martin W. Bremen. He set up a steam-operated sawmill and tapped into the need. The profusion of growing timber nearby furnished the rough product, and for a 200-mile radius Bremen became the source, perhaps the only source, for finished lumber. The local military brass and mining-camp residents turned to him for their construction needs, making Bremen's business so good it upped the number on his payroll—and his profits.[131] Piños Altos, so it seemed, was undergoing a post-Civil War boom. Apache and remoteness were impediments, but fortunes lay just over the next ridge or up the next canyon for hearty spirits not frightened off by the possibility of seclusion or slaughter.

Another nearby area was attracting no little attention. Nine miles southwest of Piños Altos, in a magnificent valley surrounded by mountains, lay *La Ciénega de San Vicente*. A Grant County old-timer eloquently paints the picture:

> ...where upon the hills that bordered it—grew dense groves of cedar and piñons, and in the early spring and summer the rich, luxuriant gramma grass grew in abundance; and, from the fertile soil of the little valley, tall and gorgeous sun-flowers grew in profusion, and which at times covered nearly the entire valley. About midway

> and toward the lower end of the valley, there flowed a number of cool, clear springs, the water from them creating an extensive marsh, from which thousands of tules grew...Here, for years and years, the Apaches, under Mangas Coloradas and his forefathers, gathered to celebrate their victories over the enemy and to hold their councils of war. Here, too, they buried their dead.... For years, too, when the valley was silent, and nothing but the voice of the morning dove or the howl of some wandering coyote broke the stillness of those eternal hills, thousands of antelope from the plains, and droves of deer from the foothills hardby, would come down in the silent nights to drink and wallow in the cool of the marshes.[132]

There can be little doubt that from time to time, perhaps only in the summers, early-day 18th-century Spanish traders may have for a short time camped at *La Ciénega de San Vicente* and, just as plainly, they moved on. Later, Mexican herders ran about 4,000 sheep and goats in the lush valley, supplying mutton and *cabríto* for ravenous miners working at Piños Altos.[133] Another crew of Mexicans—five in number—pastured many of the area miners' horses and mules at *La Ciénega de San Vicente* for $5 per head, per month and "chuck."[134] Apache were continually a threat, and on at least one occasion, "took the Mexicans prisoner, stripped them of all clothing and gave them a severe whipping with rawhide quirts, and sent them back stark naked to the mines."[135] Although charmingly eye-catching and a wetland oasis in the wildest section of the territory, the *Ciénega* remained unsettled.[136] It was—after all—*Apachería*. Covetous Americans, however, would soon modify the enchanting vale, everlastingly!

From their prospecting base at Piños Altos, several visionaries realized the sure agricultural potential for *La Ciénega de San Vicente*. William M. Milby, recently of San Antonio, Texas, along with the aforementioned Bullard brothers, John and Jim, Richard Yeamans, Dick Hudson, James McGee, John Swisshelm, Joseph T. Yankie and Andrew J. Hurlburt, cooperatively began farming the delightful valley in early 1869.[137] They did not forsake their prospecting probes, though. Some took a more active part farming than others, but all were cutting-edge pioneers, prospectors and planters. Cautiously spying from foothills nearby, the Chihenne Apaches'

One of Grant County and Silver City's earliest pioneers, John Swisshelm. *Courtesy Silver City Museum.*

psyche was jolted. Fur trappers, seemingly never satisfied in one place, triggered the steel jaws till they caught beaver no more, and moved on. Gold hunters came, exploited and went. Soldiers foolishly established, then dismissively abandoned, fortifications. Stagecoaches raced back and forth, slowing only to change sweating and worn-down teams, while jostling passengers acted as if they were chasing after or being chased by somebody. For years and years Apache warring men had watched, waited and savagely plundered Hispanic gardeners along the permanently settled lower Rio Grande Valley. Quick-witted Apache knew all too well that farmers put down roots—and stayed!

Andrew Hurlburt, "as daring [a man] as ever trod the West," pushed forward and built the first crude cabin at *La Ciénega de San Vicente*, the very first American-built structure at the location.[138] Hurlburt brought with him a Mexican wife and nine-year-old-daughter.[139] Incontestably it was risky business. Soon, others threw up rudimentary shelters. Usually one intrepid partner stood by, rifle in hand, performing duty as an eagle-eyed sentry, while cohorts plowed and planted and picked. "Even this precaution seemed inadequate protection against the Apaches, and it was arranged that two infantrymen should be detailed from Fort Bayard to protect the settlers. As Hurlburt's cabin, located in the lower end of the valley, was a large one, it was decided that these guards should be stationed there."[140] Cunning Apache could be patient, excruciatingly so! In this instance, Fate extended Indians a helping hand.

During an early morning in late March 1869, "the two infantry guards had started for Fort Bayard before the arrival of their relief, on the pretext that they were short of rations."[141] Unaware that the soldiers had already vacated their assigned post, the Bullard boys and "their partners" started for Piños Altos to restock their larder with provisions. An eerie stillness blanketed the *Ciénega*. Hurlburt's wife and child quietly busied themselves at the remote cabin. Andrew Hulburt hitched mules, went to the field and began plowing. Uncharacteristically he commenced "yee-ing" and "hawing" sans any rifle or sidearm. Those implements he had recklessly left at home. Apache smiled!

Superior in numbers and seeing no advantage in stealth, brashly and boldly the Apache assaulted Hurlburt's cabin—and family. It was easy work. From behind the mules' muscular rumps Hurlburt heard his wife's pitiable screams and the distressed cries of his precious girl child. For a moment time stood still. He was frozen with fear. Andrew Hurlburt in but a second saw what was happening but, unarmed, he was a toothless tiger. Shortly, several Apache, desirous of the mules and the muleteer's carcass, started in Hurlburt's direction, knowing the impotence of a rifleless chap. There would be no cultural shame in killing a foolish man, one who knowingly left his family exposed and vulnerable. His death would be just. Hulburt comprehended the dire predicament he was in and ran—a gut-bustin' dash all the way to Piños Altos.[142] Utterly exhausted, between gasping breaths he blurted out his sad story. Quickly a platoon of heavily armed prospectors led by Dick Hudson and Font Williams raced to the *Ciénega*.[143] The chimney-jutting proud and lone was a sad omen. In the ashes of the smoldering cabin lay the remains of Hurlburt's wife and daughter, horribly mutilated. Purportedly, at that very moment, standing before the grieving husband and disfigured bodies, each and every man swore an oath to avenge the murder and never show mercy to an Apache.[143] If those words had indeed been spoken, and had Apache prowling close by heard them, they would have rolled with laughter. On that cruel southwestern New Mexico Territory frontier, idle or boastful chitchat was a worthless commodity. Deeds mattered, talk didn't. Gritty settlers cinched their resolve tight. By damn, they'd come to stay—hell or high water!

Grant County, like most of New Mexico Territory's counties, was just too damn big for the army to safeguard with the resources and manpower at hand. Reportedly, by 1869 there were scarcely sufficient soldiers at Fort Bayard and Fort Cummings to defend the posts, much less the settlers and prospectors. Civilian *and* military travel was perilous unless in reinforced squadrons. Thoroughly aggravated with the US Army's inability to provide protection, Grant County folks turned to the territory for help. Other counties did likewise. Gov. William A. Pile, in a General Order dated Aug. 24, 1869, authorized the formation of civilian "posses." Grant County was officially allowed two: one at Rio Mimbres consisting of 32 men under the command of Captain K.K. Wardwell, another of 26 men at Piños Altos led by "the most capable and fearless Indian fighter in the Southwest," Captain John M. Bullard. Sufficient arms and ammunition were to be requisitioned at Santa Fe.[144] Such Grant County notables as Andrew Hurlburt, John R. Johnson, John Swisshelm and Joseph T. Yankie were a part of Bullard's posse.[146] The boys, as necessity arose, hunted Apache and "seemingly undaunted—caught, perhaps, like so many Southwestern miners, between the poles of greed and fear—Hurlburt and the others continued their gold prospecting."[147]

Little did they know it then but a spark was fixing to ignite, not at *La Ciénega de San Vicente* but 40 miles southwest at the other end of the Burro Mountains, near that forlorn stage stop, Grant. Although credit for the actual discovery is variously awarded to one man or the other, a loud truth rings through loud and clear: By April 1870 the boom was on at Grant—"the silver madness was going strong"—and the find was being pervasively and persuasively touted as the "the richest as well as the most extensive mineral deposit ever discovered."[148] Prospectors back at Piños Altos weren't deaf to the buoyant prattle. An investigative trip was called for—before the bubble burst!

John and Jim Bullard, Henry M. Fuson, John Swisshelm, Elijah Weeks, Joseph T. Yankie, Richard Yeamans and, perhaps, widower Andrew Hurlburt formed an eager exploratory party—well armed—and set out through the Burro Mountains for Grant.[149] Safely arriving, they were quickly made aware the camp's name was no longer Grant but instead Burro Mines. More important, the Piños Altos boys were brought up to speed on other actualities. It was good news, too! "This was not an ordinary lode, but a mountain of quartz, the base of which covered and area of somewhat more than 400,000 square yards and the height was not less than 1,000 feet..." and "...by the simplest processes of assaying the 'croppings' had yielded as high as $200 to the ton while fragments from the main body of the rock had yielded as high as $2,300 to the ton...above ground lay sufficient quartz to keep a score of mills in constant operation for a whole lifetime."[150] Already four tent saloons had popped up, and a growing throng of optimistic miners had dotted the surrounding hillsides with huts.[151] Traditionally consistent with imposition of time-honored "Miners' Law," a committee had been fashioned to ensure a modicum of general good order and restrain ne'er-do-well "jumpers" from any shenanigans.[152] Straight to the point, it was written that "the mines grew richer as they sank into the earth."[153]

News of the strike had reverberated all the way to San Francisco. The US government's surveyor working southwestern New Mexico Territory, William D. Brown, may very well have been the person liable for making the marvelous discovery, or, if that's not the case, as some assert, the rediscovery. In any case, he made sure big-money interests in California heard about it. Brown's Pacific Coast contact was William C. Ralston, "who directed the destinies of Harpending & Co., the Bank of California and the city of San Francisco itself."[154] Ralston, favorably impressed with ore samples assayed under his watchful supervision, formed a mining company, and the not-inaccurate rumors of stupendous fortunes just waiting to be made were fanned.[155] The touring Piños Altos crowd were not immune. They, too, were keyed up.

Depending on the version consulted, the quotation may be variously attributed, and Ellijah Weeks really seems the most likely candidate, but, in any event, one of the men fanatically affirmed: "Hell, boys! If that's silver ore, I know where there's plenty of it!"[156] The "where" was, of course, *La Ciénega de San Vicente*. Keeping their secret, the men saddled their riding horses, loaded the pack horses, and hightailed it for the *Ciénega* and a confirming inspection. Reportedly, on the trail headed home they met Charles F. Bottom rushing to Burro Mines intending to "lay out a townsite and stake off some lots."[157] Laughingly, they chided the "ambitious little Kentuckian," informing him that he was more than welcome to all the town lots he could plot. Whether they mentioned to Bottom the purpose of their return or remained mum goes unrecorded. Indeed, they were reasonably confident, but their jaunty demeanor was not free from a degree of apprehensive reservation.

Still, they were gold miners—not silver miners—and many times they had tramped all over hills west of the *Ciénega* "without dreaming of the wealth" underfoot.[158] By May 10, 1870, the neophyte silver prospectors were confidently exploring, picking up likely looking surface-ore samples in the "lime and iron-capped hills" due west of San Vicente Spring. At Piños Altos they handed the ore over to assayer John R. "Adobe" Johnson, and crossed their fingers. Was it to be bonanza or bust? At $60 per ton it was encouraging. They returned to *La Ciénega de San Vicente* and did the "stipulated amount of work to secure their new claims," the Northeast and Black Hawk ledges, guaranteeing the validity of their labors for at least one year. Next and, appropriately so, the impatient crew burrowed below the surface for supplementary samples, and raced to Johnson's for another assessment. On tenterhooks they stood by. They could have, and probably did, buy Johnson a beer when his finding was made known. The ore indicated a yield of at least $100 per ton. An El Dorado! They had, at last, struck it rich![159]

Eight aspiring silver moguls—John and Jim Bullard, Henry Fuson, Andrew Hurlburt, John Swisshelm, Elijah Weeks, Joe Yankie and Richard Yeamans—organized the Bullard Mining Company and the "octetoctette" [any group of eight] set in motion the very first silver mining venture in the vicinity of *La Ciénega de San Vicente*.[160] Quickly, in what would be known as the Silver Flat District west of the *Ciénega*, on May 27, 1870, the impassioned speculators started three mines, the Legal Tender and the Twin Lode No. 1 and Twin Lode No. 2.[161] And on that same day, J. D. Fresh claimed the Giant Lode. Within three days, John A. Miller, David C. Knox, Charles Kurl, George O. Strong and John D. Slocum, maneuvering as close as possible, filed the first extension on the Bullard Mining Company's Legal Tender.[162] The obligatory paperwork was filed at Piños Altos with the county clerk and the deed book was appropriately updated, James Fresh and A. [Alva] Mason attesting as witnesses.[163]

An Apache arrow burning through the breeze couldn't have carried the word any faster. The news was out! Gold miners from Piños Altos and the surrounding mountain camps rushed to the *Ciénega*. Silver miners working the Burro Mine section raced to the *Ciénega* astride fit thoroughbreds and windbroke nags. Others crammed into bump-jumping wagons and hung on for dear life. Mining is boom or bust business! First come, first served! Once those initial words leaked—no—detonated, the explosive echo was deafening.[164] From quaintly charming Mesilla and El Paso del Norte they came. From Santa Fe to San Diego, from Denver to Detroit, the mining grapevine buzzed with a new promise. The clamor wafted across the US-Mexico border, too.

Typical of the "boomers" and "stampeders," 32-year-old gold prospector Harvey Howard Whitehill and a brother-in-law, his junior by 10 years, Isaac N. Stevens—full of dreams—threw down their picks, shovels and pans. From their base in northeastern New Mexico Territory at Elizabethtown, the ambitious duo hustled toward the *Ciénega*, overtly teasing jeopardy along the way.[165] The wisdom of "gettin' there while the gettin' was good" is underscored by an informative blurb appearing in the

Las Cruces Borderer, which might have been slightly overblown: "...candles were brought into requisition, and the prospectors hunted night and day."[166] That same newspaperman penned that in but a short time after one promising discovery was made, the "hill was like a swarm of ants" with the fervent contenders scampering to and fro.[167]Journalistic hyperbole aside, the pecuniary roar emitting from old Grant County was thunderous. The vociferously blistering noise would forevermore alter and then lastingly sear its brassy and blustery page into the Southwest's history book.

Overnight shanties were scattered all over the foothills, enveloping the once-quiet *Ciénega*. In certain instances, trying to pinpoint precisely the day they arrived in the area would be a nebulously useless task. Grant County's deed books reflect the actual dates of filings, however, and so it may be accurately reported that the countryside was fast becoming a patchwork of colorfully monikered claims: the Specie Basis, by G. W. Powers, Richard Howlett, M. Riding [Redding?] and David Winterburn; the Carolina by James Corbin, Aaron R. Hackney, John R. Johnson, Edwin J. Orr and Juan N. Carrasco; the Last Chance by Hugh Flynn and James P. Flanagan; the Josephine and Green Mountain by Harvey H. Whitehill, George W. Tower, Charles Simpson and Andrew J. Hurlburt; and in the stupendously rich Chloride Flat District—two miles farther west—the La Providencia by Juan Carrasco, John Johnson, James Corbin, James E. Atkinson, Jesus Armijo and Manuel Moreno. Other area silver mines were springing up (or down) all through the Chloride and Silver Flat Districts: the Keystone, the Trinity, the Robinson, La Esperanza, El Gran Tesoro, El Benado, the Bang All, the Fanny Hilton, the George Washington, the O.K., the General Lee, the Mayflower, the Southern Cross, and the list goes on—and on![168]

This scurrying hullabaloo had a downside. Sociologically, as would be expected in any cascading influx of treasure hunters, with the good came the bad. Not everyone was a nice guy. Since the close of the Mexican War, the turbulent international border region had become sanctuary for outlaws and misfits. The section, for the most part, was yet remote and absent any hint of effectual law enforcement.[169] By simple definition, it could be reported the mere fact that a fellow was even in frontline Grant County meant he had already proved himself a "pretty tough cookie." The timid went elsewhere. Most were hardworking and honorable. Others, though, were slothful and dishonest to the core. Philosophically, the latter class were content to subsist at the expense of the former. They were all adventurers. Classifying their mutual magnetism to the place as pure greed would be untidy, historically. They did, however, share a common denominator.

Apache, ever wary, were watching. The world—their part of it—was changing. The once unmolested *La Ciénega de San Vicente* was now being raped. Insatiable miners were probing, poking and putting down holes everywhere. The shattering crack of dynamite blasts ricocheted through the canyon walls and over once-quiet hilltop crests. Displaced Chihenne lurking nearby made no a distinction between a good guy or a bad guy. All were fair game!

Following tradition rooted in generations of Americanized thinking, the ever-growing cadre of Grant County silver miners saw—in their minds—the good judgment associated with formalized organization. R. C. McLeod roughed out a survey for a new town. Land formerly preempted by the Bullard brothers, John Swisshelm, Joe Yankie and Richard Milby was divided. Milby took a 160-acre tract on the eastern side of San Vicente Spring and was soon partnered up with Dick Hudson in opening perhaps the first business in that section, the Legal Tender Corral. The Bullard boys and the others held on to land west of the spring. Big doings were in the making.

In early June 1870, a public meeting was called. The boys gathered 'round at the Legal Tender Corral. There was the inevitable back and forth discussion but, in the end, those originally holding the choice *Ciénega* real-estate relinquished any further claim in exchange for clear title to a few of the top-notch town lots previously laid out by one Harcourt, mapped by surveyor McLeod's plat.[170]A new town was born! Shamefully, though, she was nameless.[171]

The local mixture of personalities was diverse. There were Americans and Mexicans. There were European immigrants and native-born Hispanics. There were old-timers and newcomers. There were Union Army vets and even a few—very few—Southerners. There were hardrock businessmen and untried tenderfeet. US Census numbers for the town's first official count [August 17, 1870] are revealing: Of the 80 individuals enumerated, all but six were males, and two of those darling girls were three years of age. The four adult ladies who were listed as "keeping house" ranged in age from 18 to 40 and were truly homemakers—the *demimondes* would come later. None in camp had reached his 60th birthday, and most were in their 20s and 30s. Twenty-eight-year-old Jacob Bolds, hailing from Georgia, was the town's only black man.[172] Most, it may be fairly assumed lacking contrary evidence, were first-rate men. No doubt, too, for good measure some scalawags could be thrown into the mix. The Apache were not counted nor consulted.

Christening the new town was called for. A town meeting called for this purpose proved contentious. There was a faction, primarily the earliest pioneers, who wanted to maintain the name of *San Vicente.* Others thought, how ridiculous—and said so! Professed wisdom that night at the Legal Tender Corral was mind-boggling:

> They searched in Rome and they searched in Greece, even went to Egypt and back again to Spain for a name...[173]

The debate raged, and the disputants wrangled. Luckily, despite the fact that most of the exuberant crowd could undoubtedly be characterized "by youth, daring ambition, energy, recklessness, greed, contempt for restraints, and a casual view of suffering and death," the meeting did not evolve into a fisticuffs or six-shooter mêlée.[174] New Mexico Territory was well acquainted with violence—it was, in fact, for a while, a "condition of life." The recipe for a hearty meal of abrupt calamity was ever present. In a climate where all the men were contesting for an economic future, where most went armed, and where nearly everyone drank hard liquor every day—some all day—and where there was "no duty to retreat" in the unwritten code of manly interaction, the fractious meeting went rather well.[175] A consensus was finally reached.

Whether it was with tongue in cheek, or whether it was with total disdain will never be truthfully known, but Dick Hudson, upon hearing the final choice, remarked that "it was one hell of a name to call a town on a mud flat." *La Ciénega de San Vicente* was out, and a new town name was in. From then till now it's plainly just been—Silver City.[176]

Chapter 4

"From Hell to Breakfast"

A simple christening at the stinky Legal Tender Corral did not a town make. Before the young settlement could bloom, she had to suffer those "growing pains" that were so very common to most frontier communities throughout the American Southwest. Some towns lived on; others simply didn't. Silver City from the outset suffered two not trifling handicaps. First, she was planted at the hub of *Apachería*. The Chihenne Apache? Well, they could just move on—or be damned! Forcefully wrestling land away from Apache clutches would not prove a pushover, though; scores—from both ranks—would die. Second, Silver City was not an easy place to get to. She was worlds away from any semblance of urban civilization. Silver City was at the end of a tirelessly long road! To get there, one had to be going there. An arduous 1870s trip to lively Silver City was and for years to come would be chancy.

The nearest railroad connection was more than 700 meandering miles away in Colorado.[177] The topography in between was harsh. Costly mining machinery and, yes, even the basic day-by-day supplies came to Silver City only two ways: packtrain or ox-drawn freight wagon. A tortuous one-way trip could take months. It has been written, and perhaps it's true, that "the owners of the 'ox outfits' would stop at certain points on their way to the railroad to plant a crop of barley and corn, and on the return trip they would harvest the same...."[178] Mexican traders, prodding slow-moving oxen hitched to creaking *carretas*, traveled the extraordinarily hazardous and well-worn trail up from Old Mexico but, likewise, they were forever on the road.[179] Silver City was distant from. . . everywhere! In those earliest days there was not an officially designated US post office. Sending a letter from Silver City by mounted messenger to Piños Altos for a posting back East was wearisome. The overly anxious sender could

Until the advent of rudimentary railway service, necessities and niceties were hauled to Silver City by lumbering oxen or mule trains. *Courtesy Silver City Museum.*

expect a reply, depending on the weather conditions, Apache shenanigans, breakdowns, broken arms, whooping cough or lame mules, sometime within three or four months—or so.[180] There was no telegraph. There was no alternative.

Few early-day Silver City residents were full-time miners. Most, although hoping to strike it rich and retire, were forced to accept the dismal truth. Everyday survival meant everyday work. The vast majority of the new city's fortune hunters banked on sinking shafts as but a gaming sideline occupation. So, for instance, William Milby and Dick Hudson had the aforementioned Legal Tender Corral; Parker Burnham established a brickyard, an early industry of momentous and historic significance, because the close-by clay soils were exceptionally favorable; Martin Bremen kept the sawmill at Piños Altos working overtime, generating foot after foot of rough-cut boards; Ed Moulton put his trudging teams to work hauling tons of local freight; Harvey Whitehill built the town's second public corral and worked for others as an engineer; Dr. Myers H. Casson dabbled in silver mining, but earned his keep as the town's first physician;

Isaac James Stevens speculated in the mining business, but assured his livelihood in those earliest days raising vegetables for local tables; Richard Yeamans retailed groceries freighted in from the States. Immigrants from Mexico performed manual labor for $1.50 to $2 per day, while common miners were pulling down $3.50 a day working hard at others' claims. Skilled craftsmen—carpenters and bricklayers—were knocking down a whopping $5 daily wage. And lawyers, doctors, merchants, tradesmen and saloon men alike were rushing pell-mell to Silver City, intent on tapping into prosperity.[181]

At least in the beginnings, most newcomers were hindered not by a lack of sharp enthusiasm but by a very real shortage of requisite tools. The town's sheer isolation and long-delayed freight shipments were not inconsequential problems for area optimists. Not everyone—by a long shot—had been as "forehanded" as Samuel Cradlebough, who managed the trip to Silver City "with his mill, the first reductions works in the camp, a metate and a Dutch oven, strapped to the back of his burro." Another, Juan N. Carrasco, capably experienced in the silver mines of Old Mexico and somewhat more farsighted than most, brought with him an attendant workforce and "erected small adobe furnaces and by utilizing blacksmith bellows to provide the necessary blast soon began smelting the ores."[182] Presently, a dawning reality poked through: The Chloride Flat District was far superior to the Silver Flat District. Another truth punched through, too: Until a sufficient supply of tools and milling machinery could be hauled to the section, there would be more prospecting than actual mining.

Silver City's founders were full of zest and zeal, woefully short on coins and currency. An infusion of investment capital, a substantially healthy dose, would be necessary to breathe life's breath into Silver City's struggling economy. Mills were expensive and, until the area's wealth could be proficiently and not wastefully stamped out, the town's lasting future seemed rather dreary.

In stepped a powerhouse player. Lucien B. Maxwell, a millionaire land baron in northeastern New Mexico Territory, hearing the same hubbub as other speculators—rich and poor—gave power of attorney to an eminently qualified agent, Thomas L. Lowthian. Appraiser Lowthian was empowered to make rigorous assessments of the potential for profit in mining camps throughout southwestern New Mexico Territory, as well as southeastern Arizona Territory. Favorably impressed with the likelihood for success in the Silver City area, Lowthian messaged Maxwell.

Enamored with the glowing report, Lucien Maxwell entered into an agreement with the Bullard Mining Company to ship a mill—at not inconsiderable expense—to Silver City for a half interest in the Legal Tender.[183] "Maxwell sent 'a way back east' to Chicago and ordered a brand new 10-stamp mill. Now it took a long time for that mill to come from the east to its destination—six months or more."[184] Moreover, Maxwell "guaranteed to do additional development work at his own expense."[185] The preliminary accord was reached and the burdened freight wagons rolled, Silver City bound. At long last, the sparkling star of sweet success was shining overhead.

A snag soon developed, however. During fine-tuning of the business deal, one of the partners—and to this day the defector is yet mysterious—balked. Whether or not it was a pigheaded decision or a well-founded judgment goes unrecorded, but either one of the Bullard brothers, Hurlburt, Swisshelm, Fuson, Weeks, Yankie or Yeamans bolted. Deadlocked! Lucien Maxwell was, as an old-timer asserts, madder than an "Injun" and "forthwith, rather than bring the mill any further, or that it might be of benefit to anyone in the mining business, had it unloaded at Ft. Cummings, 40 miles from its destination, and there it remained for several years."[186] The once-bright sky went black for Silver City.[187] Scratching out a meaningful livelihood silver mining was still more than problematic—catch as catch can! Silver City was at the cusp of something big, they all knew. Prospectors and other hopefuls were still flocking to the burgeoning camp, madly chasing rumors and dreams. For those already there it was simply a time to hang on. They hadn't been quitters gettin' there and they wouldn't make quitters stayin' there.

But things soon went from bad to worse. Although ever since the formation of civilian Apache-chasing posses there had been a lull in Chihenne depredations, the wobbly state of affairs was now in flux. Silver City's durable residents would find fault with the US government's "slipshod" Indian policy. Their hard temperament was explicable. Scavenging raids had resumed. The military wasn't protecting the whites. Indian agents weren't feeding their wards or even watching them very closely. The bureaucrats were ineptly mismanaging tax money. It was plainly a gigantic mess. Some Warm Springs Apache had either sought a short-lived rest stop or experienced a peacefully settled change of heart and were seeking an unending sanctuary—it's arguable—at an out-of-the-way Cañada Alamosa area reservation near the San Mato Mountain's southern slope. At Silver City it mattered not a damn whit. Other Chiricahuas, Chokonens nominally under the leadership of the well-known Cochise, determined it "was time to go out and make a living."[188]

Fifteen prospectors set out from the old Burro Mines camp, which had undergone another name change and was now Ralston.[189] South of Apache Pass, some 30 miles into the Arizona Territory, Apache attacked the party on Jan. 23, 1871. Two men, Hugh O'Neil and Robert Schell, were wounded; two others managed a harrowing escape and went for help. The remaining prospectors fearfully hunkered down in a narrow defile, awaiting rescue from cavalrymen stationed at Fort Bowie. Captain Gerald "Jerry" Russell, an Irish-born career military man commanding hard-riding soldiers, galloped to the ambush scene but could not find any telling trail. Unbeknown to him, the Chokonen band had already ridden north into the Gila River country of New Mexico Territory.[190]

Whether it was this group of Apache or another was inconsequential to the folks at Silver City when, on Feb. 5, Apache stole horses and mules, almost within town limits. Captain William Kelly, at the forefront of 14 men from Company C, Eighth Cavalry, charged out of Fort Bayard in pursuit. Riding with his unit was Juan Arroyo, an adept and thoroughly steadfast scout, and a civilian mulepacker responsible for horse feed, rations and extra cartridges. At Silver City the platoon was enlarged by a compliment of seven private citizens under Jim Bullard's authority. The roundabout Apache trail, as frontiersman Arroyo deductively reasoned, was leading south through the Mangas Valley between the Big Burro and the Little Burro Mountains.[191] Joining forces with a second US Army patrol, Kelly's strength was increased to 31 rifles. Farther south, Juan Arroyo discerned that the Apache trail bent southwest, heading straight thorough the ancient Peloncillos, a narrow north-south range of 1,000-1,500-foot hills straddling the New Mexico-Arizona borderline, the San Simon Valley on the west, the Animas Valley on the east.[192] After cutting through the Peloncillos, the Apache had turned west, apparently making tracks for Cochise's favored stronghold in the foreboding Chiricahua Mountains.

Early in the afternoon of Feb. 12, Bullard's boys located the Chokonens' *ranchería*. Totally self-assured that their back trail had been obscured and that no bunch of ragtag Silver City miners or clumsy soldiers could follow, the Apache dropped their guard, failing to post a look-out. The harebrained breakdown in their cat-and-mouse tactics was uncharacteristic; it proved to be a horrific blunder. During a blinding and biting snowstorm, the whites reconnoitered and then deployed keen-eyed riflemen. Fourteen Apache died from the withering fire. Twenty were wounded. Afterward at the *ranchería* all 17 wickiups were burned to the ground, which didn't take very long. Amid the Apache property, solid evidence was found linking them to a previously executed stagecoach ambush in Arizona Territory at the ever unsafe Apache Pass. The mounts earlier stolen at Silver City were recovered.[193] Cochise wasn't around for this skirmish, however—he was over in New Mexico Territory prowling about in the Silver City country.

On Feb. 23, the Silver City miners took a tattered and ruinous page from the Apache playbook: They, too, stupidly neglected to post an alert sentinel, or any guard. For a weekly nighttime *fandango,* the attendees put their horses in Harvey Whitehill's conveniently positioned corral. Dan Rose, an old-timer reminiscing in 1917, drew from memory a fascinating sketch of the evening and of the partying folks:

> The night was dark and nothing to mar its silence save the whining grind of a "fiddle," accompanied by the plung-plang of an erstwhile melodious guitar—for a dance was on. It was "baile night," and all the people, excepting the "grouch," the feeble and blind (and they were very few) were gathered there, where the bright lights (candles and lamps) shown on fair women and brave men. "El Cabelero de Mexico" was there, with his huge sombrero, embroidered with bands of silver and gold, as were his other vestments, from his jacket of doe-skin to the buckles on his fine tan zapatas. He rarely ever danced, but stood a wall-flower, silently, with his eyes flashing from time to time, as he saw his amorous-eyed Senorita clasped in the huge maws of some boisterous giant of a "Gringo" mule-whacker. This mule-whacker was in glory, and why not? Here was a diversion fit for the Gods, and he had been "eating dirt" for three months behind an 18-mule outfit, and it was his time to yell, and "buy the shades of Old Joe Bowers" he was "a-goin' to yell," and he did. In the same set, with their ore-stained overalls, miners and prospectors pealed forth loud and long, as each one grabbed his little Senorita to "prome-nade-all." Which went to show that he, too, was willing

> to let joy be unconfined; nor were they alone—not "a-tall." The merchant was there, so was the baker, the banker, and the wagon maker. The "bad men" and the "bully" and the gambler and his pals; in fact the "hentefina" (fine people) as were the "poveries" (the poor). All were gathered in one swaggering, boisterous crowd of devil-may-care human beings as ever danced and flirted, drank and swore, fought and died in any carnival where Bacchus reigned as king.[194]

During the wee hours of the morning, when someone finally staggered to Whitehill's corral, it was learned to their total astonishment that the horses were gone.[195] Moccasin dints in soft earth gave the clue. Without delay, a posse was organized consisting of John Bullard, Sam Eckles, Ed Moulton, Joe Yankie, Amos Clark, Able L. Webb, John Jones, Tom Findley, Peter Hildreth, Hugh Flynn, Jason Baxter, Thomas Jefferson Wood and about 20 others unnamed.[196] Most of the townsmen's horses were among the missing. Luckily, before their departure, the posse located a couple of jaded nags to serve as packhorses. The broiling mad and utterly dogged civilians traveled on foot; they had spilling buckets of Apache blood on the brain. After trailing the Indians for five cold and miserable days, their dream came true. Once again during a blizzard, just across Arizona Territory's eastern boundary line in the dazzling San Francisco River country on the Mogollon Mountain's western side, the two enemies neared collision.

John Bullard, early settler and one of Silver City's founding fathers. Killed by Apache. *Courtesy Silver City Public Library.*

The Apache's secreted camp on the north side of the San Francisco River was noticed by a forward guard of Silver City's possemen. Quickly the raring-to-go outfit was split, Bullard leading one squadron and Ed Moulton heading the other. A lesser watch was detailed to protect the pack-animals. Inadvertently and all too quickly, the boys from town stumbled into a shivering Chokonen sentry. Ed Moulton fired. The startled Apache winced in pain as a bullet tore through his thigh. Almost at the very same instant, John Bullard let loose and his spiraling ball wickedly cut through the warrior's chest. From his crumpled position the Apache drew a revolver from his belt and leveled it at Bullard, who was fast approaching, trying to reload as he dashed in for the *coup de grace*. Once again shots rang in unison. The Indian's bullet ripped into Bullard's "bosom," while the projectile released by Moulton struck its bobbing target, blowing the Apache's head to "atoms." Bullard slumped to the ground, peeled back his shirt, saw the gaping hole in his heaving chest and, without a groan, died.[197]

According to Ed Moulton, "the ball began to roll" and the Silver City posse rained hellfire on the flabbergasted *ranchería*, killing 14 Apache, "giving them what was coming to them."[198] Reportedly, one of the dead was Salvadora, the Chihenne son of Mangas Coloradas, who had jarringly jumped the reservation with Cochise the previous November. Cochise, if he was there at the time of the bloody clash with an infuriated posse from Silver City—which was likely—made good his getaway.[199]

"These chastisements taught the Apaches a lesson, for never again did they make a raid upon Silver City, in fact, for several years afterwards they gave the town a wide berth. The citizens of Silver City on the other hand never forgave the Apaches for the death of Captain Bullard. Their hatred for them now became intensified into a firm conviction that the only good Apache was a dead one."[200] The ongoing punishment of a few Apache and the settlement of Silver City may have succeeded in retarding another direct assault on the town by Indians. As the Southwest's history clearly reveals and as the city's colorful story continues to unfurl, however, the seemingly incessant conflict continued to seethe throughout old Grant County's hinterland, a bailiwick that then encompassed the whole of Southwestern New Mexico Territory.

With a respite in Apache depredations, Silver City citizens refocused on their pressing problem—a lack of milling machinery. Cleverly, that "wild, indulgent and theatrical" sawmill and lumber man, Martin Bremen, jerry-rigged two old worn-out mills from Piños Altos.[201] Combining sundry parts, Bremen efficiently fashioned five good stamps, and with the ingenious combination of eight wooden barrels for amalgamation and pieces of rawhide belting, he was in the milling business. He immediately began crushing ore. The camp cheered up! Harvey Whitehill and partners jumped in too and:

> ...commenced reducing ore, by smelting, but owing to the want of good material for furnaces they could not make it pay. They then tried the Patio process and obtained $23 per ton. They next took a whiskey barrel and tried amalgamating by revolving it on axles. After the first trial they obtained from 750 pounds of ore, $64. Quicksilver being very scarce they had great difficulty in obtaining a supply, often paying as high as $2.50 per pound. During part of the time they obtained, with two arrastras and two barrels, $110 per day.... They treated about 150 tons of ore and obtained about $14,000.[202]

Productively latching on to the euphoria, William L. Rynerson and the Bullard Mining Company teamed up and brought another old mill from Piños Altos, placing Isaac James Stevens, Harvey Whitehill's father-in-law, in charge of its day-to-day operation. Other ramshackle mills, crude but functional, were refurbished and were soon churning and pounding with mechanical gusto. Mining claims and real estate titles changed hands "quite frequently, but in a legal way... as the men who founded Silver City were no beggarly crowd of drunken gamblers and cutthroats, but men of breeding who scorned

Miner in the forefront drilling his hole for an explosive "shot" is employing his single-jack, a short one-handed sledgehammer. His upright companion is using a long-handled sledgehammer, a double-jack, while the other cohort is holding the "drill steel." Thus, the slang terms "double-jacking" or "single-jacking" were the jargon often used to differentiate between a man working alone or with another. *Courtesy H. C. Stinson.*

Early Silver City businessmen Eugene Cosgrove, left, and Isaac N. Cohen, right. *Courtesy Silver City Public Library.*

quarreling and claim jumping." Harvey Whitehill and partners sold out to Arnold Wilson and Abel L. Webb, who had formed Wilson, Webb & Co. Shortly thereafter, Isaac N. Stevens, Whitehill's brother-in-law, located a "pocket of silver in the Seneca mine eight inches in thickness and 85 percent pure." The rejuvenation was good for downcast spirits and Silver City was revitalized. The boom was back on track.[203]

Success was not exclusively set aside for the hardscrabble prospectors and wealthy mining moguls. An effervescent local economy was being propped up by the population surge. There was money to be made—fortunes to be had—catering to the wants and needs of people in any setting. So, while some rushed headlong to prospect, extract and crush silver ore, others saw their destiny tightly linked with feeding, clothing, sheltering and, as has been smartly penned, merchandising "everything from wagon sheets to dynamite."[204] Eugene Golding's store was first, followed by several Jewish mercantile men: the no-nonsense David Abraham, Isaac Cohen, Henry Lesinsky and Max Schutz.[205] In short order, there were five general stores selling, as an old-timer recalled, "everything from a pin to a stamp mill."[206] Barney W. Connely was fixing and selling shoes and boots. There were two blacksmith shops and even a paint store.[207] James Copely opened a saloon, The Bedrock, and was fast stacking empty whiskey barrels out back.[208] Hotels fashioned from adobe bricks were springing up, although "most all the visitors had their camp outfit with them, and hung their hats where night overtook them."[209] Numerous were the men back East who threw caution to the wind and, with mining fever burning their souls, rushed to Silver City. Simultaneously, others, with diverse entrepreneurial ambitions, signed on for the invigorating race, too. None doubted they could grab a blue ribbon at the finish line.

Silver City's euphoric magnetism was also pulling from across the border. Mexicans, who'd long had experience mining in the northern

Chihuahua Hill overlooking downtown Silver City. *Courtesy Silver City Public Library.*

states of Chihuahua and Sonora, were notching their spot in the grueling marathon. In fact, their practical know-how was much in demand. Renowned not for mining skills but for their matchless savvy as teamsters and freighters, Mexican *arrieros* [muleteers] were also astutely aware of the very real opportunities to be had hauling tons of raw ore and other crucial cargo, and they came. *Contrabandistas* showed up too. Not surprisingly a cultural enclave soon materialized. Maintaining traditional and a time-tested style of architecture, the predominately Spanish-speaking sector came to life. Known locally as Chihuahua or Chihuahua Hill, the community evolved into a collection of adobe houses, *cantinas*, eateries serving peppery foods, and downright delightfully entertaining *fandangos* and *fiestas*. Striking *señoritas* in their fastidiously embroidered skirts strolled the dirt streets snaring gazes from visitors and hometown folk alike. Amorous men stood by taking fantasizing notice, quenching their parched thirst with fiery shots of *tequila* and *mescal*, their *sombreros* pulled down low to shade their faces and hide their lust. Crowing gamecocks and braying donkeys unmusically added to the scene. Red *chiles* hung drying under the sun's radiant warmth. It was a kaleidoscope of color. Incontrovertibly, most of the Chihuahua Hill people were hard workers. They had to be, just to survive. A few others, however, as with any subclass of humanity, chose the lazing and drinking night life, a *pistola* secreted under their blouses. Some Mexican sporting men deftly dealt *monte*; others just played—sometimes not so deftly. By any clearheaded analysis, Chihuahua Hill full well made her very real and measurable contributions to Silver City, adding to the eye-catching ambiance of a dynamic frontier neighborhood.

In those earliest days of the 1870s, the town was overrun with single males, and there were but five "white" families: the David Abrahams; Isaac James and Olive Priscilla Stevens and their not-inconsiderable brood; Cornelius Bennett; Robert Florman; and Harvey Whitehill, wife Harriet (better known as "Hattie") and their son, Harry Vance, and baby daughter, Emma Sarah.[210] The women and kids, just like their husbands and daddies, had managed the strenuous trip to Silver City risking their very lives. Dashing or plodding through harm's way was the price for cashing in on Silver City's promise. Physically, the cost of a tortuous wagon trip was demanding. Psychologically, for devoted mothers it must have been utterly maddening. Apache were not discriminate killers; women and children were fair game. When on the wearisome road, a faithful father had to absent himself from the family for reconnoitering ahead or to hunt; not infrequently he armed his wife with a six-shooter and explicit instructions: In case of an Apache attack, "she should first shoot the children, then herself."[211] It was a hard game! Actuarially, on that wild southwestern New Mexico Territory frontier, the infant morality rate was high; the natural life expectancy low. The good women who came on, forging ahead, were the caliber that could make a home out of a haunt. Speaking of those fine ladies, one who knew several of them well respectfully recalled:

> They were the ones when a friend or stranger was sick or wounded to place a mother's hand on his fevered brow and speak to him words of cheer and comfort. Burdened,

> as they were, with the care of their own brood, they never lost an opportunity to extend that mother's love to others. Fit mates they were for those rough-hewn, hard, daring men, and they clung to them as the ivy to the oak, with but one desire—to honor their God, their families and the community they called home.... Side by side with those sturdy men, they endured hardships, privations and sorrow. And if those same men built the fires of civilization, those pioneer women heaped on the fuel until its lights gleamed east and west, north and south until they penetrated the remotest part of this continent.[212]

Almost overnight, Silver City had changed. Civilization, whether she liked it or not, was being dragged to old Grant County. An Eastern urbanity was their objective, and by damn that tenacious Silver City bunch would not be sidetracked or bought off with less. A trip to the county seat or the post office at Piños Altos, although but nine miles, was yet risky business. Extended travel, say, through the Burros to Ralston, was still best made in platoons, heavily armed. Common sense still dictated carrying a six-shooter or carbine while jouncing and rebounding inside one of W. H. Wiley's passenger and mail coaches scurrying between Silver City and Rio Mimbres. Even a pleasant Sunday afternoon outing was a calculated undertaking, security-wise: "The first picnic in Grant Co. was enjoyed under a Picket Guard of 10. It was surely most picturesque—the undergrowth had been cut away by an advance guard and about 25 people enjoyed that one day in the woods."[213] In town, however, Apache were no longer a threat. An Americanized normalcy was close at hand.

On July 16, 1870, one of the city's founders, Richard Yeamans, and his Spanish-speaking bride, the dazzlingly attractive Talonia Raves, stood before Dick Hudson, who had traded in his sheriff's hat for that of probate judge, and were united in marriage. The festive ceremony was Silver City's first wedding.[214]

Other signs of civilization were at hand. Because of the burgeoning mercantile traffic with Old Mexico, Silver City now had a permanently assigned US mounted customs inspector, John S. Crouch. Piños Altos citizens were chargined after they learned legislators at Santa Fe had stripped Grant County's seat of government from them and honored Silver City with the prize; it was altogether predictable, though. Washington bureaucrats awarded Silver City a post office, too, and it sounded an early death knell for Piños Altos, which began a withering decline. Silver City was on the right track, so it seemed.

Still, there were hurdles to overcome. With the promise of opulence resonating through the Southwest, Silver City attracted more than its share of riffraff, gamblers, gunmen and girls—the latter of the working variety. Geographically, Grant County was positioned perfectly for those playing fast and loose with the law. Its near borders with Old Mexico and southeastern Arizona Territory made jumping from one judicial jurisdiction to another easy. For those running from the law it was mere child's play. Gigantic land areas under the thumb of only infant local governments' rule were alluring. Mere token law enforcement added to the draw. Silver City truthfully could boast that conscientious, honest and decent folks were in the majority, but as well she would have to shamefully confess—at least for awhile—that she was in a flash "gaining the reputation of a tough, even lawless town."[215] To deny otherwise would be kicking the teeth out of veracity. For a time it was a fast town, harboring a fast crowd recklessly fixed on chasing fast money.

Spotlighting those early days, it has been written with tongue in cheek that at Silver City "the only legitimate industry was coffin making."[216] That same historian penned, "The mining camps around Silver City, New Mexico, were tough almost to the limit of human endurance."[217] Speaking of the smoke-belching "gun-plays [that] took place quite often," a contemporary storyteller concluded that Silver City was at the time tagged with a "reputation it did not really crave."[218] Another old-timer recalled how wresting the town away from hooligans was pulled off, it being necessary to give the overworked Grant County coroner some "siftings."[219] Over a hundred years later, advantaged by decades of proficient historical research, due credit may be given an assertion that southwestern New Mexico Territory was a "gunfighter proving ground, the blistering cauldron where so many Wild West gunmen made their reputations."[220]

A common thread pulled the good men and the badmen together: the saloon. Refined to its simplest, it may be candidly conceded, "Everywhere on the frontier, nearly all men drank nearly all the time, which made nearly all men more or less drunk most of the time."[221] Resultantly, inhibitions lessened as the blood-alcohol level went up. Samuel Colt, inventor of the Colt's revolving six-shooter, is generally credited with "making all men equal." He did not, however, give all men good sense. With handy six-shooters stuffed into their waistbands, back pockets and sometimes even leather scabbards, nearly everyone went armed. This concoction of gunpowder and gut-wash, stirred with a mind-numbing dose of false courage, often spilled over into puddles of blood-splattered tragedy. Besides girls, gin and guns, gambling was recurrently cause of pointless carnage. Arguments and allegations were commonplace. Gaming was nonetheless a very popular pastime. The era when New Mexico Territory's southwestern frontiers were being peeled back "was a time of almost unlimited personal freedom and it was a loose, tolerant society with few to say that gambling was a sin, a crime or a folly."[222] Among hot spots on the gaming circuit, Silver City fast became known as a "wide-awake" town![223]

Swiftly Silver City developed its underbelly, an after-dark economy. An old-time chronicler, one who was actually there during the palmy days, sets the stage:

> ...there were between 10 and 15 saloons and three dance halls, scattered from "hell to breakfast" all over town. Of course, the dance halls were attached to the saloons.... First there was Bill McGeary's where the first court was held and before I forget it, let me redeem its wickedness if I can, by mentioning the fact that it was also used for the first church and afterwards I went to school there. So you see "Old Bill's" place turned out good after all, even if Charley Bishop did pin a Mexican's hand to a monte table with a bowie knife for trying to steal a bet, right where the pulpit afterwards stood. There was Dick Howlett's and last but not least that of Don Juan Ward.... As this particular dance hall is to play conspicuous part in the wild life that followed, I will describe it more intimately than the others, although they were all generally built alike. The building at this time was of adobe, one-story and 50 feet wide....The front part of the building at that time was a gambling department. The next was the "wet goods" and cashier's department—the bar room annex. Both of these departments covered about one third of the building while the other, with huge barn doors leading from the street into a capacious hall, was

> the "baile room," where the denizens of the little town made up of almost every color and creed gathered Monday, Wednesday, Saturday and Sunday nights to dance and carouse and enjoy the one great joy of their life....Considering the money spent over the bar and the gambling tables, not only that of Juan Ward's but the others also, one can judge that as far as money was concerned it was "sure" the best business in town....If the nights were wild and boisterous the days were none the less so, for all was bustle and confusion with the drunken brawls and crowds singing in and out of the saloons, the coarse laughter and Indian yells of the half-crazed "critters" as they drank and fought.[224]

An early snapshot of Silver City during those first two years of the 1870s exposes an authentic Southwest frontier neighborhood functioning within a much broader context. It was an incredible three-ring circus. In one circle were the industriously engaged and hard working. Twenty-four hours a day and seven days a week, the overworked and often undervalued wives and mothers—and there were but a few—resiliently sculpted hearth and home, the cozily warm refuge for adoring families. The vast majority of the menfolk worked, earning a meager living, building businesses or providing services—and copiously prospecting for and speculating in profitable and/or poor-paying mining claims. In the middle ring, for all to see, were the "sporting men," the card players and faro dealers. There was no dearth of business. The professionals slept late and stayed up all night betting and bluffing. Recreational "sports" just jumped back and forth between sin and sobriety. Some of Silver City's best were pretty springy!

Circling in that last ring were the Apache. They weren't friendly, and they weren't welcome. Chihenne and Chokonen raids had become pandemic. Rightly or wrongly, those pioneering Grant County folks had come to stay—by damn! "During the first part of 1871, the Indians in Grant County got out of hand. 'About 20 men and women have been murdered and horribly mutilated within the last three weeks', Governor [William A.] Pile wrote the secretary of state."[225]

One such outrage is paradigm. Freighter Charles Keerle, his wife, Gus Hepner, Thomas Sunderland, Charles Delard and three or four others were working their way back to Fort Bayard from an Old Mexico trip. Keerle had been to Chihuahua City to pick up wagon loads of salted bacon, contracted by the Army. At Chocolate Pass, roughly halfway between Casas Grandes and Galeana, 35 Apache attacked on the morning of March 4, 1871. The Americans were all killed, excepting one who somehow escaped. Apache "horribly mutilated" the bodies, cutting their victims' hands off, and for some odd reason, Mr. and Mrs. Keerle were beheaded as well.[226] News of the atrocity screamed throughout the Southwest—and beyond. Silver City citizens knew the Keerles as hometown folk.

Grant County's populace was fed up. A communal meeting was called and many concerned and fuming civilians came together for a hurried council at Rio Mimbres, east of Silver City. Their unanimous declaration was not ambiguous. They pledged to follow their stolen livestock wherever the trail might lead—reservation or not—and to regain it by force of arms if need be, "even at the sacrifice of every Indian man, woman and child of the tribe." Furthermore, warned Probate Judge Dick Hudson, they would deal "accordingly" with "anyone" who stood in their way, be they an Apache or be they one of their "accomplices." Messaging the Indian agent, O. F. Piper, through the public release of their resolutions, the assembly asked: "What we want to know is, whether our stock can be recovered or not from Indians on your reservation, when fully proved and identified, or if we are to be forever at the mercy of these thieving murderous Apaches, who have a 'house of refuge' at [Cañada] Alamosa; if so, the sooner we know it the better, because the citizens of this county are determined to put a stop to it, and if they carry out their programme the Camp Grant massacre will be thrown entirely in the shade, and Alamosa will rank next to Sand Creek."[227]

Perturbed and at the same time thoroughly won over to the notion that Grant County people in their desperation meant business, Territorial Governor Pile made arrangements for intervention, departing Santa Fe on May 1, 1871. His worry was that "harsh and illegal measures" would be taken by the "armed and aroused" citizens. After his grueling and dangerous trip, he arrived in Silver City and the red carpet was rolled out. The governor sympathized with the citizenry: " I know you have suffered deeply. I saw today the green tree that stands sentinel over the grave of brave Captain Bullard, whose loss you mourn, and it brought tears to my eyes when I thought of Mrs. Kerl [sic], who was like one of my family, now silent in death, a victim of Indian barbarity." Governor Pile assured the townsfolk that his administration agreed on the necessity of "immediate action" and professed his hope that a peaceful policy might yet prevail, but declared he would not be hesitant to "strike terror to the Apache heart."[228] After receiving presidential treatment, the governor promised to see that the military commands were beefed up, as well as the authorized civilian posses.[229] A committee of locals was appointed to "collect statistics of the number of people killed; and of amount of property destroyed in Grant county, during the last 18 months, by the Indians," and the governor left for Santa Fe, touring the variously scattered mining camps on the way.[230]

Area citizens were more than pleased with a personal and compassionate visit from Governor Pile, and generally it was believed there would be a "speedy adjustment of the Indian troubles."[231] Little did they know it then, but the "adjustment" would be years in the making. Another signal fact, though, they all very well knew and could count on: They had come to stay, and Silver City was going to be "Built to Last!"

Chapter 5
"That Go-Ahead Town"

Verifiable mining records at Grant County reveal by January 1872 claims had been filed on more than 300 lodes, most area prospectors financially involving themselves in multiple partnerships.[232] Preempting a strip of promising ground was relatively simple; making it pay was an altogether different and expensive proposition. Demonstrably smart men were hedging their bets, not wishing to freeze limited capital in a single gamble: John Bullard and Charles Keerle, both killed by Apache, left their co-owners, Jim Bullard, Charles Steelhammer, John Swisshelm, John Mason and William Kelly, in possession of the Santa Maria Ledge, as witnessed by H. M. Fuson and Elijah Weeks. H. B. Porter, with various other speculators and relatives, was trying his luck with the Excelsor Ledge, the California Ledge and the Nebraska Ledge. Andrew Hurlburt, one of the original Bullard Mining Company partners, was also invested in the Monmouth Lode, along with Harvey Whitehill, George W. Tower and Charles Simpson. And the sanctioned registry of joint ventures goes on and on, seemingly ad infinitum.[233]

Milling machinery was continually breaking down, and scarce parts were constantly being cannibalized for installation elsewhere. Shade-tree mechanics were incessantly at work. Quicksilver, an essential ingredient in the process, was in short supply—sometimes almost nonexistent. Due to the excessive freight rates and Silver City's remoteness, when the quicksilver shipments did finally arrive, upset miners were paying exorbitant prices—twice its worth in New York.[234] Heavy milling machinery shipped by wagon from Kit Carson, Colo., to southwestern New Mexico Territory was on the road for seven or eight weeks to Las Cruces or Mesilla, then several weeks later it was off-loaded in Silver City at great expense.[235] Speculators Parker Burnham, the city's brickyard owner, Dr.

Casson, H. M. Harshberger and Henry Lohman erected a makeshift mill in the Silver Flat District to work their claims on Ciénega Creek, the Summit, the Black Hawk extension, the Red Jacket and the Local Lode.[236] The mill worked erratically. Thereafter, the Wisconsin mill came on line—part of the time.[237] Still, that cadre of first-comers knew, in due course, mechanical troubles could and would be overcome.

Their newly found community may have been still an island in a wilderness, but those early pioneers were unmistakably focused. Silver City was not destined to be a fleeting and transitory stop on their hard-fought journey to prosperity. It was home! And therein was the dynamic factor that differentiated their outlook from many others who wandered the West hopping from one short-lived camp to the next, leaving ghost towns in their backwash.

Demographically Silver City was a mixture of Anglo-Americans and native Spanish speakers, those linked by the heredity of decades in New Mexico Territory or immigrants from south of the international borderline. Truthfully, at the time, not too many of the Americans were Southerners or Texans. They were Easterners. Some were foreign born, but the majority of them had assimilated through or grown to adulthood in the eastern United States, from Ohio, New York, Pennsylvania, Illinois, Michigan and Massachusetts. For the most part, those who claimed West Coast origins had, in fact, earlier come west from the eastern states, and then onto New Mexico Territory during the Civil War as a part of Carleton's California Column.[238] As a result, their ideas of how to build a city were not grounded in generations of an architectural style common and practically suited to the Southwest. Collectively they very well knew what a bona fide city should look like. Silver City was going to—notwithstanding Chihuahua Hill—fit that ironclad mold. Parker Burnham's brickyard made it feasible. The lit fuse was fast burning toward an authentic building boom, and it would not go unnoticed:

> Silver City is making rapid strides and progress is the watchword here. There is scarcely an idle man to be found about the town, and not a single man need be idle for there is plenty of good work for all. The mines are every day being more fully developed, and with the most gratifying results. The rattle of the hammer and saw are every where to be heard, as well as the booming of the miners' shots.... There are a number of fine brick build-

ings now in process of erection that would be an ornament to any town far east of the Rocky Mountain base, and others will be put up as soon as Burnham can turn out the brick. The first kiln of the season will be ready to open in a few days. Bricklayers are in demand here, and would find plenty of work the whole season at remunerative wages. In fact, mechanics of all trades are much needed here.... There is a large quantity of ore at all the mills, each man awaiting his turn, and if there were a hundred more stamps working here today, not one of them would be idle for want of ores to work.[239]

An early example [1883] of Silver City's built-with-brick permanence is David Abraham's spacious residence at the northwest corner of Black and Sixth Streets. *Courtesy Silver City Museum.*

Forty-eight-years old at the time, Polish-born David Abraham [Dobrzinsky] is credited with putting up the first brick building in Silver City, finished and ready for occupancy by spring 1872. The handsome edifice was a two-story; living apartments upstairs, general merchandising store on the ground floor.[240] Other brick businesses and residences were soon showing clear evidence to the peeking world that Silver City was no clapboard mining town. She was better than that, they hoped—no, they guaranteed. In every respect, Silver City was going to be an idealistically crafted and Americanized town. A city with prototypical models of American architecture, furnished with American whatnots, plumed with American accouterments, and drenched and entrenched with an American ethos. The fine art of symbolism was not lost. Historical scrutiny snared their mindset: "Brick was a reminder of home—of St. Louis, Detroit, Chicago, New York—and at the same time a boast which declared with every straight corner that what a man built in the West could look as good as what he had left in the East."[241] Adobe was cheaper, cooler, warmer, tighter, and easier to fix, but it wasn't American. It just wouldn't do! Sometimes, financially embarrassed men hid mud-front abodes with false fronts made of brick.[242] Their intent was to hew a town like Prescott, over in Arizona Territory, a town with "houses American style." The doors were to be American, fastened with American bolts and locks, and opened by American knobs.[243] Newspapermen had already made note: Silver City was "essentially an eastern town, full of live energetic and intelligent men who have come there to stay."[244] Almost overnight, so it seemed, "strangers" were admitting an "astonishment" at finding Silver City, so far out on the Southwest's frontier, to be a "real American town with fine, two-story brick buildings and a live energetic people."[245] With thumping messages proclaiming their victorious feats, Silver City peoples' pride was pumped:

> No where in New Mexico—no where in the Southwest can so striking an example of energy and enterprise be found as in Silver City.... The enterprising citizens of that go-ahead town are determined to create a city that shall prove that American genius, enterprise and intelligence has reached this isolated frontier.[246]

During that spring of 1872, David Abraham and family may have moved into their spacious new home—Silver City's first red brick—but Harvey and Hattie Whitehill had some bragging rights of their own. On March 16, their second son, Wayne Washington, was born. The delivery was significant, in a way: He was the very first "white" child to be born in the town. Births on Chihuahua Hill must have been happening too, but since records remain silent, the premium for being Silver City's first native-born son is tidily awarded to Wayne Washington Whitehill. [247] A visitor dropping by Whitehill's residence to see the newborn recalled, "Mr. Wayne Whitehill could not now get himself into the space where I first saw him: it was a tiny cradle and he a tiny baby kicking and cooing, while the dear Mother was busy with her callers, who had just come from the far off, outside world."[248]

By this time, any of those far-off visitors to Silver City from the "outside world" could now find accommodations at Samuel Eckle's 10-room Star Hotel. It had an attached corral and—maybe more important for some guests—it also had a barroom.[249] Joseph Yankie's hotel, the Keystone, was under construction and would soon be selling "good rooms and beds."[250] Some early arrivals, such as Henry "Harry" Boyer Ailman, were so financially strapped they dared not even think of paying tariff for a bed. Ailman remedied his nighttime dilemma by bunking in a crudely constructed hovel built on a vacant lot with discarded adobe bricks, sleeping on a makeshift mattress stuffed with empty coffee sacks.[251] He made it just fine!

Some other visitors to Silver City made it just fine, too, but just barely. During the pleasant September of 1872, a seven-man party was inching toward Silver City with utopian objective. Leading the squadron was Brigadier General Oliver Otis Howard, a one-armed Civil War veteran. Howard, a US Army man with unbending faith in God Almighty, was nicknamed by supporters the "Christian General" and, no doubt, by detractors as an implacable "Bible thumper." Accompanying General Howard was his aide-de-camp, Lieutenant Joseph Alton Sladen, a steadfast solider and man of evident courage as a recipient of the Medal of Honor. Three civilians traveled with the military men. One was Thomas Jonathan "Tom" Jeffords, an authentic Southwest frontiersman, but also a man of sometimes dubious dealings with Apache, at least so some surmised. Another was Jacob "Jake" May, hired as an interpreter. Rounding out the Anglo faces was a hard-drinking and wayward ex-soldier, Zebina Nathaniel Streeter, who could speak Spanish fluently and enough Apache to get by; he, too, was a man with a shady past. Two obliging paid Apache served as trail guides and optimistic emissaries, Ponce, a "thick-set, 35-year-old Chihenne" with a pronounced stutter, and Chie, a Chokonen about 21 years old, reportedly one of Cochise's favorite nephews. Howard's mission was simple: Find Cochise and make peace.[252] The party entered Silver City on Sept. 24 for an overnight stay. Lieutenant Sladen accentuates the outfit's legitimate apprehension and sheds light on their reception:

> The valuable silver mines of that region had drawn many adventurous spirits into the midst of this hostile country. The town was compactly built, and contained one or two brick houses, said to be he only ones in the Territory. But it was entirely cut off from any civilized community, and in the midst of a savage and blood thirsty band of Indians.
>
> Scarcely a day passed but some outrage was committed, and men dared scarcely venture outside the line of houses, unless in some numbers and well-armed.
>
> Our own live Indians, Ponce and Chie, belonged to the very tribes that were supposed to be committing these depredations, and we were warned by the officers at Fort Bayard that we should have to guard them very closely or we should not be able to restrain the people of Silver City from killing them, so bitter was their hatred engendered against the race, on account of the sufferings they had undergone.
>
> On reaching the town, the presence of these Indians very soon created an excitement, and we were glad to get them inside the protecting enclosure of the Corral, which was an important feature of every hostelry in that country. No attempt, however was made to molest them, but threats were many that they would not get out of town alive.
>
> The rank and standing of the General, however, had its effect, and though Ponce and Chie were confined most to the time to the enclosure, and never left without the protecting care of some of our party, no further demonstration occurred.[253]

Indian fighter and early Silver City settler, James "Jim" Bullard. A US soldier said of Bullard: "He was about as morose, insolent and foul-mouthed a brute as I ever saw." *Courtesy Silver City Museum.*

While restocking supplies and making ready for their departure, General Howard hired a local man, J. H. Stone, to accompany his peace delegation for $50 per month. Lt. Sladen, who apparently checked up on Stone's suitability for the assignment, reported the man was "ready for a fight with hostile Indians, or a dance at a Mexican *baile,* always ready for any work, always good natured, an excellent cook, a ready talker and a good shot."[254] And, according to the lieutenant, Stone was "on good terms with everybody, Mexicans, Miners, Indians or Whites" and was an "excellent addition" to their small party.[255] Departing Silver City on the 25th, the peace party moved out, heading south through the perilous Burro Mountains for a dicey meeting not with formidable Apache fighters, but with southwestern New Mexicans hell-bent on solving their problems—their way!

In country that Sladen described as "wild and dangerous," his group ran headlong into a band from Silver City, "well-armed and determined looking," working under the loose command of Jim Bullard. The two crews collided but not with cordiality. Approaching with "black looks," the Silver City boys eyed their conventional enemies, Ponce and Chie. During an uneasy parley, Howard questioned Bullard if his party had seen any Apache. Angrily, Bullard told the general that they hadn't, but if they had there would be dead Indians to show for it, and then matter-of-factly said something to the effect of "We'd like to kill the two goddamn Apache you have with you!" In the blistering-hot conversation that ensued, Howard shook his good arm in Bullard's face, and, at length, the Grant County civilians backed off and rode off—spitting in disgust.[256]

Back in town, citizens were aggressive too, hammering out their stamp of how an enlightened civilization was predestined to be. Southwestern frontier folk could well figure that when their town warranted a newspaper editor setting up shop and inking the presses, the settlement was off to a darn good start. Silver City soon boasted two pugnacious and fire-breathing newspapermen in the same town—at the same time—each voicing contrasting partisan viewpoints and doing battle with printing presses in a manner that frequently "resembled Armageddon."[257] At first the town had but one newspaper, *Mining Life*, and its vocal editor, Owen L. Scott, expressive, opinionated and sometimes even "grumpy," had no competition when he inaugurated his sheet on May 17, 1873.[258] In August the *Silver City Tribune*, a radically Republican-tilted newspaper, appeared on the journalistic scene, but before Christmas she was a dead-letter.[259] The newspaper wars, in earnest, were yet to commence for Silver City, but she wouldn't be let off from the fun!

Many family men, much like Harvey Whitehill, had made an exploratory trip to southwestern New Mexico Territory prior to moving or sending for their wives and children. So, while Wayne Whitehill may have been the first "white" child *born* at the town, he by no stretch of the imagination was the first or only child. In fact, there were a not inconsiderable number of youngsters of school age, but there was no educational facility. Shortly before *Mining Life* began its circulation, the pioneering citizens of Silver City had petitioned the Territorial Legislature for passage of a special act for Grant County, allowing them to assess taxes dedicated to the creation of a free public school system. It was the first stab by the "electorate" of any county in New Mexico Territory to do so. Legislative matters at Santa Fe regarding the inadequate territorial schools were mired in miles of bureaucratic red tape, indifference and ineffectiveness. In the interim and absent an adequate law, the "go-ahead" people at lively Silver City went ahead and sent their children to a privately funded school in a local residence. Classes were taught by Charles Shannon, who was later replaced by a Mr. Green. Newspaper editor Scott, after launching *Mining Life*, took up the harangue for a free public school system and campaigned passionately with other conscientious citizens for a workable solution. Undaunted mothers formed the Ladies Educational Society and placed at the very top of their target list the building of a suitable schoolhouse. An unselfish building committee composed of William Chamberlin, Isaac J. Stevens, John Johnson, Mrs. Robert Florman and a newlywed, Mary (Stevens) Hudson, Isaac's daughter, who had married the generally admired Dick Hudson, were appointed. A modest single-story brick structure measuring 20 by 40 feet was proposed at a cost of $2,500, to be built on a lot donated by Isaac J. Stevens. Fund-raising efforts were kicked off.[260]

Social, civic and local governmental orderliness from the structural standpoint was close at hand. Early in January 1873, a meeting was called at H. M. Porter's Hall for the purpose of organizing Lodge No. 8, Ancient Free & Accepted Masons, under the Grand Lodge of Missouri. Present at that charter meeting were such Silver City founding notables as Cornelius Bennett, I. N. Cohen, Eugene Goding, F. H. Cooper, Sam Eckles, Alexander H. Morehead, George W. Bailey, Robert Florman, R. C. True, G. S. VanWagenen, S. Green, J. R. Nichols, John I. Pantlind, John B. Morrill, J. C. Wheelock, George W. Hold, C. Robbins and Harvey Whitehill.[261] Affiliating with the Grand Lodge of Missouri rather than a previously chartered lodge in New Mexico Territory proved more than just a little controversial.[262]

There was not yet a church in town, although a Catholic priest included Silver City on his meandering circuit.[263] Perhaps, even if God's house had been standing in Silver City at that time, the number of pious parishioners sitting in pews might have seemed rather negligible when evaluated against the existent backdrop of predominately single-male inhabitants—and their proclivity for frolicsome amusement. It has not untruthfully been written that "Silver City was a town with all its hair on, its population a mixture of the most fearless and the most desperate men on the frontier. It was a town where three shifts of bartenders were needed to cope with the round-the-clock thirst of the patrons of saloons like the Blue Goose and the Red Onion or more elegant places like Joseph D. Dyer's recently opened Orleans Club on Main Street, where the high rollers sat all night with their gold and silver stacked in front of them, betting into pots running to thousands of dollars."[264]

Unsmiling bettors won and lost, bluffed and bragged—and they sometimes squabbled. Overindulgent swigs of neat whiskey coalescing with belligerent machismo and gunpowder naturally had predictable result. The upshot? Time and time again in Silver City's taprooms the flashpoint was touched and six-shooter firestorms blew up with calamitous consequences. One of Harry Ailman's traveling buddies, 23-year-old Lee Campbell, forsook prospecting for gambling. He thought he was a poker whiz! Ailman recalled about saying his last goodbye to young

Campbell: "One night he got into a dispute over a game that was settled with six-shooters, and we followed him to his grave."[265] Previously, near the back of McGary's ballroom, a drunk named Campbell—possibly the soon-to-be-deceased Lee—fought and scuffled while refusing to surrender his sidearm to an unnamed local lawman; his blue-steel Colt's six-shooter discharged. Sadly, an innocent—presumably—bystander was shot.[266] Another time, William "Billy" Wilson jerked a knife and cut Joe Dyer, the saloon owner, scarring him for life.[267] All told, for that fractious summer of 1873 there were a dozen shootings and they were still happening when the leaves started changing color.[268]

Even that plucky little "tough as nails" merchant, David Abraham, was forced to empty both barrels—or as a *Tribune* reporter penned, "give him the contents"—of his Parker breech-loader into the bowels of an intoxicated man, Robert Everett, killing him outright. This wasn't Abraham's first justifiable Silver City killin', and it wouldn't be his last.[269] Possibly it's a wee bit melodramatic, but one who was actually on the scene and correspondingly an eyewitness, wrote of Silver City's "bad men from Bitter Creek" and her "howling wolves of the lone prair-ee."[270] Quick summation of his personal assessment was that it was a "God-send" when these types punctured each other through and through with "45-bullets." Candidly the same contemporary scribe was forced into another admission—history bears him out—that "all these gun-plays" were not confined to just one class, and that a "great many occurred from disputes over gambling tables and business affairs, such as mining claims, etc."[271] *Mining Life* editor Scott railed about the senseless violence, to no avail.[272]

The Antrim home where "Billy the Kid" lived while a youth in Silver City. *An Alfred S. Addis photo, courtesy New Mexico History Museum, #99054.*

The editor likewise complained about Silver City's growing throng of unsupervised school-age boys. Scott mused that a few of the lads hellishly fixed on running life's race could "benefit by

The photograph generally used [and frequently questioned] portraying Cathering Antrim, "Billy the Kid's" mother. *Courtesy Leon C. Metz.*

coming in on the home stretch across the maternal knee."[273] No doubt the kids, free roaming, were periodically pulling off acts of tomfoolery, as would be expected of most boys. Editor Scott neglected monkey business specificity, but shied not away from bestowing them a collective nickname: The Silver City boys were the "Village Arabs." He was, even then, promoting one of his burning passions, completion of a public school.[274]

One of those boys Scott was classifying as a "Village Arab" would, in due time, garner more historic ink than all the others combined. During that summer of 1873, 30-year-old William Henry Harrison Antrim, accompanied by his new wife Catherine McCarty Antrim, 13 years his senior and suffering from tuberculosis, arrived in Silver City. The couple brought with them Catherine's two boys from a previous marriage, Joseph M. and Henry. The Antrims found a vacant cabin near the corner of Main and Broadway and quickly settled in. Catherine, sick but industrious, took in washing and an occasional boarder, and reportedly baked some of the best sweet-cakes to be had in any town. It has been written of Catherine that she was a "jolly Irish lady" and with spontaneous burst of energy she could be "full of life, fun and mischief and [who] could dance the Highland Fling as well as the best of the dancers," at the regularly scheduled weekly Silver City shindigs.[275] Her husband, by most accounts, worked intermittently as a butcher, carpenter, handyman and, always, a prospector.[276] The two boys, well, they quickly swelled ranks of the "Village Arabs."

Mining Life editor Scott continued his altruistic rant about criminal misdeeds, juvenile delinquency—or the potential thereof—and the indisputable want for a spanking-new schoolhouse. Worried citizens were listening and, for the most part, in agreement with the sermonizing news-

William Henry Harrison Antrim. Catherine's husband and "Billy the Kid's" stepfather. *Courtesy Robert G. McCubbin.*

paperman. Simply sprouting a town from near nothingness to magnificence was not easy work. Nor could it be done overnight. Silver City would have to be painstakingly built, if it were to last, brick by brick, house by house, and institution by institution. One of those crying first needs, aside from a schoolhouse, was for a courthouse—after all, Silver City was now a coveted county-seat town. Similarly there was want for a lockup—a calaboose. As an old-timer characterized early-day New Mexico Territory, "Everything in the country was rough right about then. It was, to tell the plain truth, very rough. The country was full of all kinds of bad men from cold-blooded deliberate murderers down to sneak thieves, and everybody just had to take care of himself in his own way."[277] The need for a county jail was unmistakable.

Although citizens had plans for a one-and-a-half-story brick courthouse with the basement set aside for a jail and sheriff's office, interim obligations commanded an architectural prescription less ambitious. Right then the county's needs were met by construction of a four-office adobe complex—no jail. The Grant County pokey was a separate adobe-bricked building, absent at the time any strap-iron cells but heated by "a big old fashioned chimney" and tightly secured by "heavy oaken doors."[278]

As Grant County buildings popped up, political faces changed, too. Cornelius Bennett was elected probate judge. Charles McIntosh, who should have felt "elated, as he ran against a very strong man," beat the incumbent Grant County sheriff, James G. Crittenden, who in the previous election cycle had succeeded the esteemed Dick Hudson. Harvey H. Whitehill was elected by a 67-vote majority to fill the post of county coroner, a tirelessly unthankful job—but, in light of all the killings, an important office.[279]

Silver City and her citizens and her politicos were seemingly in a state of unending transition. One phenomenon remained constant, however: Although there had been a longed-for letup in New Mexico Territory's Apache warfare—not in Arizona Territory—the calm was always teetering on the brink of heartbreak, as everyone knew. Their earlier tirades about Apache jumping the reservation near Cañada Alamosa, raiding, and then racing back for asylum under an Indian agent's wing weren't illegitimate. During that 1873 summer, while Silver City was caught up in building, electioneering, ore crushing and carousing in the downtown saloons and ballrooms, several Apache bolted.[280]

Riding hell-bent-for-leather, Apache cleared the Rio Grande River's east bank, negotiated the 5,719-foot San Augustin Pass between the San Andres and Organ Mountains east of Las Cruces, and—as was their trademark—vanished! Secreted in their lair, the majority relaxed and rested their jaded horses; others, just a few, stealthily scouted down the Organ's eastern slant, enviously eyeballing Warren H. Shedd's ranch, "a known and welcoming haven for every horse and cattle thief in southern New Mexico and a favorite water hole of Texas badmen." Shedd's San Augustin ranch was one of the "toughest places in New Mexico." Apache long familiar with *El Ojo del Espiritu* [Spirit Springs] had raided the jagged-faced mountain country for years, killing hapless travelers channeled there for want of water. Over time Shedd had shaped a wayfarers' layover complete with "a store, a commodious hotel-restaurant, a saloon, a dance-hall and a brothel." Warren Shedd pimped, pirated, pilfered and, above all else, profited.[281] As would naturally be expected in such a setting geared toward sin and sleaziness, from time to time six-shooters barked, snapping shut the quarrels, and second-place winners were buried out back or left for a buzzard's indifferent pecking.[282]

Timing their strike with precision, Apache broke from their hideaway and swooped down on Shedd's ranch, running off a herd of horses grazing nearby. Deftly, warriors circled the bunch in a wide arc and ran them back through the mountain pass, heading west. In this instance, perhaps, was it a case of thieves stealing from thieves? Regardless, after notification of the foray, the US Army questioned not morality issues but chased after Apache.

Charging out of his station, Fort Selden, on the Rio Grande's east bank just north of Las Cruces, rode Eighth Cavalry Captain George W. Chilson. Ten troopers, rationed and well-armed, followed. Captain

Chilson in an after-action report said:

> After following them four days and a half, I struck them in a cañon, tributary from the southwest of the Cañada Alamosa, where an engagement ensued resulting in the loss of one man, Corporal Frank Battling [Bratling] of my Troop, killed; the killing of three Indians out of four who were seen, and the recovery of all the stock.283

The skirmish, indeed, was hard fought. In addition to the death of Corporal Bratling, for their "service against hostile Indians" Sergeants Leonidas S. Lytle and James L. Morris, along with blacksmith John Sheerin and Private Willis Henry, received the grateful nation's highest tribute, the Medal of Honor.[284] Grant County citizens undoubtedly were proud of the soldiers' prompt and decisive action; nevertheless, they must have sighed a condescending "I told you so!" Their haughtiness was buttressed, and to a degree rightly so, when they read in the *Silver City Tribune* that Apache had been—once again—stealing horses "from the settlements between Fort Selden and El Paso." It mattered not a tinker's dam to them whether the raiding Apache were Cochise's Chokonens or Victorio's Chihennes or Mescelaros from east of the Rio Grande. They were Apache and they were to be unfeelingly scorned, stalked and slain. And too, no doubt those Silver City folks were more than a little disheartened to learn the civilian posse giving chase had been compelled to abandon the hunt.[285]

The chase for mineral wealth and social stability at Silver City was nonstop—despite what restless Apache did or did not do. The milling process, absent the proper equipment and the dependable stocking of spare parts, was yet crude. As much as 40 to 60 percent of the silver was simply not extracted due to the unrefined methods and recurrent breakdowns. Yet, even despite these very real afflictions, the camp could boast over a half-million-dollar output as autumn 1873 drew near. The richest, of course had been in the Chloride Flat District, the La Providencia and its whopping $250,000. Next from the twin shafts at the Seneca came a reported $120,000 payout. Then there was a $100,000 dividend at the El Gran Tesoro, and a not paltry $30,000 scavenged at the Dexter. The father and son team, Isaac James and Isaac Newton Stevens, were sitting on top of the proverbial "gold mine" with their stake in the

Two Ikes, but the shortage of operative and reliable machinery was rendering their mine worthless.[286]

The building boom was in full sway, and the Harvard-educated Robert Black and his brother, Thomas, were publicly marketing in newspapers that they could construct almost any type of structure from a "shanty" to "an elegant 3 story brick of palatial proportions."[287] Their claim was not deceptive advertising—they could and they did!

Reportedly, as many as a thousand emigrants from Utah alone were steadily advancing upon Silver City, and another "colony" from Colorado was likewise bound for Grant County's highly touted burg.[288] Real 1873 population figures may not be expressive of the genuine prattle echoing throughout the United States and Old Mexico, for they reflect not the region's numbers, only Silver City's head count. Residing within town limits were, by the most reliable figures, 700 Hispanics or Mexicans and 350 Anglos.[289] Outlying mining camps were sweet combs too, drawing hives of prospecting bees. Impossible to compute were the flood of transients, tourists and trekkers—here today, gone tomorrow. Fugitives from justice in other states or territories shunned being questioned or counted for any enumerator's tally. There was, especially at Silver City, an authentically identifiable housing shortage. The little municipality was fast outgrowing her britches.

Peter Ott had taken over as proprietor of the Keystone Hotel and was proclaiming the benefit of his thorough "renovations, refittings and refurnishings" and that "First Class" accommodations were guaranteed. Merchant J. A. Ketchum, a former partner with Martin Bremen, was "dealing in dry goods, clothing, boots & shoes, hats & caps, hardware, miners tools, groceries, liquors, Cigars & Tobacco." Richard Hudson was encouraging "responsible" patrons to stop by the Legal Tender Corral and lease some of his "First Class Riding Animals, Buggies and Teams" and to buy by the "pound or by the load" hay, corn, oats, barley and bran. John Brockman sold a flouring mill. The former sheriff, James Crittenden, "removed" himself from Silver City to take up farming along the Mimbres River. Jessie Coomer and Robert Newsome of Lone Mountain and Rio Mimbres respectively in separate incidents reported horses stolen, presumably by Apache. Rev. Wood, a Presbyterian and "a proper man to be sent to a frontier country like this," was on the scene performing marriages and preaching the Gospel. And Grant County Sheriff McIntosh was lauded for the "prompt discharge of his official duties," as "there had been nothing, so far, entrusted to his care, but what had been at once executed."[290] Whirlwind doings were blowing through old Grant County.

The little eight-sheet, 7-by-11-inch *Tribune* newspaper, unaware that she was in the throes of publishing death, bemoaned that New Mexico lawmakers should amend the criminal statutes, and that the "fees of officers should be regulated and raised...and that in all cases where the Territory or safety of the citizens requires any service of any officer, he should be reasonably compensated by the Territory or county."[291]

For the fall semester of 1873, and for those who could afford the $5 monthly surcharge, Jessie Anderson agreed to conduct basic classes at Robert Black's house on Texas Street. For concerned parents, it was the only workable solution for that year's few remaining months. Change—big change—educationally, was on Silver City's bright horizon, however.[292]

By late December, school commissioners reported the Silver City District had available funds to the tune of $630, for expenditure on 180 children. Proposing that if citizens would "defray the expense of rent and fuel," leaving the public funds dedicated for payment of a teacher's $50 per month salary, a free public school could open just after ringing in of the new year. Arrangements, at that time, were being made to hold classes at Bill McGary's Saloon and Hall, and to hire Professor J. Webster as headmaster and teacher. For the 119 "Spanish-Americans" and the 30 "Anglo-Americans" residing in Silver City, and the 31 others within the district but outside town limits, there would be no tuition. To qualify for admission a student had only to be between five and 15 years of age.[293]

Outside town limits travel was still risky. Apache jumped reservations, raided, and returned. Downtown, drunks and rowdies misbehaved, and with alarming regularity yanked out six-shooters and smoked each other. The doctors treated the wounded and dying. The busy coroner ruled. And, twice a year, the Third District Court's officers traveled to Silver City and adjudicated. Others just drank and gambled, then went home after a hard day's work to read weekly editions of *Mining Life* or the *Tribune*. By this time, family men were fast rising to a majority. Absenting one's self from the Silver City barrooms and bordellos was a reasonably good prescription for avoiding serious trouble. Mothers cooked, ironed, nursed the sick and stitched calm around commotion. Kids kicked cans, played, pushed each other down, and tattled. Silver City had arrived. She was, with the securely proposed opening date for a free public school, a real American town. There would be no going backward now!

Chapter 6

"Jack Has Skinned Out"

On Jan. 5, 1874, school opened. The headcount was 43 students. Many "Spanish-Americans" refrained from enrolling their children, finding it impossible to believe that classes were being offered free of charge. Moreover, scores of them could not afford the textbooks, an expense to be borne by the students' parents.[294] A partial roster of those attending would include: the Whitehill siblings, Harry and Emma; Cortie Bennett; James and Mary Davis; Alice Dyer; Carrie Bertchy; Roscoe Ginn; Richard Justice; Charles and Al Rosencranz; the Isaac James Stevens boys, Charles and Albert; Louis Abraham; Giedeon and Chauncey Truesdell; the Rose brothers, Dan and Tom; and Joe and Henry Antrim, who had adopted their stepfather's surname.[295]

After classes the lads did what unsupervised boys do. While navigating the pitfalls on the road from childhood to maturity, at least according to Louis Abraham, the footloose boys frequently hung out at the William Antrim household, eating home-baked cookies and playing.[296] Harry Vance Whitehill, one of the students, elaborates:

> The boys used to have a lot fun keeping race horses too. They would have someone be their race horse and would bet just for fun. I was Louie Abraham's race horse. Every time before a race Louie would come around with a bottle with something (I don't know what it was) in it, and say, "Lift up your foot." So I would lift up my foot and Louie would put some of the stuff out of the bottle on it. Of course, there wasn't anything to it and it couldn't help me win, but I always imagined that it would make me win and I could outrun anyone.[297]

The infamous Palace Saloon at Central City, one-time county seat of old Grant County. *Courtesy Silver City Museum.*

Other youngsters, or maybe some of these same boys, were up to just a little more than childish tomfoolery. There were several cases of petty theft, and even an instance of a saloon burglary where money from the "cash till" and several "buckets of whiskey" were taken. The blame was quickly laid at the doorstep of "obnoxious kids" whom it was editorially recommended "ought to be put to work sweeping the streets by day and locked up in the new jail at night."[298]

While kids were here and yonder playing, or perchance up to mischief, and while mothers were busy baking tantalizing cookies, Silver City's mining business underwent a revolutionizing adjustment. Silver productivity was greatly increased during 1874 when the Tennessee mill went on line. Reportedly, it was the largest mill in the whole New Mexico Territory, and, not at all surprisingly, it was the very mill Lucien Maxwell had several years before unloaded at Fort Cummings in a fit of exasperation.[299] Not unpredictably, too, was the fact it was a partnership venture. Among the investors putting up a $65,000 cash outlay were Valentine S. Shelby, Isaac J. Stevens, Thomas "Tom" Lyons, Isaac Givens, H. M. Porter and Dick Hudson. The mill was impressive, covering an area of 78 by 80 feet. With 10 425-pound stamps and six varney pans, the mill was capable of handling 50 tons of ore weekly—dwarfing the output of all the mills combined just two years before. One hundred and thirty-five men found jobs with assembly of the Tennessee. Curious bystanders from far and wide came just to see the Tennessee, "the first perfect silver mill in the Territory."[300] After the Pope mill was erected, also during 1874, Silver City could boast of seven reduction works, all told. Capacity had almost overnight increased to the point that ore was being brought to Silver City from the faraway Organ Mountains east of the Rio Grande.[301]

It was during this general time-frame that another perennial problem was cracked. Tom Lyons and John Swisshelm set up a foundry.[302] From that point forward, many of the replacement parts could be manufactured locally. With efficient mills in operation, spare parts at hand, and natural resources in the form of lumber for shaft timbers and clay and limestone for building furnaces and stacks, Silver City was, at last, in the mining business—big time!

Construction business in town was brewing and spewing too, with new enterprises springing up left and right. Dr. G. W. Bailey now had a drugstore. The Derbyshire brothers operated a furniture store and, peculiarly, since they were both under one roof, a funeral parlor. Gideon Truesdale retailed out of a two-story grocery store. The Bennetts, J. F. and Cornelius, after finishing Silver City's third brick building, opened their general mercantile store. German-born Louis Timmer bought out Sam Eckles' interests in the Star Hotel and renamed it The Exchange. As alluded to earlier, Peter Ott, the "Prince of Caterers," was running the old Keystone Hotel, but with add-on construction had re-christened the spacious hostelry The Tremont House.[303] Comfortable residential housing was at a premium, and one raconteur would soon be hyping the very real need for construction of reasonably priced rental property, predicting that such an investment "would pay better interest than any thing we know of."[304]

Father Oliver Ruellan in March 1874 founded a Silver City parish, and meticulously began laying plans for putting up the Saint Vincent de Paul Catholic Church. Sadly, as the heartrending result of a centipede sting, he died before seeing completion of the cathedral. Father Ruellan was succeeded by Father Joseph Marie Leclero, and with the talented assistance of parishioners under the guidance of Joese Trujillo and Felecito Esquival, the colossal mud-bricked walls were erected, covered over, and "a centrally placed entrance tower was built of adobe and wood, with Gothic-arched louvers and a Gothic-arched door."[305] It was impressive. It was symbolic. Silver City had come of age.

Catherine Antrim, sorrowfully, about this time removed herself from Silver City and traveled south some 25 miles to the Mimbres Hot Springs. The natural springs were known throughout the Southwest. The hot mineral waters were just the ticket for men or women suffering this or that physical malady, the healing and rejuvenating bubbling of the warm waters promising a healthful and refreshing cure-all. Farsightedly, two former Texas lawmen, A. Kuhne and William "Billy" Watts, earlier had "filed a homestead claim and built a bathhouse and hotel." Perhaps, as has been written, in her condition it was a "last-ditch" try for Catherine Antrim, her tuberculosis worsening, her strength ebbing.[306]

The celebrated Mimbres Hot Springs in a "natural state." *Courtesy Silver City Museum.*

On the other hand, her son Henry had plenty of energy. Supposedly, he took the lead in hatching up a crime. Henry proposed to fellow juvenile Charles Ernest Stevens burglarizing Matt Derbyshire's store.[307] The loot to be taken was a not-insignificant display of costume jewelry.

Charles Earnest Stevens. As a youngster, "Billy the Kid" tried to persuade Charley to commit a Silver City burglary, but Stevens got cold feet and told his daddy that the "Kid" had him "hypnotized." *Courtesy William Bishop from the Beatrice Stevens Greenleaf Collection.*

According to the plan, the boys would race to Old Mexico, dispose of the swag, and count their pile of cash on the way back to Silver City.[308] Charley Stevens agreed, then got cold feet—and snitched. He told his daddy, Isaac J. Stevens, who in turn updated legal authorities about the wayward Antrim kid, and the boys' scheme came to an abrupt end. Most probably to avoid a stern spanking, and in a desperate try at wriggling out of punishment, Charley Stevens tearfully blurted out that Henry "had him hypnotized."[309]

Some others weren't put under a trance; they were full-grown traditionalists—raiders and reprobates. Silver City was still brutal country, stocked with rough and tough frontier folk. Thomas Collins reported the theft of two horses from the vicinity of the Chino mine, east of town. He offered a reward of $25 each for their recovery. *Mining Life* Editor Owen Scott goaded potential takers to action, and in doing so reflected public opinion: "There's a chance for you, boys, you might get a scalp in the operation."[310]

And it wasn't just Apache who were accused of making off with valuable horses. One of Martin Bremen's sawmill employees, an Irishman named Kelly, and another with the obviously—but not cleverly—invented moniker of Abe Lincoln "decamped," taking three of their bossman's horses. Sheriff McIntosh saddled up and gave pursuit. In the Upper Mimbres country, the thieves misappropriated four more horses and made tracks south through Cow Springs, the sheriff riding hard about an hour behind them.[311] Whether the haggard lawman made the arrest is fuzzy. More than likely the owl-hoots made it across the borderline and, for certain, McIntosh returned to Silver City—this time.

The school semester came to an end. Then, in the spirit of an educational full-court press, Emma Norris [Noyes] succeeded Professor J. Webster for a summer session during 1874.[312] Classes for this term were held in Owen Scott's place, home of *Mining Life*.

Pulsating Silver City was abuzz with activity, not only in the classroom but downtown in the barrooms as well. Having 15 ribald saloons in town with 24/7 accessibility, Silver City saw its drinking and gambling emporiums well patronized. The self-indulgent traffic grew with the city's acquisition of long-overdue stagecoach service from the faraway "outside world." But even for stagecoach passengers there was proper imbibing etiquette. After all—as previously cited—most men drank liquor every day and since that was the case, the *Omaha Herald* charitably offered suggestions for first-time stagecoach travelers:

> If you have anything to take in a bottle, pass it around, a man who drinks by himself in such a case is lost to all human feeling. Provide stimulants before starting; ranch [stage station] whiskey is not always nectar.[313]

Silver City was not the only place one so inclined could take a drink. Whiskey and whores always seep toward profitability—no matter where. The demographic at early Silver City—a predominance of young single men—was alluring to those purveyors specializing in what is now termed traditional vice. But Silver City had competition. There was another assortment of lonesome males just down the road at nearby Fort Bayard. Grant County's first seat of government, Central City, was within a mile or two of the US Army's military outpost, and the town was "filled with saloons."[314] Drunkenness at frontier army posts was typically widespread: "in view of the isolation, lack of social opportunities, hard work and boredom, sometimes all mixed together...soldiers, both black and white, turned to drink."[315]

For a while Central City was home for "50 or so" *nymphes de paves*, entertaining locals and troops with the wiles of the oldest profession.[316] Military hierarchy normally indicted enlisted ranks for supporting the profession, many times turning a blind eye to an officer's bargain shopping for female company. With any retailing effort a want of customers is ruinous. At Fort Bayard the ready man market kept the ladies engaged in a brisk business, despite sometimes hypocritical denials to the contrary.

When top brass sporadically cracked down, putting Central City off limits, sexually deprived soldiers conspiratorially smuggled greedy prostitutes onto the post. During at least one southwestern New Mexico Territory soldierly tryst, a 9th Cavalry sergeant was embarrassingly caught in barracks gratifying licentious fantasy, writhing and tangled in a *ménage à trois*. He was disciplined—after the fact—and very well may have considered the lustful rendezvous more than worth the punishment.[317]

The Kerns & Mitchell Stage Company advertised regularly that its coaches could make the run from Silver City to San Diego in but seven days, and then all the way north to San Francisco for a mere $115. A trip to Tucson was just $30, and the line was declaring passengers would be riding in "Good Stages, and No Danger on the route."[318] The first assertion concerning quality coaches may have been true. The second claim wasn't! And the same may be said of the coaches running between Silver City and the Mesilla/Las Cruces area operated by J. F. Bennett, Henry Lesinsky and Con Cosgrove.[319] Any travel, be it by speeding stagecoach, hitching a ride on a lumbering freight wagon, or cavalierly straddling a twitching-eared horse, was an adventure. Apache marauders and Mexican bandits and Anglo brigands were all about. Stepping down from any mode of transportation and planting one's feet on Silver City's dirt streets always exacted a genuinely thankful sigh of relief.

Silver City's sheer isolation may be further amplified by the fact that US Army contracts with freighters destined for Fort Bayard and Fort Cummings demanded the highest dollar amount per 100 pounds of any shipments to military bases in New Mexico Territory.[320] Formalized religion, public education, architectural excellence and entrepreneurial penetration may have made it to Silver City, but the town was still put down at the end of the line—and it was yet a long and perilous road.

For the 1874 fall school term, an English-born, 27-year-old's application to teach school at Silver City was accepted. Mary Phillipa Richards, a multilingual intellect, fluent in German, French and Italian, began instructing her classes on Sept. 14.[321] Exactly just how long Miss Richards taught is a little foggy, but the fact that one of her pupils would become notoriously well known is not clouded.[322] Henry Antrim, in the eyes of his teacher, was "a scrawny little fellow with delicate hands and an artistic nature—always willing to help with the chores around the schoolhouse."[323]

Odd jobs around the classroom in Henry's case no doubt were suspended—at least for awhile. After nearly four months of confinement in bed, and just two days after the fall semester began, Catherine Antrim succumbed to her illness and "breathed her last breath in the little cabin."[324] Henry and brother Joe mourned. After the bereavement period Henry again lent a helping hand to his teacher, Miss Richards. He was also capable of helping himself into trouble. At the time, however, the public's law-enforcement attention was focused elsewhere. Grant County folks had worry with one of their finest.

Sheriff Charles McIntosh made a trip to Old Mexico. Reportedly he didn't intend on coming back and, allegedly, the $3,000 pilfered from Grant County coffers was going to finance his sojourn.[325] As with most any Old West story, there is room for alternative scenarios, but in this case one truism is indisputable: Grant County was in dire need of a new sheriff.[326] And, by "virtue of law," she got one. Coroner Harvey Howard Whitehill ascended to Grant County's law enforcement throne.[327] Two years short of his 40th birthday and one of the area's bona fide pioneers, Harvey Whitehill immediately assumed the responsibilities as sheriff and appointed William Price as his deputy.[328] The strapping six-foot two-inch, 240-pound Whitehill was all man—all the time. It's written he frequently went about his duties unarmed, which is only partly true, but he shied not away from hazard whether he had a six-shooter or not.[329]

Harvey Howard Whitehill, Grant County sheriff and politician. Whitehill is generally credited as the first—but not the last—man to arrest Henry "Billy the Kid" Antrim. *Courtesy Silver City Museum.*

Shortly before Whitehill was named Grant County sheriff, *The Grant County Herald*, a weekly successor to *Mining Life*, made its publishing debut under the editorial leadership of William H. Echols [Eckles]. Quickly it rivaled the Santa Fe *New Mexican*, the territory's most widely circulated and profitable newspaper.[330] The *Herald*'s journalistic outlook was made perfectly clear; it was destined to be:

> ...a moral, religious, and political reflector; it will mildly snub vice, patronizingly pat virtue on the back and encourage politicians to act as their own tumble bugs.[331]

One of those "tumble bug" politicians, the new Grant County sheriff, was from the outset earning mentions in the *Herald*: Sheriff Whitehill investigated a case where two men burglarized a man's quarters, stealing "two pistols and two needle guns" before they stole three horses and took "French Leave" of the country. In another case, Whitehill recovered one of his favorite horses, Old Ned, which had been stolen by Indians. He also safely arrested Fred Wall, a man under criminal indictment for an earlier shooting incident.[332]

It would be another episode, however, that would mark Whitehill's spot in history. The offense and the offender were really small time, contemporarily. Sadly, the tale is often how Harvey Howard Whitehill is best remembered, although he had a reasonably long, sometimes controversial, but always exhilarating career serving as a persistent lawman during New Mexico Territory's wild and woolly days: Charley Sun, a Chinese immigrant, and his partner had previously set up a laundry. Shortly before Sept. 5, 1875, their business was burglarized. The sneak thieves made off with "a large amount of clothing, blankets, and two revolvers—valued at one hundred and fifty or two hundred dollars."[333] It was felony theft, not child's play!

"Billy the Kid." *Courtesy Robert G. McCubbin.*

One of the suspects, whom Whitehill had arrested earlier for the theft of a keg of butter, was Henry Antrim, Miss Richards' scrawny little student with the delicate hands and artistic nature. He was a boy who had early on "developed a proclivity for breaking the eighth commandment." In the first instance, Sheriff Whitehill had benevolently let Henry off the hook on a promise of good behavior. But, according to Whitehill, the "nimble-fingered boy found the road too straight and narrow." Henry involved himself with an older fellow, another ne'er-do-well, George "Sombrero Jack" Schaefer. Following Henry's participation in the case of the Chinese fellows' purloined property, Sheriff Whitehill arrested him and put him in the Grant County jail. Schoolteacher Richards afterward contradicted this, the generally accepted story, saying that Henry was actually put in jail for "parading up and down Silver City streets" wearing a woman's clothes.[334] That Henry was actually picked up for cross-dressing is a dubious assertion at best. Perchance on another occasion he actually was; if so, the historical record missed it. The fact that Sheriff Harvey Whitehill arrested him in connection with the burglary is not subject to dispute.

The next part of the story has been oft repeated, but two existing first-hand sources seem to make it most clear. The *Grant County Herald's* newspaperman reported:

> Henry McCarty [Antrim], who was arrested on Thursday and committed to jail to await action of the grand jury, upon the charge of stealing clothes from Charley Sun and Sam Chung, celestials, sans cue, sans Joss sticks, escaped from prison yesterday through the chimney. It's believed that Henry was simply the tool of "Sombrero Jack," who done the stealing whilst Henry done the hiding. Jack has skinned out.[335]

During an after-the-fact interview several years later, ex-sheriff Whitehill told a reporter working for the *Silver City Enterprise*:

> One day the "Kid" complained to me that the jailer was treating him roughly and kept him in solitary confinement in his cell without any exercise. So I ordered that he be allowed to remain in the corridor for a limited time each morning. And right there is where we fell down... for the "Kid" had a mind whose ingenuity we knew not of at that time. He was only a boy, you must remember,

> scarcely over 15 years of age. Yet we made the mistake of leaving him alone in the corridor for a short half hour. When we returned and unlocked the heavy oaken doors of the jail, the "Kid" was nowhere to be seen. I ran outside around the jail and a Mexican standing on a ridge at the rear, asked whom I was hunting. I replied in Spanish "a prisoner." He came out of the chimney answered the Mexican. I ran back into the jail looked up the big old fashioned chimney and sure enough could see where in an effort to obtain a hold his hands had clawed into the thick layers of soot which lined the side of the flue. The chimney hole itself did not appear as large as my arm and yet the lad squeezed his frail slender body through it and gained his liberty.[336]

The sheriff should have known better, he said, because the "Kid" had "one peculiar facial characteristic that to an experienced man hunter, would have marked him immediately as a bad man and that was his dancing eyes. They never were at rest, but continually shifted and roved, much like his own rebellious nature."[337]

Henry Antrim aka "Kid" Antrim aka "Billy the Kid" hurriedly scampered out of old Grant County and into Arizona Territory, taking a fork in the road. The future icon of Old West outlawry took the crooked path, one straight away leading to skullduggery and killing and, more important, mythology. Sheriff Harvey Whitehill, well, he just went back to work. And there was plenty of law enforcement work to be done.

The year 1875 was ushered out with bang. On Dec. 27, John Collins "undertook to make a cold moist body" out of James "Jim" Smith. Collins shot Smith in the head. The wicked powder-burning gunshot was not lethal, but it was a face scorcher. Thankfully Smith wasn't "sent home on a shutter." Later, Sheriff Whitehill arrested Collins and, fearing that the "dogs might bite him," locked him up. Next morning, illustrious of rough frontier justice, Collins was fined $60 for carrying and mishandling a deadly weapon and sent on his way—a "mild punishment," so declared a newsman working for the *Grant County Herald*.[338]

Much as the old year went out to the sound of a six-shooter, the new year of 1876 was heralded with a holdup. Joseph "Dutch Joe" Hubert, particularly identifiable by his lisping Dutch accent, and three cohorts,

Stagecoach service to bustling Silver City. *Courtesy Silver City Museum.*

Roscoe Burrell, Fredrico Lopez and Enrique Rodriguez, at three o'clock in the morning on Jan. 12, 1876, robbed a Silver City stagecoach near Cooke's Peak.[339] The driver, a man named Lancaster, and strongbox guard Fred Kaiser were riding topside. Inside the coach were John Simpson Chisum, already widely known as "The Cattle King of the Pecos," and his attorney, Thomas F. Conway. Cleverly, Chisum hid a wad of cash in his boot and forked over but an insignificant amount to satisfy the robbers' greedy demand. The well-prepared hijackers loaded six heavy silver ingots on pack mules and fled into the fast-breaking dawn—after ordering the conveyance to be turned around and make fast tracks back to Silver City.[340] The robbers rode east toward Mesilla, their date with the Blind Mistress of Justice yet to be docketed. Now they were running with a $3,000 price tag on their heads, posted by the rightful owners of the silver bars, H. M. Porter and J. F. Bennett.[341]

Should the crooks have then been captured, their fate in court would have been in doubt—at least according to most Silver City citizens. Locals were discontented with the third judicial district judge and member of the New Mexico Territorial Supreme Court, Warren Henry Bristol, a polit-

Judge Warren Bristol. Many Silver City citizens wanted him removed from office and signed a petition aimed at accomplishing that end, but their efforts failed. *Courtesy New Mexico History Museum, #50340.*

ical appointee of President Ulysses S. Grant.[342] So displeased with the judge where they that most of the prominent citizens of Silver City angrily circulated a lengthy petition addressed to the president himself, "respectfully requesting the removal of Judge Warren Bristol from the office of Judge of the District and Territory."[343] They snappily spelled out 16 separate grievances, ranging from inappropriate and secret consultations with parties having cases before the judge to arbitrarily jailing people for contempt of court, from refusing a defendant's constitutional right to subpoena exculpatory witnesses for an important murder trial to a whole litany of allegations of malfeasance and ethical indiscretions.[344] In the end, their petition fell on a faraway president's deaf ear, and for a long while into the future Bristol would stay. No doubt many wondered if, with their failure to have him fired, they had idiotically made a powerful enemy. Still, they were purposeful Silver City folks, get-in-your-face folks. Collectively they just weren't the type to backtrack—not if wronged. And they were damn proud of it!

While the stickup artists had hightailed it toward the rising sun, legitimate players were looking in the opposite direction. Some of Silver City's stalwarts had also come to that figurative fork in the road leading to Arizona Territory. They took the respectable trail and it lead to prosperity. Robert "Bob" Metcalf, from near Clifton, had filed on, developed and sold to Silver City investors Henry Lesinsky, David Abraham, Robert Golding, J. Freudenthal and Louis Cardis the legendary Longfellow copper mine, an authentic humdinger. In the southeastern regions of Arizona Territory on Pinal Creek, near Globe, the Silver City wheeler-dealer John B. Morrill was industriously and profitably engaged, working the surface ore. On Chase Creek, Isaac J. Stevens and his sons founded the Copper King and Last Chance mines. Tom Lyons and John Swisshelm were there too. Arizona Territory, the southeastern section, was visibly experiencing a significant mining boom, and absent a railroad the extracted ore was shipped by freight wagon to Silver City for reduction. There, the emptied wagons were crammed full of spare parts, mining machinery and everyday necessities by the Silver City merchants before the return trips to Clifton, Globe and the outlying mining camps.[345] The two sections, separated only by a synthetically imposed borderline, were tightly interlocked economically and culturally, and, even more notably, philosophically. They were Americans. They were insistent. They were mulish.

In forward-looking Grant County a nervy political movement was under way, too: Secession! Silver City citizens, in fact, all of Grant County's folks, were hollering for disunion from New Mexico Territory and annexation to Arizona Territory. The clamorous racket they were generating was not hollow claptrap—they were serious, dead serious! Their festering aggravation with politicos in Santa Fe boiled over the top. On Oct. 4, 62 of Grant County's "prominent" citizens angrily met at Burns Hall in Silver City. Taking a cue from their founding forefathers a century before, the assembly proudly adopted a "Declaration of Independence," unanimously.

On Nov. 7, 1876, during the regularly scheduled election, a near undivided majority passed the proposition calculated to forevermore cut loose from the archaic system that was dominating New Mexico Territory's politics. Political hostages they would be no longer. It was, in every respect at the local level, perceived to be a strictly nonpartisan act. Grant County's highly informed electorate overwhelmingly opted to disassociate themselves from New Mexico and become Arizonans. They had collectively spit in the powerful Santa Fe Ring's face, by damn!

Their grievances were not unfounded. From the get-go, with the birth and development of far-flung Silver City, they had spiritedly campaigned for an incorporated self-rule city government; implementation of an adequate and meaningful tax structure, one that would capably and prudently support public schools; and an utterly fair system of representation in the Territorial Legislature, instead of their illegitimately crafted and superficial *misrepresentation*. The Ring's blatant political machinations were plainly not acceptable—not to Grant County people, not when they were loosing priceless seats in the legislature and their voice was being ignored.

They would not forgive nor forget the slight. Perhaps, above all else, they were "Americans" and politically attaching themselves to Arizona Territory for administrative purposes, because it was "more liberal and better suited to a progressive community such as theirs, especially since the primary interest of both Grant County and Arizona was mining," made good common sense.[346]

There were other practical matters, too. In fact, the whole wrangle about boundary lines and that $15 million Gadsden Purchase had been about the United States acquiring suitable flat land for a second transcontinental railroad. No matter how it was sliced, the Southern Pacific Railroad's tracks were going to cut clear across the southern section of their county—that was a given. The Apache, too, were a real threat. Many Chiricahuas made their home in Arizona Territory and their living in New Mexico Territory. Reciprocal nuptials between Grant County and her beguiling neighbor across the western borderline would, in many an eye, result in a unified and common defense network. As it stood, even with the US Army it was a sort of willy-nilly stratagem. Seemingly there was no downside to divorcing Santa Fe and marrying up with Prescott. At the ballot box they had proved their fidelity to the idea.

During the Ninth Territorial Legislature of Arizona Territory, Anson P. K. Safford, the governor, addressed the assembled lawmakers and advocated:

> ...that the people of Grant County, New Mexico, had expressed to him a desire to be annexed to and become a part of this Territory....They allege among other reasons, the superiority of our laws and their execution which is complimentary to the wisdom of our law makers. The trade and intercourse between that county and Arizona are already extensive, and are constantly increasing, and I consider its acquisition desirable. It seems to me that the people of that locality are the proper judges as to which government they prefer, in as much as a change of territorial limits will not add to the expense of the Federal Government. I have been asked by a committee appointed by the people of that county to call your attention to the matter, with the hopes that you will memorialize Congress upon the subject.[347]

After acrimonious debate in both houses of Arizona's legislature, the measure was finally passed and Governor Safford signed a Memorial to the Congress of the United States. Heretofore-skeptical lawmakers and Santa Fe Ring loyalists were aghast. Earlier, the southern New Mexico Territory bunch had been scoffed at by editors in pages of the Santa Fe *New Mexican* and the Las Vegas, New Mexico, *Gazette*. Somehow, now, there was no humor in possibly losing the richest and most productive mining country in the whole territory. Those folks in Silver City weren't kidding; they were ready for a showdown.[348]

In Washington, DC, an Arizona delegate, Hiram S. Stevens, absent any silly fanfare, introduced House Resolution No. 795, requesting that Grant County, New Mexico Territory, be officially annexed to Arizona Territory. The resolution was referred to the Committee on Territories—given two readings—and there it died.[349] The legislative death was not in vain. The Santa Fe Ring had taken note. Those Silver City "rebels" meant surefire, poker-playing business and, next time, the aces might show up in a different hand. At the next session of the New Mexico Legislature, Silver City's citizens were given part of what they wanted, an act allowing them to formally incorporate and fashion a legitimate city government. Questions concerning creation of a truly independent school district for the city were tabled, temporarily. Silver City by any man's calculation had "gained in prestige" despite the legislative setback.[350] She was now a power player in territorial politics.

Closer to home, however, Silver City was still—sometimes—wild and woolly. Within a short span of time Richard Yeamans, one of the early Silver City pioneers, was horrifically beaten, dumped in an abandoned mine shaft, and later died; Anselmo Pacheco killed Citor Parra and fled for Old Mexico; Delesfero Pacheco lethally gunned down Lamberto Montes with a barking Winchester; and "Dutch Joe" Hubert began laying sneaky plans for another daring stagecoach robbery. At some point in a *balie* gone wildly awry at nearby Georgetown, "Mexicans armed with sling shots" ferociously assaulted pioneer and constable Ed Moulton, and during the ensuing brawl Charles Moore was fatally thumped on the cranium. Sheriff Harvey Whitehill, in perpetual motion, was zipping back and forth between crime scenes and scuffles.

The US Army's cavalrymen were whooshing about in 1876, too. Earlier in the year, while Silver City's citizens were aching and conniving for a geographical-political divorce, Colonel Edward Hatch, the newly appointed commander of the Military District of New Mexico and leader of one of the military's post-Civil War black units, the well-known Ninth Cavalry—the Buffalo Soldiers—was also busy.[351] He journeyed by stagecoach from his Santa Fe headquarters to Cañada Alamosa for a face-to-face huddle with Victorio, the Chihenne chief.[352] There he found the Apache in an utterly belligerent mood, complaining of short rations. Despite the pleas for peace and a cessation of raiding, the headstrong Chihenne were adamantly claiming a preference of uncompromising warfare over starvation. During the talks, Colonel Hatch noted the Apache were armed with the latest models of Smith & Wesson top-break revolvers and Colt's six-shooters, along with improved carbines made by Winchester and the more common Springfield and Sharp's rifles.[353] In Hatch's own words, the Apache were "extremely defiant."[354]

Brazen, indeed, was Victorio's logic, but it was pragmatic. The now-legendary Apache strategist, backed up by other notorious war leaders, told Colonel Hatch of their soon-to-be-adopted policy for fighting and surviving. Simply, they were intent on making peace with the Mexican state of Sonora. "Victorio grimly declared they could do better by war on the United States than they could do at peace with this country and war with Sonora." Despite the hardships suffered by pioneers acquiring material possessions on the American side of the line, there were riches to be had. In Old Mexico there was not too much worth having, at least so said Victorio.[355] As with almost any parley between top military brass and warrior chiefs, Apache elders blamed their young men for many of the southwestern New Mexico Territory acts of depredation, the burning and killing. It was not an injudicious mechanism for scapegoating and, undoubtedly, it was even partly true. Horses and mules stolen north of the international line could be offhandedly bartered south of the border for sufficient greenbacks to keenly arm Apache with the latest and best examples of America's firearms technology, and with cartridges enough to feed the hungry guns. Young men may have stolen or traded for the six-shooting handguns and lever-action rifles, but make not a politically correct mistake: Victorio, Loco, Sanchez, Rafel and old Nana stuck them into their tightly drawn waistbands or slung them across the pommels of their slick-forked saddles, too.[356]

Colonel Hatch duly noted that the Apache were in a "better condition to resist than ever before" and they would require "watching." Furthermore he grumbled that they were no more "civilized" then than when they first voluntarily came into the problematic Cañada Alamosa Reservation, and, in point of fact, the place had become a "place of concealment for stolen property," and was drawing a "disreputable class of traders."[357] Vowing to kill or capture raiding Apache, and, if necessary, follow them right back onto the reservation, Colonel Hatch departed Cañada Alamosa. As history would bear witness, the Chihenne Apache weren't won over, cowed or scared. Silver City and Grant County folk, after learning of the powwow, no doubt yawned with bored cynicism: "Here we go again!" Their disparagement would be understandable, but not wholly equitable. The troops were working hard, racking up the hours on patrol and pulling escort duty, the 9th Cavalry's patrols traveling some 8,813 miles during one 12-month period.[358] Their Apache chasing wasn't all in vain, either.

On two separate campaigns, Henry Carroll, an ex-Third Army artillery veteran and more recently a captain with the 9th Cavalry, "a brave and resourceful Indian fighter," made contact with hostile Apache in the southern reaches of old Grant County's Florida Mountains, an Apache stronghold and staging ground for bloody decades.[359] During the first engagement on April 15, 1876, his command of 25 "colored" troops killed one Apache and captured 11 horses and scattered the rest.[360] During the second scouting in September of that same year, Carroll led a detachment of F Company, 9th Cavalry, in a scouring sweep of the Florida Mountain's southwestern edge, hunting for two notorious Apache raiders, Geronimo and Juh.[361] On Sept. 15 his command made contact, killed an Apache, wounded three, and once again confiscated a herd of horses. One enlisted soldier was wounded. After the nine-day, 274-mile patrol, the worn-down unit returned to its Fort Selden base near Las Cruces.[362] The targets at the top of Captain Henry Carroll's list escaped, if they were even there in the first place. Neither Geronimo nor Juh, however, would suffer any guilty pangs about making their southwestern New Mexico Territory terrorizing presence known—and feared. They were Apache. They were patient.

Chapter 7

"A Dead Game Hombre"

Throughout the frontier period, Silver City was predisposed toward two very real and unmistakably measurable phenomena. First, the young mining town, unlike her sister mining camps, was fated for longevity. That fact can directly be traced to an utterly independent mind-set and the farsightedness of her pioneering fathers. Second, she, if a feminine appellation is not too tasteless, was hellcat tough. The latter reality may be slammed down at Father Time's unyielding doorway. Hammering out stability in the American Southwest was not an easy task. In Silver City, the darn job was triply taxing. Geographical remoteness, foraying Apache and a steady influx of undesirables came near wrecking what so few had done—and were doing—for so very many. For lonesome and massive old Grant County and her budding shiretown, 1877 would prove unusually troublesome, an abnormally deadly 12 months.

An Apache raid—if not Juh's and Geronimo's bands, then their allies in war—seared down on the southeastern Arizona Territory ranch of James Hughes. The Apache quickly made off with 21 ranch horses. Military authorities at Fort Bowie were posted regarding the sortie. Second Lieutenant John Anthony "Tony" Rucker, 6th US Cavalry, riding at the head of 17 men from Companies H and L and 34 men from an Indian scout troop, Company C, along with civilian guide Jack Dunn and a combat surgeon, went looking for the Apache. It was Jan. 4, 1877. Three days later, south of Ralston in the Leitendorf Hills, an extension of the Pyramid Mountains, they found the raiders. Trying to surround them in the dark for a first-light attack proved knotty, and was made utterly unworkable when Jack Dunn and his Apache scouts opened fire too soon. After a raging two-hour battle, Rucker's side was triumphant, counting the lifeless bodies of 10 Chiricahuas. Additionally, if blood trails are taken as conclusive evidence, many more Apache were wounded. Rucker's command captured a five-year-old boy and the string of stolen horses. It was a decisive victory.[363]

To the east, just two weeks later, a six-man detachment of 9th Cavalry "Buffalo Soldiers" and three Navaho scouts, riding out of Fort Bayard under command of Lieutenant Henry H. Wright, found a Chiricahua hideout in the Florida Mountains. Undermanned and outnumbered, Lt. Wright decided on a confab rather than an out-and-out charge on the hostile Apache camp. For a half-hour the two sides squabbled. When Wright tried to remove himself to his horse, Apache blocked the way. Soldiers fired, and all hell broke loose, cavalrymen having to use their rifle butts as clubs during hand-to-hand combat. Seizing the moment, Corporal Clifton [Clinton] Greaves fought like a man possessed, "managing to shoot and bash a gap through the swarming Apaches, permitting his companions to break free." No soldiers were killed, but five Apache were. Others were wounded. The fortunate squadron, pleased to even be alive, returned to Fort Bayard with six Indian horses. For his heroic action, Corp. Greaves was awarded the prized Medal of Honor.[364] Silver City citizens cheered! Prematurely!

Apache handiwork was far from over, but Grant County folk would quickly focus on mayhem from one of their own. Richard Remine and his partner, Pat Rafferty, staked a mining claim at Georgetown and nearby shared a tiny one-room cabin—and the only mattress. Both men were hardworking. Remine was particularly well-liked, although from time to time he could and did get blinding drunk. Such was the case on March 16, 1877. During the wee morning hours before first light, Remine managed, somehow, to make it home. There to his displeasure he found Rafferty taking up all the room, lying crosswise on the bed. Remine went berserk! Picking up his single-jack, a miner's short-handled sledgehammer, Remine beat the snoring Rafferty to death. Befuddled by drink and in a state of fanatical panic, he dismembered his buddy with an ax. Then he passed out across the now-unoccupied but, nevertheless, blood-splattered bed sheets. There he was later found and arrested.[365]

At trial the jury returned a guilty verdict and Remine was sentenced to be hanged, the execution put on provisional hold by the competency of an appellate lawyer. Gaining trustee status as a prisoner, Remine was given free run of the jail—and the town. Shopping for the lockup's kitchen and frequently gambling in area poker parlors, Remine was often out way past dark. Supposedly, on one occasion Sheriff Whitehill told the prisoner, "if he didn't come back by 10:00 o'clock at night he would damn sure be locked out."[366] Maybe it's true, perhaps not, but another bunch of lawbreakers were back in old Grant County, and on the loose.

At the very same spot he had earlier robbed the Silver City stagecoach, "Dutch Joe" Hubert did it again:

> **Coach Robbed**
>
> Coach coming west was stopped by two masked men last night in Cook's Canyon, one mile this side of Fort Cummings, and passengers robbed—mail not molested. John B. Morrill, F. R. Know, Miss Maggie Wilson and Joe Kaier were aboard. Robbers captured $1.50 from John and a revolver. Morrill told them they ought to have known better than to strike such a poor crowd. They were after the paymaster. The gentlemen hid their watches.[367]

For this robbery Hubert had been accompanied by a notorious outlaw known throughout the Southwest, Robert E. "Bob" Martin.[368] Later "Dutch Joe" was arrested by a posse from Doña Ana County under the command of Deputy Sheriff Jacinto Armijo.[369] In the county jail Hubert ran his mouth. He shouldn't have. The prisoners paying rapt attention were two of New Mexico's worst *mal hombres*, George W. "Buffalo Bill" Spawn and Nicholas "Nick" Provencia. The two desperately needed to make a deal with the joyful prosecutor, and they did. Both "ratted out" and their indictments were quashed after Hurbert's 13-year prison sentence began. Honor among thieves? There ain't any!

While Anglo owl-hoots had seemingly run amuck in old Grant County, so, too, had the sassy Apache. At Richmond [now Virden] on the Gila River banks southwest of Silver City, Cisto Garcia's wagon train was attacked, and "the boys kept them off but lost one horse killed in the fight." A few days earlier the Apache had "killed quite a number of cattle" belonging to "Mr. Murring," an area rancher.[370] And farther east? Charles Whimple reported that a party of Apache had stolen eight head of cattle from the Alex McGregor ranch just two and a half miles south of the Mimbres Reduction Works.[371]

United States governmental readjustment of Apache policy demanded a relocation of Chiricahuas to the miserably hot and forlorn San Carlos Reservation in Arizona Territory. John Philip Clum, the civilian Indian agent, young and bombastic, sanctimonious and enthusiastic, courageously daring and impetuously bold, was tasked with the assignment. The ever-elusive and unmanageable Geronimo continually made his "destructive raids" into southern New Mexico Territory, Arizona Territory and Old Mexico, then slipped into shielding sanctuary near Cañada Alamosa at *Ojo Caliente,* commonly referred to as the Southern Apache Agency. After one such raid Geronimo haughtily returned to the agency with as many as 100 stolen horses "and was outraged that he was refused rations for the days he had been absent."[372] Military and civilian brass had grown plumb tired of the back and forth between raiding and rationing, killing and coddling. For the New Mexico Territory phase of his assignment, John Clum's orders from the commissioner of Indian affairs were reasonably precise:

> If practicable, take Indian Police and arrest renegade Indians at Southern Apache Agency; seize stolen horses in their possession, restore property to rightful owners, remove renegades to San Carlos and hold them in confinement for murder and robbery. Call on military for aid if needed.[373]

Agent Clum ordered the chief of Indian Police at San Carlos, Clay Beauford, a Medal of Honor recipient for his past "gallant conduct during campaigns and engagements with Apaches," to take 102 of his policemen and proceed by wagon road to Silver City, a meandering trip of several hundred miles.[374] There, Clum, who would travel cross-country with 40 Apache police, would meet Beauford. Then the whole outfit would move over to Fort Bayard for consultation with military authorities and after that polite protocol proceed to *Ojo Caliente*. The April 1877 trip in pleasant spring weather should have been a lark for Clum's squad, a holiday. It wasn't. Desert travel was tough business. The Apache, who were traveling by foot, had to resole their moccasins every fourth day. Resolutely, they relentlessly trudged through "the dust, cactus, and broiling sun."[375] At one point they were delayed 30 hours by a blinding sandstorm, a not-uncommon happening in Grant County's southern border country. At Silver City the two platoons finally joined forces, and while there John Clum bought several horses, mounting 22 of his constables.[376] After conferring with Major James Franklin Wade, who had been ordered to provide tactical support, Clum and his men struck out for *Ojo Caliente* and a planned rendezvous with 9th Cavalry soldiers on April 22.[377] Traveling the higher elevations was much more pleasant than their trip's first leg. As Clum recollected:

> During April the weather is delightful in the mountainous country over which our trail led, north from Silver City, New Mexico, where Beauford and my Apache militia company met me. Flowers, endless in variety and of rare beauty; varieties constantly changing with the varying altitudes. Antelope and deer afforded entertainment for our sharpshooters, and steaks and chops for the rest of us. Vast forest areas, the flash and song of mountain brooks, the whirr of quail, the mysterious depths of rugged cañons, here and there the soothing green of mountain meadows. Each day yielded its generous tribute of good things, in compensation for the fatigue involved in our strenuous march; each evening discovered in our camp, weary, hungry, good-natured groups about campfires, toasting bits of venison set on spits, puffing cigarettes; "telling old tales beneath a tree, with starlit skies for canopy." And ours was a democratic assembly. There was no saluting of superior officers. We were engaged in a serious undertaking. Just how much actual hazard might be involved in our mission, none knew, but each one was there for effective action in any emergency.[378]

At *Ojo Caliente,* Clum and his horseback Apache police rode in, leaving Beauford and the dismounted platoon on the Indian agency's outskirts—tucked away and out of sight.[379] Learning that Geronimo and his band were in camp some three miles away, Clum began springing the jaws and setting the trap. No doubt he also was informed that many, maybe most, Chihenne didn't want Geronimo at *Ojo Caliente*—because his omen was that of a raven, "one who always brings trouble and lives always on death."[380] With Geronimo nearby, prompt action was necessitated. The situation presented "both a problem and an opportunity."[381] Surely, if not taken into custody speedily, Geronimo would either attack the hated turncoat Apache police, or bolt and run for safe haven in Old Mexico.

John P. Clum, Apache agent, about the time he traveled through Silver City with Indian Police to capture Geronimo. *Courtesy Arizona Historical Society, #982.*

Secreting 80 of his Apache police in an empty commissary storehouse before sunup, and not daring to await arrival of clamoring and clanking troops, John Clum sent word for the notorious outlaw Apache to come in for a confab.[382] Geronimo himself later remarked: "The messengers did not say what they wanted with us, but as they seemed friendly we thought they wanted a council, and rode in to meet the officers."[383] Thinking that Agent Clum only had with him the 22 mounted policemen, Geronimo arrived at the agency office—painted for war, heavily armed and coolly defiant. Brashly, Geronimo warned Clum that he wasn't going to San Carlos, and that if the cocky little Indian agent wasn't pretty damn careful he and his whole damned Apache police force wouldn't make it back either, amplifying the threat with: "Your bodies will stay here at *Ojo Caliente* to make feed for coyotes."[384] Clum touched the brim of his tattered sombrero in a prearranged signal, and at once the storehouse doors swung open. Eighty Apache police, thumbs on rifle hammers, surrounded Geronimo and his little band. The renegades' disbelief was palpable. They had been hoodwinked. Geronimo's thumb crept slowly toward the hammer of his .45-70 Springfield carbine. Clum's hand inched toward his Colt's .45 six-shooter, another preset gesture, and Beauford and his squadron shouldered their rifles, aimed at Geronimo's heart. Clum kept his eye on the Apache's thumb; "I saw it hesitate, just before it touched the hammer of his rifle. Intuitively, I knew that Geronimo had reconsidered; that he was my prisoner; that there would be no blood shed, unless we spilled it."[385]

Clum employed an area blacksmith to fashion leg-irons from one-inch strips of metal wagon tires, connected by a heavy chains 18 inches in length. These were riveted around the ankles of Geronimo and his cadre of personal bodyguards and subchiefs, who, in the absence of a guardhouse, were placed in a barbed-wire corral that was "horse high and bull strong." Apache police stood proud as threatening sentinels inside the enclosure. Clay Beauford with 20 of his Apache police shepherded Geronimo's remaining followers—a hundred "thoroughly humbled" warriors—to their camp, forced them to collect a few belongings, gathered the herd of stolen cattle and horses, and promptly made the three-mile trip back to *Ojo Caliente* headquarters. Groundwork for the Apache removal to San Carlos was now well under way. Then, according to the dogged Indian agent, "victors and vanquished lay down together, wrapped in their blankets, under the stars, and called it a day."[386]

The next day, in rode Major Wade with three companies of the 9th Cavalry. There is little doubt that he was surprised—cheerfully—to find Geronimo's outlaw band had been scooped up absent any bloodshed. The major was likewise pleased at learning Clum had apparently slick-tongued Victorio and his Chihennes to report for a showup and head count. Clum, who usually stood on shifting sand in his relationships with Army men, seemed to take special delight in updating the major: "Sorry you were delayed with your troops. We would have liked to have had you here for the party. But I couldn't wait for you...Geronimo surrounded me with 100 of his bandits. So I had to surround him immediately with my Apache reserves. If you will walk over to the corral with me, I will be glad to introduce you to our special guest."[387]

The 25-year-old Apache agent's next manipulation was either a brash overstep of his actual authority or an obedient fidelity to orders. One account penned that the "self-assured and totally uninhibited" John Philip Clum, holding his own counsel, decided to reposition all of the *Ojo Caliente* Apache to San Carlos, not just Geronimo's band.[388] Other narratives report: "He [Clum] received telegraphic instructions from Washington April 17 to effect the removal of all the Indians, not merely the Chiricahua renegades, if he could do it."[389] Clearly, that message predated Clum's actual arrival at *Ojo Caliente*, but the gist and result of the story stay unchanged. "The only remaining task was to escort them to San Carlos. Clum wired the commissioner that the Chiricahua renegades had been captured. Since there were only 600 Indians at Warm Springs [*Ojo Caliente*] he advised transferring all of them to San Carlos. The commissioner agreed with this unfortunate and inappropriate suggestion and

The ever-incorrigible Geronimo. *A C.S. Fly photo, courtesy New Mexico History Museum, #2115.*

ordered the Warm Springs Apaches moved."[390]

Geronimo, classified as a common criminal, had no choice in the matter. Victorio and his *Mimbreño* Apache, on the other hand, voluntarily complied with the relocation plan, not happily, but peacefully. Victorio's fighting men, knowing they would be disarmed, cached their first-class firearms—and deceptively surrendered their old and malfunctioning weapons.[391] The implication is not fuzzy: Victorio and his Chihennes at some point intended on returning to *Ojo Caliente* either "in peace or war."[392] Whether Major Wade, John Clum or the Apache policemen were fooled by the stashing of arms is murky, but it seems unlikely. General George Crook would latter convey his informed opinion:

> In the first place it is impossible to disarm Indians. Individuals may be taken in certain instance at such disadvantage as to make it possible to get their arms, but with whole bands or tribes this is hardly possible. I knew that the Chiricahuas had an abundance of the best arms, and yet when they came into our camp, thinking very likely that I would demand the surrender of their arms, many of them were armed only with lances, and others with very indifferent guns, which would have been given up had I demanded them.[393]

No matter. Agent Clum and Major Wade had no time to burn digging and burrowing looking for workable Colt's six-shooters and Winchesters, which couldn't be brought into play for the long march to San Carlos. Other serious details required attention.

With whirlwind speed news scorched the telegraph line to Clum. He was advised that Ponce and 10 or 15 other renegades were on the loose in southern Arizona Territory, engaged in raiding and murder. The confusion played right into Clum's salesmanship stratagem; in fact, Ponce was at that very time standing with his legs shackled in the Apache agent's wire prison at *Ojo Caliente*. Astutely, Clum made sure Geronimo's renegades and Victorio's followers were posted on the hearsay, pointing out the real value in their being regularly counted, thus making certain a perfect alibi for those "good" Apache who had not jumped the reservation.[394] His audience nodded knowingly.

Nevertheless, Clum rationed Clay Beauford and the main body of Apache police for a 30-day campaign, arming them with 3,000 rounds of ammunition. Their instructions were straightforward: Intercept any Apache raiding between *Ojo Caliente* and the Dos Cabezas Mountains in southeastern Arizona Territory, and "convey them to San Carlos, or leave their bones to bleach in the desert sun."[395] Beauford rode out, leaving Clum behind with a personal bodyguard of 25 handpicked Apache. Wel-attuned to the fact he would need additional help with transporting 453 Apache—men, women and children—over the backtrack through precipitous mountains and across the sweltering desert to San Carlos, Clum turned to Major Wade for a manpower infusion. A 12-man platoon under command of Lieutenant William H. Hugo was detailed to accompany Clum's cumbersome expedition as far as New Mexico Territory's western border, the dividing line between military districts.[396]

Clum faced two distinct dilemmas. Geronimo and his subchiefs were wearing leg-irons, which Clum dared not remove but which prevented those Apache from straddling a horse or marching on foot. A wagon was requisite. His second quandary was the discovery that one of the Apache men had smallpox, necessitating a quarantine. He couldn't with clear conscience just leave the infected Apache behind, alone, to wither and die. Luckily, one of the Apache, who had previously suffered the smallpox scourge and was now immune, volunteered to drive an improvised "portable isolation hospital," discreetly following at a healthful distance. Burdened by the necessity of wheeled vehicles, Agent Clum divided his unwieldy command. His chief clerk at the San Carlos Reservation, M. A. Sweeney, had cautiously preceded him to *Ojo Caliente* and was now placed in charge of the main body of Apache who would cross over the mountains as pedestrians, a much shorter course. Clum himself would take a more roundabout way with the wagons and shackled prisoners. Silver City would be their rallying point.[397]

On May 1, 1877, the two processions got under way. Unfortunately: "Tis true there are [were] yet some stragglers at large; just how many we are not able to say, but they are destined to come under the same salutary rule that govern others of the tribe, or else they must, in the language of the poetic Sprague, 'wither from the land.'"[398] Some of the "stragglers" struck. Near Mule Springs northwest of Silver City, a dog and its master, A.W. Branch, were killed while George Dallas barely escaped with his life. Dallas only saw two Apache, but he guesstimated there were at least six. For sure, he did watch a "large Indian" saunter up to the wounded Branch and place a bullet through his head.[399] Later the Apache killed a "fine cow" near Andrew Hurlbut's ranch on the Gila. Shortly thereafter, two miles below the mouth of Duck Creek, three Apache fired on John Comerford and his hired hand, but luckily they weren't hit.[400] And just across the territorial line, 22 miles from Richmond, New Mexico Territory, 78-year-old Peter Davis and an unnamed helper delivering a load of potatoes to Camp Grant were killed by Apache. Either just before or just after that incident, three "Mexican" teamsters were also massacred near Ash Springs.[401] An area resident wrote the *Grant County Herald's* editor:

> Times look very bad here at present. Every time the dog barks we grab for the guns.[402]

Plainly, not all the area's Apache were on the march to Silver City with Sweeney or Clum. Wayne Whitehill later asserted that his father on at least one occasion received a contract to guard Apache prisoners moving through Silver City during a removal to San Carlos; perhaps this is that time.[403] Clearly it would not have been an unwise move. Clum's armed Apache police, traveling with several hundred other Indians, some no doubt participants in previous area raids, created no little stir, and there was good reason to be concerned for Apache safety. The likelihood of reprisal was very much on the mind of the Indian agent and his military escort.

Upon their arrival at Silver City, not unexpectedly, citizens turned out *en masse* to see the Apache up close. At the request of several local gentlemen, Sweeney agreed to treat onlookers to a "veritable Indian war dance."

Company of Apache scouts at Silver City. *An Alfred S. Addis photo, courtesy New Mexico History Museum, #98506.*

Wood was collected and placed near the Apache encampment outside of town. About nine o'clock in the evening the citizens, including the town's "fair ladies and their spouses," gathered around to witness the "novel performance," and the bonfire was lit:

> ...about twenty squaws (young and old) and bucks were congregated around a large buffalo hide, to which they each held on with one hand while they beat time upon it with long sticks in the other, accompanying their action with a monotonous sound between a shout and an attempt at song. Thus beating, holding fast to the rawhide, and singing, they went dancing around leaving the bonfire to pass each small party at the numerous camps strewn around the neighborhood. Upon their return they formed a quarter of a circle about the main campfire, with their medicine man in the center. The latter was provided with an old kettle, over the head of which was fastened a piece of rawhide or else a drum head. This old gentleman kept beating and at the same

> time leading the rest in the song which related the bold achievements in love, war and the chase, of themselves and their ancestors. The quarter of a circle gradually grew to a half and the half expanded into a complete ring, and round and round they went, old men, young men, aged and wrinkled women, young and pretty squaws, boys, children and papooses.[404]

Silver City's group of "fair daughters of American civilization" gazed with wondering eyes at the whole scene, taking in the "many colored shawls, pieces of flannel blankets, buckskin mantillas and the red, yellow and green war paint of the savages."[405] A grand time was had by all. The fire dimmed to but smoldering coals, and everyone, Apache and townsmen alike, retired to their own private worlds of reflective thought and personal perceptions. The two groups—for that night—had come together and parted peaceably.

Thankfully, there had not been outrage right there in town. After a rejoining of columns at Silver City, John Clum and his charges finally arrived at San Carlos on May 20, although they lost eight Apache along way due to infectious smallpox. At the agency's guardhouse 17 manacled "outlaw" Apache, including Geronimo, were safely locked away pending a civil trial for murder and robbery in Pima County, Arizona Territory.[406] While Geronimo languished in jail—temporarily—other bronco Apache were nimbly jumping across the San Carlos Reservation's hard-to-watch borderline, engaging in mischief and then racing back for its veiled protection. For Grant County folks it was troublesome.

Apache struck again in Grant County—after Clum's arrival at San Carlos—kidnapping Catrino Baldanado, a 10-year-old who was herding cattle at the John Bragaw ranch near San Lorenzo, on the Upper Mimbres. Also taken as a terrified prisoner was the adult herder, Andrew Fleming, "a negro." The Apache acted decisively: They released the child sans his clothes, mercilessly killed cowboy Fleming, and drove four stolen oxen and several horses before them. On the way out of the country, the Apache stole two more horses from George Shepard.[407]

Compelled to set aside civilian law enforcement and tax-collecting duties, Sheriff Harvey Whitehill was, from time to time, pressed into the Apache-hunting business. On one occasion during a punishing scout into the Burro Mountains south of Silver City he very nearly rode into an ambush.[408] In later life his second son, Wayne, recalled that his father was "out all the time while he was sheriff...had posses. He'd go out and he'd be gone a month and he'd come back and he'd have Indian scalps dangling, tied on his saddle when he come to town."[409] Support for such an assertion is somewhat offered by a blurb in the *Grant County Herald* urging that the sheriff should be "recompensed" for his Apache-chasing expenses from county funds or, if not that, by the contributions of private citizens.[410] Plainly, by any levelheaded standard the whole Silver City region was undergoing a nightmarish barrage of hostility, be it at the hands of Apache fighters or pale-faced marauders. Sheriff Whitehill was desperate for help. He strongly urged that the Third Judicial District attorney, J. F. Bennett, wire New Mexico Territorial Governor Samuel B. Axtell at Santa Fe and request authority to call up a company of militia to deal with a "large band of rustlers."[411] Bureaucratically, the governor replied that Whitehill must first exhaust his "civil power" before any militia could be fashioned or called out.[412]

One of Sheriff Whitehill's exhaustive efforts at getting an effective handle on widespread criminality was the employment of a truly audacious man-killing chief deputy. He hired Dan Tucker. The life that Tucker lived prior to his arrival in Silver City is shadowy. Reportedly he was born in Canada, raced through childhood in Indiana. By the time he appeared in Silver City during June 1877, he had already killed a man in Colorado and, perhaps, men in Lincoln and Doña Ana counties of New Mexico Territory as well.[413] At the time the sheriff's constituents thought Whitehill had put the right man on the payroll. Contemporaries pithily commented that Dan Tucker was a "dead game hombre." He was not afraid to kill when necessary, they observed; he was a man with cool unflinching eyes; he could not have been singled out as a gun-player, but he was one; and that before the "bad element had 'painted the town red' and 'shot it up at their own sweet will' but when Tucker took charge it was not quite such an easy job, especially after had had given the coroner two or three siftings."[414] Historic newspaper accounts and court records affirm those old-timers' character assessments. Dan Tucker was—if anyone in the Old West was—a gunman!

Silver City could well use his talents, or of those likewise predisposed. One set of outlaws almost had the town buffaloed. William "Wild Bill" Martin, Bob "Nelson from the Gila" Nelson, Jose M. "Portuguese Jo" Carrolla and John Orr, aka John Donaldson, were believed to have committed numerous murders, laying blame on the Apache—as many as 16 by some news accounts.[415] Men had turned up missing after coming in contact with the gang, Charley Embry to name just one.[416] Citizens' tempers flared after the killers gunned down R. N. Calhoun on John Perry's Mangas Creek ranch. During a horrendous confrontation things turned "Western." After the scorching shootout, "Portuguese Jo," John Orr and "Wild Bill" Martin were kicking up daisies and Bob Nelson's horse and blood-stained saddle were recovered by Dan Tucker. The desperado Nelson was, at that time, presumed a dead *hombre*. There is no historic evidence to shatter that supposition, although his perforated body was never found.[417]

Silver City and old Grant County were fast earning reputations they didn't want. Assuredly the prominent city dwellers, dragging their Eastern urbanity with them, didn't relish the fact that their picturesque town was fast becoming known for stagecoach robberies and barroom dustups often settled with frog-stickers or six-shooters or single-jacks. She was, after all, a mining metropolis with brick houses, picket-fenced front yards, and a steadily growing population of romping and stomping school children. Downtown businesses were ornately trimmed and elaborately stocked. Big deals were brokered, fortunes won and lost. Silver City may have been that "Diamond City in the Hills," as some articulated, but with a tempestuous wink she could also show her tawdry side. History bears witness to her interludes with wickedness, even though the prim and proper, then and now, often blush and look the other way—or sometimes deny. During those tumultuous adolescent years Silver City was as wild a town as there was anywhere in the West.

The 1877 summer was hardly over before Atanacio Bencomo was "struck by a pistol ball" fired by Dan Tucker while attempting an arrest. Bencomo died.[418] Scarcely had any time passed before Juan Garcia, after cutting an adversary from stem to stern, ran from deputy Dan Tucker, and "the bullet struck the Mexican dead-center."[419] Garcia died, too. Dan Tucker's pistol shot was justified, so ruled the coroner. Tucker shot a drunken soldier, Tom Robinson.[420] He didn't die, but did pay a fine for his rowdiness, no doubt wondering why he hadn't heeded the officer's insistence that he settle down and mind his manners. On another occasion, although it is supported by but one account, in an area taproom the ever-dangerous Dan Tucker fatally gunned down two belligerent horse thieves and wounded a third.[421]

The bloody time frame wasn't exclusively set aside for a peacekeeper's killings. Hugh Flynn, a "quarrelsome and dangerous man," was gunned down in a "Mexican House" by Silver City baker Bill Jordan, the six-shooter conclusion to a personal feud.[422] Emil Forrer, a US Army private, killed E. H. Cuddy with a "cavalry needle gun" and was arrested. And perhaps the most sensational 1877 killing was that accomplished by suspected stagecoach robber and certified man-killer Thomas "Tom" Bowe. He shot Silver City pioneer Richard "Dick" Howlett in the forehead while both fussed or kidded across a green-clothed poker table.[423] Tom Bowe had earlier killed one Silver City man, John Clark, during a saloon hullabaloo that exploded into six-shooter fireworks. He had hollered self-defense and was turned loose.[424] After popping Howlett between the eyes, Bowe ran fast—and far. The New Mexico governor at the time, Samuel B. Axtell, incensed, offered an official $500 bounty for the arrest and conviction of Bowe, or even if he was "necessarily killed in the attempt to arrest him."[425]

Sometimes those desperadoes who failed to elude hard-riding lawmen paid dearly for their slowness. That is, if an anecdotal tale is accepted straight out: Brazen thieves stole a band of horses near Lone Mountain, southeast of Silver City. A posse was speedily fashioned and pursuit was initiated. The brigands were quickly overhauled near Cow Springs and "what happened there the people never knew, except perhaps the sheriff and his deputies, but the posse returned, with every stolen horse and three extra ones with saddles on." Naturally, when questioned the possemen tendered oblique answers designed to skirt the truth, but everyone knew what fate had really befallen the wrongdoers. Of this particular instance it was penned:

> That is the way they dealt with horse thieves in those days. Their contempt and loathing for that class of men was so bitter that the stern, unrelenting old-timers rarely ever buried their bodies. It may have been inhuman, but if one will stop to think that for a man, left afoot in as dangerous a country as this was at that time, meant death for him. I will leave the reader to judge which was the most inhuman, the horse thief or the man who showed him no mercy?[426]

Illustratively, Benjamin Leggett and one Patterson, from the Tularosa country of western Socorro County, followed the tracks of suspected horse-thief Mike Gibbons and his "Mexican" accomplice to the vicinity of Grant County's Duck Creek. Leggett and Patterson were a law unto themselves and simply gunned down the pair of owl-hoots. Gibbons died on the spot and the gut-shot "Mexican" ran off to die—somewhere. The aggrieved fellows unsympathetically blew away the blue smoke pouring from their six-shooters' muzzles, gathered their misappropriated horses and coolly returned to Socorro County. No harm, no foul.[427] Other instances of old Grant County's lynch-law justice, which will be addressed later, are not nearly as sketchy, and plainly lend a degree of credit to the aforementioned models of summary judgment. It was tough country!

Despite the barroom shootings, an occasional gut-cuttin', or the biting off of an ear, Silver City was ever so slowly hammering out stability. Nonviolent 1877 happenings were taking place, too. The ever-flamboyant but nearly always thriving Martin Bremen made a move. Smartly he consolidated the Tennessee mill and the Wisconsin mill. With importation of two heavy jaw-type crushers and other machinery, Bremen increased the vicinity's ore-processing capacity to 20 tons per day.[428] Builder Robert Black had opened a most complete woodworking facility—New Mexico Territory's first—and was locally manufacturing "doors and window sashes" of first-rate quality.[429] Adding to the buzzing din of planes and saws was Samuel Carlin, turning out custom cabinets for the elegantly outfitted brick mansions. Thomas F. Cooper, a "practical watchmaker" and jeweler, was kept busy from early dawn to late at night.[430] John A. Warren and W. J. Mason were covered up with work at their blacksmith shop repairing wagons and carriages, and shoeing fidgety horses.[431] The Derbyshire brothers were doing a booming business selling stationery, books, toys and some very "fancy articles."[432] H. M. Porter's bank was financially flourishing, as was the Grant County Bank under the astute management of Newton Bradley.[433] The Bennett and Van Wagen & Company drugstore was busy "compounding prescriptions" at all hours of the day and night and, of course, dispensing pure liquor for "medicinal purposes."[434] For those not suffering a medical malady, a stiff drink could be had at several area saloons, including the Kentuck and the Centennial.[435] Joseph Buhlman, the "fashionable" boot and shoe maker, was guaranteeing a "perfect fit."[436] Charlie Sun opened a restaurant on Broadway Street, pledging to set a first-class table at moderate prices.[437] The forecast for Sam Carpenter's ice business was promising, the demand rising to meet the frosty supply.[438] A shooting club affiliated with the National Rifle Association was birthed, and 300-yard target matches were set in motion.[439] S. M. Ashenfelter had taken over as editor of the *Grant County Herald,* and was proudly boasting—justifiably so—that his broadsheet had the largest circulation of any in the whole of New Mexico, and was the only newspaper in the territory associated with the Western Associated Press, receiving daily telegraphic reports across the newly constructed and, sometimes reliable linkage with an ever-encroaching outside world.[440] Partisan regional bragging rights were fostering a not-necessarily unfounded public relations declaration: "Silver City is the only live town in New Mexico."[441]

Many merchants were blatantly violating the territory's Sunday Law, a prohibitive statute designed to forestall commercial enterprise on the Sabbath. With but a sly wink Silver City looked the other way—that is, until a prescribed date was set for all of the offending businesses to be shut down and fines paid, promptly followed by a reopening on that very same Sunday. The collected revenue went for a good purpose—the school.[442]

There had not been a spring term for the public school, but George Murray, a Methodist preacher, had opened a private institution. Later he was replaced by Reverend N. H. Gale, who opened a "select school" during Sept. 1877, with 43 students.[443] The regular term of public school began in October with classes held in the Bennett, VanWagen & Co. building on Bullard Street—between Broadway and Yankie Streets—Miss Belle Lucas the teacher in charge.[444] Silver City's public school was in "a flourishing condition," the attendance roster was "quite full" and Belle Lucas was praised for her overall excellence. There was not yet, however, an adequate public school building.

Educational interest was not solely restricted to Silver City. At nearby Georgetown, a "first-class" teacher, Mr. Pratz, was conducting classroom activities; while over near the Mimbres River at quaint San Lorenzo there were "upwards of 30 pupils" in a public school taught by the exceptionally competent and well-liked Doña Guadalupe Reyna.[445]

Trees were being planted; schoolchildren were listening—most of the time; preachers were proselytizing; merchants were making money hands over fists; brick buildings were rising from nothingness at an astounding rate; tradesmen were industriously trafficking their time; lawyers were jabbering and arguing, advocating for this or that good reason; prospectors were peeling back earth's treasures; and all the while stagecoach horses were continually galloping into town with a brand-new batch of hopefuls—dumping them and racing away to profitably pick up the next load.

Silver City was booming, blooming and busting at the seams, so it seems.

Not all news was good news, though. Not only were Clum's Apache wards suffering from smallpox afflictions, Silver City was having its bout with the dreaded curse. For a while some of the regularly scheduled *bailes* were suspended in a try at capping off the epidemic. In their hedonistic search for pastime and pleasure, however, several residents organized well-attended private shindigs; the local press had a field day exposing the partying participants.[446]

There, too, were other reoccurring ailments—the manmade variety. Very real was the need for H. M. Porter to advertise when the latest overdue shipment of "Colt's Pistols and Cartridges and a large stock of Winchester and Needle-gun Cartridges" was unpacked, degreased and made ready for sale.[447] Especially after it was learned that the second of two "Mexican boys" left for dead by renegade Apache at remote Burro Springs south of town had died.[448] Or when it was realized that nine Anglo owl-hoots, each "armed with two revolvers and a Winchester rifle, and carrying two belts with cartridges," had stopped the westbound stagecoach near Fort Cummings. Finding no cash-stuffed strongbox on board, the guttersnipes cavalierly remarked, "Well, we'll let you pass this time," and then shared guzzling pulls from an uncorked whiskey bottle in a departing toast, riding east toward the Rio Grande—and into the outlaw/lawman history books. A contemporary newspaperman noted the "gang was constantly on the road and it is time that the citizens turned out and strung them up." Reportedly, and possibly it's true, Henry "Kid" Antrim, after killing Francis P. "Windy" Cahill near Camp Grant in Arizona Territory, was riding high with this same stage-stopping bunch of misfits, the gaggle a perturbed newspaper editor wanted lynched from the nearest piñon limb.[449]

Nonetheless, as 1877 drew near its close, Silver City's family folks were laying plans for a festive holiday season, with horse and foot races, shooting contests, barbecues and *bailes*. In fact, it was to be "A Gala Day—Come One, Come All!" Sheriff Whitehill was warning, though, "that no persons carrying pistols will [would] be permitted near the race course or shooting grounds on Christmas day."[450] Eager youngsters were no doubt drooling with anticipation after eyeballing the latest shipment of Christmas toys on display at Bennett, VanWagen & Co.'s showroom.[451] Martin Maher, one of the local bakers, was proposing to turn out a rousing baking night on Christmas Eve, furnishing all his delighted customers with "fresh mince-pies, plain and fancy cakes, fresh bread, biscuits, etc.,

etc."[452] Charles Schutz, "the Broadway confectioner," was likewise busy putting up "all kinds of sweet-meat in a most artistic manner."[453]

To the southeast at El Paso del Norte, things weren't so sweet—the holiday season had turned particularly sour. History knows the bloody bedlam as the El Paso Salt War; the clear-cut truth is it was a race war, pure and simple. Without detailing the whole sordid story, Silver City's link to the mess can be quickly put in plain words: Anglo faces at Franklin, on the American side of the Rio Grande, were overwhelmingly outnumbered by a Spanish-speaking population scattered along both banks of the river. The ratio, indeed, was lopsided. Out of an estimated population of 12,000, 80 were "white."[454] With the murder of Louis Cardis, an Italian but nevertheless an incredibly proactive voice for El Paso area non-Anglos who held little political power, and the retaliatory killings of Judge Charles Howard, John McBride, John Atkinson and Texas Ranger C. E. Mortimer, all hell broke loose. And, reportedly, a corrupt Catholic priest, Father Antonio Borajo, was fanning the flames, declaring "shoot all the Gringos and I will absolve you."[455] After the looting and rioting commenced, the El Paso County sheriff, Charles Kerber, was woefully deficient manpower-wise to put a peaceful cap on the broiling turmoil. Kerber wired the governor of Texas asking for authority to "raise 100 [men] in New Mexico." Permission was granted.[456] Sheriff Kerber immediately sought aid beyond the border: "I telegraphed in every direction. Was promised 40 men at Las Cruces and 50 at Silver City." With rising confidence the sheriff wrote his father-in-law, "I expect 50 citizens from Silver City and then I will drive the scoundrels ahead of me like sheep.... You will find I will not allow the greasers to pass unpunished."[457]

At Silver City, Deputy Sheriff Dan Tucker and a soon-to-be-notorious cow-rustling kingpin, John Kinney, began shaping a fighting force of volunteers from the rougher element, a contingent later described as men who were "hard faced and battle scarred...they nearly all had reputations."[458] Twenty of those tough customers rode out of Silver City and were reinforced by 30 more from the Lower Mimbres country. Three days before Christmas, they stormed into Franklin.[459] Highlighting the behavior of the Silver City boys is not complex. Simply said, they "behaved badly"—ravishing women, taking peoples' property, breaking doors and windows, pot-shooting both chickens and several escaping prisoners. After that, they simply turned to killing each other. Certainly getting much more than they bargained for, and because they were operating

"New Mexico Rustlers." The man standing may be John Kinney, as some assert. If so, could the others be Jesse Evans and Frank Baker, as has been proffered? Or, perhaps, the notorious Jimmy McDaniels and Charles "Pony Diehl" Ray, all cohorts of Kinney? *¿Quien sabe? A Ben Wittick photo, courtesy New Mexico History Museum, #14264.*

absolutely absent any "restraint," the Silver City righters-of-wrongs were hurriedly mustered out of service on Jan. 10, 1878.[460] Not inaccurately it's been written: "Sheriff Kerber had been promised the aid of 50 men from Silver City...30 men from Silver City arrived; judging by their performance it is well that 50 did not come."[461] The people living in El Paso County thanked their lucky stars the Silver City bunch had ridden back to old Grant County; they simply couldn't stand much more of their help.[462] Back home in Silver City, the returning combatants "expressed themselves as well satisfied with their lark. No expense, plenty of fun and a measure of experience which may be turned to advantage in future campaigns."[463] Perchance the Silver City people would have preferred the "boys" to have stayed a little nearer their home turf, where they may have well benefited from a plateful of their compassionless vehemence.

Approximately 35 Apache "bucks" had jumped the San Carlos Reservation, accompanied by about 100 women and children. South of Silver City in the Peloncillo Mountains [the newspaper referred to them as the "Stein's Peak Range"] straddling the Arizona-New Mexico Territorial borderline, the "mangled remains" of Ralston's mail-coach driver, D. Kier, were found. After attacking the frightened courier, Apache had mercilessly mutilated the corpse, then cut loose the horses, rifled the mail sacks and—characteristically—vanished![464] Close by, in the mountains bordering the Lower Gila country, the body of William "Dick" Richards was discovered by Sterling Burwell and Abel L. Webb. When swooped down on by Indians, Richards had been nonchalantly and, evidently carelessly, skinning a downed deer. Six ragged bullet holes marked the Indians' accomplishment. The hurrying Apache fled deeper south for asylum in the Sierra Madres of Old Mexico. Somberly, Burwell and Webb "buried the remains, and erected a monument of heavy stones over the grave."[465]

Unbeknownst to them at the time, Apache raiders couldn't have picked a worse time or a more ill-advised section of real estate to haunt. Coming back from a dual government-sanctioned expedition into Old Mexico rode the seemingly unconquerable and indestructible Lieutenant Tony Rucker. Behind him—at the trot—were 6th Cavalry detachments from Companies C, G, H, and L, augmented by a hardened crew of Apache scouts, totaling 80 men, well-armed with single-shot Springfield rifles and long-barreled Colt's Army revolvers.[466] Somewhere in old Grant County's Animas Mountains, the two outfits crashed into each other—with force! During the ensuing fight Tony Rucker's men killed 15 Apache warriors, captured one, and recovered 60 stolen horses.[467] This time the Apache were whipped. Those that managed an escape had a debt to pay. No doubt the citizens at Silver City cheered, but incessantly reoccurring news of this or that Apache raid and the horrifying deaths were chafing, no, scalding nuisances. They were growing bone-weary with Apache reports that were always bad, and damn dog tired of Indian agents' and Army colonels' lame excuses. They had a city to build.

Chapter 8

"Popped Him and Killed Him Right There"

The first day of January 1878 was simply perfect, not a cloud in the sky to dampen spirits for a grand New Year's Day celebration. The crowds at the target range and the race course were large; many visitors from outlying camps were in town, too. J. P. Risque and C. P. Crawford took first and second places, respectively, in the long-range rifle competition, although the postures they twisted into were not "particularly graceful." At the racetrack, numerous contests were battled for by jockeys riding the county's very finest hot-blooded and best-bred steeds. There was even a race for "scrub" horses so everyone could get in on the action. Vigorous side bets in addition to the regular purse kept eager spectators on edge. For the most part all went well. There was one spectacular sideshow, however: The cinch on La Luz's saddle broke, dumping her rider. Panicked, the horse madly dashed into the crowd, scattering spectators and severely injuring Yrlneo Pacheco's hip when he was struck by the "flying mare's" hoof.[468] All and all, though, it had been a good day to be in Silver City. A welcome break to be sure, but once festivities came to an end there was serious business at hand.

Silver City incorporated during 1878—officially. As may be recalled, subsequent to Grant County's abortive stab at surgically cutting loose from the New Mexico Territory, Santa Fe politicians had acquiesced and granted Silver City the exclusive privilege of levying and collecting her own taxes, allowing city government to operate under a special charter. At the time, it was the only municipality in the whole territory so endorsed.[469] The newly incorporated city was to be mapped outward from the heart of the hectic building hubbub:

> All that portion of the County of Grant embraced with the following limits, to-wit: An area of two miles square, conforming to the points of the compass north, east, south and west, measuring from the point intersecting at right angles Broadway and Main Street in the Town site of Silver City.[470]

Fashioned after Eastern models of town government, Silver City operated under the mayor/councilmen system. In Silver City's case the mayor and two councilmen were to hold one-year terms, and two other councilmen two-year stints in office [for the first election cycle], elections to be held the first Tuesday of each April. As a body, with the mayor serving as the chief executive, the city council had limited legislative power to implement local ordinances not in conflict with New Mexico Territorial or United States' statutes, and to appoint themselves a city clerk, treasurer, town marshal, tax assessor and street supervisor.[471]

Silver City as a government was off and running. She had no permanent city office, however, so for the first few years, like an orphaned vagabond, city council meetings took place as convenience and practicability permitted, at first one place, then another.[472] The highly esteemed lumberyard and building tycoon, Robert Black, was Silver City's first elected mayor.[473]

Dan Tucker, still holding on to his deputy sheriff's commission, was named Silver City's first town marshal on April 11.[474] His no-nonsense reputation and policing proficiency soon put the brakes on what had evidently become an everyday recreational diversion: "Marshal Tucker under the city government has put a stop to the discharge of firearms upon our streets."[475] Shortly thereafter a "Mexican went haywire" and instead of firing a gun in melodramatic Old West fashion, began indiscriminately and sadistically chunking rough-edged rocks at passersby. Town Marshal Tucker was promptly notified, and rushed to the scene of disorder. Whether Tucker tendered any warning to cease and desist is not known. It is clear, though, that the policeman was not a man to monkey with. Unflappably, Marshal Dan Tucker simply unlimbered his six-shooter, pointed it at the Mexican and "popped him and killed him right there."[476] An eyewitness thought Tucker had "done a good job killing him" and echoed contemporary public opinion on the matter: "Everybody thought so anyhow."[477] Later Tucker was called to a private house where a "Mexican was murdering his wife and son," or so it was thought—he was beating them with a club. Pistol drawn, lawman Dan charged into the abode, but his Colt's revolver was smartly knocked from his hand by a ferocious whack from the suspect, who wielded a hardwood stick. Once more with his typical cold indifference, Dan Tucker reached down with his uninjured left hand, picked up his six-shooter and "shot the Mexican dead."[478] Woe be it to the one who challenged Marshal Dan Tucker or the community's resolve to skin back bad behavior. Ever so slowly Silver City was shedding her standing as a wild and woolly hell-town, though it would be a lengthy and troublesome process.

Cart loads of immigrants were arriving daily, as were freight wagons and mule trains burdened with all sorts of commodities—indispensable and frivolous alike.[479] There was still a real housing shortage: "It is worthy of notice that Silver City has no vacant houses...several parties, who, during the past week, have used every effort to secure even habitable quarters—but without success."[480] Not everyone had a good place to stay, but everyone could enjoy America's favorite pastime. Silver City had a baseball club, which sometimes even won its games.[481] The hustle and bustle may be extrapolated—albeit less than scientifically—by assessment of a plain fact: That always-industrious baker, Martin Maher, with only a one-day vacation in three years, was pulling from his hot ovens 250 loaves of bread per day, every day. Too, it was reported that during one busy Silver City week merchant R. B. Higbee off-loaded 10 tons of groceries. And stored underneath packed sawdust in the cooling houses owned by Sam Carpenter and David Abraham were 35 tons of eight-inch-thick ice, more than enough to get through the upcoming summer months.[482] Beer was cold at Silver City.

The water 25 miles southeast of town was hot. Dick Hudson, Grant County's pioneering first sheriff and an ex-county judge, in a near-legend-making deal, acquired the Mimbres Hot Springs, a transaction that included the much talked about Hotel of Accommodation and bath houses.[483] The site was known far and wide as a healthful, rejuvenating getaway spot. Although Hudson would purchase advertising space in local newspapers, he really didn't need to.[484] A laudatory and cost-free news item in the *Mesilla* Independent reported:

> Scarcely a day passes that we do not receive additional evidence of the wonderful curative properties of the waters of the Hot Springs in Grant County. So many invalids go there broken down in health, and return in a

Stagecoach at Hudson's Hot Springs [Mimbres Hot Springs] between Silver City and Deming, after the site was acquired by Dick Hudson. *Courtesy Silver City Museum.*

> few weeks strong and hearty, that all doubt is dispelled of the efficacy of the waters. Those who visit these springs in search of health and strength not only find it but are enthusiastic in their praises of the proprietor and host, Judge Hudson, and his good lady.[485]

Billy the Kid's mother wasn't alone in her effort to seek a cure bathing in the bubbling hot spring. Many were the southwestern New Mexico Territory and southeastern Arizona Territory citizens who weighed the health benefits of soaking in the therapeutic waters against the very real likelihood of inadvertently bumping headlong into a band of renegade Apache or a gun-carrying gang of scowl-faced stagecoach robbers en route. Nearly everyone opted to make the trip to Hudson's Hot Springs. Like Charles Schutz and David Abraham, the majority safely returned home, "testifying to the healing influences of the Springs." In fact, Cyrus Loomis, completely helpless from the ravages of rheumatism, regularly bathed in the bubbling mineral waters and after just a few days' treatment was "able to run a race with anybody."[486]

Another community, 18 miles northeast of Silver City, Georgetown, couldn't boast of healing properties in the nearby Mimbres River, nor could her hardworking residents crow about rivaling Silver City with a seamy underbelly, a wild and wicked night-life. In fact, relatively serene Georgetown couldn't attract that "class of individuals known as 'professional gamblers,'" having but the one saloon, and it was "conducted in the most orderly manner," most of the time.[487] Thoughtfully laid out into three well-planned neighborhoods, with the business center separating residential areas, Georgetown thrived. James A. Lucas, the proprietor of the cozy Crawford House, dished out Southwestern hospitality to overnight guests. There were several general merchandising stores, two of which were owned and operated by G. P. Armstrong and Sigmund Lindauer. Armstrong, too, was running a busy hackline between Georgetown and Silver City, using a "most commodious and staunchly built spring wagon," capable of hauling six paying passengers if necessary. George Smith was the local and "thoroughly competent" assayer. Energetic Georgetown, like her shiretown sister, was a silver-mining town. Ore from such mines as the Naiad Queen, McNulty, Satisfaction, McGregor, Uncle Sam and many, many others was hauled to the Mimbres Mining and Reduction Works.[488] Intermittently there were well-attended "evening balls" at Georgetown with many of the Silver City folks invited as special guests; the parties lasted "till the peep of dawn."[489] Those so inclined could keep up with local news through the pages of A. C. Lowery's *Silver Brick*, and between this or that Grant County six-shooter "difficulty," tracing scorching Apache footprints clear across the gargantuan county, or following political missteps and intrigues, there was plenty to read about.[490]

One of those attention-grabbing stories was taking place on the other side of the county. That southwestern New Mexico Territory wedge of ground familiarly known by so many previous monikers was undergoing another name change. Ralston was no more. William G. Boyle, "a mining engineer and a cultured gentleman" thoroughly committed to eradicating any taint of scandal, had prompted the renaming.[491] Earlier, allegations of unscrupulous fellows Philip Arnold and John Slack had set the county and the country ablaze with dreams of easy pickings and unparalleled riches. They had, if the story is actually true, perpetrated the classic mining territory con. Convincingly and cunningly they had "salted" an area surrounding 5,105-foot Lee's Peak in the Pyramid

Mexican Springs, then Grant, the Burro Mines, then Ralston, and finally Shakespeare, New Mexico. *Courtesy New Mexico History Museum, #55364.*

Mountains, not with imported gold nuggets, but with diamonds. Sample gemstones purportedly "found" by Arnold and Slack were sent to California, then to Tiffany's in New York for an appraisal. Placing a value of $150,000 on the diamonds, the jewelers unwittingly nudged the swindling rip-off onward:

> By this time everyone was practically insane with anxiety to see and test the field, and a party including one of the foremost mineral geologists of the day, Henry Janin, made a trip there. They were guided in by Arnold and Slack, who took the most round-about route.... Janin, the specialist and, incidentally, a man of undoubted integrity, pronounced the field genuine. That cinched it. A company was formed with a capitalization of some $10,000,000, Arnold and Slack were bought out for $300,000 apiece, and American's first major diamond mine seemed ready to produce untold wealth.[492]

Paying his own inspection journey to the promising field of raw and precious stones, Clarence King, a government geologist, made a most monumental finding: a diamond "already cut and polished." The bubble had burst! Without reservation King declared the hoax the clumsiest "salting" job he had ever seen and that he had seen a good many. Embarrassment washed across the country from coast to coast—many had been greedily bamboozled.[493]

Boyle's subsequent founding of The Shakespeare Gold and Silver Mining Company was to give Ralston's folks a new life and the town a new name. From then till now she has simply been called Shakespeare, a designation the US Postal Department recognized early on.[494] Shakespeare's main thoroughfare, the aptly named Avon Avenue, became beehive busy with prospectors, barkeeps, merchants, travelers and, in due time, attracted an assemblage of the most notorious ne'er-do-wells and scalawags who could be found anywhere in the Old West. Good mining news attracts newsmakers, and many—good and bad—were now flocking to Grant County's camps and towns.

Earlier in the Chloride Flat District that ever-showy Martin Bremen had acquired the 76 Mine, along with three others, the Back Bone, the Chloride and the Victoria.[495] The 76 was a whopping producer and word of its profitability spread throughout the country, at least all the way to Texas. Learning of the 76's productivity, several Lone Star holdovers from Mason County's infamous Hoo Doo War exercised their geographical options and made the move. Men such as Jacob Melborne Lacy and his son John Hancock; Joe Olney, aka Joe Hill; John Peters Ringo, sometimes simply known as "John R. Godalmighty"; and the high-handed jail-breaking and jailhouse-escaping brothers, Thomas Searcy "Tom" and William Zachariah "Bill" Redding, took up residence in old Grant County. Olney and Ringo set up in the Shakespeare neighborhood, and the Redding boys in the Georgetown precinct, declaring to a census enumerator that Bill was a stockman, and that Tom was a shingle cutter.[496]

During 1879 Bremen located the eponymous Bremen mine and, with a linkage system to the aforementioned mines through connecting "shafts, levels and drifts," the conglomeration thereafter was referred as the 76 Mine. It would become the district's largest producer and it put Martin Bremen on the path to becoming Silver City's richest mine owner, a not-insignificant achievement.[497] The value of a public relations message was not lost to Silver City's promoters, as evidenced in pages of the *Grant County Herald*, which ballyhooed the fact that Bremen's 76 Mine was "turning out better and more ore than ever before," running some $8 to the pound, and that the nearby Rescue and the old Providencia were "looking well." That very first mine, the Legal Tender, was also still "showing a fine body of first-class ore."[498] Adding to the favorable buzz was a report that The New Mexico and Massachusetts Mining Company was in the process of shipping to Silver City what would be the "largest and finest mining machinery in the Territory."[499] Not yet having celebrated her 10th birthday, Silver City saw her candles burning bright, her future assured.

The bright light for one resident, however, was snuffed out. Henry F. Dwenger disappeared. That in and of itself wasn't big-time news. Silver City was a come-and-go community. Some stayed, some prospected and played, and some simply moved on. Intuiting that there was a chance something just might be amiss in this instance, however, Sheriff Harvey Whitehill slyly quizzed Dwenger's 18-year-old son, William. The lawman was knocked back on his heels with the boy's tearful confession: The senior Dwenger had been lured to an isolated spot, and with a spiraling bullet fired from a "needle gun" held by his very own son, he had suffered a head shot from behind. Standing nearby with a six-shooter in hand, in case the lad's shot went wild, was William "Parson" Young, a man who had been "getting' kinda thick" with the dead man's wife, Dora Dwenger. The lifeless form was interred beneath "rock and earth" taken from a hastily dug "prospect hole." It was also learned that sweet Dora had been the "black widow" behind the plot to do away with her man. Piloted to the scene, Whitehill had the corpse exhumed, and the murdering teenager's story was forensically confirmed. Mother, son and lover were arrested and locked away in Grant County's jail awaiting surefire criminal indictments by the grand jury.[500] The year, not yet half over, was whirring with news, and most of it wasn't welcome.

At Arizona Territory's San Carlos Reservation, or, as some Army men called it, "Hell's Forty Acres," turmoil was ever on the front burner.[501] At this juncture tries at justifying or condemning the management or mismanagement of Apache affairs is pointless. Agent John Clum, in a spat with the US Army and his own supervisors, hurled down the challenge: If his salary was doubled he would "with two companies of Indian police take care of all the Apaches in Arizona," and then all the troops could leave the territory and go home.[502] Needless to say he didn't get the pay raise and the rest of his suggestion "fell flat." The bombastic Clum, following through on his not-idle threat, saddled his favorite horse and rode off, San Carlos Reservation and the Apache but a memory.

Seemingly there was—although it wasn't necessarily interrelated—a ripple effect. With a laundry list of reasons, Victorio bolted San Carlos. The government's vacillating policy regarding what should be done with the band once they surrendered or were run to ground was emphatically unfair to Victorio's running and hiding Chihennes. In this case hesitancy was wrongheaded. The Apache themselves wanted to return to their *Ojo Caliente* home turf, a site inexplicably off the table with civilian and military bureaucracies at Washington. Precious time and tempers burned. Accordingly, Victorio "kept his word, and the result is [was] he has laid waste and stricken terror into the whole valley of the Rio Grande.... If Victorio's band had been left at Ojo Caliente...all would have been at peace where now terror reigns and [there is] mourning, in many households."[503]

On Silver City's outskirts Victorio's raiders fell upon stockmen, killing all four and making off with 15 mules. Thereafter they killed two more cutoff unfortunates. Soldiers took to the field.[504] Chasing close on Victorio's heels were Captain Charles D. Beyer, New York born and of Dutch descent, and the previously mentioned Lieutenant Henry H. Wright, both riding out of Fort Bayard. With 46 enlisted 9th Cavalrymen, two Navaho scouts and a civilian guide, John R. Foster, the patrol set their northerly course and galloped into the mountain country. It was ablaze, on fire all the way to the Gila River's headwaters. With great difficulty and danger the army boys camped and meandered while they hunted for fresh Apache sign and trigger-finger closure with an elusive enemy.[505] The Apache were setting backfires to cover their tracks, making Foster's work all the more thorny. Determined though, the skillful guide cut a significant trail two days old. Foster figured there were 20 Apache, and the chase was on.[506]

Atop the Continental Divide on May 29, 1879, Apache and Army locked up. Hollering back and forth, the two sides bantered for advantage, but talk came to naught. Sergeant Delaware Penn, leading a squadron, outflanked the Apache. The sharp battle raged for a half-hour, during which time Lt. Wright's horse was killed beneath his knees. Racing to Wright's rescue, Sergeant Thomas Boyne "spurred his horse and executed a one-man charge. His audacity and marksmanship halted the Indian attack as abruptly as it had begun" and he saved the lucky lieutenant's life![507] After the horrific exchange and expenditure of scarce ammunition,

Victorio was forced to slip down the mountain's western slope, abandoning the Chihennes' camp and its substantial stores of "blankets, skins, hides, baskets, meat and mescal," which was quickly burned by the soldiers.[508] The scorecard? At least two of the Apache were wounded—perhaps, from the amount of spilt blood, fatally. Private Frank Dorsey was killed outright, Private George H. Moore was seriously injured, and Private John Scott was slightly wounded.[509] Again, a hard-fighting "Buffalo Soldier," Tom Boyne, was awarded the prestigious Medal of Honor for disregarding danger and rushing to Lt. Wright's defense.[510] The aging Victorio was far from through with letting southwestern New Mexico Territory off the hook and, likewise, the black 9th Cavalry's fighters weren't through earning the nation's most exalted honors campaigning against him and his ragtag band of Warm Springs Apache followers. Resonating with the acidity of utter frustration, Colonel Edward Hatch was forced to admit: "We may as well accept the fact that many of these Indians must be killed."[511]

There was, however, just maybe, one more chance. Everyone, well, nearly everyone, tried finding a piece of that elusive middle ground—the Army, the Indian agents and even old Victorio. Grant County's civilian folks were utterly unimpressed when they picked up the *Grant County Herald* and read:

> Victorio, and his entire band, delivered themselves up at the Mescalero Agency, near Ft. Stanton, on the 30th day of June [1879].[512]

They were much more excited after flipping through a few more pages of that same edition of S. M. Ashenfelter's *Herald*, and learning that Ashenfelter was also foreman of the sitting Grant County grand jury and that:

> The Grand Jury brought in indictments into court against...Victorio (an Indian) murder, Victorio (an Indian) murder (two cases) Victorio (an Indian) stealing Horses.[513]

That same grand jury brusquely returned indictments for murder in the murder of H. F. Dwenger.[514] Three other Grant County owl-hoots escaped the filing of formal criminal charges. In retrospect, there is little doubt they would have hollered "take back" and gladly walked through the jailhouse door and willingly slammed it shut behind them.

The unnamed rustlers soon stole 65 head of cattle from Dan Coomer, a Southern-bred livestock man, hard as nails and courageous as cougar.[515] Gathering his camp trappings, Dan Coomer and a friend, George Williams, a prominent black rancher from the Lower Mimbres country, set out in pursuit. Their trip lasted 24 days, taking them into southeastern Arizona Territory and then back into New Mexico Territory. Trailing though the Burro Mountains, the civilian manhunters finally caught up with their prey.[516] In "an approved Old West manner" Dan Coomer "settled their hash" when they failed to answer his heed: "Throw up your hands!"[517] Two outlaws died on the spot, while another ran for dear life before Coomer could chamber his Winchester's next round. Were they going for their Colt's six-shooters or trying to escape? An old-timer said: "I went and viewed the bodies where they lay, and if they had tried to run, they evidently hadn't gone far, as one lay partly across the other."[518] Back in Silver City, Coomer offered to turn himself in and answer any criminal complaints if necessary. Deputy Tucker said, "No way!"[519] A local newspaper editor summed up the public's outlook about Coomer's no-baloney mode of operation: "...and we say, well done Dan!"[520]

As late August 1879 approached, Silver City's parents of school-age children were industriously making ready, purchasing pencils and tablets and new clothes for the fall semester's opening day. For the first time, there was going to be a school for secondary education—a high school—but its financial support would come from private payment rather than public coffers. A. C. Lowery planned for a full 11-month curriculum with classes covering such subjects as spelling, reading, grammar, geography, arithmetic, philosophy, chemistry, geology, logic, rhetoric and composition, oratory, Latin, French and, for those really sharp students, higher mathematics. Tuition was paid monthly, $4 per student.[521] The Silver City Select School was in business, but that was not the case for the public elementary school. Due to a lack of funds, H. W. Sherry, had to delay opening until October. Many parents were perplexed and the school board was "spurred to activity" to solve what seemed a perpetual problem.[522] There, as of yet, was no decent school building.

During that first decade Silver City—before and after incorporation—was continually playing catch up. Americans' and Mexicans' interest in the town had not subsided and swelling population numbers simply outstripped the community's ability to keep pace. "Coaches from east and west [were] arriving heavily loaded."[523] There was not yet a real Protestant church completed, though one was under construction. Dedicated fire-and-brimstone ministers were not absent, however, and they were reverently spreading the Gospel, preaching sermons here and there, conducting funerals, and baptizing babies.[524] Mayor Robert Black, the city's foremost building contractor, with enthusiasm said that spring was "opening with the most cheerful prospects" and that he had already closed deals that would "keep saw and planing mills in constant operation for months to come."[525] Residential rental property was still scarce to nonexistent. Skilled craftsmen and tradesmen, those who wanted to hustle, weren't ever out of work. Merchants could barely keep their plank shelves stocked, and Martin Maher was "crowded with work" at his downtown cracker factory.[526] Those Silver City men who could afford them were smoking H. M. Porter's imported La Fama and Preciosa brand cigars, and those who couldn't were puffing away on the "Alligator, the best cigar for the price to be found in the United States." And, thankfully, after noting that George Smith had successfully and safely completed his protracted trip to "the States," he was soundly complimented for having "not acquired any foreign airs."[527] The 1870s were speeding to a close and, seemingly, all was well. Elsewhere—east of the Rio Grande—the storm was brewing; when it blew west it would hit Silver City and Grant County with cyclone fury.

The Mescalero Agency in south-central New Mexico Territory was atypical, as far as Indian reservations go. Nestled in the scenic Sacramento Mountains with an abundance of tall pines, dazzling vistas, reliable running springs, and herds of deer and elk feeding in the fog-misted valleys, in contrast to San Carlos it was "God's Forty Acres." Despite the charming setting, the Indian agent, Samuel A. Russell, was worried. Both he and Colonel Hatch had promised Victorio "protection" if he would but enroll at the Mescalero Agency quietly, and calmly remain so until a long-term bargain could be made for him and the decimated band of Mimbres Apache. Victorio had come in, but now lasting peace was dangling on a threadbare string. Russell was in a damn tight spot and wired the commissioner of Indian affairs in Washington: "Three indictments have been found against Victoria [sic] in Grant County, N. M., two for horse stealing and one for murder. There is little if any doubt but an effort will be made to arrest him."[528] What in the hell was Sam Russell to do, he wanted to know, when a sheriff showed up at the agency, doggedly intent on placing Victorio in handcuffs and leg-irons? The bewildered agent's dilemma was real. Quickly it all worked out—not pleasantly, though!

An innocent hunting and fishing trip turned upside-down the expectation of peace. Riding 18 miles east of agency headquarters were Judge Warren Bristol and Prosecuting Attorney Albert Jennings Fountain, on a pleasure excursion. Whether or not the vacationers saw Victorio is moot. Somehow, earlier, he had learned that the Grant County civil authorities were holding a "paper" for him. Now two men he knew to be a part of legal officialdom were passing through the reservation. Mistakenly, Victorio surmised they had come to arrest him, or trick him so others could accomplish the deed. Paranoid he might have been. Rightfully he knew there would be but one outcome for an Apache at a Silver City murder trial. While those excitable schoolchildren at Silver City were making ready their to-do lists, so was Victorio. He finished before they did. On August 21, Victorio bolted the Mescalero Reservation.[529] Victorio's *Mimbreños*, including old Nana, an extraordinarily witty Apache in the craft of war, jumped with him.[530]

The die had been cast for this outbreak. It would be war to the knife, knife to the hilt! On Sept. 4, Victorio with 60 comrades swept through the *Ojo Caliente*, killing five soldiers of Captain Ambrose E. Hooker's Company E, 9th Cavalry, and three civilian herders. Acquisition of 50 horses and 18 mules branded "U.S." was their reward. During the following week Victorio's hard-to-pin-down band killed nine of New Mexico Territory's horror-struck civilians.[531] Two weeks later on Sept. 18 in the ominous and foreboding Black Range northeast of Silver City, a multi-company military command and 46 Navajo scouts, all under the leadership of Lieutenant Colonel Nathan A. M. Dudley, trapped Victorio's renegades—or so they thought. The Apache turned the tables and the always-controversial Dudley found himself and his unfortunate men jammed up, unable to advance and barely capable of retreating. After killing five troopers, a civilian and two Navaho—plus 32 horses—Victorio outfoxed 'em and slipped away under the cover of darkness. Victorio's vanishing act didn't diminish the favorable light shone on Lieutenant Matthias W. Day, who in the face of a withering fire ignored an order to retreat, which would have left a wounded trooper on the field. Day rescued the downed soldier. In classic Army fashion Day's superior officer, the previously cited Captain Charles Beyer, wanted to court-martial the lieutenant for an act of insubordination, the very action he was later awarded a Medal of Honor for. "Buffalo Soldier" Sergeant John Denny, likewise "braving heavy gunfire," carried a seriously hurt comrade to safety, and he too was a Medal of Honor recipient.[532]

Before the month was over, Victorio and Major Albert P. Morrow's

Seated in chair on right, Lieutenant Colonel Albert Payson Morrow. *Courtesy Nita Stewart Haley Library.*

hard-riding detachments from Companies B, C and G, 9th Cavalry, a 6th Cavalry platoon and a squad of adept Apache scouts—190 men—brutally fought all day on Cuchillo Negro Creek. This time two soldiers paid the ultimate price, but so too did three Chihennes. Three other Apache were wounded including Victorio's son, Washington. Victorio's Warm Springs boys made off with 15 of the soldiers' horses and mules, several still saddled or carrying cross-buck packsaddles weighed down with provisions.[533]

Traveling south, Victorio's beleaguered band sensed trouble and near Lloyd's Ranch [present day Nutt, New Mexico] skillfully set a trap, turning three horses loose as bait. They then slithered into position, blending into the topography behind scarcely noticeable rises, ground that would not even qualify as low hills. There, with the excruciating patience Apache were so very well known for, they waited. From Mesilla rode a heavily armed Indian hunting civilian posse, led by Eugene Van Patten. Just after noon on Oct. 13 Van Patten's men pulled up; in the distance were grazing the three riderless horses. Cautiously the party dismounted, tightened girths, chambered rounds under the Winchester's and Sharp's hammers, and stepped back into their slick-forked saddles. Although knowing full well Apache frequently employed such a ruse, the party advanced. They were watchful, but never did they dream that the almost level ground concealed hard luck. When so close an errant shot was locked out of the equation, hidden Apache unleashed hellfire. Terrified horses gyrated and bucked. William T. Jones fell from his saddle, a bullet through the brain. Reining their mounts back under control, the possemen spun a 180-degree arc, setting in motion their horrifying flight. Apache answered escape with deadly accurate rifle fire, killing Cleto Sanches, Nepomuseno Barragan, Venceslao Lara and Pancho Beltran. Van Patten, along with Dr. William B. Lyon, J. B. Hinds, Filoman Barela, Deputy Sheriff Jacinto Armijo, N. L. Hickey and a few others, hightailed it to safety, living to tell the sad tale.[534]

Shortly the story worsened! Zeroing attention to a lumbering ox-drawn freight train near Slocum's Ranch, the Apache attacked. An "American" riding with the train "fired over a hundred rounds from his .44 Winchester before he was riddled with bullets."[535] Eleven Mexican teamsters were killed in the onslaught, their wagons plundered and set afire. Before the Apache departed the grisly scene with a captured woman and child, they heaped the Mexicans' bodies onto the blazing wagon-beds, a southwestern New Mexico Territory funeral pyre—Apache style. "They then faded southwest, into the Florida Mountains, fat with loot and happy with memories of bloodletting."[536] Perhaps this handiwork was not that of Victorio and his mixed band of Chihennes and Mescaleros; Juh, a "notably cruel" Apache, and his band of Nednhis were up from Old Mexico, too, inflicting their own havoc and hell.[537] Cynical folks throughout old Grant County could have hardly cared less; the murderous culprits in their minds were but one, and that was Apache. Victorio rode south, crossing the border, and the fighting raged on, but he was no longer—for the time—on America's side of the line. That signal fact, however, didn't mean all warring Apache had scampered south, vacating old Grant County.

In Silver City, Charles "Boston Charley" Bacthelder, the stagecoach driver for the run to Globe, Arizona Territory, was warned that the Apache were "out" and had been seen west of town. This did not deter the 21-year-old Knight of the Ribbons, as stage drivers were sometimes called. He was going to make the trip even if "all the Apaches in hell" were out and on the road. To a passenger who had wisely decided to forgo the trip, Joe Hull, Boston Charley further declared, "People may say I'm a fool, Joe, but I'm no coward."[538] Youth knows not mortality. To Bacthelder's way of thinking, if attacked, he could just cut loose his favorite mule, a gray named Molly, and make a slick getaway.[539]

On the road 15 miles south of Silver City stood the Burro Springs stage stop. After passing the night there, Bacthelder had gone but a short way before the Apache pounced. At the rifles' first crack a mule went down, as planned. Desperately Bacthelder yanked on the lines, jerking the lead mules' heads into a hard right turn, but with catastrophic effect—the stagecoach's tongue snapped. With precious few options, Bacthelder grabbed his .45-60 Winchester, jumped from the box, and raced to cut Molly loose, which he managed to do. While trying to climb aboard the dancing mule's back a volley knocked Bacthelder to the ground. He drew his Colt's six-shooter, and about the time it ran dry—so too did Boston Charley Bacthelder, life's blood dribbling into the dirt. The number of Apache was estimated at between 15 and 20, and the bullet holes in Bacthelder's body numbered 22, so it was said. "His face was not marked, nor was the corpse mutilated in any way," evidence that the Apache, who had plenty of time for disfigurement, esteemed his bravery.[540] Apache benevolence for not maiming a dying or dead man sold for zilch with the Anglos and Hispanics of old Grant County, however.

Feelings too were hardened when they learned, which surely they did, that across the borderline in Old Mexico in just one 1879 six-week period nearly 150 Mexicans paid with their lives for the benefit or blight of inhabiting a pitiable spot in *Apachería*. Previously the innocent sheepherders on both sides of the line had—more or less—been exempt Victorio's deathly wrath. No longer was it so![541]

Chapter 9
"$100 for Every Head of Any Indian"

Silver City, as well may be imagined, was not built in a vacuum. The growing town was an island of refuge in a sea of privation and peril. Townsmen within the city's boundary lines were reasonably liberated from any real hazard. For the most part, the man who absented himself from the clubroom card games, saloons and whorehouses had little to worry about. If after a hard day's work he started for home intent on relaxing and reading the newspaper, he was more likely to painfully stub his toe on the trip than he was to suffer gunshot wounds to the bellybutton or spleen. It was, of course, another story for the habitués of life's wicked pleasures downtown. They took their chances. Alcohol and attitude are volatile mixtures; abstinence and amicability are not! Wee morning hours and weapons whetted calamity.

Three ladies well known on the vibrant Silver City social scene. From left to right: Mrs. Isaac J. [Olive Priscilla] Stevens, Mrs. H.B. [Virginia] Ailman, and Mrs. Harvey H. [Hattie] Whitehill. *Courtesy William Bishop [Beatrice Stevens Greenleaf Collection]; Silver City Public Library; and Silver City Museum, respectively.*

Travel between the settled points in old Grant County could still prove risky, but even those dangers were diminishing as the 1880s decade dawned over southwestern New Mexico Territory. As a result, though plenty of wild and woolly days remained on Silver City's calendar of upcoming events, a certain refinement was starting to envelop the town. By one account, it was predicted that 1880 would be an exceptional year—an unprecedented year—for thriving New Mexico Territory's immigration on the whole and, in blooming Silver City specifically, the population numbers were predicted to double.[542]

Life in early Silver City didn't always revolve around hard work, Apache, or fractious misbehavior. Here, amateur talent performs at the Morrill Opera House. *Courtesy Nita Stewart Haley Memorial Library.*

During 1880, the Silver City Library Association was locally incorporated. With an initial capital stock of $15,000 and an elected slate of officers, share certificates were in demand. Announcement that a reading room was available on tree-shaded Hudson Street soon magnetically pulled men, young and old, to the interim library and it became a "favorite gathering place."[543] Already the Silver City Dramatic Association's amateur actors were playing to packed houses, and money was raised through private subscriptions to purchase an organ for religious, school and cultural wingdings.[544] A. S. Addis and H. W. Lucas were "marketing" photographic images of the town, distributing them far and wide, and newspaper readers were encouraged to pick up the latest "Stereoscopic views of Silver City" on sale at Bennett's News Depot.[545] Plainly, the din of sharp salesmanship was resonating.

That year also saw completion of Silver City's First Methodist Church. At the dedication ceremony Bishop Thomas Harwood introduced the church's new minister, Reverend Emory H. Brooks. Reportedly, this Methodist church was the very first Protestant house of worship "in that wide sweep of territory between Santa Fe on the north and Yuma [Arizona Territory] to the southwest."[546] An Episcopal clergyman and a renowned botanist from California, E. L. Greene, made his second trip to Silver City during 1880, and began ministering to the people "at their request." It would, however, take several more years before the devout Episcopalians had a church house of their very own. Presbyterians were, for the moment, in-between preachers, the Reverend W. W. Curtis having already come and gone, while Reverend J. M. McGauhly was yet to make his inspection trip and officially sanctify Silver City's First Presbyterian congregation.[547] At the Catholic parish of Saint Vincent de Paul, Father John Baptist Stagnon had come into the picture, and he worked tirelessly and faithfully, "extending the limits of the parish and thus serving the entire surrounding region."[548]

Talk of actually laying the foundation and mortaring some brick for a suitable public schoolhouse was being "tossed from pillar to post." Many of the necessary building materials donated years before were no more, especially the bricks. Sewing-machine salesman J. N. Lafferr, along with C. A. Shaw and Dr. George W. Bailey, were tasked with looking into the matter and reporting how and why the bricks, lumber and shingles delivered to the plot of ground donated by Isaac J. Stevens had disappeared. They learned to no little surprise that the clay-fired bricks, during the previously cited dearth of adequate milling equipment, had been "loaned" to the Pope Mill for construction of its "roasters." Times were changing, though, and the focus was now on getting a school facility built. The Silver City bunch was being chided by the fact that at nearby Georgetown, the children were already attending classes in a permanent structure, albeit a small adobe building. Regardless, it had a good shingle roof and was serving the town's need—and, even more prickling, it was the territory's first free public school building. If Silver City's schoolhouse couldn't be the first, surely it could be the best, "something much more pretentious than a one-room adobe school."[549]

The new edifice of public learning was to be 28 by 66 feet, made of brick, and two stories high. With a bid of $5,000, Black & Co. won the contract and the folks in Silver City began raising the necessary funds. For 1880, the public school limped along intermittently as it had before—the crutch of private schools propping up the town's and parents' insistence on real educational opportunity for their children.[550]

Becoming only the third daily newspaper published in the whole territory—behind the Santa Fe *New Mexican* and Las Vegas *Optic*, *The Daily Southwest* was kicked off by editors Cornelius Bennett and S. M. Ashenfelter during 1880. It was to last but six short months and then it was married to the *Grant County Herald* under a new name, *The Herald & Southwest*. That same year Henry W. Sherry shut down his foundering *Silver Record* and thereafter published and edited "a diminutive sheet" tagged the *Telegram* and another "tidy newsy sheet," the *Mining Chronicle*. At the time none were too much competition to Bennett and Ashenfelter's *Herald & Southwest*.[551]

With *mucho* news-making and long-anticipated fanfare, the milling equipment for the New Mexico and Massachusetts Mining Co. was finally hauled into Silver City. Before it could become operational it required erecting, and that was a titanic task. Early in 1880, a crew of 50 men was industriously engaged in constructing the mill and its ancillary structures—machine shops, assay office, blacksmith shop, carpenter shop, powder houses and bunkhouses for its workforce. Additional milling equipment had been purchased in San Francisco—57,000 pounds' worth—and transported by rail as far as Benson, Arizona Territory, terminus at the time for the Southern Pacific Railroad's march across the Southwest. Then it was freighted by slogging ox-teams to Silver City. Before year's end, the mill was crushing at the rate of 16 tons per day. A simple look at the project's inventory is instructive:

> [There] were over 1,100 tons of ore on hand, 75 tanks of quicksilver, 150 cords of wood, 300 pounds of bluestone, 15 tons of salt, 480 kegs of powder, and 4,200 pound of giant powder. Its assay office and laboratory were undoubtedly the most complete in the Territory.[552]

Energetic building activity was taking place right in Silver City, too. Carpenters were hammering and newcomers were hollering about the woeful shortfall in the availability of suitable living quarters. Almost overnight, 60 new houses were eagerly occupied and still the want could not be satisfied. Jumping in with both feet, several area businessmen bent to the newspaperman's evocative cry that there was real money to be made investing in "rental" property. Gorge Potten built four "brick cottages, with ornamental brick cornices," and later Max Schutz "ensured a lengthy career as a landlord with the construction of a three-unit, one-story row house," as did entrepreneur Charles Lesinsky when he built three more brick cottages nearby.[553] Profitability was surely the driving force, but unlike most other towns springing forth in the West's mining country, Silver City's construction of brick residences for non-homeowners was emblematic. The town, whatever she would come to be, was never

Silver City, an absolutely delightfully situated community progressively growing amid southwestern New Mexico Territory's harsh realities. *Courtesy Silver City Museum.*

destined for clapboard collapse—of that city councilmen made sure. They passed an ordinance, Number 75, prohibiting construction of any structure within town limits not fashioned from brick or adobe.[554]

Touted as a good fire-prevention ordinance, the restriction had two identifiable results. In the short term the law somewhat retarded the pace of housing construction, but in the final analysis it was a measure that insured Silver City's longevity. Not everyone, at the time, was pleased, though. One effusive editor with a degree of logical justification offered his take: "The effect of the ordinance is to prohibit the man of moderate means from building himself a home."[555] Other newsmen, perhaps with a slightly broader perspective, were openly and somewhat proudly boasting that Silver City genuinely looked like a "New England town," which had been dexterously transplanted to that garishly pulsating section of southwestern New Mexico Territory.[556]

Downtown trade was flourishing. In fact, as the busy 1880s began it was clear that Silver City was the undisputed supply center for all of southwestern New Mexico and southeastern Arizona Territories. Receiving "over 4 million pounds of goods annually," local merchants were having a heyday catering to both wholesale and retail needs.[557] The region's "gold and silver bullion" passed through Silver City before it was sent back East.[558] By anyone's yardstick, Silver City was the hub, the outlying mining camps and towns the strengthening spokes. William H. "Bill" McGary and Eugene Cosgrove were busily selling furniture from their store on Main Street, "the largest establishment of the kind in southern New Mexico."[559] The Schutz brothers, Max and Aaron, were promoting nearly everything imaginable from their establishment on Bullard Street, and they were claiming to pay the very "highest rates for gold dust, gold and silver bullion, grain and produce."[560] Peter Ott was offering spaciously remolded rooms—again—for overnighters at the Tremont House, the "leading hotel of the southwest" and a stopping place for all arriving and departing stagecoaches in Silver City.[561] Wing Chong, who had bought Charlie Sun's restaurant, was offering "good board" at a bargain price, $5 per week.[562] Every Saturday morning, auctioneer W.P. Carter was striking the gavel, closing on the highest bid at Meeson and Marriage's weekly livestock auction in the Exchange Stable's sale ring.[563] Doc Bailey was still filling prescriptions from his large inventory of "pure drugs and medicines" at the Post Office Drug Store.[564] And, for those requiring a different kind of dose, it could be had at the Centennial Bar, a "first-class" establishment, where "fancy drinks were a specialty" and where the heavy slate billiard tables were in "perfect order," at least so claimed pride-filled proprietors W. H. Kane and J. M. Speck.[565] Although he served "fancy drinks of every variety" if a man desired only a "plain drink" Fred Shelton could oblige at his emporium, Shelton's Sample Room.[566] Fallen angels Antoinette "Nettie" Simon, Bessie Harper, Kate Stewart, Ruby Fowler, Verdie Bell and "Big Jess" didn't advertise in the newspaper, but rest assured they and their fellow frail sisters weren't unapproachable, unreachable or very hard to find.[567] Silver City was perkin'!

South of the border it was strife that was percolating. Crossing the international border near the Portrillo Mountains southeast of Silver City, Victorio and 60 of his Warm Springs Apache warriors, forsaking a sporadically safe haven in Old Mexico, rode north on a "slashing raid into New Mexico."[568] The Mexican general commanding military forces in the state of Chihuahua, Gerónimo Treviño, had given fair warning to United States officials that Victorio was approaching and so patrols began scouring the Southwest's border country from Texas clear across New Mexico Territory and into Arizona Territory. After crossing the line, Victorio began his spate of "killing an occasional prospector, ripping down telegraph wires, fighting whites here and there," prompting a distraught editor at the *Tucson Star* to moan, "The hell-hounds are again at work in New Mexico."[569] During the previous year's jump from the Mescalero Reservation and before he had snaked across the US-Mexican borderline for a hiatus, purportedly Victorio's Chihenne had killed between 75 and 100 civilians—at least his bunch caught the blame for it. Now the outrages had begun anew.[570]

Folks in Silver City were not happy. Not happy with the flip-flopping military policy and not happy with the civilian politicos' mishandling of Apache affairs. Tersely either Bennett or Ashenfelter penned for their *Daily Southwest* the public sentiment running rampant throughout old Grant County: "We are dreaming of a golden age—a future empire—and 50 dirty, lousy Indians have us in a state of siege."[571]

There is little value in a historic setting to predict what might have happened. Indeed, there is a body of evidence that during this cutting raid Victorio and the Chihennes made peaceful overtures of surrender—if they could but be reunited with their people still encamped at the San Carlos and Mescalero Agencies, and then be settled at their preferred *Ojo Caliente* mother land.[572] Silver City people, there's little doubt, would have out of hand rejected such a proposal, and would have wielded their substantial economic and political power to quash what would seem to them an idiotic idea. The reunification and surrender, of course, didn't take place and the Silver City folks weren't reticent with public condemnation of the Apache. The Army's inability to solve their damn problem right fast, too, received no sympathy. The historic cards had been dealt!

Major Albert Payson Morrow, twice captured and once wounded by Confederates during the Civil War, with his six companies of 9th Cavalry cutting for meaningful sign in southwestern New Mexico, picked up

Victorio, Warm Springs Apache and a terror to southwestern New Mexico Territory. Indicted by a Grant County grand jury. *Courtesy National Archives.*

Victorio's trail and followed north into that imposing Apache stronghold, the Black Range.[573] On the afternoon of Jan. 12, 1880, along upper Percha Creek, Victorio and Morrow locked horns. The ferocious fight, during which Sergeant D. J. Gross and a civilian scout were killed, lasted from 2 pm. until the sun went down.[574] Then the Apache vanished, taking their dead with them—if there were any. Not exactly lined out on "old Vic's" trail, military authorities contacted Dick Hudson on the Lower Mimbres at Hudson's Hot Springs, a man they knew was always "well-informed." The ex-Grant County sheriff had no actionable news about the Apache's movements.[575] But soon it was learned that Victorio had run north, and in the San Mateo Mountains the aggressive Morrow caught up to the crafty old fighter on Jan. 17. During the ensuing battle, controversial 29-year-old Second Lieutenant James Hansell French, a West Point graduate, was killed and two enlisted men were seriously wounded before Victorio's combatants faded into nothingness absent any casualties of their own. Splitting their forces to elude pursuit and scavenge isolated ranches and sheepherders' camps, the Apache replenished their horse herd, which served the dual purposes of providing getaway mounts and filling empty stomachs.[576] Major Morrow gladly left the battlefield to recruit gaunt cavalry horses and rest his exhausted men.

By the end of the month, however, the grueling chase was again well under way. On Jan. 30 Captains Henry Carroll and Louis H. Rucker [not Lt. Tony Rucker] and hard-riding detachments of the 9th Cavalry's Companies B and M caught up with the Apache on Las Animas Creek. During a running fight the overworked cavalrymen drove Victorio's careworn *Mimbreños* into the Caballo Mountains [Horse Mountains] on the Rio Grande River's eastern bank.[577] Four days later, in an indecisive battle, Major Morrow at the head of six companies skirmished with the slippery

Colonel Edward Hatch commanded the 9th Cavalry and was in charge of New Mexico Territory for much of the Apache War. Rightly or wrongly, he frequently took a journalistic blistering in the Silver City press. *Courtesy National Archives.*

Victorio northeast of Aleman's Well in the San Andres Mountains. Seemingly the battle was tit for tat in the rough canyons and neither party suffered an authenticated fatality before nightfall swept across the White Sands and the Tularosa Basin's western gradient. And, once again, the Apache evaporated. Less than a week later, on Feb. 9, Captain Rucker was poking around the 14 east-west-running canyons of the San Andres and soon got all that he bargained for: "The troops were received by a heavy fire, under which several horses and men fell. Perceiving their advantage, the Indians charged the troops, who gave way, and retreated in pell-mell order; the Indians in turn became the pursuers and drove the troops across the river. In the retreat rations and bedding were abandoned, which the Indians secured."[578] A month later New Mexico Territory's top military man, Edward Hatch, was in Silver City trying to explain the Army's inability to put the kibosh on Victorio's raiding and to get Grant County folks off his back:

> General Hatch, the commander of this district, was in town yesterday. In conversation with one of our prominent citizens, he stated that the greatest danger from Indians is while they are divided in small bands as at present, and the only way to capture them is to allow them to get together again. Guards and troops are now being stationed at all watering places and a large supply camp has just been located, four miles from Hillsboro.
>
> The General also stated that the Indians are much

> stronger in point of numbers than generally supposed. They have lately been reinforced by Comanches, Mescalero Apaches, Hot Springs Apaches and Indians from Mexico. While in Mexico they captured a large supply of Winchester rifles and ammunition, and that the Mexicans on the Rio Grande (Canada) supply them with all the cartridges they need, as well as harbor and nursed their wounded. The troops are much hampered in their actions by the Indian department, and many renegades who have been captured in this Territory and Colorado have been returned to the agencies. All the women and children of the hostile Indians are now at the San Carlos Agency. The General also added that the troops in the Territory are altogether too weak in numbers to cope with the difficulty, and that should the Navahos, Apaches and Utes ever unite, they would have the whole country at their mercy.
>
> He concluded by saying that it would be better if the press, and public at large would abstain from severe criticism, as it only disheartens the troops; and the people have no idea of the difficulties they have to contend with in following these wily enemies.[579]

After the Silver City visit Hatch departed for Santa Fe, a fact that did not set well with the local print media. The *Grant County Herald* railed: "His departure is no wise to be regretted but—if we may be permitted to ask—what in the Devil did he come down her for?"[580] Hatch's plea for understanding fell on deaf ears, that is, if the public's opinion is reflected through the voice of *The Daily Southwest's* editor. His vociferous harangue was not ambiguous. Excerpts from the editorial—politically incorrect as they may be—are illuminating:

> We have no prejudice against the black man. At no time did we ever spell negro with two gs or believe in the divine right of any man to wallop him. But we will stoutly maintain that a colored regiment is not the proper instrument with which to put down the Indian. We will even go so far as to say, that the very virtues of the colored man are the elements that go to disqualify him for such a task. He is essentially quiet and peaceable, disliking strife or warfare. He is rarely by habit a woodsman,

> and though an orderly, obedient soldier, he has not that keenness of sense and self reliance that are essential to irregular and partisan warfare.... We simply say that these circumstance have not been such as to make the colored man, fresh from the hemp and cotton field, an available means of suppressing this Indian outbreak.... Whatever may be the speculation and reasoning as to who didn't kill cock robin [Victorio] and why he was not killed, it is beyond peradventure that he *has* not been killed; and the prospect is not bright that he will be killed, under the present military system.[581]

And that present military system—good or bad as it might have been—called for the employment of Apache scouts in the campaign against Victorio. Specifically recruited for service in southwestern New Mexico Territory was the 15th Infantry's 63-man Company A, Apache Scouts, with Second Lieutenant James Allison Maney, a West Point graduate of the class of 1877, in command.[582] "First enlisted in October 1879 from Fort Bayard, New Mexico, Maney's original company consisted of 25 scouts. These men were discharged at Fort Bayard on Dec. 31, of that year and reenlisted on Jan. 1, 1880. They were again discharged at San Carlos on March 20, 1880. Apparently, at least some, if not all of the 24 remaining scouts immediately reenlisted along with an additional 37 scouts."[583] Fighting Apache with Apache was a workable modus operandi for the US. Army and, in the long run, catastrophic for renegade Chiricahuas, be they Bedonkohes, Chokonens, Nednhis or Chihennes.[584]

Victorio's and Nana's forces grew when a few Mescalero Apache bolted the Mescalero Reservation and scooted into the San Andres' fastness. The commingled assemblage of Indians, numbering about 120 men of fighting age, smartly encamped at refreshingly reliable Rock House Spring in out-of-the-way Hembrillo Canyon, some 40-odd miles north of Las Cruces. Riding out of Fort Stanton and on the hunt for Victorio, Captain Henry Carroll with four companies of 9th Cavalry—100 men—also found water in the San Andres, but soldiers and horses were sickened, nauseatingly so, after drinking from the gypsum-polluted pool. That tale may actually be more folklore than truth, but it's safe to say the worn-down soldiers spent a miserable night.[585] Next morning, April 6, rather than returning to Fort Stanton, Carroll pushed his belly-aching men forward, looking for fresh water and warriors. They found neither and dry camped.

On April 7, at six o'clock in the evening, they finally found good water—and Apache. At first the Indians scampered and scattered, but then someone noticed the weakened condition of the parched-throated cavalrymen and their fatigued mounts. Never known for failure to exploit an opportunity, the Apache took up positions in the cliffs and crevices and pelted hellfire on the disadvantaged troopers, preventing them access to the cool spring's wet refreshment. Nighttime brought an astronomically imposed truce for joyful Apache and Uncle Sam's thirsty band of brothers. Since he chose not to run away, there is little doubt that Victorio intended on finishing off the soldiers and appropriating their horses, ammunition and trapdoor .45-70s at first light. Unbeknownst to the cunning Victorio, however, Captain Curwen Boyd McClellan, 6th Cavalry, with Company L and a contingent of Indian scouts, Lt. James Maney's Company A from Fort Bayard among them, were making a night ride to make up for lost time due to an earlier daytime delay. On the morning of the April 8, McClellan and 120 men rode into Hembrillo Canyon just as the Apache had opened the ball on Henry Carroll's men, in the nick of time. For a while the battle raged, the booming echo from Winchester and Springfield carbines dancing to the tune of agonizing screams and shrill war cries. Captain Carroll was twice wounded. Eight soldiers eventually died as result of their wounds, as did 25 cavalry horses. Perhaps the Apache lost three killed, maybe not, but they knew it was time to run, and they did. Nana ran one way. Victorio dashed the other, west, straight toward southwestern New Mexico Territory and old Grant County.[586] Victorio was running and hiding in familiar country; the soldiers were floundering in an utterly confusing maze of rough canyons, lofty mountains, and Mother Nature's well-hidden basins.

In the Cañada Alamosa section Victorio was a friend no more. It was a new day: "The old understanding between this place and the Indians seems to be broken, and those people, who, from all accounts, have heretofore benefited by the spoils brought in by the Indians, having sown to the wind or now reaping the whirlwind."[587] The Apache moved southwest.

All over the Upper Gila country Victorio "killed whoever came across his path: ranchers, sheepherders, cattle drivers and miners."[588] "Throughout May 1880 they killed and pillaged in the Black and Mogollon ranges, around Silver City, and even as far west as San Carlos, in Arizona."[589] Along Mineral Creek, they killed James Cooney and Jack Chick, their bodies "most horribly mutilated."[590] Soon a band of 25 horses was in Apache hands.[591] On Copper Creek miners, prospectors and ranchers, including Sheriff Harvey Whitehill, who was in the area on business along with his son Harry, had to "fort up" and there they remained shut in for 10 days while Apache raided, plundered and burned.[592] In the Keller Valley, Apache laid siege to James Keller's and Jim Roberts' ranch homes, and during their exhilaration killed William Willcox and seriously wounded James Murray.[593] Editor Ashenfelter of the *Grant County Herald* was there too. From the Williams' cabin—where he was pinned down—he wrote that their heavily armed cluster was prepared to repel an anticipated attack, and that it was his firm opinion that Victorio was in "command" of the Apache, but his estimate of the number of Indians ravaging the countryside was wishy-washy: "50 to 150 to 250."[594]

Quickly, teams of civilian volunteers were formed to ride for the Mogollon Mountains and rescue fellow countrymen: 85 from Silver City in one group, 20 in another; from the far southern reaches of old Grant County at Eureka, an additional platoon; and as soon as a wagon of provisions was loaded it left under a "strong guard."[595] To say most Silver City folks were miffed—rightly or wrongly—at the US Army is a woeful understatement:

> Something must be done; flesh and blood cannot long endure what we as a people are now enduring. The military arm of the government is to all appearances powerless to protect us; the wily Apache plays with the troops in the field as though they were men of straw; here today, 50 miles away tomorrow, they murder as they go and laugh at any effort of the troops to punish them; in fact, they fight the troops for pastime, when they stand in need of guns and ammunition.... If we have an imbecile in command of our forces, let us try by all honorable means to have him removed. If he does his duty he will receive our warmest gratitude.[596]

And:

> The troops under Hatch are after Victorio (in their minds).[597]

And:

> Hitchity Hatch-ity, here I come. Old Vic's after me, but you must keep mum.[598]

The 6th Cavalry's Second Lieutenant Charles Bayer Gatewood, an 1877 West Pointer who gained no little fame as a leader of Apache scouts, was not overawed with Victorio's abilities as a military strategist. Giving Victorio his due, it has been written that perhaps Gatewood confused Nana for Victorio—which seems unlikely—when the lieutenant offered his opinion on Apache chiefs: "Among the most prominent were Cochise and Geronimo of the Chiricahua Apaches, and Mangas Coloradas and Victorio of the Warm Spring Apaches. These two tribes have caused more trouble in the last 30 years than all other Apaches combined. While the other tribes fought among themselves, these two under Cochise and Mangas Coloradas, combined and fought not only the other kindred tribes, but everybody else. While the two chiefs were such in fact as well as in name, Victorio and Geronimo were such only in name. Their reputations were greater among the settlers than among their own people. From 1879 on, the real plotters of this mischief were Nana, Tomacito and Turrivio. Victorio was a palsied, aged, and decrepit chief, who was barely able to accompany the squaws and children in their forays."[599]

Undeniably, Silver City folks stubbornly intent on carving their Eastern permanency out of New Mexico Territory's southwestern wilderness saw Victorio in a different light:

> This Indian [Victorio] has unquestionably reached a most conspicuous place.... He has made his very name a terror to the white man. Aged and infirm—for he has dumb palsy and cannot light a cigarrito—he has with a handful of men made himself verily a scourge of God to the race he hates and despises. It is idle at this late date to go into the merits of the quarrel he has with the government. Much can be said on both sides, possibly. But one thing is undeniable, he has inflicted more punishment on the frontiersman than any Indian....There is not one of woman born who has shed so much innocent blood. Towards us he has had the hatred of a fiend, supplemented with the ferocity of a tiger. So far as military skill is concerned he has yet to meet the foeman that he had not thwarted, outwitted and out fought....When he has retreated it has been as though he fled through the air; and when he has stricken a blow, it has been as the bolt of death descending from the cloudless sky. Astute and tireless, cunning and sleeplessly vigilant—this old man

> has made his very name a proverb of terror. The mothers of this country use it to frighten away the crossness and peevishness of their children. So cautious and suspicious is he that it is said he will not sleep in the camp with his own men and they dread his anger so, that to provoke it is to court the doom of fate. Though his right arm shakes with the palsy of old age, it has not forgot its cunning, and his followers dread his vengeance as it were the wrath of God....Victorio so far has been evincible and he is fast cutting us off from the rest of the world. The wayfarer and stranger stops at the sound of his name. The dread of his scalping knife paralyses trade and travel from Socorro to El Paso. Not a poor shepherd goes out trembling to his duty but he prays that he may not be caught and tortured to furnish a savage holiday for the devil incarnate. There is not a road that he has not incarnadined with his slaughter, and the very wolves and vultures obscene, follow his track sure of his provision for them.[600]

With maddened civilian forces rallying forth from Silver City on Victorio's southern flank, the Chihenne fled east for asylum in the seemingly impenetrable Black Range. Chief Scout Henry Kinney Parker, a civilian Texan working for Hatch, "who told him to go out and kill one or two Indians," leading a band of 60 Apache scouts, caught up with Victorio near Brushy Mountain. Trapped in a box canyon, Victorio validated Lieutenant Gatewood's assessment. During the ensuing battle, which lasted all day, the Apache lost 30 men, women and children. Victorio was wounded in the leg, a fact the Apache scouts soon learned. Hollering their insults back and forth, Apache scouts bragged they had, at last, conquered Victorio. The Apache women, not knowing whether Victorio would die, retorted that if he did "they would eat him, so that no white man should see his body!"[601]

Having Victorio trapped, Parker sent a courier to Hatch requesting reinforcements and more ammunition. Then Parker pulled back and waited for help and supplies that never came. Two days later, disgusted, he quickly rounded up 74 of the Apache's horses and went home.[602] The military could ill afford to admit—and they didn't—that this was Victorio's most punishing thrashing, and not a single regular Army man had been involved. Silver City people weren't ungrateful. They gave Henry Parker an engraved $300 gold watch "in recognition of the fact that by his brave and tireless energy, [he] not only inflicted terrible punishment on the murderous Apaches, but...had driven them from our soil."[603] The inscription read:

> Presented to H. K. Parker, Chief of Scouts, by the citizens of Grant County, N.M., as a token of their appreciation of his bravery and successes in the Indians wars of 1880.[604]

Victorio's legions, tattered as they were, scattered and began working their way south. One group of about 25 was caught on June 5 in Cooke's Canyon by Captain Morrow with four companies of 9th Cavalry. There Buffalo Soldiers inflicted heavy casualties, wounding three and killing 10, one of whom was Victorio's son, Washington.[605] Several days later "Doc" Kane rode into Silver City with "two scalps taken from the Indians last Saturday morning in Cooke's Pass." Citizens were cordially invited to drop by the Centennial Saloon and take a look at the gory trophies.[606] Counterbalancing Gatewood's less-than-idolizing estimation of "old Vic" was the Silver City folks' measurement that the astute Apache had yet to meet his US Army "foeman." After all, hadn't he—in point of fact—slipped away one more time?

Echoing the sad commentary, General John Pope, writing to the secretary of War, was forced into owning up to reality, that in Victorio's case "the capture is not very probable, but the killing can, I suppose, be done in time."[607] Before the US Army could catch up with Victorio and do the killing, however, the old warrior skillfully outmaneuvered military pursuers and scooted back across the Mexican borderline, his safe haven—he thought.

Apache troubles whirling about them, Grant County citizens had to go on with their everyday lives, but even that necessitated killing of their very own. Louis Gaines, a black man, had been convicted of fatally stabbing a Fort Bayard soldier. About the same time, Barney O'Toole, who at the time was using the alias Charles Williams, had been convicted of mortally gunning down a "Mexican musician at Georgetown for no reason."[608] Judge Warren Bristol sentenced both men to be hanged. Although it certainly wouldn't be Grant County's first neck stretching, the August 20 executions would be the county's first *legal*

Scene of double hanging [murderers Barney O'Toole, aka Charles Williams, and Louis Gaines], on the outskirts of Silver City, August 20, 1880. *Courtesy Silver City Museum.*

hanging, and it was going to be a two-for-one affair. There was no little controversy about having a black man and a white man share the same scaffold—at the same time—but after Sheriff Whitehill, assisted by Dan Tucker, armed a few citizens as a protective posse, the execution outside of town on the Fort Bayard road before 400 spectators came off with out a hitch.[609] *The Daily Southwest* went so far as to say that the men who had been "swung into Eternity" had died without a struggle and the executions would have a "most salutary influence."[610]

The salutary influence wasn't being felt at Shakespeare. The town was fast filling up with good people, but some badmen too! Recklessly traveling back and forth across the southwestern New Mexico Territory and southeastern Arizona Territory borderlines, and in and out of Shakespeare was a cast of notoriously well-known characters, possibly unequaled anywhere in the American West, dubious men such as: "Curly Bill" Brocius; Sandy King; Johnny Barnes; "Russian Bill" Tettenborn; the Clanton boys, Billy and Isaac; Billy Leonard; Zwing Hunt; William "Billy the Kid" Grounds; Frank and Tom McLaury; "Slim Jim" Crane; Harry

Head; the Haslett brothers, Bill and Ike; Charles "Pony Diehl" Ray; Jim "Sweetheart of the San Simon" Hughes; and the aforementioned Johnny Ringo, Joe Olney and Robert E. "Bob" Martin.[611]

In increasingly violent Shakespeare, Charley Williams heartlessly and without reason killed F.W. Mollitor; William Carroll gunned down "Happy Bob" Fambro; Robert "Arkansas" Black barely escaped a lynch rope; and, reportedly, "Bean Belly" Smith mortally gutshot Ross Woods during a dispute over who would gain possession of the last hen's egg to be had.[612] At the time, "there were no churches or Sunday schools, no lodges or fraternal organizations, and no social clubs in existence at Shakespeare; so it naturally resulted that those desiring amusement or recreation gathered together at the saloon."[613] Inside the taprooms, discussion groups would argue about first this or that but generally the talk funneled into three channels: "mineral merits of different geological strata" or "about the quarrels and the feuds of long standing" or the "barbaric details of some Indian raid," which, at the time, was still pandemic.[614]

Apache were incessantly jumping back and forth across the Mescalero and San Carlos Agencies' boundary lines and the shared borderline with Mexico. "Travel on all the roads between Socorro, Silver City, El Paso and vicinity" was very unsafe.[615] Raiding and murdering Apache, who were proving a "constant nuisance," struck southern Grant County again in early September. Sixteen miles west of Fort Cummings they waylaid a stagecoach, killing the driver, Alexander Le Beau, and two passengers, Isaac Roberts and 19-year-old Emery S. Madden, the son of Captain Dan Madden, 6th Cavalry, stationed at Fort Bowie.[616] The younger Madden, who had been away at college in the "States," was reuniting with his parents after a goodbye three years earlier. The sad news reverberated throughout the Southwest. Captain Leopold O. Parker, with Company A, 4th Cavalry, chased after the Apache and the hunted became the hornets. In a sharp fight, the Apache killed one cavalryman and two scouts and wounded two other scouts, suffering no loss themselves.[617] Folks all through old Grant County, which was at the time the whole of southwestern New Mexico Territory, were hopping mad!

There is little doubt those Shakespeare prospectors and a smattering of others picked up on the tittle-tattle wafting down from the county seat. Exasperated people in Silver City were not happy with incessant Apache depredations. Taking a page from their friends south of the line, Silver City men adopted the Mexican solution, although they stamped it with their own modification. Whether the change was meant as a spiteful escalation for sending Apache an understandable message, or rather a preventive measure designed to ensure the penalty was imposed only on Indians, goes unrecorded. A reward of $100 was posted for "Every head of any Indian that is connected with the band of Fiends who are murdering our fellow citizens." Plainly, it was serious business. To adequately fund the monetary kitty subscriptions were sought and the list of willing donors contributing between $200 on the top end and $10 at the lower end reads like a who's who of Silver City's most prominent citizens.[618] *The Herald & Southwest* ecstatically proclaimed:

> The Scalp fund shows up fairly. Enough is subscribed to pay for making good Indians of at least 20 of the red devils.[619]

Chapter 10

"A Man's Life Goes for Naught"

Silver City folks rejoiced upon learning that on Oct. 14, 1880, Mexican Apache hunters, led by the chain-smoking Joaquín Terrazas, had accomplished what they, or even the US military, had been unable to do. At Tres Castillos, east of the road running between Carrizal and Chihuahua City, Victorio and nearly all of his Chihennes were run to ground. During the ensuing fight Terrazas' hard-boiled men killed and scalped 62 warriors, along with 16 women and children. The gruesome trophies were salted away for redemption—there was a state-sponsored bounty to be collected. Additionally, Terrazas made prisoners of 68 Apache and, in turn, liberated two of their wretched captives: 12-year-old Felix Carrillo and 10-year-old Felipe Padilla, both taken during searing raids into New Mexico Territory. The worn-down Mexicans lost three fighters killed in action, Nicanor Aguilar,

A Lordsburg family dressed in their Sunday best posing for a traveling photographer. *Courtesy Lordsburg-Hidalgo Library.*

Serapio Muñoz and Luis Rubio. Ten had been wounded, four seriously. Moreover the victors exultantly recouped 120 horses, 38 mules and a dozen donkeys. Accounts vary as to how Victorio met his death: Mexicans said at great risk to themselves he was courageously gunned down doing battle; Apache claimed he intrepidly cut his own throat rather than suffer humiliating capture at hands of the hated Mexicans.[620] *¿Quien sabe?* Victorio was, regardless, sledgehammer dead. Southwesterners' glee should have been somewhat tempered, though, as 70-year-old Nana wasn't among the dead or snared Apache—and like human tigers he and a few more were yet prowling loose!

North of the border, 1881 would definitively prove, in the historic context, to be one of Grant County's and Silver City's headline years. There was, however, just a little unfinished business to attend to. After learning that Richard Remine's appeals had been exhausted, Sheriff Whitehill suspended the prisoner's trustee status and locked him up. On March 14 the sheriff bought the condemned prisoner a box of cigars and several bottles of wine, which no doubt hastened the "lusterless" look in his eyes as he marched up the scaffold's steps. Dan Tucker placed the black cap over the man's head and Sheriff Whitehill gave the signaling nod. "The drop fell about a quarter before four o'clock," and 20 minutes later a physician officially declared Remine dead.[621] Before the month was out, on March 25, the process was repeated. William "Parson" Young climbed those very same steps. For his part in the Dwenger murder, he too, made the terminal plummet, the fall breaking his neck "instantaneously."[622] After their court convictions, Young's accomplices, Dora Dwenger and her son, were awarded prison time.

Those Silver City folks were not just absorbed with ghoulishly witnessing death doings; they were also downtown parting with hard-earned money—and there were plenty of places to spend it. Keeping up with Silver City's explosive growth may best be illustrated by an early 1880s newspaperman's swank:

> It [Silver City] is the supply point for all the vast mining country in southwestern New Mexico and eastern Arizona, as it is also for a large portion of the states of Sonora and Chihuahua, in Mexico, whose merchants come hundreds of miles with mule trains packed with adobe dollars to exchange for our merchandise. This Mexican trade amounts to several hundred thousand

dollars annually and is a business that no other town in the territory enjoys to any extent at the present time. We have three solid banking establishments; eight extensive dry goods and grocery houses that do a large wholesale business, some three or four of which carry from $100,000 to $300,000 stocks; two large hardware stores, carrying a full line of goods, especially those used by miners and prospectors; two wholesale liquor houses that buy their goods by car loads and handle in large quantities; two large well stocked drug houses carrying a stock of goods sufficient to meet any emergency; one wholesale and retail saddle and harness establishment; three jewelry stores, one of which manufactures Mexican filigree jewelry on an extensive scale; eight or ten handsome and well conducted saloons; four of as good hotels as can be found in the territory, whose tables are daily supplied with game from the wilds of the mountains, and also choice vegetables and tropical fruits from California and old Mexico; one of the best meat markets in the territory which with its marble-slabbed counters and windows of blooming flowers, for neatness, taste and elegance cannot be surpassed anywhere in the west; two excellent bakeries and one cracker factory, that daily turns out as good crackers as can be made anywhere west of the Mississippi, and in quantities to supply any demand; one wholesale confectionery establishment; four corral and liveries, where at all times can be procured an elegant turn-out or saddle-horses; two merchant tailoring establishments, one of which carries a large and fine assortment of goods; three barber shops, with a large and skilled corps of artists. We have two exclusive clothing and boot and shoe establishments; two photograph galleries; one cigar and tobacco house; two real estate and insurance offices; three restaurants; one carriage factory. An extensive saw and planing mill is within the city limits, and gives employment to from fifty to one hundred men in its different departments....In the professions we are well represented, having one of the strongest and ablest bars in the territory, and quite a number of skilled and experienced physicians and surgeons, and a score of mining experts and surveyors.[623]

J.P. Ownby and family. Mrs. Ownby was the first female resident of Lordsburg. *Courtesy Lorsdburg-Hidalgo Library.*

Frankly, the real Grant County news—for the time being—was not being made in on-the-go Silver City. Much of the excitement was centered south of town in that east-west stretch picked up nearly 30 years earlier, the Gadsden Purchase's wedge of ground. Also the previous year, on Oct. 18, 1880, the Southern Pacific Railroad, in its quest to lay tracks east for a juncture with the Santa Fe Railroad (which was steadily moving southwest), reached a point some two miles north of Shakespeare. At that spot a new town sprang to life. Named after Delbert Lord, the Southern Pacific's chief engineer, Lordsburg burst forth with a robust population of "railroad workers, freighters, cowboys, gamblers and merchants."[624] Quickly the new settlement, at first just a tent city, grew into a supply point for the area's ranching and mining operations and, not unexpectedly, thriving Lordsburg "siphoned settlers from Shakespeare."[625] The Chinese graders kept moving east, and by the end of the year had reached a point less than 50 miles due south of Silver City, almost in the shadows of the Florida Mountains.[626]

With pecuniary anticipation a few settlers—if the term is applied loosely—had established another tent city and grandly christened it New Chicago, thoroughly convinced the new town would be the Southwest's next urban center when the Santa Fe Railroad reached that point.[627] They were disappointed. The Southern Pacific chose a location for its depot sev-

After the coming of the railroad, Lordsburg blossomed. *Courtesy Lorsdburg-Hidalgo Library.*

eral miles west of New Chicago. Named in honor of Mary Ann Deming Crocker, the wife of railroad executive Charles Crocker, the town of Deming was born.[628] On March 8, 1881, the Santa Fe Railroad reached raucous Deming, joining tracks with the Southern Pacific, and America's second transcontinental railroad was inaugurated.[629] The merging of railroad tracks was a newsworthy feat; no longer would the Southwest and, for this story, Grant County and Silver City, be cut off from the outside world:

> Soon an army of mechanics was busy erecting round houses, station houses, railway tenements, putting down the big wells; switching yards three miles long were laid out: soon the handsome and commodious depot hotel was in course of construction—then the finest railroad building between Kansas City and San Francisco—Deming, the division point for both roads; lay over station for all Pullman employees, train crews and express messengers; everything indicated that here the railroads would make the great town of the Southwest.[630]

In the very beginnings, however, not all of Deming's early residents were particularly nice guys. Putting down steel tracks was hard work, man's work, and resultantly a class of humanity commonly known as "track followers"—the "flotsam and jetsam of the frontier"—tagged along with railroad workers, intent on tapping into their end-of-the-week wages.[631] Not all the riffraff wore trousers and high-heeled boots. Eastern journalist Henry M. Stanley wrote for the *New York Times*: "These women are expensive articles, and come in for a large share of the money wasted. In broad daylight they may be seen gliding through the dusty streets carrying fancy derringers hung to their waists, with which tools they are dangerously expert. Western chivalry will not allow them to be abused by any man they may have robbed. Mostly everyone seemed bent on debauchery and dissipation."[632] An early-day Deming saloon operator was not lovingly characterized as "the most desperate white savage in the entire valley."[633] A concerned newspaper editor offered his warning that the con men and others of disrepute were "getting the best of even one or two knowing ones from Silver City."[634] Adroitly reflecting sinful reality after all the workers' pockets were emptied is plain recognition that "when it became necessary for the early parasites to find nourishment, they went to work on specimens of their own kind with shorter priority. These in turn practiced their cannibalism on later-comers and so *ad infinitum*."[635]

Another journalist making an 1881 trip to the new town, C. M. Chase, was not at all reticent in his commentary, declaring that "Deming morals are not to be discussed in a newspaper—till she has some!"[636] With a writer's flair Chase blended the theatrical with the truth:

> But the Indians are not the worst element in Grant County society. The cowboys, or roughs and thieves, are so numerous that no man ventures any distance from the village without his Winchester rifle, ready to repeat 12 or 16 times without reloading. With this element constantly on the watch for plunder, a man's life goes for naught.[637]

One of those "roughs" haunting the Deming and Rio Mimbres section was a live wire simply known as "Six-shooter" Smith. That he was real is indisputable. That he was an authentic hell-raiser is not arguable, in fact, so much so the *Las Vegas Optic* labeled Deming's badman "Six-shooter" Smith as the "big dog with the brass collar." A Texas newspaperman characterized Smith as "one of the coolest, nerviest desperadoes" who ever marched, murdered and malingered across the Southwest.[638] Also hovering in the section was another legendary buzzard, "Curly Bill" Brocius [Bresnaham] and his cadre of misfits.[639] The whole section was snarling with trouble. During a drunken stupor Anthony "One-Arm" Price killed his best friend, not the first cut on his notch-stick.[640] And southwest of Deming in the Bootheel Country, the Haslett brothers, Ike and Bill, lay in wait behind a corral fence, successfully ambushing suspected holdup artists Bill Leonard and Harry "the Kid" Head, killing both. Revenge could be sweet, though, and shortly thereafter highwayman Jim Crane and his crowd "waylaid and killed" the Haslett boys.[641] The Grant County grand jury urged Sheriff Whitehill to damn quickly get the situation under control, nudging him with the rejoinder that should he not, perhaps, it would turn to "a higher and more powerful authority."[642] Whitehill, an astute politician, quickly deciphered the not-so-veiled implication.

Taking deputies Dan Tucker and James K. Farrell with him, Whitehill fell on Deming. Making his presence widely known, and that it was going to be a new day in the untamed railroad town, Whitehill shortly returned to business in Silver City, leaving Tucker behind. Strolling the streets with a double-barreled shotgun and sporting his no-nonsense approach to law enforcement, Tucker solidified an unambiguous certainty, "if he wanted to arrest a desperado he was sure to either arrest or kill him."[643] Owl-hoot Charley Hugo didn't get the message, evidently, and began "deporting himself in a riotous manner." Dan Tucker, not allowing lawlessness to take a foothold, "narrowed the dimensions" and killed him.[644] Another scalawag, an ex-Texas Ranger by the name of Jack Bond, rode his horse up onto the Harvey House veranda at the railroad depot. Tucker, shotgun in hand, told Bond to "reach for the sky." Bond, probably drunk as a lord, demurred. Tucker "without further discussion" cut loose and nine buckshot knocked Bond out of his saddle, a dead man falling. Picking up on the story, a reporter for the *Wichita Daily Eagle* offhandedly added to Tucker's contemporary reputation: "A darn fool went and rode through the dining-room in the railroad hotel at Deming flourishing his pistol. And frightened the lady passengers bound west nearly into fits. Dan Tucker found the fellow on the street, covered him with her [the shotgun] and called 'hands up.' The blasted idiot makes a motion for his six-shooter and Dan filled him chuck full of buckshot. He failed to get there, Eli,

In contrast to Silver City, much of Deming's residential construction was wood frame, and many homes were quite elegant. Note the windmill in backyard and, interestingly, the man in the center of the photograph is holding a guitar, not a Winchester that would repeat 12 or 16 times. *Courtesy Deming Luna Mimbres Museum.*

and now peacefully sleeps beneath the daisies."[645] During another dustup Tucker was powder burned during a melee with three drunken soldiers and two Indian scouts from nearby Fort Cummings, but nevertheless he made the arrests "as he usually does" according to the newspapermen writing for *The New Southwest & Grant County Herald*.[646] At faraway El Paso it was written that Dan Tucker during one 20-day timespan "arrested 13 of the cowboy gang" at Deming.[647]

Specifically, one of those "cowboy gang" members was William Rogers "Russian Bill" Tettenborn, a ne'er-do-well with a "fierce blond mustache and blond hair which hung to his shoulders; carrying a six-gun at each hip and a long knife in his boot, and was always telling how tough he was."[648] Tettenborn stole a horse at Shakespeare and Tucker nabbed him; possibly, he wasn't so tough after all. Whether Tucker did or did not know what was to become of "Russian Bill" is not provable. He turned Tettenborn back over to the Shakespeare folks and returned to Deming. What happened next made both the El Paso and Silver City newspapers:

> Two "rustlers," "Russian Bill" and "Sandy King" from the southern part of Grant county, were arrested last week by Deputy Sheriff Tucker and lodged in jail at Shakespeare last Monday. They were taken from jail that night by the citizens who overpowered the guards, and hanged. "Russian Bill" has often declared that no man living could arrest him, but when he found Tucker was on his track he gave himself up without any resistance. Their fate has no doubt engendered the enmity of the element to which they belonged against Shakespeare and the people there will organize a safety committee as a means of protection. The two men hanged were noted horse and cattle thieves.[649]

There in fact was no jail nor hangman's scaffold at Shakespeare, but the folks had a simple remedy. Taken from a room where they were being guarded, King and Tettenborn were quickly strung up to a ceiling cross-beam in the town's Grant Hotel, where King "died game" and Tettenborn "begged for his life," but in vain.[650] The bodies remained suspended overnight, and the next day a curious passer-through inquired: "Why were they hanged?" According to folklore, and it's a darn good story, the traveler was smartly informed that one of the swinging corpses was that of a horse thief and the other was guilty of being a "damned nuisance."[651] Later, in keeping with the rough frontier humor, when poor Tettenborn's mother inquired as to the fate of her missing son, the written response was: "Dear Madam, Your son has died of throat trouble"—at least that's how old-timer Johnny Evensen told the story.[652]

Deming, indeed, was a hell-to-pop town. But just like her older sister up the road, Silver City, there was another side to Deming's infant story. Planted as she was 750 miles south of Denver and 1,149 miles from Kansas City, in spite of her forlorn geographical location Deming was blossoming. There were in addition to Fred Harvey's depot hotel, some 40 "houses or shanties, all business places." Charles H. Dane was the postmaster, at first sorting mail in an abandoned boxcar, but shortly thereafter in a "shanty on a village lot." J. E. Currier, a frontier newspaper editor, had set up his little four-column sheet, the *Deming Headlight*, and was steadily cranking the press. Naturally there were the saloons with 15-cent drinks and gambling dens galore, but in the Old West where were

As in Silver City, 20th-century progress was coming to Deming—slowly. *Courtesy Deming Luna Mimbres Museum.*

there not? Deming bricklayers were knocking down $5.50 a day, and carpenters $4 even. A local physician was charging $3.50 for an examination whether he got the diagnosis right or wrong, notwithstanding the cure. Potatoes were bringing $3.50 a bushel, and butter 45 cents a pound. Town lots were selling for up to $325 and, for sure, the future for Deming town was looking tiptop! So good, a prospective speculator thought an investment in real estate alone might yield as much as 1,000 percent.[653] The railroad assured her future. If it lasted, so, too, would Deming. Frontier growing pains were to be expected, endured and overcome.

Recognizing Deming's potential for growth and the momentous impact it would have not only on Hudson's Hot Springs, but Silver City as well, Dick Hudson opened a "good corral" and placed "Doc" Gilpin in charge.[654] Travelers intent on making the trip from Deming to Silver City, with a stop at "The Celebrated Hudson's Hot Springs" could now, riding in a comfortable six-horse Concord coach, make the trip in but eight hours over the "shortest, quickest and cheapest route." [655] Tobacco-spitting teamsters and bullwhackers with a railroad connection just 50 miles from Silver City were capable of flooding the mining town with commodities, and they did. Traffic on the well-worn road between the two points mushroomed, profitably and progressively. Silver City, for all practical purposes, was still an end-of-the-road spot, but that byway shortened by coming of the railroad guaranteed her Eastern urbanity its sustaining breath. She was yet an Old West town, sometimes still wild and woolly, but at her very doorstep lay the avenue to refinement and municipal maturity. Silver City's enlightened movers and shakers began harboring thoughts of a railroad branch line. They set to work exploring the possibilities and options, as did cigar-smoking railroad executives who could smell the perfume of prosperity.

Another aroma wafted across town on a cloud of smoke, and it wasn't pleasing. The New Mexico & Massachusetts mill caught fire. It was totally destroyed. Although it had been farsightedly covered by a comprehensive insurance policy, and the owners were pledging to rebuild, it never happened. The site was eventually leased to the Silver City Reduction Works.[656] The Meeson & Marriage stage stand, valued at $15,000, likewise but during a wholly separate conflagration burned to the ground.[657] The owners vowed to rebuild—at another location—and they did.

Work at another place was, for whatever reason, stymied. The incomplete status of Silver City's public school building was drawing ire not only from parents but from newspaper editors who were declaring that the situation was fast creating a "serious detriment to the town."[658] According to contractor Black, there were cost overruns to the tune of $809. Although construction was behind schedule, a commitment was made to have the new schoolhouse completed by the first day of April the following year [1882].[659]

Outside of town, Tom Lyons and Angus Campbell filed preemption claims on public lands along the Middle Gila section southwest of Silver City.[660] Their individual tracts were separated by the cattle ranch of pioneer R. V. Newsham. For a purchase price of "something over $12,000" Lyons and Campbell bought Newsham's ranch, brand and entire herd of cattle.[661] With the buyout the two partners' lands were joined. Two weeks later Lyons was on the road headed for Kentucky with plans to acquire 1,000 head of English cattle to mix with the 900 already grazing their range.[662] The foundation for one of southwestern New Mexico Territory's legendary livestock operations, the LCs, was being laid.

Farther south in the Bootheel section, another renowned ranching empire was in the making. Michael Gray, Tennessee born and Tombstone tough, along with his sons Dixie Lee "Dick" and John Pleasant, two daughters and a pioneering wife, eyed undeveloped and underpopulated grazing land in the Animas Valley:[663]

> We [paid] Curly Bill the rustler, three hundred dollars for his squatter claim on the land and also [received] a written contract or guarantee from Bill that he would uphold our rights against all claimants. It being unsurveyed land, possession of course was the only title possible, but we paid the sum to Curly Bill for the sake of peaceable possession of the land in a country where law officers seldom if ever ventured and self preservation was the only law to follow....We were there to stay.[664]

Another aggressively minded person was also industriously at work. After Victorio's death, surviving Apache in Old Mexico, under the leadership of the wily if aging Nana, licked their wounds and likewise licked in revenge scores of Mexicans. Feeling the pressure of pursuit and needing time to collect his thoughts, Nana led his people into the Mogollon Mountains of New Mexico Territory for the winter of 1880-81. Near Horse Springs they camped, undetected.[665] During the early part of January 1881, they forewent privacy for plunder. Striking the mining town of Chloride, Nana and his second-in-command, Kaytennae, led Chihenne in a scalding raid that left hopeful miners named McDaniels and Overton dead, and a third man "badly wounded." Working their way south through the Black Range's protecting slopes with stolen horses, the Apache managed the trip to Fort Cummings'

The seemingly unconquerable Warm Springs Apache tactician, old Nana or "Little Old Boy Dwarf." *A Ben Wittick photo, courtesy New Mexico History Museum, #16321.*

Kaytennae, an Apache marauder of the first order. Later, however, he productively undertook assignments at the behest of General George Crook. *A Ben Wittick photo, courtesy New Mexico History Museum, #15902.*

vicinity. On Jan. 20 they "killed four men on the Silver City-Mesilla road," before losing themselves in the Florida Mountains on the outskirts of Deming and then scampering on, into Old Mexico.[666] From within the Sierra Madres' secreted vales, Nana began concocting plans for his next move. It would not be long in coming!

On June 28, 1881, Nana and 15 warriors blistered forth and attacked the Upham survey party some 40 miles south of El Paso, killing five. Hours later and 20 miles away, Nana's incredibly destructive band ambushed the El Paso-Chihuahua stagecoach, killed the driver and made off with a terrified customer. The next day they attacked a freight train and killed three teamsters.[667] South of the Mescalero Reservation in Alamo Canyon on July 17 the Apache struck a small pack train, wounding Chief Packer [John DeWitt] Burgess and an assistant packmaster, making off with three mules and their tightly lashed cargo.[668] The small pack train had been detached from 28-year-old Lieutenant John Francis Guilfoyle's command to pick up a payload of fresh vegetables to supplement his Buffalo Soldiers' blandly routine diet. Upon learning of the ambush, the young lieutenant straight away rallied manpower and made ready for the chase.

Riding hard behind Nana, who had by this time picked up a few—30 to 40—Mescalero Apache allies, were Guilfoyle and the 9th Cavalry's Company L, 20 troopers strong. The Maryland-born Guilfoyle, a four-year veteran of Southwestern frontier duty, was accompanied by a well-seasoned Civilian Chief of Scouts, Frank P. Bennett, and Company B Apache scouts. Frank Bennett's 1st Sergeant was 60-year-old Chihuahua, a

Chokonen "who spoke passable English" and was himself rawhide tough, a hardened warrior generally well-regarded by both "hostile" and "tame" Apache.[669] Chihuahua made clear that Nana's outlaws were making tracks west, heading for southwestern New Mexico Territory and their favorite haunts of days gone by. Across the Tularosa Basin and near the White Sands, Nana's bunch killed Jose Provencio and his stepson Victoriano Albillar. Traveling with them had been a 16-year-old girl and her husband. She was found dead and "horribly mutilated." His sad whereabouts went undiscovered.[670] The Apache continued their western flight.

On July 25, after a grueling chase, Guilfoyle's doggedly determined command caught up with Nana in the San Andres Mountains. During a stinging engagement both sides suffered wounded personnel but no fatalities. After crossing the San Andres the outlaw Apache raided the little farm of José Montyoya and killed two workers, stole horses, and raced for the San Mateo Mountains. During the mad-dash trip, near Cantarecio, Nana's band killed two miners and four sheepherders.[671] Nana and company made good their getaway, crossing the Rio Grande and scampering into the San Mateo Mountains, after killing two more miners and a "Mexican" and then "killing more Mexicans in the foothills."[672]

Lt. Guilfoyle hastened to Fort Craig for refreshment and refitting, his men and horses fatigued after the punishing two-week chase under a blistering summer sun's scorch. Hiding in Red Canyon, the Apache tried to catch their breath, too. For a moment they were lulled into a false sense of security, but soon tuned into the fact they were also being pursued by a squadron of hopping-mad civilians—36 men strong—from the mining towns of Chloride and Winston, now poking around in Red Canyon below them. The waylaying was perfect: Popping up from bushes Apache waved scary-looking blankets at skittish horses, and within seconds had killed one civilian, wounded seven, and stampeded and captured 38 remounts and repasts. Killing another horror-struck "Mexican" on the way out of Red Canyon, the Apache—freshly mounted once more—scooted ahead of meaningful pursuit. "The posse walked out of Red Canyon."[673]

At Monica Springs, near present-day Monticello, the seemingly indefatigable Lt. Guilfoyle and his detachment again ran up against Nana's hard-pressed band. On August 3, the Buffalo Soldiers or the Apache Scouts wounded two of Nana's warriors and recaptured 11 horses, but Nana's slippery force melted away.[674] Military minds were sure Nana would make for the Black Range. He didn't. On August 9 he "swept out of the mountains" far north of Monica Springs and attacked the sleepy village of Garcia. There his Apache killed six Hispanics and misappropriated 117 horses. A couple of days later, two more hapless men paid with their lives, and a woman was carried away into slavery.[675]

Nana went one way searching for more blood and booty; Guilfoyle went the other for rest and refurbishment. West of Sabinal, New Mexico Territory, 25 miles or so, deep within Carrizo Canyon, Captain Charles Parker, 9th Cavalry, with Company K composed of 19 troopers, clashed with Nana's Apache and Mescalero warriors, who held a two-to-one manpower advantage. The August 12 battle raged for an hour and a half before the Apache characteristically disengaged and vanished. Two troopers, Farrier Guy Temple and Private Charles Perry, lay lifeless on the battlefield among three of their seriously wounded comrades and nine dead cavalry horses. Thanks to the courageous actions of Sergeant Thomas Shaw, an ex-slave from Covington, Kentucky, who had "made a stand in an exposed position and forced the Indians back, preventing them from surrounding the patrol," the soldiers were saved from wholesale annihilation. The sergeant received the Medal of Honor. For his heroic actions in this instance, and an earlier skirmish, Sergeant George Jordan was also awarded the enviable Medal of Honor.[676]

Farther south, near Cañada Alamosa, Nana's renegades killed and mutilated an area rancher's wife and her three small children.[677] When notified of the pitiless outrage, from his camping spot at *Ojo Caliente* Lieutenant Gustavus Valois sent a subaltern, Second Lieutenant George Ritter Burnett, and 15 troopers from the 9th Cavalry's Company I to confirm or contradict the report.[678] Sadly, it was true. Approximately 30 "mounted Mexicans" who were friends and relatives of the victims joined the military at the horrible crime scene.[679] Lt. Burnett gave chase, trailing Nana's band south along the Black Range's eastern face, and sent a courier, Private John Rogers, back to update Valois. At Cuchillo Negro Creek, near modern Chloride, New Mexico, Nana used the rocky ground to military benefit and repelled the best efforts of both US Army officers. At one point four cavalrymen were cut off, and were boldly rescued by a twice-wounded Lt. Burnett, Sergeant Moses Williams and Private Augusts Walley. All three earned the Medal of Honor.[680] Nana, of course, could have cared less; after nightfall he disappeared—again!

The Apache raiders uncharacteristically "shot their way through" the small mining-tent city of Gold Dust, doing no real damage. Farther south they did manage to kill Perry Ousley, burning his ranch house and outbuildings to the ground. They also set fire to the Irwin Ranch three miles above Lake Valley.[681]

Obviously, Nana was by this time racing south for the international borderline and Sierra Madre sanctuary. East of the Mimbres River on the southern flank of the Mimbres Mountains, Nana's renegades bivouacked in Gavilan Canyon. Their tracks, however, were detected by Lieutenant George Washington Smith, riding from Fort Cummings with 9th Cavalry Companies B and H. At the canyon's mouth the military command was joined by a 20-man Apache-chasing posse led by George Daly, superintendent of the Lake Valley Mining Company, who had gathered up men at Lake Valley's Cotton Saloon.[682] By one account the civilians were "half-seas-over," meaning that they were drunk: "Some of the men were so much the worse for tarantula juice they could hardly keep their saddles."[683] Perhaps! The two parties—drunk or sober—parleyed. Somewhat muddled are the accounts between civilian and military versions, as both were trying to save face. Writing for *The New Southwest & Grant County Herald*, a newsman penned:

> The pursuers then followed the trail into Gavilan Canyon until they reached a point about eight miles out from Brockman's mill, where the advance scouts gave notice of the proximity of Indians. At this point, accounts conflict somewhat, but it seems certain that Lieut. Smith ordered an advance and the entire command marched into a deadly ambush. Smith fell at the first fire but was subsequently helped on his horse. He then ordered the command to dismount and "take to the rocks," and he and Daly made a dash as though to disperse the ambushed Indians, but were both shot dead from their horses, within a few feet of each other. Besides Lieut. Smith and Geo. Daly, two soldiers and one citizen were killed. Seven or eight were wounded, one of whom subsequently died at Jno. Brockman's ranch. The rest of the command took to the hills near by, and kept up the fight from behind rocks and hastily constructed fortifications from 10 o'clock a.m. until 4 p.m., when the Indians withdrew, having evidently been warned of the approach of the reinforcements which arrived a half hour later. The bodies of the dead were then recovered. That of Lieut.

> Smith was horribly mutilated but the rest had not been touched.[684]

At the death of Lt. Smith, Sergeant Brent Woods, Company B, took command, deploying men and generally holding things together throughout the disaster. For Woods' gallant action, another Buffalo Soldier received the prized Medal of Honor. Nana gathered up about 30 of the US Army's milling mounts "with full accouterments, and fully 1,000 rounds of ammunition," and reconstituted his galloping tear for the border.[685]

> The original summary of these engagements says that the hostiles "were defeated after a very severe fight," but does not explain on what ground it concludes this. On the record the decision was the other way around. Lieutenant Smith was killed as were four of his men and George Daly, a civilian member of a posse which joined the fight. Three other troopers were wounded, which amounted to about 50 per cent casualties and left the raiders in command of the field, scarcely a resounding victory for the soldiers![686]

Nana's southwestern New Mexico Territory work was not quite finished. Racing for Old Mexico the Apache made another bloody stop, just a tad north of Fort Cummings:

> On Friday the Indians took in the entire party of wood choppers at work for S. P. Carpenter in Cooks' Cañon. Desiderio Herelda and Petronillo Chacon were killed, Manuel and Juan Chacon, aged 12 and 14 years respectively, were captured, and two others who are reported missing were without doubt killed, although their bodies have not be found.[687]

And the following evening, between Victorio [Peak] and Eureka in the southwestern desert of old Grant County, just a few miles shy of the international border, the Apache killed another miner and wounded his partner.[688] Then wily Nana, 70-plus years old, crippled and infirmed, and his tattered band of Chihenne and Mescalero raiders eluding American military and civilian pursuit, slipped across the line. Unable at the time, to make cross-border incursions, the US Army was hampered with "positive orders from the government" and abandoned the chase after Nana. "In about six weeks this aged warrior and a few dozen hardy Apaches had covered 1,000 miles through enemy territory, fighting off pursuers and living off the country. They had killed 50 men or more, captured or stolen several hundred horses, and evaded at least 1,000 troops as well as hundreds of civilians."[689] Again and again, cavalry officers reported wounds inflicted on the Apaches, but Nana left neither dead nor wounded behind. In fact, it is likely that Nana's losses were few. [690]

Chapter 11

"Well Mounted and Armed to the Teeth"

Peeking in on 1881 New Year's Eve merriment might be revealing, and surely there were celebrations galore, but the first week of 1882 in Silver City was rather humdrum and mundane for an Old West town with such a wild and woolly reputation. At the year's first Grant County Commissioners' meeting there was not a quorum, and therefore not any accomplishment. The editor of *The New Southwest & Grant County Herald,* with tongue in cheek, was postulating that Silver City's citizens should make a solemn New Year's resolution to attend church—at least once—during the upcoming year. It was also, he thought, exceedingly important for the clergymen to sermonize "that hell ought to be preached whether there is one or not." His serious motive was simple: Good churches and good schools encouraged "a high class of immigration" and for that reason alone, he said, the institutions should receive "hearty support."[691] Evidently the positive public relations message was getting out: "Travel on the coaches running into this city is increasing. We also notice many prairie schooners on our streets."[692] Another thing the newspaperman wanted to see in Silver City was a railroad connection. Editorially he began jabbing that it would never happen unless some of the leading men were awakened from their apathy.[693] Another editorial poke at community lethargy pointed out the fact that Grant County, as late as February 1882, didn't even hold clear title "to the block on which the jail and other county buildings are [were] erected."[694]

Nonetheless, fortunes were being made and Silver City was booming. A degree of pretentiousness was to be expected, and in a capitalistic society wealth is measured by materialistic possessions, lavish furnishings and fancy abodes. Hartford Meredith and his partner, Henry B. Ailman, the man who at one time was sleeping on a makeshift mattress stuffed

Silver City folks proudly posing for an 1882 photograph at their "go ahead" town. *Courtesy Silver City Museum.*

with coffee sacks, divested themselves of their Georgetown mining interest. With the proceeds they opened a bank, and built two personal residences with identical floor-plans. Contractor Robert Black was doubtless told to spare no expenses associated with building the side-by-side houses on Broadway. They were elegantly ostentatious. They were "Eastern." They were mansions for a Southwestern frontier city. The twin brick structures were quickly recognized as the "most stylish private residences in town."[695] Unsurprisingly, other successfully inclined Silver City entrepreneurs followed suit. C. P. Crawford had a "stately Queen Anne style house" constructed on Ninth Street; Isaac N. Cohen, the mercantile and mining heavyweight, built a "fine brick Italianate home" on Bullard Street; and John A. Miller, moving into Silver City after the $100,000 sale of his Lake Valley ranching and mining properties, had his eye on building where the city cemetery was. No problem! Money talks! Politicians listen! After receiving the say-so from Silver City's town council, at his own expense Miller exhumed the bodies—notably for later generations including that of Catherine Antrim, whom an eventual historic marker at the new location would identify as "Billy the Kid's Mother"—and laid them back to peaceful rest in a new memorial park outside municipal limits. This act gained Miller an unencumbered deed to the original graveyard real estate. Miller's fancy new home, built at a cost of $15,000, was indis-

Silver City bankers Henry [Harry] Boyar Ailman [L] and Hartford [Henry] M. Meredith [R], long days after Harry Ailman was forced to sleep on a makeshift mattress stuffed with coffee sacks. *Courtesy Silver City Public Library.*

putably the finest house on Santa Rita Street, and probably the "most elaborate" private residence in Silver City.[696]

With such a vibrant business economy and social standing as one of the most lively towns in the whole of New Mexico Territory, no wonder Silver City would magnetically attract a swarm of vociferous newspapermen. Journalistic goings-on in the town marked their apex during 1882. By the end of the year, Silver City could boast of six locally published newspapers: *The New Southwest & Grant County Herald*; *Mining Chronicle*; the semi-weekly *Watchdog*; the *Grant County Sentinel*; the *New Mexico Mining Gazette*, a semi-monthly folio aimed at the mining, manufacturing, industrial and railroad readership; and the *Silver City Enterprise*, arguably the most important and certainly the longest lasting. There would be mergers and failures, personnel comings and goings, ups and downs, but from the very outset Silver City and Grant County folks were never short-sourced for newsy and gossipy columns or for a newspaperman's witty partisan opinions.[697]

Downtown merchants, who for years had been profitably catering to the manly crowd by promoting Colt's six-shooters, Winchesters and Marlins, cartridges and cuspidors, saddles and spurs, dynamite and single-jacks, began finding a more refined market with the ladies. Advertisements for Singer and White sewing machines; "fine flavored natural leaf Japan tea"; the latest styles of flower vases; Saxony yarn in all shades; plated and solid and engraved silverware; along with "smoked halibut and salmon" or "nice fresh Wisconsin Creamery butter," were sophisticated barometers that Silver City was on the march.[698]

And finally, at long last, those Silver City kids could be marched, too—off to the new public schoolhouse. During April, Silver City's wives and mothers, the real driving force behind the clamor for a good public school, sponsored a fund-raising party in the 32-by-70-foot hall at the new Meredith and Ailman building, "and a more auspicious opening it could not have had. The music was excellent, and the dancing good and the management perfect. The supper was contributed by the ladies present, each one bringing a little and was most excellent. The dancing was kept up until 4 a.m., when the company dispersed, tired but well pleased."[699] The shindig raised $136.25, which was turned over to the school commissioners, and the well-attended affair served as an informal dedication ceremony. Officially there were no dedicatory exercises for the school's opening, the first of its kind in Silver City and, in fact, the best built in the whole territory.[700] A Mr. Hardenbrook was hired as teacher and principal, assisted by a teacher identified as Miss Shannon. With 125 smiling students, Silver City's public school was in session. Already the

The long-awaited public school building. Construction was completed in 1882. *Courtesy Silver City Public Library.*

physical plant was too small, and quickly it was recognized that the upstairs hall [not hallway] would have to be used as a classroom.[701]

During that very same April some guys in Arizona Territory learned their lessons, too. The "Earp boys" and a few of their cohorts decided it was time to vacate Cochise County, in a hurry! The aftermath of the previous year's shootout near Tombstone's O.K. Corral had not boded well for the Earps: Brother Virgil had been bushwacked and seriously injured, while brother Morgan was assassinated while playing pool by a bullet fired through a window pane. Wyatt and "Doc" Holliday and a few of their pals committed some retributive killings of their own, becoming murderers themselves. Officially they assumed the role of devious fugitives when they ran ahead of legally drawn warrants. Indeed it was "a unique spectacle; a posse of federal lawmen forced from their district."[702] It's been perceptively written that ol' Wyatt's appearance on the Tombstone stage left "indefinitely open to debate whether he had been part of the problem or part of the solution."[703] The rights and wrongs of their actions are contested mightily even today, over a century after the six-shooter hubbub. For the context of this Old West story—Silver City's part—the facts, however, generally go unchallenged. On their flight to avoid lawful prosecution for homicides committed in Arizona Territory and, while riding on the dodge, the Earp crowd smartly forwent a quick Southern Pacific Railroad train ride and a trip through pulsating Deming. Knowledge of the posting of Dan Tucker at Deming was widespread. The fleeing Earp bunch opted not to put Dan Tucker and his steady companion, a W. Richards double-barreled shotgun, to the test.[704]

That the Earps of Tombstone had contemporary fame as halo-wearing lawmen is a ludicrously imposed myth, manufactured for 20th-century audiences.[705] "And, irony of irony, Wyatt Earp, the most well-known shootist or gunfighter in America's past, was never in a man-on-man gunfight or duel. It is true that because of his presence (the famous shootout; the Tucson rail yard, etc.) certain dead bodies were found, but how they were killed and by whom has never been established with certainty. This is indeed a lamentable record for America's premier 'gunfighter.'"[706] At the time, many believed the Earps were pimps, gamblers and assassins, not lily-white town tamers. In fact, the editor of the *Deming Headlight* referred to their actions rather explicitly: "The Earp party riddled Frank Stilwell with bullets last. [sic] Murder is the order of the day in Tombstone and Tucson."[707]

On horseback the dubious outfit obliquely cut through Mule Creek and alighted in Silver City. They came not as feted cavaliers, but as sneaks. Perhaps they too wished not to sample Sheriff Harvey Whitehill's true grit as a Southwestern frontier lawman! Slyly using fictitious names, the fugitives stayed but one anxious night, and their presence was not duly noted till after they'd gone:

> Last Saturday evening at about 10 o'clock the Earp boys' party and Doc Holliday arrived in Silver City. They went at once to the Exchange hotel to find the stage agent to make arrangements to leave the next morning on the Deming coach. [The Deming stagecoach stopped at Fort Cummings, and from there northbound passengers could make the short hop to Nutt for a Santa Fe Railroad connection, bypassing Deming completely.] They slept in some private house up town and took breakfast next morning at the Broadway restaurant, and as they had not registered at any hotel it was not known they were in town until after their departure. The party came horseback, and put up at the Elephant corral. They were all well mounted and armed to the teeth. One of the men, when asked his name, answered John Smith, and another Bill Snooks. This excited the suspicion of Mr. White, proprietor of the corral, and the next morning when they offered to sell him their horses, he refused to buy them, fearing to get himself in trouble. They offered six of their horses for $300 but as the horses were worth much more than that, this offer was also looked upon as unfavorable to them. They finally sold the six horses to Mr. Miller, who about to start a livery stable here. This done, they spoke to Mr. White about hiring a team to take them to Fort Cummings, but he advised them to go by stage, which they decided to do. The saddles and two horses they failed to sell were left here with Charley Bagsby.[708]

The "Earp boys" made good their getaway. They deceptively handled a trip to Colorado. Thereafter the misfits effectively schemed to avoided extradition and a facing of the music in Arizona Territory. The Blind Mistress of Justice was simply outfoxed. The Earps' and Holliday's stories have been repeated, rehashed and regurgitated, but chiefly during the 20th century. Melodramatic chronicles—in this instance—have been the glorified and often fictionalized work product of overzealous scriptwriters and movie producers trafficking in mythology and money. Sadly, sometimes absent the slightest hint of historic fidelity, rubbish has overvalued reality. Silver City folks, in truth, during those Old West days paid the scampering scalawags not too much mind. Fleeing felons weren't the only newsmakers that April of 1882. Apache were about!

Renegade Apache under the leadership of Chihuahua, Nachez, Chato and, perhaps, Geronimo, breached the international border from their lair in the state of Sonora, Old Mexico. Riding hard the Apache dashed onto the San Carlos Reservation. Wisely they cut the telegraph line between the agency headquarters and Globe, Arizona Territory. In an act of wanton butchery they murdered the chief of Indian Police, Albert D. Sterling, and also killed his first sergeant, Sagotal.[709] By at least one account the insurgent Apache cut off Sterling's head and "played with it like a football."[710] Then, dependent on the umpteen versions available and the preferred scenario selected, Loco and his followers were either hoodwinked or forced at gunpoint to jump the San Carlos Reservation. So, while the Earp crowd was racing for their lives, hurrying and hiding in remarkably rough mountain country dividing southeastern Arizona and southwestern New Mexico Territories, so, too, were several hundred Apache—a few of whom were not particularly inclined toward friendliness.

On April 21, 1882, the Apache struck the freighting outfit of O. K. Smith about a mile or so above Clifton, Arizona Territory.[711] They killed five teamsters, one of whom was the previously mentioned Tom Redding, that Texas boy of Mason County War fame.[712] In extraordinarily short order the renegade Apache attacked a six-man mining coalition near Gold Gulch [sometimes called Rattlesnake City], east of the New Mexico-Arizona line in the Burro Mountains, killing all half-dozen of the prospecting party.[713] The next day another group, 12 Mexican muleskinners, was caught wholly unawares and mercilessly massacred. Early on the death toll was approaching half a hundred and rising. Burial teams from Silver City alone interred some 30 who had fallen victim to the pitiless Apache depredations.[714]

Veteran Indian fighter Lieutenant Colonel George A. "Sandy" Forsyth, survivor of the legendary siege at the Battle of Beecher's Island, was stationed at Fort Cummings with his companies of 4th Cavalry. Patrolling southwestern New Mexico Territory and searching for the

Apache, Forsyth dispatched Lieutenant David N. McDonald and two cavalrymen, along with a civilian guide, Yuma Bill, and seven Indian scouts to explore west toward the Stein's Peak Range straddling the New Mexico-Arizona borderline. Picking up a likely hot trail, the advance guard followed it into the nearby Peloncillo Mountains. Into a single-file canyon they started—until even the Indian scouts balked. Calling them low cowards, McDonald proceeded up the narrow defile alone. Shamed, the others tucked tail and hesitantly tagged along. Only minutes later, at the first volley fired by concealed Apache, three scouts went down doornail dead and McDonald's jaw was creased by a whizzing bullet. Yuma Bill fell from his horse, fighting his last battle, Apache falling before his wickedly accurate rifle fire. The small reconnoitering party had simply been outnumbered and overcome. There were some 150 hard-edged warriors—at least by one report. McDonald ordered a courier, who probably needed to be told only once, to ride like hell and hustle up Forsyth with reinforcements. In the afternoon Forsyth made the scene, riding at the head of Companies C, F, G, H, and M. Keenly aware of the demographic shift in manpower, the Apache wisely altered their tactics, setting fires and backfires, and began their time-honored practice: As the scorching temperature went up and wisping smoke climbed skyward, the Apache seemingly melted into the ground underfoot. Visible for a gruesome headcount, however, were the aforementioned Yuma Bill, the three Indian scouts and a sergeant and private killed; along with Lieutenant John W. Martin, five more soldiers were seriously wounded, as was another Indian scout.[715] The Apache racked up the marks on their scorecard.

Silver City folks were keeping count, too. The tally book had naught to do with Apache, though. Despite the murders and mayhem thereabouts, baseball "fever" was sweeping through town. With anticipation of fielding a first-class team for a "match game" with El Paso players, the local team was pitting first and second stringers in hotly contested practice games. Apparently a little real competition was being sought, as the Silver City team during one game got the best of the Fort Bayard boys, outscoring them 71 to 19.[716]

Other residents were agape at another show, one of technological progress. At Bennett & Baily's Drugstore, for the very first time in Silver City, there was a July demonstration of the power of electricity; an incandescent light bulb was turned on![717] The Brush-Swan Electric Light Company of Cleveland, Ohio, already ahead of Southwest competition in the electricity-supplying game, was eyeballing Silver City and its promising potential for paying customers.[718]

Clearly, Silver City was vibrating with eagerness in the boardrooms and on the playing fields. At Deming, however, the sporting activities were played for keeps: "A party of roughs stood a man up in broad daylight for his entire team and outfit. Deputy Sheriff Tucker hearing of the fact, got down his trusty gun and ran the whole gang off."[719] The next month Tucker ran off to Silver City. He shouldn't have!

Lawman Dan Tucker's world turned upside-down the night of August 24 inside the celebrated Centennial Saloon, in an encounter with a fellow

Silver City's Centennial Saloon, the site of relaxation, business deals, and an occasional shooting. *Courtesy Silver City Museum.*

from Paschal. Located some 15 miles southwest of Silver City, Paschal was actually the first mining camp in the Burro Mountains. Three years before [1879], John W. "Jack" Fleming, along with early area pioneers John Swisshelm and Jim Bullard, had located the St. Louis mine. A year later Pascal R. Smith of Deming and Frank Marshall of Denver organized the Valverde Copper Company, and a whopping success it proved to be. A post office was opened on Jan. 23, 1882, with John W. Fleming as postmaster.[720] By mid-year Pascal had bragging rights to a population of 1,000, the Paschal Hotel and Gem Restaurant, the Foote and Booth Store, two swinging-door saloons, a livery stable and a host of colorful characters. One of those frontier boys in Paschal was particularly well-thought of. Carrying an official commission from Sheriff Harvey Whitehill as a part-time Grant County Deputy Sheriff was a Brownwood, Texas, native, 22-year-old James D. Burns—an irregularly looked-for deputy sheriff, but a full-time night watchman at the Valverde.[722] On the night in question, he, too, was inside Silver City's Centennial Saloon, roaring drunk and, not unexpectedly, armed with his Colt's six-shooter.[723]

The gist of the story is short and simple. During a slobbering-drunk toot, the youthful lawman from Paschal overplayed his hand, arguing with full-time Deputy Dan Tucker, also the town's current marshal; Glaudius W. Moore; and a *sometimes* Grant County deputy sheriff, William "Billy" McClellan, who owned the unsavory reputation "as notorious a horse and cow thief as ever lived."[724] Once again, booze and bullets muddled and blood was spilled. This time it was James Burns' misfortune. He lay stone cold dead on the barroom's hardwood floor. Three fellow "peace keepers," Tucker, Moore and McClellan, were standing by looking on, smoking six-shooters still in their hands. All three had fired; all three were arrested.[725] Tucker was highly irritated that anyone would even question his assertion of self-defense, declaring the query an unspeakable injustice. During a fit of exasperation he pathetically whined to a nonaligned *Silver City Enterprise* reporter:

> Dan Tucker informs us that in the course of his duty as deputy sheriff he has been obliged to kill eight men in this county, besides several in Lincoln and Doña Ana counties and the killing of Burns, in which he was implicated, was the first time he was ever put under bonds to await examination.[726]

Ultimately criminal cases lodged against the three defendants would be resolved absent legal penalty, but the ever volatile Dan Tucker seemed always to be sitting on a powder keg. Before year's end he would be seriously wounded by six-shooter blasts while dilly-dallying at a Deming whorehouse.[727] Rather dryly an editor for *The New Southwest & Grant County Herald* surmised that Tucker "fell among those unfriendly to him."[728] Deming's dangerous Dan somehow survived the nasty gunshot wounds, but just barely.

But Dan Tucker's sordid little story paled in comparison to the bigger news. Earlier in the year, the Silver City, Deming and Pacific Railroad Company had been incorporated with a $50,000 subscription raised by Silver City's wealthiest mining magnates and merchants. More money was needed, though, to the tune of $3 million, and of course with help from "Eastern" shareholders it would be forthcoming.[729] The company's straightforward objective was to connect Silver City with the transcontinental railway system lying 47 miles south.[730] Grant County was buzzing with activity in response. Advertisements were taken out in the local newspapers for men to "cut ties and telegraph poles."[731] With the prospect of passenger and freight-moving railroad connections, the perpetually vigorous Silver City was once more being widely touted as "the coming city of New Mexico, the future metropolis of the Southwest."[732] For Grant County and Silver City the railroad's coming was a big deal!

> We are authorized to state that in view of the fact that wealthy eastern capitalists have agreed to furnish the remainder of the money to build the above road [SC, D, & P RR], it will probably be built as a narrow gauge road—and not as a broad gauge as was at first contemplated. Mr. [Edmund G.] Shields the chief engineer will meet Mr. [J. Parker] Whitney the President of the road in Boston and they will together purchase rails, material and rolling stock. The first locomotive to be used in construction will be borrowed or purchased from the Denver and Rio Grande Rail Road. All the money required for the road will be at once placed to the credit of the company, and unless some unforeseen delay should arise while the construction is in progress the road will be running order within four months.[733]

There was no little consternation over the fact that the new railway line would not be of broad gauge as initially planned, but newspaper editorials were gradually bringing a skeptical public around: "This is not as important a matter as it is generally believed to be. What we need is a railroad, be it broad or narrow gauge!"[734] With Grant County's happy folks the positive prattle about newly laid steel rails and the authentic likelihood of chugging trains in their near future was unanimous—well, almost.

Rancher Pope Black in southern Grant County was hell-hornet mad. A Santa Fe train near Florida Station, 14 miles northeast of Deming, had run over several head of his cattle. Those dumb cow-brutes, well acclimated to the trains' regular schedule and not in the least frightened by a locomotive's whistle blasts, simply failed to get off the tracks and were tipped where they stood, everlastingly. Whether or not the Santa Fe engineer could have stopped the train, or actually took sadistic delight in playing a bowling game of knocking down cow-pins, goes unrecorded. Pope Black's cows were cold-anvil dead, and he had payback on the brain. Black sneakily placed some type of obstruction on the train tracks, intent on causing a wreck and exacting revenge. Whether or not he got caught bragging about his dastardly plan or was actually eyeballed by a tattling witness is likewise indeterminate for this Old West saga. It is known, however, that Deputy United States Marshal Louis Kennon, Jr., a spirited young man who was characterized as toting "two or three six-shooters" and sporting a "broad-brimmed sombrero," was sent to arrest Black.

When the two finally collided, they stood eye to eye, toe to toe, and in an archetypal Western gunfighting duel at close range, barked it out with fire-belching six-shooters. Pope Black came in second. Deputy Marshal Kennon was indicted by a Grant County grand jury for murder. Feeling in the community was running high against him. Most thought it was a pure case of cold-blooded murder. Others were suggesting that the US marshal, Alexander L. Morrison, Sr., should himself be right fast criminally indicted for appointing such a showboating deputy as Louis Kennon.[735] Later, after the murder charge was dismissed due to a dearth of convincing evidence, Kennon resigned or was fired from his position as a deputy US marshal, but he didn't lay off his six-shooters with his new employment as a guard at the Lake Valley, New Mexico Territory, mines.[736]

The Silver City, Deming & Pacific Railroad's pledge to reach Silver City in double quick time spurred the joy and jubilation of area miners, cattlemen, legitimately minded business opportunists—and not just a few gamblers and "daughters of joy." From all appearances it was going to be another banner year for Silver City and old Grant County. "The mining outlook seemed brighter than ever; over 400 mining locations were filed at the Grant County Clerk's office in the first 10 days of 1883."[737] Reflective of the region's prominence is the fact that Silver City was indisputably the "center of mining activity in New Mexico" and even two years later an official government assessment affirmed that "Silver City is yet regarded as the principal mining center of New Mexico."[738]

Enlightened "Eastern" progress was peeking over the horizon. The Brush-Swan Electric Light Company obtained permission from the city's

Progress in transition at Silver City. Telephone lines overhead, muddy streets underfoot for freighters' laboring teams. *Courtesy Silver City Public Library.*

administrators and began laying wires to light Silver City's streets under a 20-year contract.[739] Other commercially inclined businessmen began planting poles and stringing a sometimes-sagging telephone line between Silver City, Fort Bayard, Georgetown, Santa Rita and San Jose.[740] Renowned Southwest gambler Frank Thurmond opted to purchase a wholesale liquor house in Deming. Mrs. J. D. Maloney opened the Kansas City Restaurant on Broadway in Silver City, and with her two daughters, Mollie and Josie, was "untiring in efforts" intended to make patrons happy and comfortable. Misses Lena Leuningen and Katie Ryan, previously residents on the "East Coast," opened their dress-making business. Amateur thespians, the Mohawk Minstrels, performed admirably at an "entertainment" in the local schoolhouse and, in fact, did much better than most of those "traveling troupes" passing through town. The Methodist minister, E. L. Allen, after reconciling the church's debts and building up a congregation numbering 45 worshipers, was transferred.[741]

For the moment, most of the news was good news. Prophetically, though, one editor was forward-looking and proffered a dire warning:

> When it is remembered that the mountains north and west of town constitute a watershed of great magnitude and a drainage therefrom covering an area of nearly one hundred square miles, it is not surprising that the waters in time of heavy rains come rushing down this valley in such immense volumes and with mighty fury. We are inapt to underestimate the gigantic force with which it rushes through these streets. Since the town has become more compact and the avenues of escape for the water compressed within a smaller limit, its forces and fury will be correspondingly increased. Citizens who have lived here in times of these floods know that an ocean steamer could scarcely withstand the force of those torrents.[742]

About 11 miles west of booming Silver City, John W. "Jack" Fleming, "a prominent, enterprising citizen" located the Old Man mine. The Old Man was a whopping success, a silver mine with would-be limitless productivity. Almost overnight a town sprang to life. At first it was tagged as Bonanza City, but shortly thereafter was respectfully renamed and christened Fleming, in honor of Jack.[743] An eight-man crew, drawing wages of $3 per day plus board, was immediately put to work grading a wagon road from Fleming to Silver City. From the outset Fleming town could boast of two saloons, a fully stocked mercantile store, a boardinghouse, 40 slapdab houses, 150 tents, something over 400 busy residents and a United States Post Office, Jack Fleming, Postmaster.[744]

A scant half-mile south of Fleming, three Silver City fellows, M. B. Mikesell, Thomas Kendall and a Mr. Ross, founded another town, Penrose, and again with astronomical speed a butcher shop, bakery, store, more saloons and a corral with blacksmith shop were up and running.[745] The stamped mail, however, was worked out of the Fleming Post Office.

Lest the casual reader be lulled into a sense of peacefulness, it is obligatory to register that the whole of southwestern New Mexico Territory was still a terrific model of the proverbial wild and woolly Old West. In Silver City, Billy the Kid's brother, Joe Antrim, bopped B. W. Tait over the head with a six-shooter and ended up paying a $50 fine.[746] [Billy himself had been gunned down by Sheriff Pat Garrett in Fort Sumner the previous July, ending his brief but colorful career and beginning his ascension into Wild West mythology.]

Near Fort Bayard, three Chinese immigrants were brutally robbed and killed. A fourth Chinese man, a witness, was outside nearby, but too far away to actually see the crime. He did, however, identify the strident voice of Carlos "Charlie" Chaves as being one of the murderous culprits, and so told law-enforcement authorities.[747] Competently employing his investigative skills, the then-Sheriff James B. "Jim" Woods located an additional witness, Luther Carey. Problematically, though, Luther Carey was but 10 years old and a deaf mute. With his mother serving as an interpreter, kid Carey fingered Chaves, Abel Duran and Aurilio Lora as the guilty parties. All three were described as being "well known as very hard characters to the officers of both Silver City and Central and have for months past lived, it is claimed, by the sweat of other people's stock."[748] The murderers were arrested and placed in the Grant County calaboose under $10,000 bail bonds, which they were unable to post. Later, the defendants were found guilty during their first trial, but on appeals alleging faulty sign language interpretation, the New Mexico Territorial Supreme Court remanded the case for a new hearing. For the second go, the jury was once again convinced of the validity of Carey's hand-gestured testimony, and after an eight-hour deliberation returned their verdict: Guilty as charged![749]

For sure, area lawmen were busy. O.L. Hale, who in fact was really Doc Conway, a fugitive from Iowa, was arrested and locked away.[750] And, over in Georgetown, William Lang, an engineer at the Naiad Queen mine, who under the influence of liquor had "turned on a full head of steam and was running the engine at its utmost capacity, notwithstanding the fact that the boiler was almost empty," was gunned down by night watchman J. M. Wood during the dispute to forestall the wrecking of mining machinery.[751]

Away from the settlements it was even worse. "During early February 1883, cattle stealing reached an all time high in southern New Mexico, and local newspapers reported 'there was hardly any use engaging in the stock business there.' The herds along the Rio Grande and from the Texas line to Paraje have been cleaned out. Lincoln and Grant counties have been plundered too."[752] At the territory's nerve center, the widespread cattle rustling and murder led the Santa Fe *New Mexican* to call southern New Mexico Territory a "wasteland."[753] So troublesome had the cattle pilfering become that Governor Lionel A. Sheldon declared unmitigated war on rustlers. He vowed to eradicate the heretofore unchecked cow-thieves and make New Mexico safe for the honest and hard-working citizens or "depopulate the whole damned Territory."[754] The governor's orders to his subaltern, Major Albert Jennings Fountain, commander of the Second Cavalry Battalion, New Mexico Territorial Militia, were not hard to understand:

> The band you are in pursuit of are in combinations and constitute armed marauders or banditti. They are armed against society, and their acts and crimes are numerous and are calculated set at defiance all law and government. They must be treated not as individual criminals, but as foes of the public. While I wish them arrested, tried, convicted and punished by the courts, you must treat the cases as the manifestation requires and as public security demands....[755]

The focus of their no-nonsense housecleaning efforts was primarily a cold-hearted and proven mankiller, John Kinney, whom the *Silver City Enterprise* characterized as "the chief mogul of the gang of rustlers."[756] If ever there was an organized crime kingpin in the Old West, John Kinney qualified. Reigning at the head of an illegitimate empire, John Kinney oversaw the wholesale theft of livestock throughout the Southwest. Those cattle not driven on the hoof to distant markets were killed in one of his slaughterhouses and delivered by the carload lot to butchers at retail meat-markets and classy restaurants. Reportedly, and there is little reason to doubt it, just to El Paso alone he was daily delivering 84 quarters of hanging beef.[757] Again, if the often-used numbers are indeed accurate, Kinney's highly sophisticated rustling operation barefacedly moved 10,000 head of stolen Texas, New Mexico, Arizona and Mexican cattle in

John Kinney, "King of the Rustlers." *Courtesy Robert G. McCubbin.*

a single month, January 1883.[758] Then he was simply known as the King of Rustlers—now he would be labeled a Godfather, "the most feared gangster of the time" It was written that "up against his rifles the bean-shooter civil law was powerless."[759]

With vengeance Fountain's various companies struck, making arrests and, in several cases, shooting down escaping prisoners. A listing of the imprisoned and dead are not absolutely germane for telling Silver City's story. Simply, it may be reported that finally John Kinney was run to ground, and locked into an abandoned boxcar at Lordsburg. There he "begged like a Mormon elder for his captors to spare his life."[760] They did. Finally he was shipped to Mesilla for trial, where he caught five years, to be served in the Kansas State Penitentiary as inmate number 2923.[761] New Mexico Territory had not yet built a penal institution.

No sooner had the "Rustler War" been checked before another erupted. During a whirlwind series of raids the Apache hiding out in Old Mexico killed five Mexican teamsters and then crossed the international borderline and wreaked more havoc. Near historic Willcox, Arizona Territory, they murdered two men at Point of Mountains [Dibble and Bateman], and others were heartlessly massacred near the Total Wreck mine, 10 miles from the Whetstone Mountains.[762] Then the band of Apache, under the nominal leadership of a future US Army-employed Indian scout, Chato, and the recalcitrant Bonito, killed S. E. James and C. M. Thorndykeson at the Contention mine. Next they zigzagged through southeastern Arizona Territory and attacked J. J. Howard and M. C. James as they were shoeing horses in an isolated brush corral. Luckily Howard's rifle fire drove the Apache back, while James prudently stood by—holding his fire—ensuring that one Winchester would always remain fully charged.[763] For awhile the raiding Apache secreted themselves in the Dos Cabezas Mountains on the eastern side of the Sulphur Springs Valley, resting their weary horses. Then, avoiding detection, they made a blistering night ride across the vale, and disappeared into the fastness of New Mexico Territory's Burro Mountains. The hoary story was about to take its Silver City turn:

Lordsburg, N.M. March 27, 1883.

> A Richmond, New Mexico, special says: "The Indians attacked the camp of Palmer and Emerick, about ten miles east of York's ranch at three o'clock yesterday. Jack

> Haynes and a stranger were killed, and John Emerick is missing, and is supposed to have been killed. The other men in the camp escaped to York's ranch. The military telegraph line between this point and Fort Bayard and Fort Cummings has been abandoned, thus cutting off direct communication between the military at those posts and the settlers in the exposed vicinity. It is reported that a large band of Indians are secreted in the mountains north of and west of York's. Brit.
>
> Richmond, 1:30 a. m.—George Parks has just arrived and reports that Indians in large force attacked Swan's station at 8 o'clock this morning, seven miles south of York's ranch and killed five men.[764]

Hamilton C. McComas, a Silver City attorney, was messaged that his legal talents were needed regarding litigation for the Pyramid Mining and Milling Co. near Lordsburg. Recognizing her chance to personally inspect the scenic Burro Mountains, which she had not yet done, Juniata McComas, Hamilton's wife, decided to make the trip also. The couple determined to leave their two older daughters under the care of friends in Silver City, but to take their six-year-old son, Charley, with them on what they concluded would be an enjoyable family outing. For seven dollars per day, McComas rented a buckboard and team from John Graham proprietor of the Stock Exchange Corral. Juniata packed the picnic basket and clothes hampers, while Hamilton loaded his Colt's six-shooter and Winchester, making certain there wasn't an empty loop on his cartridge belt. Having frequently traveled the Silver City-Lordsburg road over the preceding three years without incident, however, had lulled McComas into a sense of false security. News was out that renegade Apache were on the loose, but McComas was not deterred. Somewhat foolishly he chose to ignore a generic warning published in the *Southwest Sentinel*.[765] The happy family, unabashedly flirting with bona fide peril, departed Silver City for their mixed business-pleasure excursion. It was March 27, 1883.

Julius Caesar Brock the next day was riding atop a rim and looking down on the Burro Mountains' Thompson Canyon. For an inexplicable reason he shot at a hawk. Noise of the gunshot echoed through the canyon and danced over the ridges. Nearby the lurking Apache must have heard, too. Perhaps thinking a lonesome hunter was prowling about with plenty of cartridges and a good rifle, they warily scouted toward

Thompson Canyon looking for easy pickings—plunder and prestige.[766]

The McComases, after overnighting at a "roadside hostelry called Mountain Home" some five miles south of Paschal, were back on the primitive thoroughfare marking tracks for Lordsburg when the on-the-move Apache discovered them. The lightning bolt from hell struck. Hamilton and Juanita were quickly killed, and young Charley was plucked from the wagon's bed, a captive, never to be seen again by Anglo eyes.[767]

Judge Hamilton McComas, wife Juniata, and son Charley. The parents were murdered by Apache and Charley was whisked away, never to be heard from again. *Courtesy Silver City Museum.*

After learning of the attack, Deputy Sheriff Herbert E. Muse rushed to the scene:

> I went ahead of the rest of the party and found Mrs. McComas on the ground with her hair about her face and clotted with blood. She was stripped of her clothing and I took off my coat and covered her body before the rest reached us. I put her in the wagon and started to look for the Judge [McComas]. I found him about 50 yards away. He had been shot three times and he was also stripped. We never did find the boy [Charley], he was a very bright child.[768]

Later, when Lieutenant Colonel Forsyth was notified of the massacre he opted to make a personal inspection at the grizzly scene rather than pursue Apache who at the time were known to be breaking south for sanctuary in Old Mexico. Purportedly one dynamic southwestern New Mexico Territory citizen, George Parks, offered his guide services to

Chato [front and center] led the attack on the McComas family. *Courtesy National Archives.*

Forsyth, as he could pinpoint with precision the fleeing marauders' exact escape route. Parks advised the Apache could easily be overtaken, and that they were but just a couple of hours ahead, having already crossed the Southern Pacific Railroad's tracks heading south. Nonetheless, Forsyth still opted to confirm the deaths rather than chase Apache, eliciting Parks to issue the lieutenant colonel "the worst cussing that he had ever heard a man receive," according to a witness, Bramble B. Ownby.[769]

The scorched-earth raid had lasted but six days and covered hundreds of miles, rivaling old Nana's earlier foray. During that short span of time 26 Apache killed 26 hapless southeastern Arizona and southwestern New Mexico citizens. Reportedly Chato never slept during the entire campaign, excepting for "the naps he could get in the saddle; when the party stopped to rest he stood guard until they were ready to ride again."[770] Once more Grant County folks were dead at the hands of Apache marauders, and once more overwrought citizens were disgustingly dissatisfied with the actions—or lack of action—by the United States Army.

Chapter 12

"I Fired One Shot... as They Passed the Corner of the Corral"

The first quarter of 1883 had witnessed the downfall of rustling kingpin John Kinney and the abduction of young Charley McComas. That was old news in a setting where speeding events unsympathetically and without a second look backward washed away yesterday's happenings. Silver City's destiny lay in building a future, not muddling and moaning about what went before. Those early-day Silver City and old Grant County pioneers were damn proud of yesteryears' triumphs—there were many—and sorrowful about past tragedies—and there were many—but all were optimistically focused on one thing: spotlighting tomorrow's progress.

Downtown city lots were selling for as much as $2,500 and the two daily stagecoaches arriving from the East were "loaded to their utmost capacity."[771] Uptown, bricks were hurriedly stacked as impatient new owners looked on, anticipating the day their elegant residence would be put "in the dry." Charles Ashton's new red brick dwelling at the west end of Broadway, near the site of the future courthouse, was "built after a very handsome pattern."[772] One early resident added a special touch:

> Fred Shelton has a beautiful aviary at his cozy residence on Yankie Street. He has about 30 beautiful canaries that make the air about the premises resonant with the music of the feathery songsters.[773]

The new office for the Silver City, Deming & Pacific Railroad was relocated to an upstairs office in the Grant County Bank Building, and was declared the "handsomest office room in town." New construction at the

The Southern Hotel in Silver City. *Courtesy Nita Stewart Haley Memorial Library.*

Southern Hotel was well underway; the dining room was being extended 25 feet, and 16 guest rooms were being added. Over at the Palace Hotel, due to an almost guaranteed increase in the occupancy rate, plans were on the drawing board for an impressive two-story addition. And, not to be outdone, R. B. Higbee was putting an entire new front on his business and adding a story, in an effort to make it "the handsomest building in the territory."[774]

There were the previously mentioned Catholic and Methodist houses of worship and, now, a prestigious $12,000 "cut stone building" was being erected by the Episcopalians. A $30,000 courthouse at the end of Broadway was under construction, with a scheduled completion date in October 1883. There was even talk of a public sewer system to "run down one of the main streets, and thus rid the city of the floods that sometimes pour down the valley, much to the annoyance and loss of property to the inhabitants." Looking into the future, contemplated improvements also included a water works company, gas light company and an enhanced electric light company.[775] Real change, positive change, was near at hand.

As spring 1883 approached, so, too, did tracks being laid for the Silver City, Deming & Pacific, which by April 7 had already reached two miles west of the Mimbres River. At the switching-yards in Deming about 70 passenger and boxcars—and two engines—were inventoried and made ready for use when the new line was completed, which was just around the corner.[776]

Make no mistake, with "a complete and effective city government" Silver City was fashioned not after a Western town model: "The administration of the law is thorough, and in no city of the east is public order better maintained than here."[777]

Not everyone was behaving nicely, however. A quick headcount for just one justice of the peace precinct reveals monetary fines were levied for: drunkenness and disorderly conduct, 29 cases; keeping a bawdy house, four cases; fighting, six cases; using a deadly weapon, three cases; vagrancy, two cases; and using indecent language, one case. At the jam-packed Grant County Jail, prisoners were busily amusing themselves telling fortunes with the pasteboards. "The jailer had his future predicted twice and both times he ended on the gallows."[778] To the south at Lordsburg it was a wee bit more serious. Saloon man John [Thomas] Welch killed his business partner, a man named Galvin, while he slept. Welch pled self-defense to a lynch mob, but hopelessly. On April 29 his accounts were squared, and although he maintained his innocence until the very end, he was hanged from an awning post in front of a downtown business. A warning note was pinned to Welch's shirt daring anyone to cut the body down before high noon. He swung until the 12th chime rang.[779]

Out and about the countryside it was still chancy. Apache inhabiting the dismally forlorn San Carlos Reservation continually "jumped," becoming marauders for awhile before returning, usually outrunning and outdistancing pursuit. From within the Sierra Madre's unexplored recesses came Apache from south of the New Mexico-Arizona borderline on hit-then-run-away raids. Even as track-layers were inching toward Silver City from Deming, Apache were busy making their living, too. While camped on the banks of the Gila, P. J. Clark and five companions lost all of their picketed horses. The wily Apache simply "cut them loose" and fled west, traveling too fast to be overtaken. On the very same night Jack Fleming lost 20 head of good saddle horses.[780]

Electric lights may have been shining downtown, but by any level-headed analysis Silver City and old Grant County were still firmly fastened to an emblematic Old West. Most men drank neat whiskey every day and many carried six-shooters, five-shooters or derringers. No-nonsense deputies and marshals prowled the streets and barrooms, *sometimes* enforcing the law. Cowboys whooped and hollered on their few and far-between trips to town. Harlots hustled. Greedy frontier gamblers grabbed. Gold-buttoned "Buffalo Soldiers" and their white officers chased hither and yon, wearing out grain-fed cavalry horses and backsides. New Mexico Territory, if any place in the whole world qualified, was indisputably and legitimately "Western"—most particularly its southwestern section, old Grant County.

Silver City residents had no time to cogitate about what their relative position might be in Old West annals yet to be published. On the ground they were busy. The big day was coming—and with it the railroad. Industriously they began building two side-by-side platforms—one for Fort Bayard's military band and the Centennial Saloon's toe-tapping ensemble, the other for prominent speechmakers and railroad executives. Contributing his part to the upcoming gala, the wealthy Martin Bremen contracted with a local jeweler to fashion a silver spike from an ingot he supplied, cautioning that the job should be kept secret.[781]

Amid the hoopla and high spirits, Silver City folks gathered 'round on May 12 for the "day of days" that would forevermore connect their town with the "outside world." At an appropriate time the final steel rail was laid, and all but one remaining spike was driven home into the last cross-tie. The jovial throng of celebrants looked on as Mr. Scott of the construction crew remarked to Silver City's Mayor Black that he was only one spike short of finishing the work. Miraculously, Martin Bremen fished into his pocket and—lo and behold—he offered Scott the silver spike that would signify completion of the railroad line. Symbolically representing all the Silver City people, Mayor Black stepped up, and once the silver spike was positioned, he "tapped it in place."[782] Then, as befitting an absolutely perfectly directed cue, Engine No. 1, the E. G. Shields—"decorated with tricolor ribbons and flowers"—came into view. Both bands cranked up and the crowd cheered.[783]

Travel between mining camps, as it always had been, was still risky and necessitated hay-burning power, but now, a trip to faraway Chicago could be made sans ever stepping into a stirrup or jostling inside a dust-churning stagecoach. Within a week the *Southwest Sentinel* was boasting with chest-thumping pride:

> Passenger and freight traffic on the Silver City, Deming and Pacific railroad is exceeding the expectations of the

> officials of the road. So far, the company is making a handsome margin on its investment.[784]

As an *Enterprise* editor headlined, indeed, Silver City was "connected with the civilized world"—but the town and county were still hell-to-pop frontier bailiwicks. Cursory inspection of the jailhouse roster is informative. While there was dancing in the streets heralding the arrival of the railroad, sitting in the calaboose were Frank Allen, Gasper Pern, T. F. Gallager, Carlos Chaves, Aurilio Lora, Abel Duran and Charles Gasiner, all charged with murder. George Mathews didn't kill his man, but he had tried, and was only charged with assault to murder. There is no need to enumerate the others, whose criminal charges included forgery, grand larceny, stealing livestock [horses and mules] and robbery—not counting the drunks and other misdemeanants.[785] Indisputably, everybody was not yet "civilized" and those choosing to expose themselves to hazard could easily hear the crack of a six-shooter or a Winchester's deafening roar. Even those innocent schoolchildren sitting in brand-new classrooms got the chance to bear witness to big booms!

"While blasting for the school cistern Monday, a huge rock weighing fully 75 pounds was thrown into the air, and descended on the roof of the school building. It broke through the roof and ceiling and badly damaged a platform on the upper floor."[786] The unfortunate accident was a man-made phenomenon. But Mother Nature had one in store for Silver City's schoolchildren, too! During the predictable summer "monsoon season," a thunderstorm hurled her spears of lightening bolts. One charge of plummeting electricity stuck a "powder house" all too near the school. The explosion was horrific. "The shock broke all the windows in the school building, created a panic resulting in Gertrude Rivers suffering a broken arm, and several of the smaller children being knocked down and trampled upon."[787] Apparently, at frontier Silver City both studying flash-cards and playing real cards could sometimes prove hazardous to one's health.

So, too, could riding a train. Between Lordsburg and Deming stood Gage Station. William Gage and his partners, active in developing mining interests in the Victorio Mountains three miles southwest of the railroad tracks, are generally credited with founding the settlement. Overnight it became an important shipping point for the nearby mines—so much so that the little burg was granted a post office on April 27, 1882,

Jesse B. Gunnels, postmaster in charge.[788] Aside from its significance as an ore-freighting hotspot, Gage was awarded another less-desirable distinction. For chronicles of Old West banditry it would go down in history as the closest depot to a murderous train robbery—perhaps New Mexico Territory's first![789]

On Nov. 24, 1883, five miles east of Gage Station, four masked bandits robbed the eastbound Southern Pacific train. In the process, one of the outlaws mercilessly gunned down the train's engineer, Theopholus C. Webster. The fireman, Thomas North, ran for his life. Sadly, the Tucson-based Webster died, crumpled next to the steam-spewing locomotive's wheels. Thomas Scott, the train's brakeman, ran the other way, straight for Gage Station and help.[790] The robbers failed to take notice of his departure and proceeded to loot the passengers:

> The alacrity exhibited by some of the passengers in secreting their valuables is said to have been wonderful....Watches, rings and other valuables were dropped in the water coolers, in the coal boxes, behind the hot water pipes, in the pillow boxes, and in fact in every conceivable place in the coaches and sleeping car. One man went so far as to attempt to secret himself in the linens in the sleeping car.[791]

The hijackers shot up the mail-car, a bullet narrowly missing the postal agent, W. O. Swain. One of the robbers' masks slipped during the robbery, and Swain got a good look at his face, as did the express messenger, Thomas C. Hodgkins, but as neither had ever seen him before they knew not whom he was. One of the other outlaws' bandanna didn't slide down, but when he turned his head and exposed the back of his neck it was a plain and irrefutably worthwhile clue—he was a black man. Gathering up their plunder, the four brigands, a murderer among them, mounted their horses and scampered for parts unknown.[792] At long last, news of the train's crew and frightened passengers' plight was made known. At Deming, deputy Dan Tucker fashioned a posse, but as a newspaperman reported, it was "thought that the desperadoes had too far a start and were too well mounted to be overtaken."[793] The owl-hoots made good their getaway, and the whodunit work in their wake began.

Traveling to the area were two privately paid detectives, James B. "Jim" Hume of Wells, Fargo & Company and Leonard "Len" Harris, representing the Southern Pacific Railroad.[794] Quickly both companies posted $1,000 rewards on each of the bandits, $8,000 in the aggregate.[795] The two detectives sought additional help, hiring the well-regarded civilian scout Frank P. Bennett from nearby Fort Cummings to nose around for the unidentified robbers.[796] The smell of freshly minted greenbacks prompted other manhunters—professional and amateur—to join the chase.

MURDERERS! & ROBBERS!

$8,800 REWARD !

On the evening of November 24th, 1883, four outlaws wrecked the East bound Express train, at a point about four miles East of Gage Station, 15 miles west of Deming (New Mexico.) and ruthlessly murdered T. C. Webster, the Engineer and then robbed Wells, Fargo & Co.'s Express of $518.00 in coin and $312.00 Currency. They also robbed the Conductor of $100.00 coin and a silver watch; and R. O. Gaskill, a passenger, of $155.00 Currency. They also rifled the mail car but took nothing of value; the robbers were mounted on a small class of horses and left in a northerly direction toward Cow Springs.

Wells, Fargo & Co. offers a reward of $1,000 each for the arrest and conviction of the murderers; and S.P.R.R Co. offers a like reward on same terms. The P.O. Department has a standing reward of $200 each for conviction of mail robbing.

On saturday evening Dec. 8th, 1883, O. W. Sample alias Big Red, Dan Dowd alias Big Dam, John Kelly alias Yorkey, Willis alias Tex, and W. E. Delaney, entered the town of Bisbee, Cochise Co., A. T. robbed Castenadas store of $2.500, coin Currency & Mexican silver, & shot and killed three men and one woman. The three first named have been arrested and are now in jail at Tombstone; the two last named being still at large.

The prevaling opinion based on Press Reports, etc., and the known bad reputation of the persons named, is that they were the parties, who robbed train and murdered the Engineer, near Gage, on Nov. 24th, 1883. We have AN ABUNDANCE OF POSITIVE EVIDINCE, that at the VERY MOMENT of the Gage affair, the men named were at San Simon Station, 74 miles from Gage and en route for Bisbee.

THE GAGE MURDERERS and ROBBERS, ARE STILL AT LARGE, and unknown, and the reward offered will be promptly paid.

The undersigned will co-operate with any person who obtains any clew and desires to obtain assistance without claiming any abatement in matters of reward. Any letters or dispatches sent in care of Col. A. A. Bean, Division Supt. S. P. R. R. Co., Tucson, will be promptly forwarded. All communications strictly confidential if so desired. If any of the above robbers are arrested in any of the states or territories or Mexico, they will be conveyed to the place of trial without cost to those who make the arrests.

LEN. HARRIS, Detective S. P. R. R. Co.

Tucson Dec 22nd 1883. J. B. HUME Special officer W. F. & Co.

Wanted poster for the Gage train robbers. *Courtesy New Mexico State Records Center and Archives.*

Complicating matters even more was the fact another vicious crime had taken place in Arizona Territory, the Bisbee Massacre. On the night of Dec. 8, four innocent citizens [and an unborn child] were senselessly and mortally gunned down during a robbery of the Goldwater-Castaneda Store in Bisbee.[797] After their bloody work, the "swaggering desperadoes" and "crimson-handed villains" speedily climbed aboard their gyrating and panicked horses and rode out of town, followed by "a volunteer party of true-blue men."[798] For a spate of time both the Bisbee bandits and the Gage train robbers were on the loose, some persons even inaccurately supposing that both crimes had been the gruesome handiwork of a single gang. That notion was quickly dispelled by the astute investigative work of Harris and Hume.[799] Eventually all the Bisbee outlaws would be run to ground. One, Daniel "York" Kelly, was taken into custody at a quiet

Deming barbershop by that poisonously dangerous and seemingly indefatigable Grant County deputy sheriff, Dan Tucker.[800] The final accounting for the Bisbee killers played out in Arizona Territory's Cochise County. An even half-dozen unrepentant murderous misfits met their Maker at the end of a rope; five were legally hanged—one lynched from a handy telegraph pole.[801]

Meanwhile, investigative leads began coming together in old Grant County. Through reasonably slick detective work, clues coalesced leading to four prime suspects. Branded as participants in the Gage train robbery and the killing of engineer Webster were: Christopher "Kit" Joy, an ex-employee of Harvey Whitehill; A. Mitchell "Mitch" Lee, a 21-year-old cowboy from central Texas; Frank Taggart, less than 30 years old and characterized by "a large mouth, which, while in conversation was always wreathed in smiles"; and George Washington Cleveland, "a large ugly looking negro, about six-feet in height, as black as Erebus."[802]

Ex-Sheriff Harvey Whitehill, working for a share of the reward monies, learned that Cleveland had left the area and was working as a dishwasher at a Socorro, New Mexico Territory, hotel. Taking his oldest son, Harry, Whitehill traveled to Socorro and captured George Washington Cleveland at gunpoint. Using a time-proven interrogative technique, Whitehill took the offensive and outright accused his prisoner: "Oh, I've got you, you cowardly son-of-a-bitch, you've killed that engineer." Moreover he bluffed Cleveland again: "Your God Damned cowardly friends Mitch Lee, Kit Joy and Frank Taggart all say you killed him." The accusatorial quizzing worked! Almost in tears, Cleveland blurted out: "No, I did not, Mr. Whitehill. I'll tell you all about it." And, thinking the others were already in custody—which they weren't—George Washington Cleveland "let his milk down"—in other words, he confessed.[803] Cleveland was hauled back to Silver City and placed in the Grant County Jail. One down, three to go.

Hungry for another piece of the bounty, Whitehill, again with Harry but this time also accompanied by proven mankiller John W. Gilmo, traveled to St. Johns, Arizona Territory, where they supposed fugitive Frank Taggart was laying low. He wasn't. But Gilmo successfully tracked him back into New Mexico Territory and confronted him at a line-cabin on the Jewett Ranch. As Gilmo later related:

> On going in I saw him, Frank Taggart, standing with his back to the fire place. I then drew my Six Shooter and

> covered him with it and told him to surrender and not move until I disarmed him. I walked up with my 6 shooter cocked and took his 6 shooter out of the waistband of his pants. I then led him out to my horse where my handcuffs were and hand cuffed him and told him to not be scared. I stayed there all that night and guarded him.[804]

The old Grant County Jail, the scene of numerous successful escapes. *Courtesy Silver City Museum.*

Gilmo took Taggart back to Silver City. The manhunt was halfway pulled off.

Kit Joy and Mitch Lee, after a night or two "carousing the saloons" around Alma, New Mexico Territory, moved farther north, camping at Horse Springs on the western edge of the Plains of San Agustin. Learning the wanted men were there, a part-time deputy sheriff, Andrew J. "Jack" Best, and a young cowman, Charles C. Perry [who would later own a dubious reputation] cooked up a plan to snare the fugitives. Working undercover, Best and Perry induced Joy and Lee to join them in an adventurous plan to free convicted murderer Joel Fowler from the jailhouse in Socorro. The bad guys accepted the challenge, and all started for Fowler's rescue. At an overnight stop, Joy and Lee were disadvantaged, surprised, and made prisoners by Best and Perry. Like the others before them, they, too, were straightway handed over to the Grant County Jail's gatekeeper at Silver City.[805] The Gage train robbery case was all wrapped up—or so it seemed at the time.

The brouhaha over catching train robbers hadn't bothered Louis Timmer one iota. While all that outlaw mess was hogging the news, he was industriously engaged in making a three-story addition to the Exchange Hotel, transforming it into a showcase facility with a new look and a new name, The Timmer House. It was, for the Southwest frontier, a sight to behold. Louis Timmer was not frugal with his cash outlay. Innovative for the time period to be sure, The Timmer House had a steam-powered elevator system, steam heating and an electric bell communicating with all 105 guest rooms and suites. The whole place was ornately and opulently bedecked with "fancy bric-a-brac work" and, according to astute architectural historians, it easily became southwest New Mexico Territory's most luxurious hotel. It is said by those experts on Silver City's blueprints, however, that "the *piéce de resistence* of the hotel was the dining room, with ornamental raised plasterwork on its ceiling and columns, and 12 life-size statures decorating the room."[806] The whopping freight bill just to ship a "huge and faultless" barroom mirror to Silver City exceeded $400; the fancy cornice for the hotel cost $5,000 in Chicago plus $9 per 100 pounds for delivery to Silver City.[807] Transportation between the new Silver City, Deming & Pacific depot and The Timmer House was furnished by Timmer's bus, "an elegant affair" necessitating an expenditure for team and harness in "the neat little sum of $1,250."[808] Clearly ostentatious, The Timmer House was Silver City's premier hotel, but the others, the Broadway, the Southern and the Tremont House were not slouchy places to spend the night or sign on for an extended stay, either. The fact that Silver City, in its geographically secluded setting, could boast patrons enough to sustain four first-rate hotels is indicative of the city's standing in the frontier Southwest.

Unlike so many Wild West towns, Silver City also felt the gentle touch of delicate and caring feminine hands. A group of Irish Catholic nuns somehow managed to construct a two-and-a-half-story brick convent and parochial school, the Academy of Our Lady of Lourdes. Esthetically, because of its architecturally sophisticated finishing touches, it was much more impressive than the free public school.[809] A second group of public spirited ladies, recognizing the fact that Silver City had not a hospital, likewise went to work:

> ...a group of local women in August of 1883 turned their sewing circle into the Grant County Charity Hospital Society. A frame cottage donated to the Society by a local lumber dealer became the hospital, and Dr. W. M. Slough performed its first operation. A hole in the roof let in sunlight for illumination, a local wholesale liquor dealer administered the chloroform, and Mrs. Elizabeth Warren, secretary of the hospital society, served as doctor's assistant. The operation, which began at 1 p.m., turned out to be a long and tiring process; as the sun left the patient's body, Warren grabbed a heavy mirror and held it so light could reflect onto the operating table. Despite the lack of supplies and experienced help, the operation proved a success—as did the desperately needed hospital.[810]

During that terrific boom year of 1883, "Silver City never presented a more busy or bustling appearance" and the merchants were all "busy and good humored." The hotels were full and, despite The Timmer House's grand opening, there was "little if any room to spare." Saloons and restaurants bustled with activity. The editor of the *Southwest Sentinel* boasted that Silver City had a "class [of people] that spends more money" than those in the surrounding mining camps.[811]

The new Grant County courthouse had opened close to on schedule, and by the end of the year its "by no means diminutive" hall was utilized by the town's upstanding ladies for a festive end of the year ball. It was by all accounts a grand affair, well-attended, and the dancing "was kept up until a late hour."[812] No doubt while couples dressed in their Sunday best were promenading on the improvised dance floor, others gossiped about the rash of rumors flashing about: Atchison, Topeka & Santa Fe Railroad executives were toying with the idea of a buyout, and stockholders with the Silver City, Deming & Pacific Railroad were all ears.[813] Who knew what was in store for 1884?

One scenario played out during that year's first quarter, and it proved to be high drama of the Old West shoot-'em-up variety. On the crisp morning of March 10, train robbers Mitch Lee, Frank Taggart, Kit Joy and George Washington Cleveland broke jail. The quartet was accompa-

Diamond A chuckwagon and cowboys near Gage, New Mexico. *Courtesy Silver City Museum.*

nied by condemned murderer Carlos Chaves, and by an accused but not yet convicted horse-thief, Charles Spencer, 24 years old. Arming themselves with Winchesters, six-shooters and a scattergun taken from the sheriff's armory, the escaping jailbirds raced downtown to secure mounts for their getaway. Using the guns as leverage, the outlaws quickly made George Chapman at the Elephant Corral a deal he couldn't refuse. The escapees got six horses and Chapman got naught. Mounting up, the brigands began their dash out of town, but Jack Fleming, sensing the trouble, had raced home to get his shotgun. He returned just in time to cut loose with both barrels. The thunderous muzzle-blast caused Cleveland's green-broke horse to buck and the rider tumbled into the street.[814] By now Deputy Sheriff Tom Hall was on the scene. He'd later pitch in his two cents' worth about the action: "...about this time the train robbers passed out as the east gate of the Elephant Corral all mounted. The Nigger Cleveland being thrown from his horse was taken up behind Kit Joy and the six prisoners started north mounted on five horses. I fired one shot at them as they passed the corner of the corral."[815]

The escapees had a slight head start, but they were soon being chased by a hard-riding platoon of Silver City's hopping-mad citizens, armed for bear and determined to recapture the thugs or, if need be, nail their wretched hides to the jailhouse door. Earlier Kit Joy had been overheard to remark that "they would do away with the negro Cleveland before they were too many miles from town."[816] On the outskirts of Silver City, the "first thing they did was shoot George Washington between the eyes."[817] George Washington Cleveland had caught the "snitch rap" and the bullet. The other five continued hightailing it for the Pinos Altos hills.

The ever-plucky Dan Coomer, by himself, took the right flank, while J. C. Jackson, Ed Mayer, Frank Andrews, Joseph Lafferr, Charles Shannon and T. E. Parks maneuvered for the left side. When the guttersnipes realized Coomer was all alone, he was in a tight spot. They wheeled about and charged his position. Coomer later recalled:

> They fired about 15 shots at me and after running about 30 yards I got behind a stump after jumping from my horse. They still came towards me and I fired a shot at them which turned them a little to the left. The next shot I fired the Mexican [Chavez] fell from his horse to his knees and the next shot I fired I killed one of their horses. There they stopped to pick up the Mexican and I jumped out from behind the stump and took right after them and ran about 80 yards firing at them about every 10 steps.[818]

An enraged posse and the fleeing felons closed about two miles out of town on the road to Fort Bayard. A furious gun battle took place, "as noisy and bloody a fight as ever pictured on the Hollywood silver screen."[819] Dan Coomer shot Mitch Lee, through and through, "from side to side, just above the hips," but Lee wasn't dead yet![820] Chaves, already wounded, was finished off by some posse member in the ferocious exchange of gunfire. The popular school-board trustee and sewing-machine salesman Joe Lafferr chased Kit Joy up a side canyon. Lafferr paid with his life, gunned down from ambush by Joy with the shotgun pilfered from the jail. Now, possemen were seeing blood red! Outlaw Frank Taggart milked his six-shooter dry and then, defiantly surrendered, saying that he damn sure would have kept fighting had he any more "loads." Floundering in the boiling cauldron, in way over his head, horse-thief Charles Spencer simply gave up. The scorecard? Owl-hoots: Carlos Chaves and George Washington Cleveland, dead; Frank Taggart, gut shot but alive, kicking and screaming; Kit Joy, on the dodge, whereabouts unknown; Mitch Lee and Charles Spencer, hides intact and under guard.[821] Good guys: Lafferr, already a widower and the father of five, stone cold dead.[822] For the pitiless killing of Lafferr someone had to pay, but his killer was long gone. Train robbers Frank Taggart and Mitch Lee, however, were handy:

> It was here determined without a dissenting voice that Mitch Lee and Frank Taggart should, by request, attend a neck-tie party and a vote should be taken as to what disposition should be made of Spencer.... The crowd, which was increasing rapidly, was about evenly divided as to Spencer's fate, and it was decided to return him to jail.[823]

Resigned to his doom as he and Taggart stood in a wagon bed, ropes cinched tight around their necks, Mitch Lee confessed unsmilingly that it was he who had killed Southern Pacific engineer Webster during the infamous Gage train robbery, "By God!" His Maker looked down as the wagon rolled out from under the piñon's sturdy limb. Lee gave up the ghost punctually, but Frank Taggart "died hard of strangulation—a throat disease that is becoming extremely common among their ilk in this section."[824] Back at Silver City the desperadoes' bodies were put on public display as trophies of the day's work and as icily cold warnings to any others bent on taking to a life of outlawry.

Long overdue, a resolute Silver City town council passed Ordinance No. 84: "That it shall be unlawful for any person to carry either concealed or otherwise any deadly weapons in the town of Silver City.... Deadly weapons shall consist of all kinds of guns, pistols, knives, slungshots, metallic knuckles, concealed rocks and other weapons by whatever name known with which dangerous wounds can be inflicted."[825] Throughout the frontier Southwest such well-intentioned measures were *supposedly* complied with, and *selectively* enforced. After all, it was yet the wild and woolly West!

And, besides, one of those murderous train robbers was yet running loose, somewhere. Kit Joy, who surely could have run off to parts unknown, changed his name and lived life as a "square dude," didn't. He remained in the Upper Gila country living by hook and by crook, for awhile. Eventually Joy was shot at long range by Erichus "Rackety" Smith wielding a .45-60 Winchester, and was forced to suffer the amputation of a leg. After several months Joy was finally convicted in Sierra County [on a change of venue] and sentenced to imprisonment in Santa Fe, which by this time was home to the spanking new Territorial Penitentiary.[826]

In Silver City there were prison plans, too. Abandoning the old Grant County Jail, the county commissioners ordered that the new courthouse's basement should be home for their local lockup. The old 16-man "chilled steel cage" and a new eight-man strap-iron cell were quickly and neatly installed, to supplement the "eight brick cells and two brick dungeons."[827] Old Grant County would never suffer a shortage of inmates, nor, the commissioners hoped, further nightmares associated with trying to securely confine wrongdoers. "The new jail is not as well arranged, perhaps, as it would have been had it been built especially for the purpose, but it is perfectly secure and will no doubt save the county something in the matter of guard hire."[828] Hardly!

Crime-wise, Silver City, was under control for the moment. Business-mined persons quickly turned their heads to listen for the latest prattle. The financially active Atchison, Topeka & Santa Fe had, in fact, acquired the Silver City, Deming & Pacific Railroad. With the acquisition came a new plan: Widen to broad gauge the tracks from Deming to Silver City; spider-web new narrow-gauge tracks from Silver City to selected mining camps throughout the area; take down and remove a railroad station building in Deming and resurrect it at a new depot site in Silver City.[829] The consequential development of Silver City's railroad connection to that "outside world" or "the States" should not be undervalued. Aside from the occasional train-robber, good things came with the train, too.

Robert Black imported an ice machine. Silver City changed forevermore, for the better. The newfangled contraption, according to a cool newspaperman, became one of the "permanent institutions of the city," producing cheap ice clear as crystal, and in great supply. It was predicted that nearly everyone would "enjoy the comfort to be derived from ice in the household during hot weather." In short order, Black & Co. was delivering close to 2,000 pounds of ice per day. The cash being generated from the contracted ice deliveries of expressman J. C. Jackson kept local money circulating in Silver City.[830] And that very concern—keeping local money at home—the very next year would bubble into trouble.

Chapter 13

"New Mexico . . . Produces the Champion Breed of Liars"

Leaving an utterly rosy impression of Silver City during the 1880s would constitute a fraudulent and revisionist reworking of history. The city was to suffer—as most cities do—economic, political and cultural hiccups. Now and again the discomfiture was long-lasting and often pitiably acidic. Southwestern New Mexico Territory was not immune from the natural ebb and flow of the national marketplace, nor was the area impervious to its sometimes mismanaged and idiotically imposed corrections. Likewise, smart dispensation and imposition of competent governmental policy had its positive effect on Silver City and old Grant County—although in many instances it trickled down, rather than flowed. Illustratively, during the 1870s the market for silver took a nosedive, especially after passage of the Fourth Coinage Act, which halted minting of the standard-weight silver dollar, "although a heavier silver dollar was still produced for foreign trade."[831] As the production of silver increased throughout the American West, the price paid per ounce was further devalued. The Bland-Allison Act, passed in the late 1870s, helped by allowing the Secretary of the Treasury to purchase up to 2 million ounces of silver per month for coinage purposes, but still overproduction retarded a price spike.[832] There were still huge fortunes to be made locating silver mines, however, especially after the railroad came to Silver City. For those fortunate enough to catch the high tide of supply and demand, affluence was assured. But there were also real fortunes to be lost if Lady Luck took a holiday. Mining business was, as it always had been, a highly speculative venture.

The influx of disposable cash invested in Silver City drove interest rates sharply downward and stripped a viable profit from the banking business. This combined with overextended credit lines for some borrowers caused several of the local financial institutions to fail.[833] At a "trustees sale" the entire stock of the Derbyshire Brothers establishment was put on the auction block: a complete line of undertaker's goods, a piano and stool, two billiard tables, a 2,000-pound safe, carpenter's and engraver's tools, 7,000 undelivered bricks and assorted additional whatnots.[834] Further tangible signs of enlightened improvement were for the moment discontinued during an 1885 time-warp: The once rapid rate of expansion seemed to be stymied. Silver City's first electric company went belly up and was "defunct" by the end of the year. Herculean labors were expended—and wasted—trying simply to maintain the continually sagging and snapping telephone lines.[835] Those type of forward-looking marches toward an Eastern mode of civilization would plainly have to wait.

Investment in a less grandiose enterprise, though, could pay big dividends. One of the biggest innovations to please Silver City's folks was the opening of a skating rink. The management "spared no pains to make the place inviting" and gave assurance that the rink's respectability would be maintained at "all hazards." Not only that, there was an especial and absolute promise made to the ladies that no "rowdyism" would be tolerated, whatsoever![836] Even in such a wild and woolly frontier town as Silver City, not everyone was decked out in broad-brimmed Stetsons with twin Colt's six-shooters appended to their hips:

> A number of the young fellows in town have adopted a skating costume of blue knickerbockers, with a gold braid stripe down the leg and gilt buttons at the knee, red stocking and red plush cap, and a white flannel shirt. [837]

Some other fellows were wearing their traditional outfits and "skating" about southwestern New Mexico Territory—once again, the Apache were "out." At the San Carlos Reservation, the ever-intractable Geronimo—no longer in chains and free from all but a hint of civil arrest—and other Apache had gotten horrendously drunk on *tizwin*, their homemade alcoholic brew. The next day, suffering cotton-mouthed hangovers and after defiantly daring a young West Pointer, Lieutenant Britton Davis, to do anything at all about their howling night of fun, or even about their customary practice of backhanding wives, they

Chihuahua, an Apache subchief. He roamed and raided throughout old Grant County. *Courtesy Nita Stewart Haley Memorial Library.*

"jumped."[838] Besides women and children, the number of fighters was approximated at 50 men and teenage boys, including Geronimo, Mangus, Chihuahua, Naiche and that deadly formidable guerrilla-war tactician, old Nana.[839] It was the middle of May 1885. Instead of making expeditious tracks for south of the territorial border, as anticipated, the bronco Apache straightaway raced for camouflage in one of their most favored haunts, New Mexico Territory's mountains—the ruggedly wild and relatively modestly explored Mogollons and the Black Range.

From his base in Arizona Territory, General George Crook made the breakout known to his counterparts in New Mexico Territory and, in turn, the civilian population of old Grant County. He messaged Fort Bayard:

> About 50 Apaches under Geronimo are reported to have left reservation near Fort Apache about dark last night and are thought to be making for Mexico. Troops from [Fort] Thomas, [Camp] Grant, [Fort] Bowie, and [Fort] Huachuca are out endeavoring to intercept them. Would it not be well to send out a detachment from your post to their usual point of crossing the border?[840]

In roughly 18 hours the fleeing Indians managed 95 miles and temporary sanctuary in the Mogollons.[841] On the way they killed the Lutter [Luther] brothers, George and Chris, as well as ranchman Jim Montgomery and another fellow named Smith, acquiring horses, guns and ammunition.[842] Never a very popular personality, even within Indian ranks, Geronimo found himself embroiled in bitter dissension with other

White Mountain Apache scouts: Sergeant Jim [left], Bonito [seated], and a "Renegade Negro." *A Ben Wittick photo, courtesy New Mexico History Museum, #102053.*

Apache. The acrimony fractured any chance at harmony, and the renegades split into fragmented subgroups, each going its separate way. Disgustedly yet dangerously, Geronimo's band began snaking toward the border with Old Mexico; Chihuahua and a few others opted to stay affixed to the Mogollon country.[843]

Hard-riding after the Apache were Captain Allen Smith and Lieutenant James Parker, 4th Cavalry, with Companies A and K. For awhile this force was supplemented by Lieutenant Britton Davis and his contingent of Apache Scouts, but they soon returned to Fort Apache to recruit and enlist additional scouts; it was going to be a long campaign, as the Mogollons were exceptionally rugged. Remaining with Captain Smith, however, was the near-legendary Lieutenant Charles B. Gatewood and his 12-man squad of loyal White Mountain Apache auxiliaries.

About 10 miles north of Alma, New Mexico Territory, on Devil's Creek, the hunters became the hunted. While taking a welcome break, stretching aching limbs and restoring circulation to chafed backsides, the dismounted soldiers were fired on by Chihuahua's secreted fighters. Steep 600-foot bluffs overlooking the creek offered the Apache an advantage. Unrelentingly they pelted the pinned-down cavalrymen with bullets, killing two horses and wounding Privates Haag and Williams, plus an Apache Scout. Finally, Gatewood and Parker led an assault on the Indians' concealed positions. They were successful—in a way. Chihuahua and his practiced boys—in approved Apache style—simply slithered away unmolested.[844]

The chronology may be somewhat awry, but according to Jim Cook,

The legendary leader of Apache Scouts, Lt. Charles Gatewood, 6th Cavalry [right], with M.F. Goodwin, 9th Cavalry [left], at Fort Bayard near Silver City. *Courtesy Arizona Historical Society, #19615.*

manager of the WS Ranch near Alma, the Apache also killed Nat Luse and Calvin Orwig before other members of their party hightailed it for safe ground.[845] By all accounts Geronimo was heading for Old Mexico with his ragtag band, but Chihuahua was raising pure hell in old Grant County, killing "a number of whites within three miles of Silver City."[846] At least one news rendering set the number of the Apache's victims at 24 between the settlement of Alma and the town of Silver City.[847] Antagonism toward the Apache was further incited and Silver City's resentments stirred after learning of another depredation:

> SILVER CITY (N.M.), May 28—Some particulars of the killing done by Geronimo's band near Silver City are learned....The family consisted of Phillips, wife and two children, aged three and five years. This morning Geronimo's band attacked him and his family, killing the entire family excepting the oldest child, a girl, whom they hanged on a meat-hook. The hook entered the back portion of her head, in which position she was found, still alive, by a rescuing posse of citizens and brought to Silver City, but only lived a few hours. The citizens think this is pretty rough, occurring within sight of a 10-company military post, and at present departmental headquarters.[848]

Sometimes contemporary nonfiction Old West writers, in an understandable climate of sociologically obliged political correctness, tend to look askew at reports of such an atrocity. Old-timers writing of those early days were not so mincing of their words. Jim Cook noted in his autobiography: "...the Indians killed a number of persons within three miles of both Fort Bayard and Silver City. Sixteen in all, I believe, was the number murdered by the Apaches between Devil's Park and Fort Bayard upon that occasion, several of them being women and children. One or two of the children were tortured to death by being hung up on spikes outside their houses."[849] The following rendition of the above cited killings given by Wayne Whitehill, an on-site teenage witness, must stand or fall on its own merit:

> Well, I was down here on the street right across from, oh, just about where that Masonic building is, I was right along there one morning, one day, it was that morning. There was a Mexican come running right down the street. I knew him well, he's got some children down there in Columbus [New Mexico] now. Old, what was his name now? He was coming running down and had a little rifle in his hand like this. I run out and I could see he was all excited and then with this gun I went out. He stopped and all he could say was Indios, Indios, Indios, Indios, Indios. And so people began to gather around seeing him there with a gun there began to think that he'd killed somebody or some sort and so people came over there to see what it was all about and I said he said it was Indians, Indians. [Whitehill acknowledged he could speak Spanish.] Oh, sure. And so they began to scatter, people did, and there was express wagons around to deliver with, horses and mules them stores, and they began to unhitch these horses and get on them. They went in the hardware store, you know, and got guns and first thing you know here the whole town [Silver City] was going out. Ya and I was right in the gang. Of course I was afoot, me and a whole bunch of kids, a lot of kids. And we got out there and here was all these people that lived in one little house. There was a little child about two or three years old and there was big meat hook, a big old iron meat hook, and this little child was hooked right on that hook like that. It was dead. And the mother of that child, oh, that was the father that come to town, the father of this little girl. He had six or seven

> children, old Reyes Rascon his name was. And all around there they had little shacks, used to be a little spring out there and it's still there yet just below where you used to live up there...[about four miles from Silver City]. Right in there was where they was killed. One Mexican was hobbling around there. He was shot right through the hips here.... He was still alive. But there was 14 of them, women and children, I forget how many men, but there was 14 counting all the children. Well, they hitched up wagons there and put these bodies in and took them to town. Over on Chihuahua Hill there used to be a big old adobe house and they took them all over there and laid them out and so this old girl, what was her name now? [Silver City whorehouse madam Bessie Harper]....Bessie Harper, ya. Well, she went in there and dressed all these bodies and bought clothes and fixed them all up and paid the whole funeral expenses to bury these people. [in response to an assertion that 22 people were killed during this Apache outbreak]...Well there was 14, 14 of them right there. Oh, they killed a lot of people all around here that time.[850]

An impartial reader must not be fooled. Apache undoubtedly were not disinclined to torture or kill their prisoners, man or woman, young or old. But apparently Grant County folks, at least some of them, were sometimes fully capable of less than inspiring deeds, too! A blurb in the *Silver City Enterprise* is insightful: "The Indian papoose captured in Doubtful Canon, was raffled off at Lordsburg. This is the first red kid that we ever heard of being worth raffling for."[851] Clearly, Silver City citizens were embittered. Many actually thought "the military are doing nothing."[852] In fact, it's been written that a not insignificant number of Grant County people simply had no use for soldiers whatsoever, not even showing them the common courtesy of calling them by name: "People hated them so bad."[853] Reciprocally, a few military men vehemently rebuffed allegations of inaction, but did blame a panicked and hyperventilated civilian populace for instigating "wild goose chases." One US Army officer, Lieutenant Charles P. Elliott, was not reticent about his feelings:

> My duty while waiting at Deming was to collect and forward to General Crook all information possible about the

> movements of the Indians, especially that gathered from the employees of the two railroads running into Deming. The shameless lies told by some of the employees, who would go into the most minute details about seeing a band of Indians breaking camp and moving south, caused me to ride many useless miles in the hot sun and to learn by experience that residence in New Mexico and Arizona, if too prolonged, produces the champion breed of liars. Lack of veracity on the part of the civilians in reporting movements of Indians was frequently the cause of unnecessary loss of life among themselves, by causing the troops to go on a fruitless search in the wrong direction for Indians raiding and killing elsewhere. In a sparsely settled country with few railroads, few roads, high and very rough mountains, with water long distances apart, information was hard to obtain, and when wrongly given, many weary miles were necessary to discover the error.[854]

Whilst Lieutenant Elliot may have proffered a reasonable-sounding argument, a salient detail was not lost on that "champion breed of liars" in Silver City: Geronimo and other Apache scooted south, right past the Southern Pacific's railroad tracks—almost under the lieutenant's nose—and scampered straight across the border, once again taking refuge in Old Mexico's formidably inaccessible Sierra Madres. From the best evidence, it seems that the soldiers "seldom" even got a "glimpse" of the wayward Apache, but possibly they did see dead bodies of at least 17 civilians—perhaps more—or part of the 150 horses and mules "worn out and killed or abandoned" during the raid before the Apache bid old Grant County a short-lived adieu.[855]

History unfolds not in vacuity, so while Apache were screening themselves from the US Army's relentless pursuit in Old Mexico, everyday life—and death—went on in Silver City. There was so much public interest in races held at the skating rink that the *Southwest Sentinel* printed results and placement of finishers under bold type banner headlines—more than once.[856] A New York songstress, Miss Jennings, was performing at the Exchange; the hotel and saloon men were doing a "rushing" business. The Ladies Hospital Aid Society was routinely meeting and settling financial accounts. All were invited to a Sunday evening concert at the Methodist

Church. Silver City's mayor was proposing that businesses houses be shut down on the day of General Grant's funeral. And the Grant County administrators were not nearly as saddened by the death of William Reed, "a well known character" and "a dependent on the county."[857]

Hardly had Grant County folks settled down for a few months of calm before some other "well known characters" were back for some September work. Reportedly a "band of seven bucks [20 by other accounts] and 11 squaws" were driven out of Old Mexico's mountains by Lieutenant Britton Davis and his squadron of Apache Scouts. Regardless of the reason, the hostile and hell-bent Apache crossed somewhere between Deming and El Paso and were now in old Grant County. Once again General George Crook was put in the uncomfortable position of cautioning the citizens of "Clifton, Silver City and Duncan" to constantly be on the watch, for "they are liable to come in on them when least expected."[858] Near Lake Valley the Apache killed Brady Pollock, a cattleman. In the vicinity of sleepy San Lorenzo they ambushed Avaristo Abeyta, who was in the act of "cutting poles." Then on the Mimbres they attacked George Horn and his companions, the young sons of John McKinn, Martin and Jimmy. Horn died, as did 16-year-old Martin, "his head split open" and his body mutilated.[859] Adolescent Jimmy was captured:

> There are no tidings yet of the 12-year-old son of John McKin[n], carried off by the Indians at the time they killed the elder brother and George Horn, on the Mimbres. His father is strong in the belief that the boy is with the Indians and well cared for. His mother is a Mexican and he talks the language fluently, and as the Indians talk Mexican well, he will have no difficulty in getting along, and as he is so young the Indians will try to rear him as one of their own. Soldiers and citizens on the trail of the Indians are warned to watch out for the boy as he is liable to turn up almost any day.[860]

Whether or not it's actually the case, Geronimo is generally credited with leading the raid and capturing Jimmy McKinn, whom the Indians later referred to by his Spanish-translated first name, Santiago. Running hard and heading south, the Apache near Deming "attacked a frame store, looted it of flour, sugar, molasses and bacon, and then left the building in flames." Before crossing the border they killed a hapless and

Jimmy [Santiago] McKinn, Apache captive [front and center], taken from Mimbres River area during 1885; his teenage brother was killed. Later liberated by General George Crook. *A C.S. Fly photo, courtesy New Mexico History Museum, #11649.*

alone teamster. Then they skipped across the line and, for the moment, made good their getaway to Old Mexico—where the process of Indianizing an adaptable Jimmy McKinn began.[861]

Apparently emboldened by this scorching September foray, in early November 1885 "came a slashing raid that rivaled the greatest such adventures in Apache history."[862] Approximately a dozen warriors under the loose leadership of Josaine [Ulzana], a brother of Chihuahua, united with a band of 16 Apache already north of the borderline. Secreting themselves in the Florida Mountains near Deming, the renegades staged a number of risky raids, killing several unwary New Mexicans.[863] Two that barely escaped were the highly regarded New Mexico Territory lawman, Dan Tucker, and his partner in some speculative mining business, William Graham. The ill-equipped pair were poking around 11 miles east of Deming.[864] A contemporary Silver City newspaper account told the brisk little story, an almost-tragedy:

> Dan Tucker, formerly deputy sheriff here, and a partner were prospecting last Tuesday a few miles from Deming, near Zuni siding, when a small party of Indians suddenly came on them. Tucker and his part-

> ner had no arms except six-shooters, and they were driving a buggy or buckboard. They drove as hard as they could until they came to the siding, where a box-car was standing, into which they climbed. The Indians kept them there for some time, riding around the car, but keeping carefully out of shot. Seeing that they would be unable to do their intended victims any harm so long as they chose to remain in the car, they finally rode off, and Tucker and his companion made their escape to Deming.[865]

Josanie's renegades split into two elusive bands. The Apache stealthily appropriated and assaulted and assassinated in both Arizona and New Mexico Territories. Near present-day Pleasanton—north of Silver City—Josanie and nine warriors hid themselves along Little Dry Creek. Chasing around the Mogollons had been Lieutenant Samuel Warren Fountain, in command of Company C, 8th Cavalry. Near Alma, the fatigued officer opted to take the road to Fort Bayard for a quick layover to replenish supplies and rest his worn-down men and used-up government horses. Nearing Little Dry Creek, Fountain's 10 Navajo scouts either sensed impending trouble or scampered at the first shot. Regardless, they disappeared abruptly! Not so lucky were Privates Wishart and Gibson, who died outright during the initial volley. Apache bullets also wounded Corporal McFarland and Assistant Surgeon Thomas J. C. Maddox. The next hellfire killed the company's blacksmith [Collins] and knocked Lieutenant DeRosey C. Cabell out of his standard-issue McClellan saddle, wounded but not fatally. Most unluckily the good Dr. Maddox caught a second round, this time to the head, and he give up the ghost. Suddenly but belatedly, the Navajo scouts "reappeared and pushed the Apaches off the ridge."[866] Josanie's fighters simply melted into mountain shadows, heading south for the border, no doubt. The score was Apache, zero casualties; soldiers, five killed and two wounded.[867]

Taking a cue from old Nana, during a blistering four-week raid Josanie and his gang had blanketed southeastern Arizona Territory and southwestern New Mexico Territory with terror. They had covered upwards of 1,200 meandering miles, killed approximately 38 persons, and had "stolen and worn out 250 horses—all with the loss of only one man."[868] And then, not surprisingly, Josanie and his haggard renegades made good their escape to Old Mexico.

In Silver City, townsmen provisionally shelved their concerns about defiant Apache and redirected it elsewhere. Regrettably, the behavior of many was less than admirable. The cesspool of racial insensitivity mired some of Silver City's most elite old-timers in the swamp of stinky bigotry. The near-insatiable demand for colossal numbers of cheap laborers once needed for breakneck railroad construction had evaporated. Many Chinese immigrants liberally imported for those projects found themselves without meaningful or profitable work. The majority, so it seems, were not yet ready to return to their homeland and, resultantly, countless Chinese workers fanned out through America's West looking for employment or business opportunity. "In the process of dispersion within the country there was a great influx of Chinese into Silver City. During this time Silver City was a great mining district, therefore creating employment for the Celestials."[869]

Throughout the United States the laboring classes of Irish and German immigrants howled that they were being robbed of jobs by such an incursion of people willing to work for next to nothing, 75 cents to $1 per day. Voices representing trade unions were loudly prattling that soon Americans would be laboring only in the "kitchens or restaurants." Something had to be done about the "yellow scourge" and by damn, it had to be done right fast.[870] Pliant politicians in Washington, DC, feeling the nudge during an 1882 legislative session, had passed the National Restriction Act [also called the Chinese Exclusion Act], which banned the future immigration of Chinese workers.[871] For those already in country—in most cases—there was not the belly-burning desire to carve a notch of permanency in the United States, but only to make enough money in three to 10 years by frugally saving wages, then returning to China well-fixed for living the good life. Therein lay the rub. Hard currency was being exported, not circulated. Particularly in Silver City there were not—in reality—all that many Chinese, perhaps, only 1.5 percent of the population, say, about 35 people.[872] Sadly, in other places throughout the West the discriminatory pressure was on, and several groups of Chinese fleeing one locale hopped to another hoping things would be better, but they weren't:

> Several Chinamen arrived in this city [Silver City] during the past week [November 1885] from Socorro. It is getting too warm for them there. There has been more or less talk here about running them out of town.[873]

And in that very same edition of the *Silver City Enterprise*:

> It is estimated that the Chinamen of this city [Silver City] ship to their friends in the flowery kingdom about $3,000 per month. If white men were employed in their places all this money would be in circulation.[874]

Everything, apparently, was just fine as long as the Southwest's overall economy was booming and the bankers were banking. But when a spiraling economic downturn during the 1880s was felt in Anglo pocketbooks, the scapegoating began. A substantial number of Silver City folks were not inclined to buck popular opinion. They willingly jumped headlong into the bottomless pit of prejudice and persecution:

> There will be a meeting of citizens on Tuesday evening at Crown Hall for the purpose of taking into consideration the advisability of ordering the Chinese population to remove [get out of Silver City], for the following reasons: first, they monopolize work that our needy populations desires; second, they have paid but $12 into the treasury as city taxes during the year, and shipped through known sources during the past year $150,000 out of the county; third, they are no benefit to our merchants, importing in the main their food and clothing from China; fourth, they breed pestilence by their filthy habits and their opium dens, and are a source of ruination to the young of both sexes of all races; lastly, the work they do can be accomplished by our own people in a manner satisfactory to all interested.[875]

The meeting was well attended. The gathering's purpose was not fuzzy: "...the advisability of earnestly requesting the Chinese residents to leave the city."[876] The three-pronged upshot of the town hall meeting was extraordinarily simple. Resolutions were argued about, then approved. All Chinese residents living inside Silver City's municipal limits as renters must declare that they had become United States citizens or intended to do so; otherwise they must leave town within 24 hours. Those holding property of a value exceeding $1,000 were allowed 30 days per each $1,000 valuation before they would be forced to comply with the removal order, a thinly camouflaged measure allowing "whites" sufficient time to finance their acquisitions of Chinese-held property and businesses. Lastly, to ensure compliance, the Committee of Ten was formed—its membership roster another veritable who's who of the town's movers and shakers.[877] A supplemental rationale of the Committee of Ten was to guarantee acts of physical aggression would not be aimed at the Chinese population during the expulsion process. Much to his credit, the then Grant County sheriff, Jim Woods, stepped up and in no uncertain terms echoed his no-nonsense sentiment: Any violence would beget a fast trip to the calaboose. Although not adopted as a formal resolution, nonetheless, it was also affirmed that all Chinese-owned businesses should and would be boycotted.[878] Let the reader not be fooled, not everyone in town or at the meeting was in favor of forcing the Chinese from town, and at times the meeting had been fractious. Afterwards a blistering string of pro and anti letters was printed in several local newspapers. The Chinese, well, most couldn't read English, but they did sense the hurtful pinch.

Soon, the tactic of shying away from Chinese businesses began to have its desired outcome:

> The Chinese agitation which has been going on in this city has influenced public opinion in some respects to a considerable degree. One of the ways in which this is shown is the loss of patronage suffered by the Chinese restaurants. Most of them have lost nearly all their customers. In consequence the restaurants conducted by white people have sustained large increases of business.[879]

Seemingly the anti-Chinese movement in Silver City was nonviolent, although such could not be said for other parts of the country: In Rock Springs, Wyo., perhaps as many as 38 persons were slain and 15 wounded during a racially ignited spate of catastrophe.[880] In Silver City many Chinese rushed to the courthouse to began the process of becoming naturalized citizens of the United States. Many, after filing the appropriate applications, then enrolled in private English classes being taught by the local Methodist minister, Reverend Coates.[881] The assimilation progression of Chinese immigrants was well under way and hard-core feelings against them began to sputter and fizzle.

Not unexpectedly, awareness quickly focused instead on a reoccurring nightmare: Apache! Harvey Whitehill and his partner in a ranching enterprise, Homer Tarbell, sold a herd of cattle to stockman John

Brockman. The beeves were free roaming and grazing the open-range pastures in the Upper Gila country. The sale necessitated a cattle gathering, counting and delivery. Homer Tarbell bossed the cowboys, which included Whitehill's sons, Harry and Wayne, along with Tarbell's 17-year-old nephew, Ethel Harris. Del Hudson, the Whitehill brothers and other cowboys would sweep the surrounding countryside, pushing cattle inward while Tarbell and Harris loose-herded them toward the Middle Fork of the Gila. Little did the unsuspecting cowmen know it at the time, but nearby Apache had already killed two upper-country ranchmen [Lilly and Prior] and two freighters [Kinney and Clark]. The next installment of murder and mayhem was just another chapter in the same old well-worn story:

> Harris was riding on one side of the cattle they were driving and Tarbell on the other, and at the first fire Harris was struck twice. Tarbell saw him throw up his hands, first to his head then to his breast and as the latter dashed off to escape the flying bullets he saw the poor boy fall from his horse. Tarbell escaped by jumping his horse over a bluff near by and thinks the cattle, which were between him and the Indians, saved him. Getting out of range beneath the bluff, Tarbell hastened down the gulch to Papinaw's cabin, about a mile distant.[882]

The community mourned. Ethel Harris had been the sole support for his widowed mother. Like so very many before her in southwestern New Mexico Territory, she was "distracted with grief over the loss of her son."[883] During this raid, which lasted a little over a week, the Apache had killed five Grant County folks before evaporating into the chasms of elusiveness.

Life is for the living, however. As the year wound down, hopeful spirits celebrated the 1885 Christmas holiday season in fine fashion. Fancy meats "rolling in fat and in prime condition" were displayed at the hometown markets; local merchants furnished patients at the Ladies Hospital with a sumptuous Christmas dinner, consisting of oysters, turkey, pork roast, sausage, fresh fruits, savory and sweet herbs, fine cakes and pastry and, maybe best of all, bottles of "light wines." For dance-minded celebrants, the floors were "well waxed" and parties were held in Georgetown and Silver City, with many Deming folks taking in the sights, too.[884]

Old Saint Nick might have visited the little children of Silver City, but clearly some of the older Grant County crowd had giving gifts of a different stripe on their uneasy minds. Hardly had the new year began before the Southwestern Stock Association met at the Timmer House. The meeting was well attended by area cowmen. The hot topic for mutually agreed discussion was the outlandish frequency of Apache raids on their vulnerably exposed cattle ranges. Cows and dollars were synonymous. Israel King chaired the meeting, with J. A. Moses acting as secretary. The attendees adopted a resolution naming a five-member committee to select one of their fellow members for a trip to Washington, DC. There, he was to lay at the doorsteps of the Secretary of War and the Secretary of Interior their concerns regarding "the true state of Indian troubles, and ask that they take immediate actions ridding our sorely afflicted people from the hostile Apache Indians at present devastating our country, killing our unprotected people and destroying our property." Ranchman G.G. Posey was selected, declaring he would do everything in his power to make the president and his cabinet aware of the untenable Apache troubles constantly brewing and spewing in southwestern New Mexico Territory. A subgroup was appointed to "gather data in regard to every person killed, loss of stock, and depredation of all kinds committed by marauding Apaches at present devastating" portions of old Grant County. The outraged cattlemen, through their association, further pledged a $250 bounty for Apache scalps. Carrying that proposal a step further, Tom Cobb offered $50 as an "extra inducement" for the first scalp brought in and the LCs Ranch's owners [Lyons and Campbell] pledged $300 specifically for the bloody topknot of Geronimo.[885] Flexing political muscle, the assembled cattleman urged the Grant County Commissioners to action:

> Resolved. That it is the sense of the taxpayers of Grant county that the county commissioners be requested to appropriate $250 per head as a reward for each and every hostile Apache Indian killed by citizens. This reward not to extend to soldiers of the U.S. Army.[886]

The meeting adjourned on a sanguine note: "So scalp hunting, if at all successful, is very profitable." The Grant County commissioners, in due time, accepted the cattlemen's challenge and did their part:

> **$250 Reward**
>
> The above reward will be paid by the Board of County Commissioners of Grant county to any citizen of said

> county for each and every hostile, renegade Apache killed by such citizen, on presentation to said board of the scalp of such Indian. By order of the board.
> E. Stine, Clerk[887]

There is no hard evidence to support an assertion that any Grant County scalp-hunters actually collected a dime. "Undoubtedly, in the final analysis, posting of a bounty for Apache scalps was much more an act of symbolism than a genuine solution."[888]

Journalistically recapturing the final days of Geronimo's rambling about is not requisite for telling the rest of Silver City's territorial story. Others have accomplished that task in magnificent fashion. Simply it may be said the intractable old Apache warrior finally capitulated to the US Army's and General George Crook's demands.

One sidebar relating to Geronimo's surrender has a Silver City twist, however. During the negotiations especial notice was paid to one youngster: "Wildest in the rough sports of the bronco boys was one figure which you would single out at a glance." The child, "scaly with dirt, wild as a coyote," was none other than the now "absolutely Indianized" Jimmy McKinn. When told that he would be reunited with his parents, pathetically Jimmy began "boo-hooing with great vigor." Acting like a "young wild animal in a trap," Jimmy spurned any inducements and was, in the end, forcefully placed in a wagon for the return trip to New Mexican "civilization."[889] In Deming the liberated McKinn was reintroduced to his father. Father and son took the train to Silver City. Upon arrival they were greeted by a large crowd of well-wishers and curious citizens, imparting the impression to Jimmy that he was now a celebrity. Jimmy's newfound status was not ill-founded; the *Silver City Enterprise* was mentioning him as "the lion of the hour." And not just a few Grant County folks were cogitating about the possibility of using Jimmy as a witness in a criminal trial for Geronimo. After all, he had personally watched his brother's murder and mutilation by Apache. The senior McKinn quickly hustled his son aboard a stagecoach and the pair headed for their home on the Mimbres and relative obscurity from prying eyes or a newspaperman's questioning.[890]

Debating today whether or not Geronimo was treacherously bamboozled into giving in is interesting, but wasteful. On the other hand, acknowledging that an assemblage of reasonably loyal Apache Scouts was

General George Crook, flanked on the left by Dutchy and on the right by Alchesay. *Courtesy Robert G. McCubbin.*

hoodwinked is not arguable. One and all they were imprisoned and forced to take the long railroad ride to banishment—first in Florida, then to Oklahoma's Indian Territory.

For the most part Geronimo's removal from the Southwest ended Grant County's incessant warfare with Apache. To say, however, that all bronco Apache volunteered for leg-irons and subjugation is historically fraudulent—provably, too! Deep within the Old Mexico's Sierra Madres, disillusioned hold-out Apache yet lurked. "Yes, the life—the free roving life of Apache raiders—would continue on in these mountain redoubts. They would never be tamed. They swore they would never wear the white man's number. They would never accept a white man's name. They would never change—they would never surrender."[891]

Just how wild and woolly old Grant County's Bootheel section was [and is] may be more fully recognized after learning that well into the 20th century renegade Apache were still making cross-border horse-stealing raids and committing murder in the isolated border country of New Mexico.[892] On one such 1924 raid they caught Frank Fisher, "a cowboy and part-time prospector," alone and poking about in southwestern New Mexico's Big Hatchet mountains. "Quickly and callously they shot him to death, took his mule, gun and provisions and eased north through the 5,500 foot San Luis Pass into the Animas Mountains of New Mexico."[893]

Apache shenanigans aside, there was yet plenty of time left for Silver City and old Grant County to cut more marks onto their notch-sticks of pistol plays and hemp-rope doings. Undeniably, though, even if ever so very slowly, southwestern New Mexico Territory—especially Silver City—was maturing into a community of modern refinement and updated enlightenment.

Chapter 14
"Notoriety for Shooting and Shooting Scrapes"

Searching for little historic nuggets to bolster the fact that Silver City was still a lively frontier town even in the latter third of the 1880s is not intensive labor. Take the case of the constable for precinct number three, J.A. Buquor. During a night of merriment he tumbled or was thrown from a box seat in the Gem Theater's balcony. The sudden impact with the floor stunned the lawman so much it was several days before he could "understand or speak." As his health steadily improved, though, it was Buquor's passionate desire to make darn certain the *Silver City Enterprise* duly noted that he emphatically was "not drunk at the time."[894]

Another area peace officer was not so lucky. Thomas Hall, the steadfast Grant County deputy assigned to Pinos Altos, who was also commissioned a deputy United States marshal, had been ordered by Sheriff Jim Woods to investigate the murder of Aguilar Santiago. The courageous Santiago had been callously gunned down while defending a 15-year-old girl, Reyes Alverez, from being abducted by a group of "Mexicans." The outlaws—by at least one account—whilst firing 14 shots at Reyes' distraught mother, inadvertently killed Reyes' younger brother.[895] During the grueling course of deputy Tom Hall's prowling around, he came upon the bloodthirsty kidnapers and the cowering victim traveling the winding road between Pinos Altos and Silver City. Reyes didn't cry out, fearing calamity. Not wishing to tip his hand, Hall rode along with the group, making "small talk" while awaiting his chance to make arrests. Badman Pilar Perez, wise to the lawman's game, bumped his reins, slightly checking his horse's forward movement. With gendarme Hall now in front of him, Perez jerked out his Colt's six-shooter and heartlessly hammered two bullets into the unsuspecting deputy's back and arm. Hall tumbled from the stock-saddle. The owl-hoots rode on. Tom Hall lay in the dirt, breathing his last. By 2 a.m. the "brave and valiant officer," a married father of five children, was dead.[896]

Reyes Alverez, according to most reports, managed to get away when the shooting started, and was the next day located at the home of a Mrs. Fessler in Silver City. Traumatized, the young girl had remained mum about what had actually happened out of worry the killer would return and take her life. Upon proficient quizzing, though, she did finally identify Perez as the shooter. An impaneled coroner's jury could not find holes in her story, and the manhunt was on for Perez. Although many unsolved crimes were laid at his doorstep, Perez was not to be found—for the time being.[897] The killer had simply taken a cue from the Apache and evaporated.

The "Gay '90s" may have been fast approaching, but in old Grant County it was yet still—from time to time—a wild and woolly frontier theater. The four-horse Georgetown stagecoach was stopped by masked bandits; the driver was shot, the passengers were robbed, and the Wells, Fargo & Company's strongbox was taken. Deputy Sheriff Pete Spence, a man with a more than dubious reputation throughout the Southwest, led a posse after the hijackers for four days, but came up with naught.[898] In the Upper Gila country a stockman named Forbes was gunned down, along with ranchman Frank Hill. It was generally believed that "desperadoes were hired to do the killing that a cattle company might get the ranches."[899] And, as befitting any stylish Western badman, James McLaughlin—wanted for murder—rode through Grant County heading straight south for Old Mexico appropriately decked out: "His person was adorned by two ivory-handled 45's, while a repeating rifle swung in its scabbard on his saddle. Mounted on a magnificent horse and thus armed he rode out."[900] Yes, southwestern New Mexico Territory was the emblematic Old West—at its very best and at its very worst!

All through the territory Silver City's progressive evolution was being noticed, however. Some less-imaginative communities seemed to effectively screen their green-eyed jealously and own up to reality. On the heels of a Silver City tax hike, the *Las Cruces Republican* said publicly what so very many were well aware of:

> Silver City has carried the special school tax measure by an overwhelming majority, and has thereby covered itself with that peculiar glory which belongs to true

> progress and civilization. Wisdom has uttered her voice and her proclamation has gone forth to all the inhabitants of earth that a town, city, state or nation that wishes to be civilized, enlightened and socially happy must be willing to pay special taxes. We may not generally be aware of the fact, but it is nevertheless true that the social condition of human life in this world is largely a question of taxes. Civilization and taxes are a sign of a well ordered social state in which to raise a family.... It is the inevitable law of human life that those who want the conveniences, immunities and advantages of well organized social surrounds must consent to pay the cost. Let every town in New Mexico follow the example of Silver City and then we shall not be ashamed to say to all the world that New Mexico is a good place to move to.[901]

Clearly times were a-changing. Entertainment-minded folks were more than pleasantly enthralled with prospects of a Professor LeRoy's upcoming show. The "athletic looking young gentleman" was going to make a hot-air balloon ascension and then, according to the plan, jump out of the contraption wearing a parachute. When asked about the danger, the foolhardy "Professor" declared: "I fully realize the danger in my business, but at the same time, there is danger in every walk of life. Why! Do you know I wouldn't couple a [train] car for any money. There are thousands of railroaders killed every year, and yet people become so accustomed to it that they think nothing of it." The daredevil naturally goaded the *Silver City Enterprise* reporter to make the plunge, proclaiming that the sensation would be akin to dreaming one was falling over a cliff and then waking up in cold perspiration—which would "tend to enhance the sensation." Not unexpectedly, the newspaperman declined.

Other Silver City folks were planning on attending the Stetson Dramatic Company's performance at John B. Morrill's Opera House. For those people wanting to witness the sideshow of humanity, Silver City was a fit place to be. There was—within a 10-day period—a Mexican Circus; Stanselle's Miracle Works, featuring a blind man with an organ and a female tambourine accompanists; a band of Gypsies with a dancing bear and a money-grabbing long-tailed monkey; New Mexico's champion wrestler from Pinos Altos, James McClain, challenging all comers to the "best two out of three falls" for $200; and, for the bigger and naughtier boys, the "upper crust of the *demimondaines* entertained their gentlemen friends at a masked ball and it proved to be a recherché affair with everyone in attendance having a cat and monkey time of it." Speaking in a clear voice about the cross-section of available Silver City amusements, a contemporary journalist simply said: "You paid your money and took your choice."[902]

Somebody who didn't have a choice was Pilar Perez. The desperate murderer of Deputy Tom Hall was finally located by one of newly installed Grant County Sheriff Andrew "Andy" Laird's informants. The fugitive was working on a sheep ranch near Flagstaff, Arizona Territory. Using a Mexican *baile* as a ruse for luring Perez to town, Arizona lawmen were successful with their trickery and locked up the brigand. Perez never denied his true identity, claiming that he didn't kidnap Reyes Alverez, but had won her over to love, and it was Tom Hall who had fired first, forcing him to kill the deputy out of self-defense. Arizona authorities didn't believe him then, nor did the Grant County trial jury when they heard the case after his handcuffed return to Silver City. They deliberated but "a few minutes." The execution, Grant County's fifth legally sanctioned hanging, took place on July 6, 1888, before a crowd of 60 "invited" guests. In a classic understatement it was penned: "...there was not a single expression of sympathy.... It was evident that the murderer had no real friends among the spectators." Pilar Perez's neck was broken by the drop. The law was "vindicated" and the death of Tom Hall was "avenged."[903]

With Perez's body cut down and irreverently interred, attention quickly focused on an upcoming event. It was to prove a real scorcher—a horse vs. bicycle race. The main purse was $2,500; the side bets were unknown and maybe incalculable. The two contestants leaving from Silver City's Timmer House were to make the 49-mile mad dash to Deming's Harvey House Hotel at the depot, winner take all. On Sept. 13, 1888, the crowd gathered: "The band was playing, the flags waving and excitement, as well as the odor of booze and beer, oozed from every pore." Unexpectedly, Cipriano Baca rode up on a scrub-looking Pinto cowpony and asked to join in, just for fun! Baca, Jeff W. Clayton and his racehorse Rattler, and H. J. Kennedy, representing the Ramblers Bicycle Club from Denver, Colo., anxiously fidgeted at the starting line. A Colt's hammer fell, the starter's gun sounded and the race was on. Three hours and 45 minutes later, before throngs of cheering spectators in Deming, late entrant Cipriano Baca took the first-place ribbon; Clayton was awarded the second-place prize [and the purse]; and a near-exhausted Kennedy, riding a bicycle with a wobbling six-foot-high front wheel, took third. Money changed hands and a grand time was had by all.[904]

Aside from sparks of pure fun, real doings—permanent and positive—were taking place at Grant County's shiretown. Earlier an agreement had been struck with George H. Utter to establish a workable waterworks for Silver City. The 50-year contract called for construction of a reservoir above town and a complicated spider-web system of pipe delivery. Residential and business customers were to be charged for their use of tap water, but churches, schools and city offices were exempt from the levy. Somewhat unusual, the impressive waterworks building on Little Walnut

The Silver City Waterworks [constructed with stone rather than brick] on Little Walnut Road. *Courtesy Silver City Public Library.*

Road was constructed of native stone rather than Silver City's symbolic red brick. "Water was pumped from a 60-foot well on the premises to a reservoir on the hilltop just east of the waterworks, and from there it was piped into town. The engineer of the plant resided with his family at the waterworks."[905] After a demonstration at the courthouse, where a stream of water was sprayed over the building's roof, signifying sufficient pressure for fighting a fire, Silver City's town council called it a done deal.[906] Down the road at Lordsburg the city "hose company" put on a sham firefighting show for an insurance company representative, who duly noted that the "waterworks threw as effective a stream as did the Silver City waterworks." Mr. Warren, the insurance man, pledged he would make a favorable report to the underwriters, guaranteeing that Lordsburg folks would have their "rates lowered."[907]

In Silver City the uncertainty of water was always an acute problem; there was either not enough of it, or too much. The summer of 1889 was an example of the latter. It rained and it rained—then rained some more. The torrential Sunday downpour and resultant runoff did considerable damage. William Lawson's house was washed away. A horticulturist, Mr. Allen, had his entire vineyard destroyed, along with 1,500 fruit trees and a barn. Jeff Christian's place on Bear Creek was completely swept away. Downtown, with the floods commencing, O.C. Hinman decided to sell furniture at "COST and just a little more" to avoid financial catastrophe. At Silver City's Episcopal Church the Sunday evening services were suspended, the soggy congregation prevented from attending by the rising flood waters. John Coleman's house three miles east of town was "badly washed out" by the Sunday night flood, too.[908] It was a damn mess! It was also a damn perennial event! Ever so slowly, Main Street was visibly washing away.

Apart from the flood Silver City was undergoing a few changes. The historic little log cabin once home to the Antrims was being fixed up and converted into a "boot and shoe making establishment." Pure ice cream could be had at the Vienna Bakery. A new saloon, the Monarch, was promising nothing but the "best wines and liquors." An earnest temperance movement was getting under way in nearby Georgetown, Thomas Philpin in charge. And, almost comically, Nettie Munger, "a lady with an unenviable reputation," insolently horsewhipped Jo E. Sheridan, a prominent Silver City businessman.[909]

Indisputably Silver City was the pulsating nerve center for southeastern Arizona and southwestern New Mexico Territories, but a plain truism must not be overlooked: Most of those hopeful early day pioneers put down roots in Silver City intending to remain. Therein was the phenomena that separated Silver City from so very many of the boom or bust towns in the American Southwest. The underpinnings of her foundation were strong. The rock-solid implication that all of those early day denizens stayed, however, is misnomer. For reasons purely economic or, perhaps, kinship reunifications, Fate's gentle hand nudged some few farther west, while others were quietly prodded back toward their eastern upbringing. For several, whatever the reason, that tempestuous Mistress of Fortune slapped hard, harshly sending some away against their will. Adroitly it's been written that Silver City's "least permanent element" was the people themselves.[910] Such an assertion is not erroneous. Circumstances dictate the rise and fall of population levels. Silver City's chance at durability may be traced to that early commitment to build with brick and to an unwavering pioneering spirit. The trail to permanency was straight, dead on! Not everyone left town, not even during the hard times. The trying 1890s would test their resolve and challenge their innovative sharpness.

As early as January 1890 a Silver City attorney, H. L. Pickett, was in Santa Fe. Ostensibly the chief reason for his visit was to argue a case before the Territorial Supreme Court, but he also was deftly paddling on the undercurrent sweeping through the legislative hallways. The sentiment for statehood was growing. Lawyer Pickett, a veteran advocate with previous experience in the Tennessee Legislature, was vocally haranguing about the lopsided advantages of admission to the Union: Capital and immigration would inevitably pour in; taxable property would increase considerably in amount and value; home rule would be obtained; and a state of New Mexico would have her own voice in the councils of national government.

In doing her share toward that end, Grant County could proudly boast of many upbeat achievements. There were within her confines 28 individual communities with public schools. Willing outside capitalists were still chafing at the bit to invest mining money. There was a viable railroad network. And Silver City, Georgetown, Deming, Lordsburg and other auspiciously enlightened southwestern New Mexico Territory towns were triumphantly hanging on, hammering out stability on a wild frontier.[911]

That "wild frontier" part was the thorny sticking point. During the very time-frame barrister Pickett was in Santa Fe vociferously clamoring for statehood, incarcerated behind bars in Silver City at the Grant County Jail were 13 inmates charged with murder.[912] Percentage-wise, for the county's population the ratio ideally should have been smaller. Luckily, at least for Grant County's sake, her 1890 violent crime statistics were not out of whack territory-wide. Overall, though, the numbers accounting for violently inclined inmates in New Mexico Territory for that year were noticeably higher than the United States' national average.[913] As Father Time marched forward, and as a generic taming of the old Southwest began taking place, not unexpectedly the statistical violent crime gap between New Mexico Territory and that of the previously admitted states narrowed. Even if it hadn't, however, many influential Easterners held a perception that west of the Pecos River in the New Mexico and Arizona country it was still as wild and woolly as ever. One Grant County episode heaped fuel on the fire of that outlook.

On the outskirts of Georgetown a "worthless character" and suspected horse-thief, Manuel Galindas, was fatally gunned down by a masked horde numbering near 20. The dead man was an ex-member of Pilar Perez's gang of cutthroats and stock-thieves. Rightly or wrongly it was vigilante justice. Officially empowered authorities did nothing, offering lame excuses that it would have "been impossible to raise a sufficient posse at night to capture an armed band of 20 or 25, and such an effort might have resulted in the loss of life." For a few of Grant County's fed-up folks the episode was simply an overdue case of "he got what he deserved."[914] But it was a happening that did not sell well with lawmakers intent on adding another number to the collection of "civilized" states. A newspaperman's commentary gave fodder both to those with an uncompromising lynch law mentality and to wary lawmakers legitimately questioning New Mexico's readiness for statehood:

> While the *Enterprise* does not endorse mob law, in this instance it did the right thing, and still has a fair field of labor before it. The Upper Mimbres country has long been headquarters for a band of desperate Mexican thieves and the sooner they are cleaned up the better. A little more of such effective work in others sections of the county would result beneficially to the community at large.[915]

Headlines of a slightly different nature did not bode well for statehood-minded folks: "Indians Out." Although it had been four years earlier that Geronimo had surrendered and was brashly whisked away, the occasional "jump" from the San Carlos Reservation was not necessarily a thing of the past. During the spring of 1890, just across New Mexico Territory's western borderline, Apache killed Benjamin "Ben" Crawford, the former sheriff of Graham County, Arizona Territory, and his unnamed companion. At least so said the telegraphic reports received at Fort Bayard. There is little doubt that the same band of Indians, operating farther south in New Mexico's Animas Mountains, near the Gray ranch, struck again. The Apache brazenly ran a horse wrangler off in sight of cowboys holding for shipment a herd of 1,600 fat steers. The cattle drovers were preoccupied with preventing a stampede, and woefully watched as the Apache spirited away their remuda, unscathed and not pursued. Soon thereafter, in Arizona Territory's Chiricahua Mountains, the Apache killed Los Angeles attorney Robert Hardie and nearly took off his partner, Francis Haynes. Then, as Apache did, they simply faded away.[916]

Livestock rustling was seemingly back in fashion, and members of the Southwestern Stock Association once more pledged bounty monies to be paid for the "arrest and conviction" of "Goddamn cow-thieves."[917] Adding to the Grant County crime commotion was the frequency of the "cutting and shooting scrapes" in the vicinity of Separ, an unruly cattle-loading station for the Southern Pacific Railroad, about 20 miles southeast of Lordsburg.[918]

Meanwhile, in Silver City—though it could have happened anywhere—one of Grant County's most prominent and controversial personalities, Thomas "Tom" Lyons, "smelled a mouse."[919] He caught Johnny McMannigil in his house, with his wife. Putting into play his fire-belching Colt's six-gun, Lyons deftly tapped out the interloper's running lights—for keeps. McMannigil in an instant departed this world; Lyons came clear, legally.[920]

Thomas "Tom" Lyons, a prominent Silver City pioneer and rancher. He killed the man who was "keeping company with his wife." *Courtesy Silver City Museum.*

Perhaps, with shootings in town, shootings outside of town, near pandemic cow stealing throughout the whole county, and patchy acts of criminality by Apache, the debate about statehood should have been tabled.

That's what many politicos thought—and that's what happened. Evidently, a not insignificant number of citizens back in the "States" concurred—that is, if due credit is awarded certain published remarks:

> This feeling of insecurity is strengthened by the impression that abounds with eastern people, especially who look on territories as inhabited by a lot of wild, unruly creatures made up largely of the criminal class, who prefer to live in and seek the country where the laws are loose and vice and immorality receive little or no check. Whether all this be true or not, still such is the belief east and elsewhere, which results greatly to our disadvantage.[921]

What happened next in Silver City is not surprising, not in the light of governmental tinkering and public skepticism. After acrimonious debate and *mucho* discussion, the town council revoked George Utter's section of the waterworks contract set aside for the payment of fire protection fees. Many of the town's movers and shakers testified, including the city's premier insurance agent, Mrs. O.S. Warren. She reported that just in Silver City the premiums for fire indemnity collectively cost citizens between $18,000 and $20,000 per annum. Furthermore, after carefully examining the fine print and the "devil is in the details" nuances, she unhesitatingly declared: "I don't know really whether we have had protection or not." Regarding water pressure, H.G. Noel pitched in his two cents' worth: "I think the council is perfectly right. We pay an exorbitant price for what we don't get. I think it is time for the people to kick, and I think they have a big strong kick coming." O.C. Hinman commented on the supply: "By God! I was out of water for three weeks before I went on a hunt, but my water bill went on just the same." Perhaps Dr. W.M. Slough summarized the majority of the citizens' mindset best: "When we need the water the most we haven't got it, and when nature provides it we don't need it."[922]

Likewise, other troubles related to governmental matters gushed to the forefront. There was a scandal at the courthouse. Big time! Numerous Grant County officials were indicted for sundry reasons. In the vast majority of instances the criminal charges were later dismissed or juries ended up rendering "not guilty" verdicts. Apparently, the jurors either saw the criminal causes as purely inspired by partisan politics, or wholly

Diamond A chuckwagon, 1895. Left to right: Jim Reynolds, Dick Hudson, Herbert Bishop, unknown, unknown, unknown, Louis Bishop and Charles Holson. *Courtesy William Bishop.*

deficient from an evidentiary standpoint to sustain a "beyond reasonable doubt" conviction.[923] The whole dismal mess was an embarrassment for a town teetering at an economic crossroads.

The price of silver was flat. The national economy was precariously perched. Any chance bump could tilt the heavily invested profiteers' fortunes up or down in a heartbeat. Many in Silver City worried. Not surprisingly, then, for a populace so long accustomed to suffering privation and peril, collectively they began exploring alternatives. For the moment a new interest was kindled in cutting sign for the promise of new mineral riches. There, too, surely, were other ways to eke out a living wage or the reasonable return on a dollar without throwing in the towel and abandoning ship. Southwestern New Mexico Territory was still home, despite the pitfalls and financial risks. Grant County's folks redirected their efforts.

Prospecting for gold was revived in the section's Mogollon, Pinos Altos and Burro mountain ranges.[924] Fresh curiosity and capital were attached to that earlier ranting and raving of John "Turquoise John" Coleman about the green-hued riches to be found along the Burros' St. Louis Canyon. That discovery 15 years before was no secret, but now it seemed especially relevant. And those very same Burros could, if properly worked, cough up profitable quantities of copper, gold, silver, manganese and fluorite.[925] There were other mineral deposits to consider—or reconsider: fluorspar, lime, onyx, serpentine, kieselguhr. A hard look was also being cast in an easterly direction toward *Santa Rita del Cobre* and her seemingly bottomless cache of copper.[926]

Another hard look was focused on southwestern Grant County, which, if anyplace in the world was, was turning into one hell-to-pop neighborhood. In Hachita, in New Mexico Territory's Bootheel section roughly 25 miles southeast of Lordsburg, Pat Hines was mortally gunned down in front of a saloon "just to see him kick." "Poor Hines never kicked."[927] Twenty-one miles northwest of Lordsburg, at the Summit Section House along the railroad tracks running to Clifton, just three miles shy of the New Mexico-Arizona borderline, an unidentified "Chinaman" was pulled from the water well. He had been fatally whacked in the head with an ax.

Hardly had that news wafted back to Silver City before another story broke at that livestock loading and pistol play hot-spot, Separ, "the little railroad station... that was gaining notoriety for shooters and shooting scrapes."[928] Two "hard characters" went on a wild six-shooter tear. William "Bronco Bill" Walters—a soon-to-be-infamous Old West badman—and Mike McGinnis "tried to kill a miner there awaiting the train and inaugurated a reign of terror at the depot, much to the annoyance of the lady operator [Alice Brewer], who during all this time had been wiring dispatch after dispatch to Lordsburg for aid." Another version—it doesn't contradict the first scenario—adds that before she could lock herself in a railway office, the drunken deadbeats took pot-shots at Alice Brewer's clothes after betting between themselves that they "could cut her skirts with a bullet."[929] Luckily, Sheriff Whitehill, who had by now been reelected, was in Lordsburg and, along with Robert Black, rushed to Separ—only to find the intoxicated owl-hoots already in a comatose stupor, sleeping it off at Armstrong's Rooming House. Poking sawed-off double-barreled 12 gauges under their snoring noses, the lawmen not politely awakened "Bronco Bill" Walters and Mike McGinnis. Bronco Bill went for a Colt, but it had scooted down toward his foot and was somewhere lost in the blankets. Nursing what must have been horrendous hangovers, the disorderly duo were shackled and taken to Silver City for lockup.[930]

An unrelated episode at Separ, too, caused heartburn for area lawman. Rosalio Hidalgo horribly cut two men, one of whom cashed in his chips.

Hidalgo hightailed it for parts he hoped were unknown, but was later nabbed. Arresting officers earned the adulation, but, too, Separ warranted her spot as a Grant County bailiwick where there were many nasty cuttings and shootings.[931]

Identified only as "Frenchy" in photographic archives, the image is most probably that of Charles "Frenchy" Baine, who was trained in scientific farming, saw military service for France in Egypt, and was later a notorious Southwest smuggler. Twice he was a widely known resident in Silver City. In El Paso he shot his paramour between the eyes and then "suicided." *Courtesy Silver Ciy Museum.*

Another tragedy soon caught Silver City's citizens off guard. Charles "Frenchy" Baine, educated in France as a scientific farmer, a former French Foreign Legionnaire with service in Egypt, and of more recent times a contraband purveyor, suspected of supplying Genronimo with oodles of hard-to-come-by rifle cartridges, was the key player. After paying a $15,000 bribe to escape punishment for smuggling this or that commodity into or out of Old Mexico, "Frenchy" for the second time settled in Silver City. There he took up two pastimes: working as a first-class gardener and horticulturist, and not secretly keeping company with Lucy Croenne, "a tall, stylish, good looking dame of French extraction," who for the previous year had been in charge at Nettie's Place on Hudson Street. What caused his mental stress is indeterminate, but "Frenchy" Baine grabbed his .41 Colt's six-shooter and he and Lucy Croenne struck out for El Paso. Dame Lucy shouldn't have gone. At the

St. Charles Hotel, inside a room littered with champagne bottles, "Frenchy" shot Lucy between the eyes and then "suicided."[932] Then as now, blood gets the ink.

As that first year of the 1990s decade closed, there were 19 prisoners celebrating their Christmas holiday locked away in the Grant County poky. A clever but curt newspaper reporter prophetically remarked that the "offenses are rather grave [and] the probability is that the majority will do time for the territory."

Another journalist, one with nationwide name recognition, was thoroughly fascinated by what he had learned about wild and woolly southwestern New Mexico Territory. Capitalizing on iniquitous six-gun dustups and bronco Apache depredations, utilizing real-life Silver City people as fictionalized characters, and wisely playing to the time and the place, the popular author produced another in a successful string of semi-historical novels:

> *Miss Nobody of Nowhere* is the title of a new novel by Archibald Clavering Gunter, author of *Mr. Potter of Texas*. The scene of this wonderful story is laid at Silver City, New Mexico, while Lordsburg, Clifton, the Gila box canyon and York's ranch frequently occur.[933]

While the rest of the world eyed Silver City from a sometimes anecdotal and often less than trustworthy perspective, those down-home old Grant County folks forged ahead. They were particularly focused—as they always had been—on educational matters. Throughout the county, revenue dedicated to public school coffers ebbed and flowed in correlation with the rise and fall of tax roll valuations. Just after the new decade's dawning, however, one group was sluggishly digging in its collective heels, dodging accountability and somewhat retarding educational progress. The gambling fraternity was in arrears for payments of their "license fees," money wholly dedicated to the public school's kitty. Traditionally the Silver City newspapers, as well as other Grant County broadsheets, had always been close allies with schoolchildren's concerned parents and the overworked and undervalued teachers. The professional "sporting men" were to feel the newspapermen's wrath, and certain governmental minions were not genteelly prodded to set things right and by damn collect those delinquent fees: "Many of the gambling tables owe

One of the driving forces behind Silver City's selection as a spot for the Normal School [now Western New Mexico University], John W. "Jack" Fleming. He was truly a self-made mining success and long-term mayor of Silver City. *Courtesy Silver City Public Library.*

licenses in large amounts not only in this city but all over the county. They will be compelled to pay those back due licenses or close up their games and in the future no license will be issued until the cash is paid therefore."[934]

Other public-spirited citizens were also interested in Silver City acquiring an institution of higher learning. Elizabeth Warren, certainly ahead of her times, and probably the Southwest's most productive writer of insurance polices, had traveled to Boston in a "faithful attempt" to persuade the Methodist hierarchy to locate a college in Silver City. Although she was treated in a "discourteous and even rude manner" by Bishop Foster, she was not deterred from the purpose of her altruistic mission. The Methodists weren't interested, but others were, and Mrs. Warren succeeded in raising $10,000. In Silver City the College Board, ever intent on accomplishment, hammered away at other options.[935]

To sweeten the pot and increase the probabilities, John W. "Jack" Fleming, truly a self-made mining magnate and Silver City's long-term mayor, donated 20 highly desirable acres on a stunningly situated hilltop at the town's western edge as a site for a campus. In Santa Fe, Fleming then lobbied for passage of a bill that would allow Silver City people to "realize their long-time dream" and have a beautiful college campus "visible to all who came into town."[936] Fleming's—and others—efforts were not in vain. During the 35th Territorial Legislative Session, Councilman Albert Bacon Fall introduced Council Bill No. 20, *An Act to Establish and*

Provide for the Maintenance and Government of the Normal Schools of New Mexico, specifically naming Silver City [and later Las Vegas] as the site for what was then considered a teachers' college, but what is now Western New Mexico University.[937] Local building contractors William Laizure and Richard W. Grabe were tasked with making the college a reality, for a bid of $10,800. Interim classes were to be held at the Presbyterian Church, and Silver City's college was up and running.[938]

At the national level, politicians were running, too. President Grover Cleveland was racing to undo what a previous Congress had done. During October 1893 he succeeded in pushing through a repeal of the Silver Purchase Act, which had somewhat guaranteed a market for silver. The government was no longer in the business of propping up the silver-mining industry and, not unanticipated, that once-viable market crashed. Silver City, birthed as a silver-mining camp, would suffer the bureaucratically inflicted hamstringing, but with cast-iron character would persevere. Certainly some small businesses went under, new construction was scaled back and, now, there were plenty of vacant houses available for a persnickety renter to choose from. Silver City's population figures precipitously declined. Nonetheless, many of those early Silver City and old Grant County stalwarts weren't quitters. They'd cut their teeth on adversity. They'd find the road to permanency. The town and the county were bootstrap tough. Maybe too tough for statehood, in fact.

The 1890s decade was but half lived out, and once again a fracas at Silver City fractured well-meaning arguments being made to Easterners that the locale was "civilized," enlightened and a wholesome place to live. It was Old West drama—*déjà vu*!

Charles L. Cantley was Silver City's town marshal. He was 37 years old and a Texan by birth. By most folks' standards C.L. Cantley was thought to be a pretty damn good peace officer—except when he was drinking, which was often. Then he became "aggressive and arbitrary."[939] At Silver City's White House Saloon the drunken city lawman met his comeuppance in the form of one of the town's most prominent and practiced attorneys, James S. "Jim" Fielder. The fact that Cantley instigated the hubbub is indisputable. By all accounts Fielder assumed the role of a gentlemen, and Cantley the cocksure bully. After a verbal and profane tirade, Silver City's finest jerked out his Colt's revolver and began shooting at lawyer Fielder, who actually wasn't very far away. Aside from altering his good sense, the alcohol interfered with Cantley's good aim. He outright missed his mark. Nonchalantly Fielder shifted a stubby cigar from one corner of his mouth to the other, and then, through the cigarette, cigar and gun smoke, shot Cantley dead.[940] The justice of the peace, after noting that Charley Cantley should have been a conservator of the peace rather than the reverse, ruled it a simple case of justifiable homicide. Self-defense, pure and simple.[941]

Chapter 15

"A Dirty Deuce in a New Deck"

The errant behavior of Silver City's police chief and the self-confident exploit of a pistol-packin' lawyer weren't the only anxieties served up on the town's publicity platter. The stumbling march toward statehood, an economy leaking like a sieve, a not trivial downward demographic shift, and the atmosphere's niggardly withholding of precious moisture from range land pastures were just a few of the pessimistic entries on old Grant County's tablet of 1895 tribulations. Another pressing development

Eugene Cosgrove's well-stocked hardware store in Silver City about 1900.
Courtesy Silver City Public Library.

had the county in a tizzy: Nearly 20 years before, independent-minded Grant County folks had pluckily bucked the system and tried to disassociate themselves from New Mexico Territory. Now, active citizens in that southern stretch of real estate around Deming were seeking their own divorce from Grant County. Certain politicos were closed-door scheming. They wanted a county of their very own. Such a move was nothing new. It was natural, very much predictable and wholly understandable: "Electioneering and political maneuvering became a consuming passion in the southwestern territories.... County building was a favorite sport of budding politicians in both [New Mexico and Arizona] territories."[942]

The squawk was getting hot notice in Silver City. Fretfully, a do-something meeting at the Tremont House was called. That night several committees were put together. One was tasked with soliciting expense funds for a delegation traveling to Santa Fe so they could ardently "oppose the division of the county." Two attending citizens, C.F. Grayson and L.A. Skelly, were selected to make the trip without delay and look after the interests of Grant County. Supplementing the list of word warriors to fight any proposed borderline trifling were the politically connected Jack Fleming and Dick Hudson, who at the time were already in Santa Fe on unrelated business. After realistically analyzing the probable effects the division might have on Grant County's taxpayers, it was near-unanimously decided "to make a determined fight and leave representatives constantly in Santa Fe."[943] For the interim their all-but-panicked plans forestalled the dreaded enabling legislation.

Political squabbling and downtown six-shooter dustups weren't the focal point for everyone. Aaron Schutz was marketing the latest style in straw hats; the Silver City Social Club gave a dance at Newcomb's Hall; enthusiastic Odd Fellows sponsored an ice-cream luncheon; the local bicycle club made a Sunday excursion to the Burro Mountain turquoise mines; and

> Brag Knox made his *debut* into society Saturday evening last. His cow-servant friends gave a dance in his honor which was attended by only invited guests. It was very select, so much so, that only five couples participated. They composed the *crème de la crèm*e of the bronco busting fraternity, with their best girls.[944]

Other big doings had been on tap. The Normal School held its introductory commencement exercise at Morrill Hall. Standing on a stage decorated with "flowers and growing plants" and before a large audience "paying strict attention," the institution's very first graduate, the nearly 18-year-old Miss Belle [Isabel] Eckles, delivered her essay. After other distinguished students and educators had had their say, Miss Eckles was surprised to be the recipient of a handsome gold watch, a gift from the delighted citizens of Silver City. Overcome with gratitude, she was "only able to reply briefly in thanks."[945] All and all, it was starting off to be a good summer. That quickly changed.

Toward the end of June and the beginning of July the newspaper reports were almost carelessly making mention of interrelated meteorological events, but clearly they weren't connecting the dots: "Several heavy rains are reported as having fallen in the western part of the county since our last issue and the chances are favorable for a downpour..." and "several heavy rains have fallen in the northern portion of the territory during the past week. Our turn will come presently."[946] And come it did!

> At 8:45 last Sunday evening the long prayed-for rain came and came in torrents. The somber clouds which for hours had hung threateningly over the Pinos Altos Range, precipitated their pent-up gloom upon the steep hillside adjacent to Chloride Flat, which gathered the waters into a compact volume, from which place it swept down the narrow gorge with terrific force upon the town of Silver City. This flood, which attained its maximum in force and volume at 10:30, was the largest ever seen at Silver City up to that hour, carried away the walls of the Broadway hotel and worked general destruction. The waters of the first flood had receded below the danger limit at 11:30 when the great bank of black clouds which darkened the sky to the northwest came in contact with the towering peak of Bear mountain, the highest in all Pinos Altos range. As if the bottom of a sea were punctured by the peak, a vast volume of water descended, accumulating in force as it converged in streams from the mountain side, making a river in the canyon which leads through the town. At 11:45 this flood struck the town, in an immense wave, 12 feet in height and 300 feet in width, carrying with it everything moveable in its path.[947]

The horrendous deluge was not a one-day happening; it was divided into three barrages, spread out over three different days. Highlighting all of the destruction is not requisite for telling the pitiable story. A plain sampling will suffice: The railroad tracks and a bridge were torn away, $20,000 worth; a rear corner of the Timmer House was knocked out; the Elephant Corral was washed away, along with four horses and several buggies; Morrill Hall was a total wreck; water filled the basement and first floor of Doc Bailey's drugstore, ruining everything; obliteration at the Broadway Hotel was complete; all the outbuildings at the Tremont House were simply gone. Other citations of damage are just too voluminous to enumerate.[948]

As with any natural disaster, there were human-interest stories. The then-sheriff, Baylor Shannon, assisted by physician Will T. Williams and J.R. Johnson, rescued A. J. Loomis and family. The good doctor, while carrying a Loomis child, was himself thrown down by the water's force—he went completely under twice—the young boy desperately clinging to his neck. When the storm broke, Adam Kujnz, a butcher, was sound asleep in a back room at the Cottage Saloon. "The bed on which he was asleep floated round for a while then turned over. The cold water awakened him and he escaped in his night clothes, well drenched." Dell Potter couldn't open the outside doors of his residence due to the raging current's pressure. Because of fast-rising water inside he was forced to take an ax and chop a hole through the ceiling, providing his family an escape passage to safety on the roof. Harvey Howard Whitehill, the ex-sheriff, accompanied by Herbert Martyr and T. N. Childers, hearing the cries of Mrs. Scott, her daughter Gertie and two smaller children, stubbornly fought their way through the wall of water. They saved the petrified family "just before the rear of the house fell in."[949]

These were, by anyone's measurements, not ordinary seasonal rains. The sheer magnitude of the drenching may be calculated, quantifiably. Just one of the floods, on July 21—the last of the three—dumped 190,548,483 cubic feet of water onto an already thoroughly saturated Silver City. This flood, four times greater than that of July 9, "would have filled a dam or reservoir one mile square seven feet deep.... This water came from a water shed of about 45 square miles.... The total of the three floods was 259,446,231 cubic feet... and [would] fill [a] one-quarter of a mile square 37.3 ft. deep."[950] The flow was estimated to be traveling at 15 miles per hour, "bringing with it boulders, debris and fallen timbers that acted literally as battering rams against the downtown buildings."[951]

Silver City's Main Street after the flood of 1902, and the resultant "Big Ditch."
Courtesy Silver City Public Library.

Previous downpours had appreciably lowered Main Street. This series of floods cut the channel deeper, and subsequent rain events [1902 especially] would put the icing on the cake. What was once Silver City's heart-and-soul thoroughfare was reduced to an arroyo of momentous import—wide and in some places 50 feet deep—down to the bedrock. In due course the gigantic chasm would physically split the town. This gash cutting through Silver City earned its own moniker. For a hundred years it has simply but descriptively been known as the Big Ditch.[952] Illuminating the townsmen's solution for dealing with the erosive phenomenon is another example of their grit: They built high, arched wooden bridges across the gorge, allowing foot and wheeled traffic to pass back and forth. Then, over time, instead of sniveling, bemoaning and whining, they turned Mother Nature's unsolicited bestowal into somewhat of a tourists attraction, bragging about the Big Ditch and their practically applied ingenuity. In fact, on at least one occasion a circus high-wire artist stretched a tightrope across the defile and put on a spectacular exhibition. Later, many herds of cattle were driven via the Big Ditch to the stockyards on the outskirts of town, children and adults alike standing on the high banks to take in the traditionally attired cowboys' show.[953]

Those leathery-faced young cowboys and, perhaps more important, their bosses the cowmen were to play an integral part in staving off a stomping for old Grant County during that stampede of dwindling capital. Until the 1890s the demand for Grant County-raised cattle by and large had been for the regional marketplace. The folks in Silver City, Deming, Lordsburg and the other area settlements fostered a healthy demand for hanging beef. Add to this the availability of hometown contracts or subcontracts awarded to keep the US Army supplied with fat steers, plus the even more profitable business of furnishing cattle to the largest market of all, the New Mexico and Arizona Territories' Indian reservations.[954] Southwestern New Mexico Territory, aside from the high mountain country, was cattle country, open-range country. "You could go through Silver City and go north to Colorado and never open a gate, and you could go west to Arizona and never open a gate, and you could go south to Mexico and never open a gate, and you could go east to El Paso and never open a gate unless it was some little gate that fenced around some fella's house or a trap for saddlehorses.... But as far as a pasture fence there was no such thing."[955]

According to the article in an early day edition of the *Silver City Independent*, the first "Eastern" shipments of cattle from Grant County weren't made until 1894. After that the local beef industry grew by "leaps and bounds."[956] The listing is not all inclusive by any means, but Grant County was home to such well known livestock operations as the Diamond A; the GOS, operated by Vic Culberson; the LCs, owned by Tom Lyons and Angus Campbell; the T. W. Holson Ranch at Lone Mountain; the Diamond Bar on the Upper Gila; Harvey Whitehill's ranch at Mowry City; the S Bar Cattle Company south of Separ; Lee and Tom Upton's O Bar O; and Tom Hyatt's A Bar T in the Florida Mountain section, just to name a very few.[957] There were so many cattle on Grant County's open ranges that poor land management practices such as overstocking and the resultant soil erosion—coupled with severe droughts—sometimes generated ground that was "bare and sere, and cattle began dying by the thousands."[958] Particularly noting how the countryside was cut by arroyos, an old-timer was asked if it had always been that way? The answer and the reasoning are insightful: "There wasn't no arroyos [in] those days. No, there was no washes. You could drive a wagon across any place everyday."

The "Real McCoy!" Ranchman Jerry McDonald on a trip to Silver City posing in front of the celebrated Tremont House. *Courtesy Silver City Public Library.*

And in response to why it changed, he said: "Oh, on account of cattle grazin' and... there's no way to hold the grass back [in place]."[959]

As cowmen readjusted their estimation on how best to utilize Grant County's terra firma to their most profitable advantage, other thinkers turned to the very real possibility of exploiting tourism as a partial bailout for the section's sagging and anemic economy. There was no little interest in the area's hunting potential. Trips to the higher mountain country were possible now that Apache had been subjugated. In fact, the "predatory wild animals were very hard on the cattle" and not much thought was awarded to such a notion as an endangered species. Out-of-state big-game hunters took due note:

> A hunting party consisting of C.D. Hasford, Mr. Elliott, [Dr.] John C. Barron, Con P. Sullivan and Thomas Lyons

left this week for the Mogollons on a bear hunt. The first three gentlemen are from New York, and have hunted the royal Bengal tiger in India, and the white elephant in Africa. They are hunters from away back, and will have fine sport in the Mogollons.[960]

An after-the-turn-of-the-century fishing and hunting excursion in the Mogollon Mountain country. Jake Reidlinger [left] and Silver City's former mayor, Robert Black [right]. *Courtesy Silver City Museum.*

Other outdoorsmen found duck hunting along the Mimbres River's banks excellent sport, one lucky shotgun devotee bagging 26 in but a single outing.[961] In the mountain fastness there were many black and grizzly bears, as well as elk and deer—and lions. The Gila River and its crystalline forks were brimming with fish. At the lower elevations antelope were in abundant supply, as were quail and other gamebirds. For the zealous sportsman Silver City and old Grant County were a good place to be—and that fact was being advertised.[962]

Unquestionably southwestern New Mexico Territory's clean dry air was healthful. The advent of railroad connections had removed the major obstacle preventing travel by affluent sightseers or less-vigorous persons seeking a cure by bathing in the area's celebrated naturally hot mineral

A pleasant turn-of-the-century family outing—southern New Mexico Territory style. *Courtesy Carol Marlin.*

waters. The hotel at Hudson's Hot Springs had earlier burned to the ground. Dick Hudson wasn't carrying an insurance policy, and therefore opted to quickly cash out. Andrew R. Graham, a wealthy Midwesterner, bought the place and erected a commodious 48-bedroom [each with a private bath] hotel, barber shop and billiard room, all pleasantly and lazily surrounded by inviting long porches dotted with wooden rocking chairs. An enthusiastic visitor said that "the building seemed to roam all over the desert and that it had miles of verandah." In short order the Casa del Consuelo [House of Delight] was favorably known from East Coast to West. In fact, A.J. Spaulding, owner of the Chicago White Stockings ball club, chose the hot springs for a spring training spot. He soon learned, however, that the players were more interested in enjoying the cool breeze while visiting with patrons under the porch's overhang and watching stagecoach passengers arrive from its short hop to the depot, than they were in tiresome batting practice or tagging third base.[963]

The tumultuous 19th century, unlike the lethargically disposed baseball players, was running—fast—approaching its deadline. Before she exhausted herself and tumbled into the arms of inquiring historians, there was one brandish of unfinished business.

Far away in Havana's busy harbor, the *USS Maine* was anchored near Buoy No. 4. On the night of Jan. 25, 1898, at 9:45 p.m., Marine Private William Anthony advised the ship's captain, Charles D. Sigsbee: "Sir, I have to inform you that the ship has blown up and is sinking."[964] And sinking it was! More than 250 sailors and marines perished. Figuratively, as the boat went down Americans' temperature for war went up. And William Randolph Hearst's *New York Journal* and Joseph Pulitzer's *New York World,* supplemented by jingoistic US congressmen, were fanning the fever.[965] Throughout the country the war cry was heard: "Remember the *Maine,* to hell with Spain!" The folks in old Grant County weren't deaf. So, when the three regiments of cavalry—the Rough Riders—"composed entirely of frontiersmen possessing special qualifications as horsemen and marksmen" were called for, 36 from Silver City signed on.[966] Bombastically it was written of the volunteers that "they would sweep every living thing before them leaving only death and destruction in their path. They are the best shots in any country."[967] By May 10 the Silver City boys, part of a 340-man volunteer unit from New Mexico Territory, were encamped near the Exposition Building at San Antonio's picturesque Riverside Park, the designated marshaling point and training ground. A citified reporter for the *San Antonio News* who had been dispatched to make some firsthand observations of the Rough Riders, reportedly penned: "Intermingled with these attention-getters were such characters as Rocky Mountain Bill, who had supposedly lost a piece of his ear fighting a bear. Another volunteer, an ex-marshal from Dodge City, had an ear bitten off, but not by a bear."[968] The majority of Rough Riders, indeed, were from the West, and

> Most of the boys could ride anything in reason, for we were recruited mainly from Arizona, New Mexico and Oklahoma. But instead of good old reliable caques and hulls [saddles] like they'd been raised on, they hadn't anything between the ends of their backbones and those buck-jumping broncs but those dinky little Army saddles. A man might as well be bareback when a pony is spreading himself as on one of those postage stamps.[969]

Nineteen days after their arrival in the Alamo City, the New Mexico volunteers and the others were hustled aboard a troop train for a 52-hour ride to Tampa, Fla., the disembarkation point for Cuba.[970] The Rough Riders were seasoned and tough fellows, but living conditions in Tampa were horrible, causing one disgruntled recruit to complain that "he had been bitten by mosquitoes, stung by a tarantula, felt a touch of malaria, ran his bayonet into his hand, sat on an ant's nest, stepped on an alligator, found a snake in his boot and felt like a dirty deuce in a new deck."[971] Of the whole miserable experience a youthful Silver City area cowboy,

Frank Brito, later remarked that most of his memories of the war were of "bad food and worse sanitary conditions," especially noting that "the flies were horrible."[972]

An abbreviated and informal history of Silver City and old Grant County is not the format to retell a story of the July 1 blistering battles on Cuba's San Juan Heights or about the gallant charges up San Juan and Kettle Hills. The bloody day was long; the "splendid little war" was short. The Grant County boys, glad to be shed of Armour's spoiled canned beef and the subtropical climate, finally headed back to their southwestern New Mexico Territory mountain and desert homes. When they arrived in Silver City and before they dispersed, all were awarded premier status as the heroes they rightfully were. There were—as with any war—those soldiers eager to see action, but who saw not. These hearty volunteers, likewise, were "just as dear to New Mexicans as any" who were in the units that did.[973] A grand ball and scrumptious banquet at the Timmer House was hosted in their honor.[974]

Pleased as strawberry punch with the valor of their fighting men, still, Grant County folks and, indeed, the whole of New Mexico Territory's populace, stood in wonderment: Other territories across the American West were being welcomed into the sisterhood of states, why weren't they?

Certainly by that last turn of the 19th century Silver Citians had much to be proud of, and they hoped the rest of the world would take notice. By 1900 there was already reasonably dependable electric service right there in town.[975] After fencing off the reservoir "so that solid matter" would be excluded, previous difficulties at the waterworks were being soundly managed—particularly if fitting credit is banked for a rhythmical newspaperman's *Silver City Enterprise* rattle:

> No more comes the kid with kittens to drown,
> Nor the skunk from his burrow to bathe,
> Nor the Mexican's *pero* to paddle aroun'
> Nor the water consumer the company to scathe.[976]

On par with "any metropolitan gallery," the graphic talents of Mrs. Bryant were being favorably critiqued as she prepared to move kit and caboodle all of her "latest and most approved photographic accessories" into a revamped art studio on Bullard Street.[977] There was even in that first year of the new century a gasoline-drinking horseless carriage protectively parked inside Goodell's Corral, and it was attracting no little attention. Spectators were "afraid to touch it for fear of pressing some hidden button which might cause it to run amuck in the corral."[978] Another sign of the 20th century's progressive march into town was a grand opening: The Silver City Beer and Ice Company was in business.[979]

William D. "Keechi" Johnson, a Grant County deputy sheriff murdered along Raw Meat Creek in the Mogollon Mountains. *Courtesy Roy B. Sinclair, Jr.*

There were other measurements hovering reasonably close around that turn-of-the-century mark, though, some of a more wicked sort. Ida Miller, "a member of the Lordsburg *demimonde,*" somehow robbed Nick Hughes and was placed in Grant County's lockup.[980] In nearby Santa Rita, badman George Stevenson recklessly killed an inoffensive gambler, Billy Woods.[981] Notable Southwest lawman George Scarborough, the man who killed the man [John Selman] who killed the man [John Wesley Hardin] was himself gunned down and died at his Deming home on April 5, 1900.[982] The aforementioned Stevenson and another legit *mal hombre,* James Brooks, broke out of the Grant County Jail with four others that same year.[983] And in August another area six-shooter tragedy took place. William D. "Keechi" Johnson, a Grant County deputy sheriff, was heartlessly gunned down while making a cattle-rustling investigation along

Raw Meat Creek, deep within the Mogollon's wilderness. To make sure southwestern New Mexico Territory maintained her shamefully untamed reputation, Ralph Jenks, Keechi Johnson's alleged murderer, was likewise the victim of six-gun diplomacy. Jenks was killed by a lawman's bullet—while in custody.[984] An early 1900s southwestern New Mexico Territory ranchman's wife distilled the rough reality: "Our County Seat is Silver City.... There the feuds are settled with six-guns."[985] The outside world knew it, too!

Long had many Easterners looked at New Mexico Territory with utter disdain. Much earlier it had been written: "If to be indolent is a virtue, and to be ignorant is bliss, then are the natives of New Mexico the happiest and most virtuous people on the globe. If religion consists in rendering homage to a God of gold, they are the most devout nation in Christendom. Education with them is eminently practical and consists of three lessons, pilfering, stealing and robbery."[986] Clearly such remarks are manifestations of transparent racism and preconceptions, yet even more moderate thinkers in a more modern era still presumed New Mexico and Arizona were wild and woolly frontier territories, much too so for statehood. Six-shooter dustups such as the well-publicized Lincoln County War, the Colfax County War, the Farmington Feud, the criminality of William "Black Jack" Christian's gang, and the birth and death of a southeastern New Mexico sin-town, Phenix, one of the Old West's most tarnished assortment of whorehouses and gambling dens—packed plumb full of authenticated gunmen—were all so very real.[987] Add the baffling disappearance and murder of political powerhouse Albert Fountain and his six-year-old son Henry into the abysmal equation, and New Mexico Territory's uphill struggle for sympathetic recognition becomes clear. All of those troubles were now just past memories, but not distant ones.

Even for an admittedly Western-focused story, aside from such violently exposed episodes, it may be truthfully told that New Mexicans politically shot themselves in their own foot regarding statehood. A legitimized state was required to have an acceptable constitution. Therein lay the rub. New Mexico as a territory didn't have one, nor need one. Vying for statehood changed things. Partisan voices in both the Democratic and Republican parties were jockeying for advantage; after all, two US Senate seats would be up for grabs upon entering the union. In 1890 a state constitution had been drafted and proposed, subject to ratification by the people. The debate was impassioned:

> If you elect to remain as a territory hereafter, your condition will be self imposed slavery. Your position today is that of peons of the eastern aristocrat.... By voting against the constitution you admit the slanders which have been fulminated against your capacity for self government. No wrong was ever righted by silence.[988]

An electorate seemingly more concerned with maintaining party loyalties [Republicans for, Democrats against] watched the proposed state constitution go down to defeat by a two-to-one margin, 16,180 to 7,493. The referendum carried in Grant and Valencia Counties, but nowhere else.[989] Statehood, at that time, was a dead letter matter. Now, with dawning of a brand-new century, interest was rekindled in gracing New Mexico with statehood. It seemed difficult, but achievable.

The first part of those transitional 1900s saw big goings-on in old Grant County. First the county's geography shrank. Behind-the-scenes manipulations had been brewing for years and they finally produced a payout for campaigners on March 16, 1901. Luna County was created and Deming was named the county seat.[990] By any man's book, old Grant County was still a whopper, size-wise—7,300 square miles.[991] The second fact to impact the region, and more specifically Silver City, was simply what many had so very well known for years: It was a healthful place. Previously cited visits to the area's celebrated hot springs did not abate, but a new health-related industry was launched. Silver City began billing herself as a natural sanitarium for those suffering tuberculosis. The high, dry climate was just the ticket for those so afflicted. The bold assertion, in fact, became an integral part of the *Silver City Enterprise*'s masthead: "Silver City—the World's Only Sanitarium."[992]

An army physician, Dr. Earl Sprague Bullock, prevailed on Mother Mary Paul O'Grady at Silver City's St. Joseph Hospital to "convert her institution into a sanatorium, with the Sisters of Mercy continuing to serve as nurses."[993] Later, through the sterling fundraising efforts of Nellie Wilson, whose son Wayne was tubercular, establishment of the New Mexico Cottage Sanatorium was brought to fruition on a nearly 300-acre tract three miles north of Silver City. The institution was first-rate in every regard, but not inexpensive. Promptly and profitably catering to the patient less affluent, other quality sanatoriums—though less sophisticated—such as the Sunnyside, the Pines and the Africo-Tubercular

St. Joseph's Sanitarium, Silver City. *Courtesy Silver City Public Library.*

Sanatorium, were soon rendering their contribution to the hacking and wheezing healthseekers in search of relief. Enterprising Silver City residents even rented rooms to distressed patients, turning spare space into needed income, allowing the sick to skirt expenses of more formalized care at a sanatorium. Patients partaking of the cure in Silver City proved, in many cases, to be beneficial to the local economy as well as the regional culture. More than just a few stayed on, making Silver City home and, besides spending hard-earned healthcare dollars: "They contributed significantly to the ranks of physicians, attorney, merchants and clergymen, and provided at least one newspaper editor."[994]

Unquestionably Silver City was coming of age. The arrival of a railroad had hastened the town's progression toward 20th-century technology. No longer was the city taking baby steps. Industriously the old temporary train depot was replaced by a new one—already built and painstakingly moved along the tracks to its designated site. Blueprints for a workable sewer system were on the drawing board. The keen fascination with electricity, telephone and reliable water services was not unappreciated, but those improvements were becoming more and more commonplace. Throughout Grant County social, educational and fraternal organizations had taken a firm foothold. Seemingly statehood and stability were near at hand.

Moving the Santa Fe Depot to Silver City, a Herculean task. *Courtesy Silver City Public Library.*

But there were yet, even in the 20th century, a few rough spots of the Old West type playing out in old Grant County. A Mexican national, José Sanchez, gunned down Catrino Alemandarez during a dispute over personal property taken from his camp along the road between Santa Rita and Georgetown. Another Grant County killing in the broadest context was not necessarily all that newsworthy, not to the outside world. What made this case a tad more prickly to those Easterners peeking in on New Mexican affairs was that Sanchez, whom a local editor characterized as a man of "a low type of intelligence and [who] has but small appreciation of the enormity of his crime and of the doom which awaits him," was scheduled to die. So widespread was Sanchez' dementia that he was hurtfully nicknamed "Loco Joe." Crazy or not, the jury took but 30 minutes to bring in a guilty verdict, and Judge F.W. Parker had sentenced Sanchez to forfeit his life of 28 years. The court's remedy and the hanging ended the pathetic story.[995] There were, however, those nagging questions about just how far had New Mexico Territory and a frontier populace really come:

> He [Sanchez] did not for an instant appear to appreciate the fate which awaited him, or if he did he certainly gave no manifestation of his feeling. He at one time expressed a wish to have the hanging over with in order that he

> might "get out into the country." Whether this was intended as an effort to demonstrate his insanity, or whether it was an utter ignorance of what hanging meant will never be known. From his conversation at times, it would almost seem that he did not know what death was.[996]

Wasn't New Mexico Territory tamed yet? Perhaps not! In that wild Bootheel country south of Lordsburg, smalltime ranchers Tess and William "Push" Hoffman engaged in an altercation with Bonito Canales over the alleged theft of a piece of watermelon. Tess whacked the "Mexican" over the head with his Colt's handgun and then "beat him badly" using the barrel as a bludgeon. There the matter ended, so thought the Hoffman brothers. They were wrong, dead wrong! After nursing his broken head, Bonito Canales rounded up a partner, Navarro Sanchez, and the pair, armed with six-shooters, went on the hunt for Tess Hoffman. At a grading camp things turned "Western." Standing toe to toe, face to face, Canales and Sanchez emptied their revolvers at the Hoffman boys as fast as they could slip the single-actions' hammers. Tess and Push were not idle, nor were they tucking tail and running away. Instead, at that very same instant they were blazing away, too, retuning the fire, givin' as good as they were gettin'. Eye to eye, the closeup exchange was hell-horrific. All four had plenty of grit and gristle. All four were damn good shots, obviously. All four died on the spot.[997]

Even with all her refinements Silver City was not to be let off the hook for Old West gunplay. Howard Pickney Chenowth, a Diamond A cowboy, and friends rode their ranch horses into town for a night of fun. Chenowth and his chief drinking companion, Martin "Mart" Kennedy, formerly of Abilene, Texas, poured them down and howled at the moon. At one point it was such a jovial visit that Chenowth unsuccessfully undertook to ride his favorite Diamond A horse, Bonito, into the Palace Saloon. The clock had been turned back 25 years! Sourmash and six-shooters and youthful hot-tempers, then as now, are the recipe for mishap. During a snarling cat-and-dog struggle, Chenowth shot the eye-brows off his foreman, Pat Nunn. His aim was somewhat better for the next target. He cutdown on and killed a former Grant County constable and ex-United States marshal, Perfecto Rodriquez. Then Chenowth turned his six-gun on Silver City's town marshal, William H. Kilburn, who had raced unarmed to the scene of trouble. As if poleaxed, Kilburn

After the turn of the century, on a stupendous drinking tear, Howard Chenowth "ran amuck" and killed two men on a Silver City street, one of whom was the Town Marshal. *Courtesy Amos and La Dorna Chenowth.*

fell to the ground paralyzed, the bullet tearing a gaping hole in his neck and shattering his spinal column. Kilburn died. Chenowth was wounded and arrested, but later during a daring jailbreak made good his getaway.[998]

Certainly it may be proffered that through the early 1900s six-shooter settlement of personal quarrels and outlaw/lawman mèlées sometimes dominated the news, but step by step those "Western" get-togethers began to taper off. Silver City and Grant County were becoming downright "civilized." Statehood's drumbeat was deafening!

Delving into the machinations and intrigues, melodramatically scripting imaginary conversations held in smoke-filled back rooms, or otherwise scrutinizing New Mexico's quest for shedding its territorial skin is not necessary for bringing this chronicle to an end. There were efforts spent to bring Arizona Territory and New Mexico Territory into the union joined at the hip as a single state, but that failed. Too, others were even advocating the historic territory's name be changed from New Mexico to "Acoma," which likewise didn't pass muster. After it was all said and done, President William Howard Taft signed the Hamilton Bill on June 18, 1910, granting New Mexico the provisional license to apply for statehood. After the politicians and people fashioned an acceptable state constitution it was a done deal, and on the sixth day of January 1912, New Mexico was a territory no more.[999]

It is true that Silver City, in her maturity, has grown into the 21st cen-

Turn-of-the-century Silver City as it looked on New Mexico's march to statehood. *Courtesy Silver City Public Library.*

tury with vim and vigor, forbearance and friendliness, an incontestably durable community in the Southwest's mélange of alluring neighborhoods. Today she is modern, enlightened and even progressively tilted, but she cannot hide—nor should she—from her extraordinarily thrilling past. Appreciably, from the perspective of an Old West notion, Silver City during her palmy days could and did rivial Dodge City, Deadwood or Tombstone for legitimate stories featuring gunfighters and gamblers, outlaws and owl-hoots.

Her history, however, seems in a broader sense much more inclusive. Indians, Spaniards, Mexicans and Americans had traipsed all through her geographic surroundings long after a prehistoric people had already come and gone. Beaver pelts and glistening gold were pulled from shimmering mountain streams and zigzagging rivers. Prospectors changed her pleasing landscape forevermore as the mines went down and the mills went up. Resilient pioneers built with brick, watched much of it wash away, and proudly built again. Frontier wives and mothers mended broken hearts and skinned knees, and brushed back the tears when compelled to peacefully lay an infant in its premature last rest. Cowboys dragged slobbering and bawling calves to the branding fires as their bossmen penciled the year's increase into a tattered-page tally book. The Apache Wars took place in Silver City's, Deming's and Lordsburg's very own backyards. Distinguished US cavalrymen—black and white—scooted and skirmished throughout the colossal county earning medals of honor and, sometimes, hard words. Trite-sounding as it may be, during those territorial days it really was wild and woolly.

There, of course, are other places deserving the richness of historic recognition. But, to liberally paint with a brush's broadest stroke, in the stirring and colorful annals reserved for the American Southwest, few environs would ever contend with, nor could they put Silver City and/or old Grant County in the shade as emblematic models for bona fide Old West drama. To this end, then, succeeding generations are in debt. Their ancestors were cut from the right stuff, sturdy as oak. Whatever they'd been before or wherever they'd started from, there was a common denominator for those early southwest New Mexico Territory front-line settlers: Hardship and hazard or not, they'd transformed themselves into Westerners and they'd come to stay—they weren't quitters!

NOTES

Chapter 1

1. As of this time, there is no single source that adequately covers the illustrious history of Silver City and of old Grant County. A practically inclusive study must include Jeanette Bennett Ashenfelter's 1904 paper, "Founding of the Town of Silver City, New Mexico," and Lettie Bennett Morrill's 1908 paper, "Early Days in Silver City," both presented to the Jacob Bennett Chapter of the National Society of the Daughters of the American Revolution in Silver City. Two early-day newspapers series should also be reviewed: the *Silver City Enterprise* 1902 serial, "Silver City Years Ago," and "Early Days of the Great Southwest" by Dan Rose, carried in multiple 1917 editions of the *Silver City Independent.* The most scholarly detailed, although not readily accessible for generalized use, is Conrad Keeler Naegle's "The History of Silver City, New Mexico, 1870-1886" (master's thesis, University of New Mexico, 1943). The oral histories recorded by Lou Blachley during the 1950s are a treasure trove of historical data concerning the region but are not readily available for widespread use. Additional information may be found in Williams' (Myres, ed.) *Pioneer Surveyor—Frontier Lawyer, The Personal Narrative of O. W. Williams, 1877-1902,* specifically, Part II: "Miner in Early New Mexico" and Part III: "Refuge in Silver City." Another little volume, insightful but also hard to locate and not annotated, is *The Silver City Book, Wild and Woolly Days,* Volume I, edited by Susan and David Nelson. Of more recent vintage is Ailman's (Lundwall, ed.) most capably and carefully annotated *Pioneering in Territorial Silver City: H. B. Ailman's Recollections of Silver City and the Southwest, 1871-1892.* Unger's compilation of 1882 and 1883 newspaper articles in *True Tales* offers a capsule glance at the everyday goings-on in Silver City for those years. Area law enforcement issues are handled in the author's *Dangerous Dan Tucker: New Mexico's Deadly Lawman* and the quotation "blistering cauldron" is taken from the Introduction by Leon Metz. Also see the author's *Silver City Stalwart: Harvey H. Whitehill—An Old West Lawman on the New Mexico Frontier* for a reasonably inclusive look at crime and violence in Silver City and old Grant County during the frontier era. Also see Ball's *Desert Lawmen, The High Sheriffs of New Mexico and Arizona, 1846-1912* and *The United States Marshals of New Mexico & Arizona Territories, 1846-1912.* The "catch basin for rogues" comes directly from Gordon Owen's *Las Cruces, New Mexico, 1849-1999: A Multicultural Crossroads.* For Grant County executions, refer to Gilbreath's *Death on the Gallows: The Story of Legal Hangings in New Mexico, 1847-1923.* The quotation "built to last" is taken directly from Berry and Russell's *Built to Last: An Architectural History of Silver City, New Mexico,* a must-read for understanding the unique longevity of this frontier mining community. For generalized reading regarding Apache and U.S. military conflicts, Thrapp's *Conquest of Apacheria* and Worcester's *The Apaches* are compulsory. For three brilliant biographies of Apache leaders specific to the Silver City area, see Thrapp's *Victorio and the Mimbres Apaches,* Sweeney's *Mangas Coloradas, Chief of the Chiricahua Apaches* and *Cochise, Chiricahua Apache Chief.* For two admirable works aimed at specific Apache raids, see Simmons' *Massacre on the Lordsburg Road* and Lekson's *Nana's Raid: Apache Warfare in Southern New Mexico, 1881.* For accounts of Apache incursions and warfare as reported in a contemporary newspaper, see, Mullane's (ed.), *Indian Raids as Reported in the* Silver City Enterprise, *1882-1886.* For insightful data regarding the US Army and its postings throughout New Mexico Territory, see Billington's *New Mexico's Buffalo Soldiers* and Giese's *Forts of New Mexico.*

2. Berry and Russell, *Built to Last,* 3-6. Also see: Giammattei and Reichert, *Art of a Vanished Race.* Also, the *Grant County Herald* noted the historic significance of the area's prehistoric culture; see the July 22, 1876, edition.

3. Ibid.

4. Forbes, *Apache, Navaho, and Spaniard, 126*: "As it has been demonstrated that the Western Apaches were in the Flagstaff-Little Colorado region in the 1580s, 1590s and early 1600s, it seems certain that the historic regions of the Apache in Arizona and southwestern New Mexico were occupied by them in this period." Also see Laumbach, *Hembrillo,* 105: "When the Mimbres Apache were first encountered by Europeans is not known, but they were likely the group referred by Benavides as the 'Apaches de Xila,' located west of the Rio Grande. Apache raids are credited with the abandonment of the now lost pueblo of Senecu on the southern Rio Grande in the 1670s. Campaigns against the Apache began as early as 1683, and by the 1770s, Spanish military expeditions were sending significant numbers of troops to New Mexico."

5. Ball, *In the Days of Victorio,* xiii.

6. Spicer, *Cycles of Conquest,* 21: "But the natives of the invaded regions were not literate people, and therefore what they thought and said about what was happening to them was never adequately recorded. Especially in the earlier periods, there are no accounts by natives of their reactions and to the contacts with the invaders.... It was a rare Spanish chronicler who was equipped for the exacting task of even moderately objective reporting. Spanish accounts have the inevitable bias of writers from one culture looking through the barriers of language and cultural difference at the

members of another. There is no way in which this bias can be corrected....It is especially in the earliest phases of contact that the record is so one-sided. One searches in vain for records of the Indians' first impressions of the Spaniards to match the Spaniards' first impressions of the Indians." Also see Sweeney, *Mangas Coloradas*, 32: "The Apaches had no written records.... Unfortunately, unlike other Indian tribes, Chiricahua Apaches have little oral history on any individual before 1870."

7. For early entry into New Mexico by Europeans, see Weber, *The Spanish Frontier*, and John, *Storms Brewed*. Also see Spicer, *Cycles of Conquest*. Although somewhat dated, Bolton's *Coronado* and Horgan's *Great River make for an interesting supplemental read.*

8. Weber, *The Spanish Frontier*, 46; Bolton, *Coronado*, 57; John, *Storms Brewed*, 15.

9. Julyan, *The Place Names of New Mexico*, 56. Also see Moorhead, *New Mexico's Royal Road*, 55: "For more than 200 years the Camino Real was the life line of New Mexico, and for almost half of that time the province was held by the merchants of Chihuahua in a state of economic dependence."

10. Reinhartz and Saxon, *The Mapping of the Entradas*, 142: "It was not until the early 18th century that the Spanish again began to explore the far reaches of the Greater Southwest."

11. Weber, *The Spanish Frontier*, 98.

12. John, *Storms Brewed*, 75.

13. Ibid.

14. Berry and Russell, *Built to Last*, 6: "Benavides wrote that they (Apache) were a nation so bellicose, all of it, that it has become the crucible for the courage of the Spaniards."

15. Matson and Schroeder, "Cordero's Description of the Apache—1796," 340-341.

16. Berry and Russell, *Built to Last*, 6. Also see Spicer, *Cycles of Conquest*, 238: "In 1756-57-58 four expeditions to the Gila River were carried out. They resulted merely in the random killing of the few Apaches encountered."

17. Weber, *The Spanish Frontier*, 221.

18. Ibid., 233.

19. Cortes, *Views from the Apache Frontier*. The quotation is from Cortes' 1799 report. The book's editor is not hesitant with establishing a date for Spanish discovery of the copper mine (23 and 128): "Although tradition has it that Spaniards began exploiting the Santa Rita del Cobre only in 1800, the site was obviously known to Spaniards by 1785."

20. Terry Humble, unpublished manuscript on the history of Santa Rita del Cobre copper mine. The bilingual researcher cites the statement made by retired Lieutenant Colonel Jose Manuel Carrasco to the Deputacion de Mineria in Chihuahua on Jan. 3, 1805, during a dispute over mining claims.

21. Cortes, *Views from the Apache Frontier*, 128; interview with Grant County historian Terry Humble, July 22, 2004; and Smith, *Borderlander*, 257: "Spaniards knew about the site as early as the 1780s. A grateful Gileo revealed it to Colonel Don Jose Manuel Carrasco in 1800, according to tradition." Also see Julyan, *New Mexico Place Names*, 186. Still a prominent Silver City area landmark, the Kneeling Nun may be observed at the northern end of Ben Moore Mountain, near Bayard, New Mexico, and indeed, the visual similarity between this geological outcropping and a living nun kneeling before an altar is striking.

22. Smith, *Borderlander*, 33, quoting the *Rio Grande Republican* of Oct. 26, 1889.

23. Batman, *James Pattie's West*, 148-149.

24. Ibid. Also see Berry and Russell, *Built to Last*, 6.

25. Ungnade, Guide to the *New Mexico Mountains*, 28.

26. Ibid. Also see Batman, *James Pattie's West*, 149, and, Smith, *Borderlander*, 257: "They produced 20,000 mule-loads of copper annually—nearly all of the copper used for manufacturing purposes in the internal provinces of Mexico." Logically, 20,000 mule loads "annually" is not realistic. If 20,000 mule loads did in fact depart Santa Rita del Cobre, it would have been over a period of years. For a thoughtful analysis of the traffic between the mine and Chihuahua, and for the source of the bewildering arithmetic, refer to the Humble manuscript on Santa Rita del Cobre's history. For weight of the ingots and another description of the Santa Rita del Cobre copper mine, see Cleland, *This Reckless Breed*, 170-172.

27. Humble, *Mining History Journal*, 93.

28. Max L. Moorhead, The Presidio: Bastion of the Spanish Borderlands, 101. And see Weber, *The Spanish Frontier*, 229. Also, Sweeney, *Mangas Coloradas*, 16. And, Berry and Russell, *Built to Last*, 6: "Finally, in the late 1700s, a policy of buying off the Apache with liquor and antiquated firearms more or less succeeded, and the close of the century saw a tenuous peace." Spicer, *Cycles of Conquest*, 240, offers added conformation: "...they [Apache] should be encouraged to use liquor as much as

possible, so that they would increasingly want it. They should also be given firearms, of poor quality as compared with those of the soldiers, but nevertheless adequate for hunting wild game. They should also be encouraged to trade among themselves and with the Spaniards so that their desire for the things possessed by the Spaniards would increase. In this way they would become more and more dependent on the Spaniards and would gradually give up their hostility. However, whenever hostility developed between bands the Indians should be encouraged to fight among themselves."

29. Griffen, *Apaches at War and Peace*, 78-79: "As the complexity of peaceful Apache affairs increased, the problem of Apaches living at peace in one place and poaching in another constantly confronted peace establishment administrators. This was a dilemma officials would never completely solve. It stemmed partly from the fact that warriors at peace were unable to give up old habits and partly because of an active market for stolen booty in the hinterland with hostiles and possibly with Spaniards."

30. Batman, *James Pattie's West*, 126-189, and, Smith, *Borderlander*, 24-40.

31. D.C. Cole, *The Chiricahua Apache, 1846-1876: From War to Reservation*, 10; Sweeney, *Mangas Coloradas*, 4-10; James L. Haley, Apaches: A History and Culture Portrait, 191; Smith, *Borderlander*, 256.

32. Thrapp, *Encyclopedia of Frontier Biography*, 2:731.

33. Smith, *Borderlander*, 70.

34. Sweeney, *Mangas Coloradas*, 73.

35. Sweeney, *Cochise*, 37.

36. Dunn, *Massacres of the Mountains*, 315, and Sweeney, *Mangas Coloradas*, 75-79. Also, Worcester, *The Apaches*, 38: "By cutting off the supply trains from Chihuahua the angry Mimbreos forced the Mexicans to abandon the copper mines."

37. Spicer, *Cycles of Conquest*, 241: "There are no figures on the number of captive Spaniards taken by Apaches, or vice versa, but the practice was common, as it was farther north in New Mexico. Women and children were taken by both Spaniards and Apaches and kept as servants." Also refer to Thrapp, *Conquest of Apacheria*; Worcester, *The Apaches*; and Sweeney, *Mangas Coloradas*. And see Sweeney, *Cochise*. For a biography of an infamous scalp-hunter, James Kirker, see McGaw's *Savage Scene* and Smith's *Borderlander*. Also see Smith's "The Scalp Hunt In Chihuahua—1849." These sources nimbly paint the picture of the period's Apache/Mexican conflict.

Chapter 2

38. David Nevin, *The Mexican War*, 13-53.

39. Ibid.

40. Metz, *Border*, 9.

41. Nevin, *The Mexican War*, 17.

42. Metz, Border, 9.

43. Myers, "Military Establishments In Southwestern New Mexico: Stepping Stones to Settlement," 5.

44. Greer, *Colonel Jack Hays*, 228.

45. Ibid., 229.

46. Ibid. The letter was dated June 5, 1849.

47. Ibid. According to the author, at El Paso del Norte lodging and pasturage were cheap, foodstuff highly priced, and bacon impossible to find at any price.

48. Thrapp, *Encyclopedia of Frontier Biography*, 2:564.

49. Faulk, *Destiny Road*, 78.

50. Greer, Colonel Jack Hayes, 237.

51. Ibid., 240. And see Thrapp, *Encyclopedia of Frontier Biography*, 2:572: "Eventually he [Gordon] 'married' an Indian girl, learned their language, and joined Apache raiding parties harassing Mexican settlements, coming ever more securely into the Indians' confidence." And see Sweeney, *Mangas Coloradas*, 175.

52. Austerman, "The English Apache," 43: "His [Gordon's] clever schemes for plunder and savage hatred of the Mexicans appealed to them [Apache], and they happily followed the buckskinned Briton on forays against the Rio Grande settlements."

53. Thrapp, *Encyclopedia of Frontier Biography*, 3:1363. And see McCall, *New Mexico in 1850*, 167: "...in which he [Steen] had several engagements with them [Apache], and was once severely wounded."

54. Ibid. For recently [2004] published material on Jack Gordon's criminality, see Selcer's *Legendary Watering Holes*, 126: "They [William McElroy and Jack Gordon] took refreshments in the

bar of Bill Ford, to whom they bragged that they planned to return to El Paso the next day for the purpose of robbing and killing Ben Dowell."

55. Greer, *Colonel Jack Hays*, 240.

56. Ibid., 242. And see Ungnade, *New Mexico Mountains*, 144.

57. Ibid., 244.

58. Thrapp, *Victorio*, 22.

59. McCall, *New Mexico in 1850*, 18.

60. Utley, *Frontiersmen In Blue: The United States Army and the Indian, 1848-1865*, 85.

61. Ball, *Army Regulars*, 4.

62. McCall, *New Mexico in 1850*, 18; Horn, *New Mexico's Troubled Years*, 21.

63. Metz, *Border*, 10.

64. Ibid., 18. For an insightful examination of the race to California for mineral riches, see Marks' *Precious Dust.*

65. Averell, *Ten Years in the Saddle*, 107. Averell recorded in 1857, nearly a decade after the survey had begun, that "[t]he reports of US Engineers who had run boundary lines, or of officers of the army in charge of exploring expeditions, had afforded interesting, but fragmentary glimpses of the wonderful topography of these vast regions which had been under the dominion of the Government of the Untied States only about nine years."

66. Metz, *Border*, 44.

67. Myers, "Fort Webster on the Mimbres River," 48.

68. Sweeney, *Mangas Coloradas*, 229.

69. Cremony, *Life Among the Apaches*, 58-66.

70. Lopez shot the unnamed Apache just six days before the New Mexico Territorial Legislature formally embraced the American system of criminal justice. See Tittmann, "The Last Legal Frontier," 219: "It was on the 12th day of July, 1851, that the legislature of the newly organized Territory of New Mexico adopted the following provision: 'In criminal cases, the common law, as recognized by the United States and the several states of the Union, shall be the rule of practice and decision.'"

71. Cremony, *Life Among the Apaches*, 66-71.

72. Sweeney, *Mangas Coloradas*, 240.

73. Giese, *Forts of New Mexico*, 15, and Frazer, *Forts of the West*, 106. Myers opts for the date of Jan. 23, 1852, rather than 1851 reported by Giese and Frazer, 48.

74. Frazer, *Forts of the West*, 106.

75. Michno, *Encyclopedia of Indian Wars*, 14. Sweeney, *Mangas Coloradas*, 246-7, places the date of the counterattack as Jan. 26, 1852.

76. Ball, *Desert Lawmen*, 11; Julyan, *New Mexico Place Names*, 113.

77. Faulk, *Destiny Road*. 53. Contention regarding the Gadsden Purchase was hard fought in the United States Congress. The originally agreed-to purchase price of $15 million was reduced to $10 million in large part due to remarks by a senator that the land in question was "only fit for jackrabbits and coyotes, and could most probably be purchased in a private transaction for $6,000."

78. Price, *Pioneers of the Mesilla Valley*, 98.

79. Ball, *Desert Lawmen*, 11. For additional data on the legendary Bean family, see Sonnichsen, *The Story of Roy Bean*, 15: "The boys (Bean brothers) were stocky powerful fellows—ambitious, energetic, and determined. They were the kind of boys who would be comforting to have around in an Indian fight but who would be poor risks at a tea party. Any one of them could have been a Captain Kidd or a Commodore Vanderbilt or a Davy Crockett, and all three left a mark on their country." Also see McDaniel, *The Saga of Judge Roy Bean*, 21: "Sam (Bean) was a bull-whacker, a driver of freight wagons between San Antonio and Chihuahua City, Mexico."

80. Julyan, *New Mexico Place Names*, 230, 317.

81. Myers, "Fort Webster on the Mimbres River," 49: "This experiment apparently died aborning, for Washington failed to ratify the treaty and the food and other supplies that Lane had ordered were halted, and the disgruntled Indians returned to their former savage economy, dependent upon the warpath and raids on encroaching civilization." Also see Giese, *Forts of New Mexico*, 16: "The soldiers knew better: only old men, women, and children settled on the Apache farms in the Mimbres Valley."

82. Ibid., 50. And see Giese, *Forts of New Mexico*, 16. Also see Frazer, *Forts of the West*, 105. And for additional data on Colonel Joseph K. F. Mansfield's inspection trip through New Mexico Territory, see Ball, *Army Regulars on the Western Frontier*, 25-6.

83. Giese, *Forts of New Mexico*, 16. And, Myers, "Fort Webster on the Mimbres River," 50.

84. For data regarding stagecoach traffic across southern New Mexico see Austerman, *Sharps*

Rifles and Spanish Mules. Also see Ralph Moody's *Stagecoach West*. And see Rathbun and Alexander, *New Mexico Frontier Military Place Names*.

85. Sweeney, *Mangas Coloradas*, 369.

86. Finch, *A Southwestern Land Scam*. By far this is the most critical and well-documented historical look at the scheme to fraudulently promote Mowry City. And see Ellen R. Cline, "Mowry City." Also, Bell, "The Fabulous Frontier."

87. Allen, "Pinos Altos, New Mexico," 303. Julyan, *Place Names of New Mexico*, 268, identifies Birch as Thomas "Three-Fingered" Birch. Pike in *Roadside New Mexico*, 261, gives Birch's first name as "Henry." Also see Ungnade, *New Mexico Mountains*, 131: "The Pinos Altos (Tall Pines) Mountains 12 miles north of Silver City are part of the Mogollon Volcanic Plateau and composed chiefly of Miocene volcanic rocks. The small northwest-southeast range rise to an altitude of 9,025 feet at Black Peak."

88. In *Precious Dust*, 38, Marks places the discovery of gold in southwestern New Mexico a year earlier than most storytellers: "In the Southwest, prospectors fanned outward from an 1859 strike at Pinos Altos, New Mexico Territory."

89. Ibid.

90. Sherman and Sherman, *Ghost Towns and Mining Camps*, 169.

91. Tevis, *Arizona in the '50s*, 192.

92. Ibid., 199-200.

93. Anderson, "... Memoirs of Hank Smith." 89.

94. Ibid., 90.

95. Tevis, *Arizona in the '50s*, 198.

96. Ibid., 203. For a profile of Swilling, see Thrapp, *Encyclopedia of Frontier Biography*, 3:1394. And for an examination of Swilling's alleged involvement in a stagecoach robbery, see Wilson's *Encyclopedia of Stagecoach Robbery in Arizona*, 79.

97. Marks, *Precious Dust*. The author's treatment of criminality and violence in a chapter titled "No Law but Miners' Law" is an astute assessment of crime and punishment in the early-day mining camps. Correctly she reports (256-7) that "one-on-one fistfights, knifings, and shootings—reflected the youth, masculine pride, drinking habits, and impetuousness of a large portion of the stampeders.... Because combativeness was pervasive and accepted, stampeders sometimes failed to address the violence that resulted... Otherwise, people didn't concern themselves with the results of one-on-one violence, particularly within the confines of a saloon."

98. Tevis, *Arizona in the '50s*, 203.

99. Anderson, "... Memoirs of Hank Smith," 92.

100. Ibid., 93.

101. Reynolds, *Trouble in New Mexico*, 3:90.

102. Allen, "Pinos Altos, New Mexico," 307.

103. Anderson, "...Memoirs of Hank Smith," 93.

104. Ibid.

105. Price, *Pioneers of the Mesilla Valley*, 99.

106. Sonnichsen, *Roy Bean*, 42. For thumbnail sketches of the legendary Bean brothers, see Thrapp, *Encyclopedia of Frontier Biography*, 1:79-80.

107. Thrapp, *Encyclopedia of Frontier Biography*, 1:188-9.

108. Reeve, "... A Soldier's Memoirs," 54-55.

109. Thrapp, *Encyclopedia of Frontier Biography*, 3:1327. Also see John R. Hutto, "Mrs. Elizabeth (Aunt Hank) Smith," *West Texas Historical Association Year Book*. October 1939, 40-47.

110. Sherman and Sherman, *Ghost Towns and Mining Camps*, 170; Allen, "Pinos Altos, New Mexico," 304.

111. Sweeney, *Mangas Coloradas*, 415-416. Also see *Grant County Herald*, July 22, 1876: "Cachise (sic), who, it is said, has since boasted of the exploit, but avers that if he had forty men like those eight he would be invincible."

112. Rathbun and Alexander, *New Mexico Frontier Military Place Names*, 44 and 170. Also see Anderson, "... Memoirs of Hank Smith," 81: "Not a man escaped. Bill Page and Levi Johnson, former chums of ours in the mines and well known by the Indians in former prospecting trips, were hung up by the heels to a cedar tree and burned."

113. Anderson, "With the Confederates in New Mexico...," 65. For a full-length exploration of Hank Smith's thrilling adventures, see Curry, *Sun Rising on the West*.

114. Giese, *Forts of New Mexico*, 16-8. Also see Ferris, *Soldier and Brave*, 223-6: "...was a key post [Fort Bayard. in the Apache Wars..." and "Several expeditions and many patrols set out from the fort

[Fort Cummings., 223-226. Also see Myers, "Military Establishments," 29-40. Fort Cummings was named in honor of "Major Joseph Cummings, 1st New Mexico Cavalry, killed by Navahos near Bonito Cañon August 18,1863." Fort Bayard was given its name in honor of "Brigadier General George D. Bayard, who died on December 14, 1862, of wounds received at Fredericksburg." See Frazer, *Forts of the West*, 95-8.

Chapter 3

115. Thrapp, *Encyclopedia of Frontier Biography*, 3:1255.

116. Horn, *New Mexico's Troubled Years*, 127.

117. Ibid.

117. Ibid., 128. Also see Price, *Pioneers of the Mesilla Valley*, 161.

119. Naegle, "History of Silver City," 2.

120. Julyan, *Place Names of New Mexico*, 324.

121. Murray, *The Gila Wilderness*, 2.

122. Berry and Russell, *Built to Last*, 3.

123. Alexander, *Dangerous Dan Tucker*, 21.

124. Murray, *The Gila Wilderness*, 18-22.

125. Naegle, "History of Silver City," 3. The author makes mention that it is usually written that the first term of district court was held at Piños Altos, or even in some instances at the yet to be founded Silver City, but his inspection of courthouse records clearly reveals it was Central City. And *Grant County Herald*, July 22, 1876: "April 26, 1868, at which John K. Houston was chosen Probate Judge. Dr. A. Brand County Clerk, and Richard Hudson sheriff..." Also see Ball, *Desert Lawmen*, 94. For Joab Houghton, see Elliott, *Mexican War Correspondence ...*, 251. For a thumbnail sketch of Thomas B. Catron, see Price, *Pioneers of the Mesilla Valley*, 122-4.

126. Ball, *Desert Lawmen*, 246-7.

127. *Silver City Independent*, June 5, 1917.

128. Billington, *New Mexico's Buffalo Soldiers*, 16-17. Also see Michno, *Encyclopedia of Indian Wars*, 220.

129. Hill and Hill, "Alias Shakespeare: The Town Nobody Knew," 211-228. Also, Thrapp, *Encyclopedia of Frontier Biography*, 1:475. And, Emma M. Muir, "The Stage to Shakespeare," *New Mexico Magazine*. July 1948, 25-27, 52 and 59. Also see Hill, *Then and Now*, 5. Also, Stanley, *The Shakespeare, New Mexico, Story*, 5. "Shortly after the war Johnny Evensen and Jack Frost were sent to the Southwest to open new stage stations along the National route. Frost remained to care for the Cow Springs station while Evensen located at a spring in the broken country of the Pyramid Mountains, two and half miles from the [future] site of Lordsburg. He first called it Pyramid Station but the popularity of General Grant was at its height in 1867, so he gave it the name of Grant." The Pyramid Mountains are a 22-mile-long and three-to-seven-mile-wide range located directly south of Lordsburg, NM. The two major peaks, North Pyramid Peak and South Pyramid Peak, are of the 6,000-foot sort. See Ungnade, *New Mexico Mountains*, 166.

130. Naegle, "History of Silver City," 3.

131. Ailman, *Pioneering in Territorial Silver City*, 152. And, Berry and Russell, *Built to Last*, 11: "...the tall pine and oaks of the Pinos Altos mountains made the running of a sawmill both practical and lucrative."

132. *Silver City Independent*. May 29, 1917. Also see Nelson and Nelson, *Wild and Woolly Days*, 1:5.

133. Anderson, "Memoirs of Hank Smith," 104.

134. Ibid., 109. Also see Morrill, "Early Days in Silver City," 1: "La Cieniga de San Vicente was a favorite camping place for both Mexicans and Indians before the 'white man' dreamed of such a valley at the foot of the slope from Pinos Altos..."

135. Ibid., 105.

136. Berry and Russell, *Built to Last*, 6.

137. Ibid., 9. And, Naegle, "History of Silver City," 9. Naegle, based on work examining Grant County deed books, adds James McGee to the list of early La Cienega de San Vicente farmers.

138. Nelson and Nelson, *Wild and Woolly Days*, 7.

139. Ashenfelter, "Founding of Silver City," 2.

140. Naegle, "History of Silver City," 10.

141. Ashenfelter, "Founding of Silver City," 2.

142. *Silver City Independent*, May 29, 1917.

143. Ashenfelter, "Founding of Silver City," 2.

144. *Silver City Independent*, May 29, 1917. In continuing with the newspaper account, it goes on to say about the alleged blood oath, "Whether that oath was kept can better be left to those old Indian fighters, who in after years [from time to time] exhibited quietly a peculiar tuft of hair with long strands, that resembled somewhat the flowing locks on an Indian brave."

145. Naegle, "History of Silver City," 69. And see Horn, *New Mexico's Troubled Years, 143:* "Posses were formed in 12 frontier counties to pursue and, if necessary, exterminate all marauding bands of Indians off their reservations. Guns and ammunition were issued from the Governor's Palace to citizens for use by the posses."

146. Ibid.

147. Berry and Russell, *Built to Last*, 9.

148. Hill and Hill, "Alias Shakespeare: The Town Nobody Knew," 214. Also see Ashenfelter, "Founding of Silver City," 3.

149. Naegle, "History of Silver City," 15.

150. Hill and Hill, "Alias Shakespeare: The Town Nobody Knew," 214, quoting the April 2, 1870, *Tucson Weekly Arizonan.*

151. Ibid.

152. Ibid., 215.

153. Ibid., quoting the May 19, 1870, edition of the *Tucson Weekly Arizonan.*

154. Stanley, *The Shakespeare, New Mexico, Story*, 5.

155. Ibid.

156. Nelson and Nelson, *Wild and Woolly Days*, 8, credit Weeks with the remark, which seems likely since he was a generally acknowledged mining expert. Their conclusion is based on and/or confirmed with the remarks of Dan Rose in the May 29, 1917, edition of the *Silver City Independent.* Naegle, "History of Silver City," 16, gives the Bullard brothers credit. Berry and Russell, *Built to Last*, report: "Upon examining the riches at Ralston, [John] Bullard is reported to have said, 'Well, if that's silver ore, I know where there's plenty of it!'" Their assertion is favorably weighted by an excerpt from the Aug. 2, 1879, edition of the *Grant County Herald*: "...and examining the ore, one of the party remarked (and tradition says it was John Bullard), 'Well if that is silver ore, I know where there is lots of it.'" Correctly, authors Berry and Russell, in an endnote, acknowledge the improbability of a conclusive attribution, 9 and 79.

157. *Silver City Independent*, May 19, 1917.

158. Naegle, "History of Silver City," 17.

159. Ibid.

160. Ibid., 18.

161. Ailman, *Pioneering in Territorial Silver City*, 150. And, Berry and Russell, *Built to Last*, 9.

162. Naegle, "History of Silver City," 112.

163. Grant County Clerk, Grant County Deed Book No. 18: Legal Tender [144-145]; Twin Lode 1 [146-147]; Twin Lode 2 [145-146].

164. Ibid., 18.

165. United States Census, 1870 Silver City, Grant County, New Mexico Territory. Also see *Santa Fe Weekly New Mexican*, Feb. 7, 1871. For a complete biography of Whitehill, see Alexander, *Silver City Stalwart.*

166. Naegle, "History of City," 18, quoting the *Las Cruces Borderer*, March 16, 1871..

167. Ibid., quoted by Berry and Russell, *Built to Last*, 10.

168. Naegle, "History of Silver City," 122-116.

169. Ball, *Desert Lawmen*, 180.

170. Ashenfelter, "Founding of Silver City," 4. Also see Morrill, "Early Days in Silver City," 2.

171. Naegle, "History of Silver City," 20.

172. United States Census, Town of Silver City, County of Grant, New Mexico Territory. Aug. 17, 1870.

173. *Silver City Independent.* May 29, 1917.

174. Utley, *Billy the Kid—A Short and Violent Life*, 4.

175. Ibid. The author is not addressing the Silver City meeting in particular, but is presenting a broad overview of violence and its causative dynamics as they apply to life on the American Southwest's frontier—New Mexico Territory during the 1870s specifically.

176. *Grant County Herald*, July 22, 1876. *Silver City Independent*, May 29, 1917. Naegle, "History of Silver City," 21. Berry and Russell, *Built to Last*, 10. Nelson and Nelson, *Wild and Woolly Days*, 8.

Morrill, "Early Days in Silver City," 2.

Chapter 4

177. *Silver City Independent*, May 29, 1917.

178. Ibid.

179. Pioneer Foundation Interview. Number 502. Wayne Whitehill to Lou Blachley. University of New Mexico, Zimmerman Library, Southwest Collection, Albuquerque.

180. Naegle, "History of Silver City," 125.

181. Berry and Russell, *Built to Last*, 10-11. *Silver City Independent*, August 19, 1919. Alexander, *Silver City Stalwart*. Also, Naegle, "History of Silver City," 119.

182. Naegle, "History of Silver City," 121.

183. Ashenfelter, "Founding of Silver City." 5.

184. Nelson and Nelson, *Wild and Woolly Days*, 9.

185. Naegle, "History of Silver City," 117.

186. *Silver City Independent*, June 5, 1917.

187. Ashenfelter, "Founding of Silver City," 5: "Maxwell, disgusted at the rejection of so generous an offer, left the camp and stopped the train bringing in the mill. Thus the Silver Flat Mining District got its first and most serious setback."

188. Sweeney, *Cochise*, 305.

189. Ibid. Also see Hill and Hill, "Alias Shakespeare: The Town Nobody Knew," 216: "Ralston Post Office—named after William Ralston, President of the Bank of California—was opened at the Burro Mines December 8, 1870, with Henry O. Rogers as postmaster." And Julyan, *New Mexico Place Names*, 332: "...the village's name was changed to Ralston."

190. Ibid. And see Thrapp, *Encyclopedia of Frontier Biography*, 3:1251.

191. Ibid. The author equates Arroyo's scouting ability on a par with the legendary Merejildo Grijalva. For an insightful and interesting look at Grijalva, see Sweeney's *Merejildo Grijalva*. Also see Ungnade, *New Mexico Mountains*, 135.

192. Ungnade, *New Mexico Mountains*, 168.

193. Sweeney, *Cochise*, 306.

194. *Silver City Independent*, June 5, 1917.

195. Naegle, "History of Silver City," 71. Also see Marie Stevens Milliken's unpublished "Isaac James Stevens: His Experience as a Pioneer," 12: "About 1871 the Apaches raided the town, stealthily crept up to Harvey Whitehill's corral, opposite where the Post Office now stands, and drove off his herd of valuable horses." Also see Alexander, *Silver City Stalwart*. The author reports that Whitehill was not in Grant County at the time of this Apache incursion. Whitehill had gone back to Elizabethtown to remove his wife and two children to Silver City; see *Santa Fe Weekly New Mexican*, February 7, 1871, "Some of the silver ore brought up from Silver City by Mr. Harvey Whitehill of Elizabethtown has been assayed..." Also see *Silver City Independent*, August 19, 1919. Sweeney, *Cochise*, reports the animals were stolen from Fort Bayard instead of Whitehill's corral, 306: "While Kelly was hunting Indians, a Chiricahua raiding party from Cochise's group stole sixteen horses from Fort Bayard....the post commander issued arms and provision to 30 citizens so they could follow the Indians." If, indeed, the horses were US property, stolen from a US Army fort, assigning civilians the exclusive charge of recovering the herd seems peculiar. Most contemporary old-timer accounts remark the livestock was taken from the Whitehill corral. Quien sabe? Nelson and Nelson in *Wild and Woolly Days*, 13, opt for the traditional story.

196. The list of posse members is a synthesis of several versions. Nelson and Nelson, *Wild and Woolly Days*, 14; McKenna, *Black Range Tales*, 77; Silver City Enterprise, February 17, 1888 and January 16, 1925; *Las Cruces Border* March 16, 1871; Naegle, "History of Silver City," 72; *Silver City Independent*, August 19, 1919; and interview with Bill Wood, grandson of Thomas Jefferson Wood, May 27, 2003, Silver City, NM.

197. *Las Cruces Border*, March 16, 1871; *Silver City Independent*, June 5, 1917. Also see Rathbun and Alexander, *New Mexico Frontier Military Place Names*, 24: "Without reloading his rifle he was approaching a wounded Apache when he was fatally shot." For minor discrepancies regarding the date of Bullard's death, see Naegle, "History of Silver City," 71-73.

198 *Silver City Independent*, August 19, 1919.

199. Sweeney, *Cochise*, 307: "Not long after the battle Piper [Indian Agent] obtained the Indian version of it, confirming that Bullard had run into Cochise."

200. Naegle, "History of Silver City," 74.

201. Berry and Russell, *Built to Last, 12:* "In Silver City, the first mill was owned by the ener-

getic Martin Bremen, who jerry-rigged two older mills from Pinos Altos into a semifunctional phenomenon."

202. *Mining Life*, May 17, 1874.

203. Naegle, "History of Silver City," 111-36.

204. Berry and Russell, *Built to Last*, 12.

205. Ibid.

206. *Silver City Independent*, June 12, 1917.

207. Naegle, "History of Silver City," 22.

208 Ibid.

209. *Silver City Independent*, June 12, 1917.

210. Ibid. Also see Milliken, "Isaac James Stevens," 1. And see *Colorado Families*, 510-1.

211. H. A. Hoover, *Tales From the Bloated Goat—Early Days in Mogollon*, 40.

212. *Silver City Independent*, June 12, 1917.

213. Morrill, "Early Days in Silver City," 6.

214. Naegle, "History of Silver City," 21.

215. Berry and Russell, *Built to Last*, 18.

216. Casey, *The Texas Border*, 313.

217. Ibid.

218. *Silver City Independent*, June 5, 1917.

219. *Silver City Enterprise*, Oct. 17, 1902.

220. Alexander, Dangerous Dan Tucker, 4.

221. Utley, *High Noon in Lincoln*, 176.

222. DeArment, *Knights of the Green Cloth*, 4.

223. Ibid., 113. The author notes the premier Western gambling towns: Deadwood, SD; Virginia City, NV; Omaha, NE; Cheyenne, WY; Denver, Leadville, Pueblo and Trinidad, CO; Dodge City, Wichita and Kansas City, KS; Albuquerque, Taos, Silver City, Santa Fe and Las Vegas, NM; Tucson, Tombstone, Phoenix, Globe and Prescott, AZ; and San Antonio, Tascosa, El Paso, Austin, Dallas and Fort Worth, TX.

224. *Silver City Independent*, June 12, 1917.

225. Horn, *New Mexico's Troubled Years*, 144.

226. Sweeney, *Cochise*, 451.

227. Worcester, *The Apaches*, 127. The author cites "Judge B. Hudson," but assuredly it was Grant County Probate Judge Richard "Dick" Hudson. For additional comment regarding the Grant County folks' attitude toward the Apache living on, and sometimes off, the Canada Alamosa Reservation, see Stout, *Apache Lightning*, 4: "All along the New Mexican frontier trouble was brewing among the irate civilians. Fearful of the real and imagined consequences of quartering warlike Indians on reservations within their midst, these local citizens threatened to act in the name of peace if the government did not." And see Thrapp, *Victorio*, 104: "...calling attention to the 'deplorable condition' of folks in Grant County 'on account of Indian depredations'...wrote to the new governor, William A. Pile." And, quoting a letter from Charles E. Drew, "From information received from reliable sources, I am compelled to believe that [parties] in the lower country [Grant County] is [sic] strongly opposed to any attempt to make peace with the Apaches, and especially to placing of them on a reservation."

228. *Las Cruces Borderer*, May 18, 1871.

229. Horn, *New Mexico's Troubled Years*, 144.

230. *Las Cruces Border*, May 18, 1871.

231. Ibid.

Chapter 5

232. Naegle, "History of Silver City," 115.

233. Grant County Mining Deed Records, Book Number 18, 19, 141, 142, 342, 178, 386.

234. Naegle, "History of Silver City," 124.

235. *Las Cruces Borderer*, Nov. 22, 1871, "Machinery for S. C, Silver City. We learn that Mr. Coleman's stamp mill is on the road from Kit Carson [Colorado]. Also, that the mill for the company of which Mr. Starnberg is agent, is at Kit Carson [Colorado], and that teams have been engaged at Santa Fe for its transportation." And, the edition of Jan. 24, 1872. "Freight, Kit Carson to Mesilla, seven weeks."

236. Grant County Mining Deed Records, Book Number 18, 20.

237. Naegle, "History of Silver City," 127.

238 United States Census, 1870, Silver City, Grant County, New Mexico Territory.

239. *Las Cruces Borderer*, April 24, 1872. And see Berry and Russell, *Built to Last*, 11.

240. *Silver City Enterprise*, March 9, 1894.

241. Berry and Russell, *Built to Last*, 11.

242. Ibid.

243. John G. Bourke, *On the Border With Crook*, 158.

244. *Las Cruces Borderer*, March 16, 1871.

245. Naegle, "History of Silver City," quoting the *Las Cruces Borderer*, Nov. 2, 1872.

246. *Las Cruces Borderer*, August 24, 1872.

247. *Colorado Families*, 597.

248. Morrill, "Early Days in Silver City," 3.

249. Berry and Russell, *Built to Last*, 13.

250. Ibid., 14.

251. Ailman, *Pioneering in Territorial Silver City*, 37.

252. Sladen, *Making Peace with Cochise*, 3-24. Additionally: for Howard, Jeffords, and Streeter, see Thrapp, *Encyclopedia of Frontier Biography*, 2:683 and 723 and 3:1378; for Ponce and Chie, see Sweeney, *Cochise*, 410, 426 and 457.

253. Ibid., 44-4.

254. Ibid., 47 and 144.

255. Ibid. Whether this subject, J. H. Stone, and John Finkel Stone were related is undetermined at this time. The former was unquestionably well thought of in the Silver City, Fort Bayard and Pinos Altos area; the latter "...had some kind of business arrangement with the miners at the Pinos Altos works of New Mexico" and was later killed by Apache near Dragoon Springs in Arizona Territory. See Thrapp, *Encyclopedia of Frontier Biography*, 3:1373-4.

256. Ibid., 48. Thrapp, *Encyclopedia of Frontier Biography*, 1:188, asserts that Bullard later regretted his behavior during the verbal exchange with General Howard.

257. Marks, *Precious Dust*, 257.

258. Naegle, "History of Silver City," 157; the author says *Mining Life*'s one-year anniversary edition was May 21, 1874, acknowledging an 1873 startup. Berry and Russell, *Built to Last*, 18, attribute the first edition as being printed on May 17, 1873. The minor discrepancy is irrelevant—*Mining Life* was Silver City's first newspaper. Terminology referring to Scott as "grumpy" comes straight from Weddle's *Antrim Is My Stepfather's Name*, 9.

259. Ibid., 161.

260. Ibid., 140-2. And see Milliken, "Isaac James Stevens," 13.

261. Harland, Mickelson and Robertson, ... *A Century of Freemasonary at Silver City*, 8.

262. For an insightful examination of this dispute, see R. W. "Ron" Brinkman, Honorary Past Grand Master, A "Paper," on the history of Silver City Lodge, Number 8. Presented at the celebration of 125 years of Masonary in Silver City on Oct. 24, 1998, Homecoming and Past Masters' Night.

263. Naegle, "History of Silver City," 163.

264. Nolan, *The West of Billy the Kid*, 21. The author's notable lifetime of research into the life and adventures of Billy the Kid resulted in this most comprehensive and superbly annotated biography of an Old West legend.

265. Ailman, *Pioneering in Territorial Silver City*, 40.

266. Nolan, *The West of Billy the Kid*, 21.

267. Ibid.

268 Weddle, *Antrim Is My Stepfather's Name*, 10-11.

269. *Silver City Tribune*, Nov. 8 and 15, 1873. Also see Metz, *Encyclopedia of Lawmen, Outlaws, and Gunfighters*, 1-2.

270. *Silver City Independent*, June 5, 1917.

271. Ibid.

272. Weedle, *Antrim Is My Stepfather's Name*, 11.

273. Ibid., 9, quoting *Mining Life*.

274. Ibid.

275. Kadlec, *They "Knew" Billy the Kid*, 1.

276. Nolan, *The West of Billy the Kid*, 22-23. Also see Jacobsen, *Such Men as Billy the Kid*, 14:

"The family set up house in Silver City, a mining camp high in the mountainous southwest corner of the territory, where Antrim hunted for the advertised silver."

277. Meadows, *Pat Garrett and Billy the Kid*, 28.

278. *Silver City Enterprise*, Jan. 3, 1902.

279. *Mining Life*, Sept. 6, 1873. Also see Ball, *Desert Lawmen*, 359.

280. Michno, *Encyclopedia of Indian Wars*, 268.

281. Nolan, "Saga of the San Augustine Ranch," 43-52.

282. Ibid. Also see Metz, *Encyclopedia of Lawmen, Outlaws, and Gunfighters*, 220.

283. Thrapp, *Victorio*, 160. For an interesting and insightful glimpse of Captain Chilson's post of duty, see Caperton and Cohrs, *Fort Selden*. For a biographical sketch of Chilson, see Thrapp, *Encyclopedia of Frontier Biography*, 1:263.

284. O'Neal, *Fighting Men of the Indian Wars*, 28.

285. *Silver City Tribune*, Nov. 8, 1973.

286. Naegle, "History of Silver City," 126.

287. Berry and Russell, *Built to Last*, 14. Also, Ailman, *Pioneering in Territorial Silver City*, 162.

288. Nolan, *The West of Billy the Kid*, 23.

289. Berry and Russell, *Built to Last*, 15.

290. *Silver City Tribune*, Nov. 8 and15, 1873.

291. Ibid., Nov. 8, 1873.

292. Naegle, "History of Silver City," 141.

293. Ibid., 142.

Chapter 6

294. Ibid., 143.

295. Weddle, *Antrim Is My Stepfather's Name*, 11 and 53. Louis Abraham is added to the school list from Kadlec, *They "Knew" Billy the Kid*, 1: Louis Abraham said: "From school each afternoon we made straight for the Antrim home to play." That Joe and Henry adopted the name Antrim may be found in numerous primary and secondary source material; *Grant County Herald*, Sept. 1, 1877; *Mesilla Valley Independent*, Sept. 1, 1877; Utley, *High Noon in Lincoln*, "Like many another drifter, he gave a false name, William H. Bonney, but he also took his stepfather's surname and answered to Henry Antrim, Kid Antrim, or just Kid"; and see Rasch, "The Bonney Brothers." And, Utley, *Billy the Kid*, 6: "Now known by his stepfather's name as well as McCarty, Henry ran with the other boys and did little to set himself apart from them."

296. Kadlec, *They "Knew" Billy the Kid*, 1.

297. Semi-Centennial Celebration Interview. Harry Whitehill. Silver City Museum.

298. Nolan, *The West of Billy the Kid*, 26, citing *Mining Life* editions of Feb. 7 and March 8, 1874.

299. Campbell and Hill, *Triumph and Tragedy*, 22.

300. Naegle, "History of Silver City," 127-8.

301. Ibid., 129.

302. Campbell and Hill, *Triumph and Tragedy*, 25.

303. Berry and Russell, *Built to Last*, 12-4.

304. *Silver City Enterprise*, Nov. 23, 1882.

305. Naegle, "History of Silver City," 163-4. And, Berry and Russell, *Built to Last*, 17.

306. Nolan, *The West of Billy the Kid*, 27. Also see Julyan, *New Mexico Place Names*, 130.

307. Pioneer Foundation Interview, Number 502. Wayne Whitehill.

308. Nolan, *The West of Billy the Kid*, 27.

309. Weddle, *Antrim Is My Stepfather's Name*, 17.

310. *Mining Life*, Sept. 5, 1874.

311. Ibid.

312. Naegle, "History of Silver City," 143. Campbell and Hill, *Triumph and Tragedy*, 1, assert that the teacher for the school term starting in May 1874 was Emma Olive Noyes. There is no reason to doubt their statement.

313. Fradkin, *Stagecoach*, 43, quoting the *Omaha Herald*.

314. Billington, *New Mexico's Buffalo Soldiers*, 166.

315. Ibid., 165.

316. Ibid., 166.

317. Ibid. 10th Cavalry Sgt. Mailton Ross was caught on post at Fort Cummings with Daisy

Shropshire and Luella Brooke, "women of admitted bad repute" who had "remained overnight."

318. *Grant County Herald*, Dec. 1 and 15, 1877

319. Milliken, "Isaac James Stevens," 11.

320. Miller, *Soldiers and Settlers*, 377-378.

321. Nolan, *The West of Billy the Kid*, 30. Naegle, "History of Silver City," 143-4, has school commencing on Sept. 16, 1874, and declares that Richards "apparently did not teach all winter as she 'resumed' her work in the school on May 31, 1875." Also see McGaw, "Billy the Kid's Teacher Saw Him as Sensitive, Effeminate, Fearful Youth." McGaw interviewed Patience Glennon, Mary Richards Casey's daughter, who said her mother "finally landed by stagecoach in Silver City in 1873, to become the first teacher in the town's first school." Certainly Richards was not the city's first teacher, but she did teach during the school's infancy.

322. See above citation. That Richards was Henry Antrim's teacher, at least for a time, is historically firm.

323. *El Paso Herald Post*, Dec. 17, 1960.

324. Nolan, *The West of Billy the Kid*, 27.

325. Ball, *Desert Lawmen*, 359: "McIntosh absconded..." Also see *Silver City Independent*, June 12, 1917: "The way that Harvey Whitehill became sheriff of Grant County, while being fortunate in one sense, it was unfortunate in another, for the reason that a man by the name of McIntosh had been duly elected sheriff of the county, but there was 'a streak of yaller' in him somewhere, for one day he appropriated the county funds for his own especial benefit—$3,000 or more. He saddled his cayuse and hit the trial for Mexico, somewhere between dark and daylight."

326. Alexander, *Dangerous Dan Tucker*, 18.

327. *Grant County Herald*, April 4, 1875. "Coroner Whitehill is now, by virtue of law, the acting Sheriff of Grant county."

328. Ibid., April 11, 1875.

329. For a full-length biography of Harvey Whitehill, see Alexander's *Silver City Stalwart*.

330. Naegle, "History of Silver City," 158. And, Berry and Russell, *Built to Last*, 18.

331. Ibid., quoting the *Grant County Herald* of March 6, 1875.

332. *Grant County Herald*, April 11 and 18, 1875.

333. Ibid., Sept. 5, 1875.

334. *El Paso Herald Post*, Dec. 17, 1960.

335. *Grant County Herald*, Sept. 26, 1875.

336. *Silver City Enterprise*, Jan. 3, 1902.

337. Ibid.

338. *Grant County Herald*, Jan. 2, 1876.

339. Bryan, *Robbers, Rogues and Ruffians*, 46.

340. *Grant County Herald*, Jan. 16, 1876. Also see Clarke, *John Chisum*, 45, and Keleher, *The Fabulous Frontier*, 52.

341. Ibid., Jan. 23, 1876.

342. Thrapp, *Encyclopedia of Frontier Biography* , 1:170.

343. *Grant County Herald*, Jan. 30, 1876.

344. Ibid.

345. Naegle, "The Rebellion Of Grant County, New Mexico in 1876," 233-234. And, Milliken, "Isaac James Stevens," 18: "Eventually he [Isaac J. Stevens] made his home in Clifton, where he with his sons Ike, Charlie and Albert located some of the best mines in that region, among them being Chase Creek, the Copper King and the Last Chance, in all about 300 claims." Also see Barnes, *Arizona Place Names*, 99 and 180. And, Varney, *Arizona Ghost Towns and Mining Camps*, 82-91: "Bob [Metcalf] and his brother Jim came back to the canyon years later, named the stream 'Chase Creek' in honor of the captain who led them on that fortuitous mission, and filed the Metcalf claims. They called their first mine the Longfellow, reportedly because they discovered the ore on the poet's birthday. It turned out to be the first mine to tap into one of the richest, longest-lasting copper deposits in the United States. Nevertheless, the Metcalf claims were sold to the Lesinsky brothers in 1872."

346. Ibid., 231.

347. Kelly, *Arizona: A Legislative History*, 75.

348. Naegle, "The Rebellion of Grant County," 236.

349. Ibid., 237.

350. Ibid., 240.

351. Utley, *Frontier Regulars*, 359. For a brief sketch of Colonel Edward Hatch, see Thrapp,

Encyclopedia of Frontier Biography, 2:629.

352. Billington, *New Mexico's Buffalo Soldiers*, 47.

353. Leckie, *The Buffalo Soldiers*, 177.

354. Thrapp, *Victorio*, 175.

355. Ibid., 176.

356. Ibid.

357. Ibid.

358. Billington, *New Mexico's Buffalo Soldiers*, 47.

359. O'Neal, *Fighting Men of the Indian Wars*, 74. And see Thrapp, *Encyclopedia of Frontier Biography*, 1:231, for a succinct profile of Henry Carroll. Also see Ungnade, *New Mexico Mountains*, 162: "A few small caves in the Florida Mountains contained evidence of prehistoric occupation. In later times these mountains were Apache territory, lying on the Apache Trail between the Black Range and the Sierra Madre Mountains in Mexico."

360. Ibid., 75.

361. Michno, *Encyclopedia of Indian Wars*, 299.

362. Ibid. There has been, and is, no little confusion regarding Carroll's campaign in the Florida Mountains, O'Neal crediting him with two distinct engagements, while Michno limits it to but one. Historically for this text the inconsistency is irrelevant; the Apache were running throughout Grant County and the Silver City citizens were fuming because of numerous Apache depredations. In fact, Thrapp is clearly troubled by the confusion: "The chronology may be open to question, but it is difficult to correlate the events any other way [than by dead reckoning.. The various authorities seem to confuse 1877, 1878 and 1879 completely and to ignore their now obvious discrepancies." See Thrapp, *Conquest of Apacheria*, 179.

Chapter 7

363. Michno, *Encyclopedia of Indian Wars*, 302.

364. Ibid., 303-304. And, O'Neal, *Fighting Men of the Indian Wars*, 32. And, *Grant County Herald*, Feb. 24, 1877.

365. *Grant County Herald*, March 18, 1881. And, Gilbreath, *Death on the Gallows*, 80-82. Also, Alexander, *Dangerous Dan Tucker*, 60. And see Williams, *Pioneer Surveyor—Frontier Lawyer*. Williams confuses the name Winterburn for Rafferty, 188.

366. *Silver City Independent*, Sept. 22, 1931. Also see Pioneer Foundation Interview. No. 503. Wayne Whitehill. "And while they was holdin' him [Remine] there in jail, why he done all the kitchen work, the cookin' in the kitchen for the prisoners. But he done all the tradin', went out to the stores.... He was a trusty, yeah. He'd do all the trusty work out, buyin' groceries and everything.... He'd go right down to any place he wanted to, a privileged character."

367. *Grant County Herald*, May 12, 1877.

368. Bryan, *Robbers, Rogues and Ruffians*, 44-53. For a first-rate biographical sketch of outlaw Martin, see Cool, "Bob Martin: A Rustler in Paradise."

369. Ibid. And see the June 2, 1877, edition of the *Grant County Herald*. "Deputy Sheriff Armijo captured 'Dutch Joe' at Santa Barbara, near Fort Thorn, who is doubtless one of the party who robbed the coach some two years ago in Cook's Canon; also on May 9th near Cummings."

370. *Grant County Herald*, May 12, 1877. Richmond [now Virden] and now located in Hidalgo County, is situated on the Gila River about 30 miles northwest of Lordsburg. See Julyan, *Place Names of New Mexico*, 373.

371. Ibid.

372. Worcester, *The Apaches*, 199.

373. Clum, *Apache Days and Tombstone Nights*, 21, and Thrapp, *Conquest of Apacheria*, 172.

374. Ibid. As a first sergeant in Company B, Fifth Cavalry, Clay Beauford won the Medal of Honor during campaigns against Apache during the 1872-1873 time period. See O'Neal, *Fighting Men of the Indian Wars*, 28. Thrapp asserts that Beauford's true name was Welford Chapman Bridwell, 167. And see Thrapp, *Encyclopedia of Frontier Biography*, 1:168: "...he joined Lee's Army of Virginia as a drummer boy, giving his fictitious name to avoid parental detection, the name Clay Beauford, being used by him for many years."

375. Clum, *Apache Agent*, 207.

376. Worcester, *The Apaches*, 201. And, Clum, *Apache Days and Tombstone Nights*, 121: "The distance by trail from San Carlos to Ojo Caliente is something like 350 or 400 miles, and the greater part of my little army of Indians measured the entire distance of the round trip on foot." And, Lockwood, *The Apache Indians*, 219: "Clum and his police met Beauford and his militia at Silver City

as planned." Also, Clum, *Apache Agent*, 213: "I told Captain Beauford I would take with me 22 of the Apache police for whom we had obtained horses at Silver City."

377. Ibid. And for additional data on Major Wade, see Thrapp, *Encyclopedia of Frontier Biography*, 3:1493. And, Kenner, *Buffalo Soldiers*, 9: "Although regular officers who transferred to the black regiments received a one-grade promotion, Lieutenant Colonel Wesley Merritt (Second Cavalry) and Major James Wade (Sixth Cavalry) were the only regulars of note to switch to the Ninth Cavalry."

378. Clum, *Apache Agent*, 212.

379. *Grant County Herald*, May 12, 1877.

380. Aleshire, *The Fox and the Whirlwind*, 149: "Many said Victorio should not let Geronimo stay [at Ojo Calentie...." And, Lockwood, *The Apache Indians*, 222: "Up to this time Victorio had been inclined toward peace, and had sometimes taken Geronimo to task for his raids."

381. Worcester, *The Apaches*, 201.

382. Debo, *Geronimo*, 105: "The reserve police arrived at about four o'clock in the morning and were concealed in the commissary building."

383. Barrett, *Geronimo's Story*, 131. Geronimo goes on to say he was "met, disarmed and arrested by soldiers," which was clearly not the case. Perhaps he was somewhat embarrassed by having been taking into custody by fellow Apache, who thought of him as nothing but an outlaw renegade. And see Roberts, *Once They Moved Like the Wind*, 168: "Geronimo himself was vague about the event....Yet both Geronimo and other Chiricahuas admitted that somehow he had been tricked into imprisonment, and that he was carried to San Carlos in leg-irons. Perhaps Clum's account is essentially truthful after all. To be grandiose is one thing, dishonest another, and few men ever called Clum dishonest."

384. Clum, *Apache Agent*, 218.

385. Ibid., 219.

386. Ibid., 228.

387. Ibid., 235.

388. Billington, *New Mexico's Buffalo Soldiers*, 52.

389. Thrapp, *Victorio*, 188.

390. Worcester, *The Apaches*, 203-204.

391. Ibid. The practice of warehousing weapons and other essentials for later use was a widely known practice of Apache. And, Adams, *Geronimo: A Biography*, 203: "Above all things, Victorio loved the land around Canada Alamosa, but he did not want war with the Americans."

392. Thrapp, *Victorio*, 193: "General Crook often mentioned this custom in support of his conviction that disarming them was virtually impossible, and in any event, would be unwise."

393. Ibid., 358.

394. Clum, *Apache Agent*, 244-6: "He [Clum] explained that Ponce, being present at the 'count' each day, could prove, by the agency records, that he had not been with the raiders.... The renegades understood, nodded heads to one another."

395. Clum, *Apache Days and Tombstone Nights*, 129. And, Clum, *Apache Agent*, 244.

396. Ibid.

397. Ibid., 130-133.

398. *Grant County Herald,* April 28, 1877. This edition also carried a telegram from Colonel Edward Hatch: "The troops are now out for straggling braves."

399. Ibid., May 5, 1877.

400. Ibid., May 12, 1877.

401. Ibid., May 19, 1877. Davis' first name is given as "David" in another account.

402. Ibid.

403. Pioneer Foundation Interview. Number 502. Wayne Whitehill. The interview is a somewhat jumbled reconstruction of events and, admittedly, Wayne Whitehill asserts his father contracted to guard Apache removed from the Mescalero Reservation and transported to the San Carlos Reservation. Whether he confused the Ojo Calentie with the Mescalero is unclear, but in any event, it would have been practical to guard Apache prisoners from any civilian retribution while passing through the Silver City area.

404. *Grant County Herald*, May 12, 1877.

405. Ibid.

406. Clum, *Apache Days and Tombstone Nights*, 133. Clum, *Apache Agent*, 249, places the number of prisoners locked in the San Carlos Agency's guardhouse as 19.

407. *Grant County Herald,* May 26, 1877.

408. Ibid., April, 4, 1877.

409. Pioneer Foundation Interview. Number 501. Wayne Whitehill.

410. *Grant County Herald,* Oct. 27, 1877.

411. Letter, Samuel Axtell, Governor, to Harvey Whitehill, Sheriff, June 23, 1877. Territorial Archives of New Mexico, Roll 98, frame 772. New Mexico Commission of Public Records, State Records Center and Archives (SRC&A), Santa Fe. And, Alexander, *Silver City Stalwart.* Also see Ball, "Militia Posses: The Territorial Militia In Civil Law Enforcement In New Mexico Territory, 1877-1883," 47-69.

412. Letter, Governor Samuel B. Axtell to J. F. Bennett, June 23, 1877. Roll 98, Frame 773, SRC&A.

413. Alexander, *Dangerous Dan Tucker,* 9, 103 and 167. For brief biographical sketches, see DeArment, "Deadly Deputy," and Thrapp, *Encyclopedia of Frontier Biography,* 3:1442-3. And see Metz, *Encyclopedia of Lawmen, Outlaws, and Gunfighters,* 250: "Numerous press clippings document Tucker's wide-ranging law enforcement activities in Grant County. None, however, make derogatory comments, which is somewhat unusual for a time when partisan politics played such a significant role in any sheriff's or marshal's administration."

414. *Silver City Independent,* June 12, 1917, and Sept. 22, 1931. *Silver City Enterprise,* Oct. 17, 1902.

415. Hertzog, *Outlaws of New Mexico,* 11, 30, 33 and 34. William "Wild Bill" Martin should not be confused with the aforementioned Robert E. "Bob" Martin or with William A. "Hurricane Bill" Martin. And see Alexander, *Dangerous Dan Tucker,* 24.

416. *Grant County Herald,* June 23, 1877.

417. By another account, Nelson was killed by posseman Thomas Jefferson "Tom" Wood. Interview with Bill Wood, Tom Wood's grandson, Silver City, May 27, 2003. And see *Silver City Enterprise,* Jan. 16, 1925, "Wood and Parker fired from close range, Parker killing the Portuguese, while Wood missed Nelson. Nelson fired a second shot, which also went wild and as he tried to escape was shot from his horse and killed by Wood."

418. *Grant County Herald,* August 18, 1877.

419. *Silver City Enterprise,* June 6, 1917 and *Grant County Herald,* Sept. 1, 1877.

420. Alexander, *Dangerous Dan Tucker,* 27. And, Metz, *Encyclopedia of Lawmen, Outlaws and Gunfighters,* 250.

421. *Silver City Independent,* Sept. 22, 1931. And see DeArment, *Deadly Dozen,* 68.

422. Ailman, *Pioneering in Territorial Silver City,* 148. And, *Grant County Herald,* August 18, 1877.

423. *Grant County Herald,* Aug. 11, 1877. And see Alexander, *Dangerous Dan Tucker,* 28.

424. *Grant County Herald,* Jan. 2, 1876.

425. Governor's proclamation and invoice reflecting Harvey Whitehill's payment to the *Grant County Herald* for publishing the reward notice. Roll 98, Frame 789, SRC&A.

426. *Silver City Independent,* June 19, 1917.

427. *Grant County Herald,* April 28, 1877.

428. Naegle, "History of Silver City," 132.

429. Berry and Russell, *Built to Last,* 14.

430. *Grant County Herald,* Nov. 3, 1877.

431. Ibid., Oct. 27, 1877.

432. Ibid.

433. Ibid., Nov. 3, 1877.

434. Ibid., Dec. 8, 1877.

435. Ibid., Dec. 15, 1877, and Oct. 27, 1877.

436. Ibid., Nov. 3, 1877.

437. Ibid., Nov. 24, 1877. And see Berry and Russell, *Built to Last,* 17.

438. Ibid., Dec. 8, 1877.

439. Ibid., Oct. 6, 1877, and Nov. 3, 1877.

440. Naegle, "History of Silver City," 160.

441. *Grant County Herald,* Feb. 24, 1877.

442. Naegle, "History of Silver City," 145. Inspection of old docket books at the New Mexico State Records Center and Archives plainly reveals the regularity of arrests for the so-called "Sunday Law" violations. Many of Silver City's most prominent merchants and businessmen were consistently fined.

443. Ibid., 146.
444. *Grant County Herald*. Oct. 6, 1877.
445. Ibid., Nov. 3, 1877.
446. Ibid., Feb., 24, 1877.
447. Ibid., Nov. 24, 1877.
448. Ibid., Oct. 6, 1877.
449. Ibid.
450. Ibid., Dec. 15 and 22, 1877.
451. Ibid., Dec. 8, 1877.
452. Ibid., Dec. 22, 1877.
453. Ibid.
454. Charles Francis Ward, "The Salt War of San Elizario, 1877," master's thesis, University of Texas, Austin, 1932.
455. Sonnichsen, *The El Paso Salt War*, 49-58. Also, Alexander, *Dangerous Dan Tucker*, 35-46.
456. United States House of Representatives Executive Document No. 93, 45th Congress, 2nd Session, 1878.
457. *Galveston Daily News*, Jan. 6, 1878.
458. Sonnichsen, *The El Paso Salt War*, 58.
459. *Grant County Herald*, Dec. 22, 1877.
460. Alexander, *Dangerous Dan Tucker*, 41.
461. Ward, "The Salt War of San Elizario," 122.
462. Ibid. Also see Boardman and Cunningham, *Revenge!* Specifically see Paul Cool's chapter, "The Many Lives and Suggested Death of Jim McDaniels," 31: "They were a gang with badges, perhaps the first southwest border area criminals to be sworn in on a large scale to fight a 'local' war. The 'Kinney gang's' actions in the Rio Grande Valley were as much nuisance as criminal, but they established a precedent for future 'wars' from Lincoln to Tombstone." And see Brand, "Sherman W. McMaster(s), The El Paso Salt War, Texas Rangers and Tombstone."
463. *Grant County Herald*, Jan. 26, 1878.
464. Ibid., Dec. 15, 1877.
465. Ibid., Dec. 22, 1877.
466. Michno, *Encyclopedia of Indian Wars*, 316.
467. Thrapp, The *Conquest of Apacheria*, 178-179.

Chapter 8

468. *Grant County Herald,* Jan. 5, 1878.
469. Naegle, "History of Silver City," 174.
470. *Grant County Herald,* March 23, 1878.
471. Naegle, "History of Silver City," 175.
472. Ibid., 176.
473. Berry and Russell, *Built to Last*, 19. And see Ailman, *Pioneering in Territorial Silver City, 161:* "Robert Black was the first mayor of Silver City, elected in 1878, 1879 and again in 1883."
474. Alexander, *Dangerous Dan Tucker*, 47.
475. *Grant County Herald*, July 20, 1878. And see DeArment, *Deadly Dozen*, 70.
476. Pioneer Foundation Interview. Number 503. Wayne Whitehill.
477. Ibid.
478. DeArment, *Deadly Dozen*, 69. And, Alexander, *Dangerous Dan Tucker*, 51. Also see *Silver City Independent*, Sept. 22, 1931.
479. *Grant County Herald*, June 15, 1878.
480. Ibid., Sept. 21, 1878.
481. Ibid.
482. Ibid., Jan. 26, 1878.
483. Julyan, *New Mexico Place Names*, 130. The author correctly places Dick Hudson's purchase of the property in 1878, and that the name of the springs was later changed to Hudson's Hot Springs.
484. *Grant County Herald*, Sept. 21, 1878.
485. Ibid., picking up a story from the *Mesilla Independent*.

486. Ibid., Sept. 11, 1878.

487. Ibid., June 15, 1878. Also see Julyan, *New Mexico Place Names*, 146: "At the community's peak around 1888 Georgetown had 1,200 people."

488. Sherman and Sherman, *Ghost Towns and Mining Camps*, 91. And, Cannon with Lape, "Silver Boom Town," 23, 45 and 47.

489. *Grant County Herald*, December 28, 1878.

490. Sherman and Sherman, *Ghost Towns and Mining Camps*, 91: The name of Lowery's newspaper was changed to the *Georgetown Courier* in August 1881.

491. Hill and Hill, "Alias Shakespeare—The Town Nobody Knew," 221.

492. Thrapp, "Shakespeare's Lively Ghosts," *Westways*, March 1961, 18.**NOT IN BIBLIO.** For an excellent analysis and an article adroitly raising historic questions concerning "The Great Diamond Hoax," see Rita Hill, "Mysteries Set with Diamonds," *True West*, September-October 1980, 44-47.

493. Ibid.

494. Hill, "Then and Now," 13.

495. Naegle, "History of Silver City," 130.

496. Johnson, "The Redding Boys," 7-18: "In the Spring of 1877, we heard of the great silver strike at the 76 Mine at Silver City, New Mexico." Also see Johnson, *John Ringo*, 107-8: "The party [Olney, Ringo and others] left for Silver City and reached Mesilla without incident...Ringo and Olney left the [wagon. train at Silver City and headed south..." And, 133, "The latter [Ringo] signed the bill-of sale as 'John R.' 'John R. what?' 'John R. Godalmighty,' retorted an exasperated Ringo..."

497. Naegle, "History of Silver City," 131.

498. *Grant County Herald*, Sept. 6, 1879.

499. Naegle, "History of Silver City," 132.

500. *Grant County Herald*, March 1 and 15, April 5, and July 19, 1879. And see Grant County Civil and Criminal Cost Docket Book and Register of Prisoners Confined in the County Jail of Grant County (both SRC&A). Also see Alexander, *Silver City Stalwart: Harvey H. Whitehill*, Chapter 5, and Gilbreath, *Death on the Gallows*, 83-87.

501. Davis, *The Truth about Geronimo*, 31.

502. Thrapp, *Victorio*, 192.

503. Ibid., 211, quoting the *Arizona Star*, March 29 and April 6, 1880.

504. Ibid., 216.

505. Billington, *New Mexico's Buffalo Soldiers*, 88. And see Thrapp, *Encyclopedia of Frontier Biography*, 1:104.

506. Ibid.

507. O'Neal, *Fighting Men of the Indian Wars*, 32.

508. Billington, *New Mexico's Buffalo Soldiers*, 88.

509. Michno, *Encyclopedia of Indian Wars*, 323-324.

510. Ibid. For gallant heroism under fire, Lieutenant Wright, guide John Foster, Navaho scout Hostensorze, Sergeants Delaware Penn, George Lyman, along with Privates Isam Malry and [?] Ridgely received medals. See Billington, *New Mexico's Buffalo Soldiers*, 89.

511. Thrapp, *Victorio*, 214.

512. *Grant County Herald*, July 19, 1879.

513. Ibid. Also, Grant County Criminal District Court Book. Posting of Indictments. #573 and #574 Victorio (an Indian) Murder; # 576 Victorio (an Indian) Stealing Horses. July 17 and 18, 1879, SRC&A.

514. Ibid.

515. Alexander, "and we say, well done Dan!," 5-11.

516. *Silver City Enterprise*, Oct. 1, 1886.

517. Alexander, *Lawmen, Outlaws and S.O.Bs*, from the introduction by renowned outlaw/lawman historian, author and editor Chuck Parsons, 3. A reasonably complete biographical sketch of Dan Coomer may be found in this volume, Chapter 13. For a brief profile of Coomer, see Metz, *Encyclopedia of Lawmen, Outlaws, and Gunfighters*, 51-2.

518. *Silver City Enterprise*, Dec. 26, 1902.

519. *Grant County Herald*, Oct. 11, 1879.

520. Ibid., Sept. 20, 1879.

521. Ibid.

522. Naegle, "History of Silver City," 147.

523. *Grant County Herald,* May 3, 1879.

524. Naegle, "History of Silver City," 167.

525. *Grant County Herald,* March 15, 1879.

526. Ibid., July 19, 1879.

527. Ibid., April 5, 1879.

528. Thrapp, *Victorio,* 217.

529. Ibid., 218.

530. Ball, *In the Days of Victorio,* 71: "When he [Nana] took my little sister in his arms no one could have believed him to be the fiercest and most implacable of all Apaches, but that was the verdict of my people. Certainly he was considered the shrewdest in military strategy, surpassing Victorio himself.... No young warrior excelled him in endurance, and at that time neither his age nor his broken foot seemed to handicap him."

531. Leckie, *The Buffalo Soldiers,* 211.

532. O'Neal, *Fighting Men of the Indian Wars,* 32-3.

533. Billington, *New Mexico's Buffalo Soldiers,* 91.

534. Johnson, *John Ringo,* 106.

535. Aranda, "An Episode From Victorio's War," 15-9.

536. Thrapp, *Conquest of Apacheria,* 186.

537. Ibid. And see Thrapp, *Encyclopedia of Frontier Biography,* 1:753: "...he [Juh] was notably cruel. He was described as six feet or more tall, dark-skinned, weighed about 225 pounds, had a speech impediment."

538. Nelson and Nelson, *Wild and Woolly Days, 36.* There is considerable conflict as to the exact date—and even the exact year—that this attack took place; however, there is little doubt it happened, and probably close to the way it was remembered by old-timers.

539. Nunn, "Boston Charlie's Last Stand," 47, 63. Nunn opts for the spelling "Batchelder," which seems reasonable, since later a George G. Batchelder, a former editor of the *New York Maritime Register,* was in Silver City on a business trip.

540. *Silver City Independent,* July 3,1917.

541. Worcester, *The Apaches,* 224.

Chapter 9

542. *Grant County Herald,* March 20, 1880.

543. Ibid. July 31, 1880. Also see Naegle, "History of Silver City," 172.

544. Naegle, "History of Silver City," 173.

545. Berry and Russell, *Built to Last,* 20. Also, *Grant County Herald,* April 12, 1880.

546. Naegle, "History of Silver City," 167.

547. Ibid., 164-6.

548. Ibid.

549. Ibid.

550. Ibid., 150.

551. Ibid., 161-2.

552. Ibid., 133.

553. Berry and Russell, *Built to Last,* 20.

554. Ibid.

555. *Southwest Sentinel,* August 25, 1883.

556. Berry and Russell, *Built to Last,* 20, quoting the *Silver City Enterprise* of July 23, 1886, which was in turn picking up comments from the *Santa Fe New Mexican.*

557. Ailman, *Pioneering in Territorial Silver City,* 166.

558. Ibid. "Before the Southern Pacific Railroad was completed, copper from the mines at Clifton, Arizona, was shipped through Silver City."

559. *Grant County Herald,* Jan. 29, 1880.

560. Ibid., July 31, 1880.

561. *The Daily Southwest.* August 7, 1880.

562. Ibid., March 10, 1880.

563. Ibid., April 12, 1880.

564. Ibid., March 10, 1880.

565. Ibid., August 20, 1880

566. *Grant County Herald,* March 6, 1880.

567. Moynahan, *Talkin' About Sportin' Women,* 29: Listing Western frontier madams the author identifies "Big Jess" at Silver City, which possibly could have been Bessie Harper, but such an assertion is speculative at best. Also see *Silver City Enterprise,* June 1, 1888. And see Berry and Russell, *Built to Last,* 32-3. For discussions of prostitution in America's frontier West, see Butler, *Daughters of Joy,* and Seagraves, *Soiled Doves.* Also, Moynahan, *Fifty Years of Prostitute Photos.*

568. Leckie, *The Buffalo Soldiers,* 214.

569. Thrapp, *Conquest of Apacheria,* 190. The assertion that Victorio crossed near the Portrillo Mountains may be found in Laumbach, *Hembrillo,* as was the reference to his having 60 warriors with him, 121. The Portrillo Mountains are a small range of hills between modern-day Columbus, NM, and El Paso, TX, see Ungnade, *New Mexico Mountains,* 161.

570. Ibid., 194.

571. Worcester, *The Apaches,* 227, quoting the *Daily Southwest.*

572. Laumbach, *Hembrillo,* 122: "The context of Kelley's letter make it probable that this incident occurred in January 1880. It is illustrative of Victorio's efforts to arrange an amicable settlement."

573. For brief biographical sketches of Albert Payson Morrow, see Thrapp, *Encyclopedia of Frontier Biography, 2:*1019, and O'Neal, *Fighting Men of the Indian Wars,* 176-177.

574. Michno, *Encyclopedia of Indian Wars,* 328-329.

575. Thrapp, *Victorio,* 261.

576. For James Hansell French's earlier participation in the Lincoln County War, see Nolan's comprehensive *The Lincoln County War,* 362: "For all his youth, French was something of a firebrand, and also a heavy drinker." And other citations throughout. Also see Maurice G. Fulton's *History of the Lincoln County War,* edited by Robert N. Mullin, 313-317. And, Thrapp's *Encyclopedia of Frontier Biography,* 1:520: "French was reported to be 'overbearing and quarrelsome, especially when under the influence,' but he was cleared by a board of officers of alleged abuses against McSween adherents."

577. Michno, *Encyclopedia of Indian Wars,* 330.

578. Thrapp, *Victorio,* 263. And, Ungnade, *New Mexico Mountains,* 147: "They [San Andres] are 6-17 miles wide and drained by 14 east-west canyons.... These mountains between the Tularosa Plain and the Jornada del Muerto extend 80 miles from Mockingbird Gap to San Augustin Pass."

579. *The Daily Southwest,* March 10, 1880.

580. *Grant County Herald,* March 27, 1880.

581. *The Daily Southwest,* March 26, 1880. Discussion of US-Mexican Indian policy at the time of Victorio's campaign is skillfully explored by Dinges, "The Victorio Campaign of 1880: Cooperation and Conflict on the United States—Mexico Border," 81-94.

582. Thrapp, *Encyclopedia of Frontier Biography* , 2:934.

583. Laumbach, *Hembrillo,* 156.

584. For a thorough discussion of this tactic, see Dunlay, *Wolves for the Blue Soldiers,* 165: "No Indian scout units achieved more contemporary and historical fame or generated more controversy than the Apache scouts of Arizona.... They furnish probably the best documented example of two of the most striking features of the Indian scout phenomenon: the way in which formerly hostile Indians became instruments of white conquest and assimilation, and the readiness of some Indians to serve against their own people."

585. For discussion of the generally written account that the soldiers were sickened by drinking foul water, and for a questioning opinion, see Laumbach, *Hembrillo,* 173.

586. Michno, *Encyclopedia of Indian Wars,* 331-2. By far, the best account of this Apache-US Military melee is found in Laumbach's *Hembrillo.* For a profile of Captain Curwen McLellan, see Thrapp. *Encyclopedia of Frontier Biography,* 2:918-9.

587. *Grant County Herald,* May 8, 1880.

588. Billington, *The Buffalo Soldiers* of New Mexico, 94.

589. Utley, *Frontier Regulars,* 362.

590. *Grant County Herald,* May 8, 1880.

591. Thrapp, *Conquest of Apacheria,* 198.

592. *Silver City Enterprise,* Dec. 14, 1906.

593. Semi-Centennial Celebration Interview. Harry Whitehill, SCM.

594. *Grant County Herald,* May 8, 1880.

595. Ibid.

596. Ibid.

597. Ibid.

598. Ibid., June 12, 1880.

599. Cozzens, *The Struggle for Apacheria*, 213-23, quoting in its entirety Charles B. Gatewood, "Campaigning against Victorio in 1879," *The Great Divide*, August 1894. Also see Thrapp, *Encyclopedia of Frontier Biography*, 2:543-4.

600. *The Daily Southwest*, March 31, 1880.

601. Michno, *Encyclopedia of Indian Wars*, 334.

602. Thrapp, *Victorio*, 280.

603. Thrapp, *Encyclopedia of Frontier Biography*, 3:1112.

604. Ibid.

605. Michno, *Encyclopedia of Indian Wars*, 334.

606. *Grant County Herald*, June 12, 1880.

607. Leckie, *The Buffalo Soldiers*, 210, quoting General John Pope's 1880 Annual Report to the Secretary of War.

608. Gilbreath, *Death on the Gallows*, 76. And see *The Daily Southwest*, July 27, 1880. Also, *Grant County Herald*, Feb. 12, 1881: "Barney O'Tool was the real name of the man who was executed here last August under the name of Chas. Williams. His father lives some 20 miles east of Wheeling, West Virginia."

609. Alexander, *Dangerous Dan Tucker*, 58-59. Also, *Grant County Herald*, July 31, 1880. And see *Silver City Enterprise*, Oct. 27, 1949.

610. *The Daily Southwest*, August 20, 1880.

611. Alexander, *Dangerous Dan Tucker*, 54; the list is not inclusive.

612. Ibid. And, Hill, *Then and Now*, 30-4 and 44-6.

613. Williams, *Pioneer Surveyor—Frontier Lawyer*, 122.

614. Ibid., 123.

615. Cruse, *Apache Days and After*, 54.

616. Thrapp, *Conquest of Apacheria*, 207.

617. Michno, *Encyclopedia of Indian Wars*, 336.

618. *The Herald & Southwest*, Jan. 29, 1881. Those who kicked in for the Apache bounty fund were: $200 donation, Meredith and Ailman; $100 donation, A. S. Addis, E. P. LeDoux, C. Bennett, H. H. Whitehill, G. W. Bailey, C. P. Crawford, Gideon Truesdale, N. M. & T. Co., Black & Co., Max Shutz, Evans & Holt, Conway & Risque; $50 donation New Bradley, Luke Bros., L. D. Miller, Louis Timmer; $25 donation, S. M. Ashenfelter, E. Stine, James Corbin, W. C. Ross, Charles O. Butts, Hull & Williams, J. H. Mills, Martin Maher; $20 donation, William S. Smith; $10 donation, William H. McGary, J. S. Crouch, J. E. Coleman, H. D. Gilbert, S. Butschofsky, William Chamberlin, Howlett & Morris, George W. Sly, Sam Eckstine, and W. B. Gibson.

619. Ibid.

Chapter 10

620. Thrapp, *Victorio*, 293-307. Also, *Grant County Herald*, Oct. 23, 1880. And see Utley, "*The Buffalo Soldiers* and Victorio," 47-54.

621. Primary and secondary accounts of Remine's execution are abundant: *Grant County Herald*, March 19, 1881; *Silver City Independent*, Sept. 22, 1931; *Silver City Enterprise*, Oct. 27, 1949; Register of Prisoners Confined in the Grant County Jail; Williams, *Pioneer Surveyor—Frontier Lawyer*; Gilbreth, *Death on the Gallows*; Alexander, *Dangerous Dan Tucker*; and Pioneer Foundation Interview, Wayne Whitehill.

622. Gilbreth, *Death on the Gallows*, 83-4, quoting the March 26,1881, *Santa Fe New Mexican*.

623. Unger, *True Tales*, 2, quoting the Nov. 16, 1882, *Silver City Enterprise*.

624. Julyan, *New Mexico Place Names*, 208: There are several theories as to how Lordsburg got its name; the author reports that the one cited in this text is "the most likely." For a contrasting assertation see *In the Shadow of the Pyramids*, 105, which declares Lordsburg was named after Doctor Charles H. Lord. Or, Willard E. Holt [Chamber of Commerce], Service Record Book of Men and Women of Hidalgo County, 40: "There was a man by the name of Lord who had a string of eating houses along the line of the Southern Pacific from the west, and it was for him that the town was named." Also see Myrick, *New Mexico's Railroads*, 60.

625. Pike, *Roadside New Mexico*, 349.

626. Myrick, *New Mexico's Railroads*, 60.

627. Unpublished typescript with notation, "Dr. Jeffrey Brown's historical survey of downtown buildings—1986," courtesy of Art Roman, Deming Luna Mimbres Museum Archives. Deming. Pike, *Roadside New Mexico*, 345, attributes the name "Little Chicago" to the new settlement. Julyan, *New Mexico Place Names*, 108, opts for "New Chicago."

628. Alexander, *Dangerous Dan Tucker*, 70 and 80.

629. William Greever, "Railway Development in the Southwest," 163.

630. Edward Pennington, unpublished 1902 typescript on the history of Deming. Pennington was the former editor of the *Deming Headlight*. Courtesy of Wayne B. Humphrey, Deming.

631. Ball, "Militia Posses, The Territorial Militia In Civil Law Enforcement In New Mexico Territory, 1877-1883," 48.

632. Keith Wheeler, *The Railroaders*, 101.

633. Gustafson, "Dan Tucker, Deming's Lethal Lawman," 8.

634. *The New Southwest & Grant County Herald*, April 9, 1881.

635. Casey, *The Texas Border*, 189.

636. Chase, *The Editor's Run*, 127.

637. Ibid.

638. Philip J. Rasch, "'Six Shooter and Three Shooter Smith." And, Bartholomew, *Western Hard-Cases*, 75. Also see Keleher, *Violence in Lincoln County*, quoting the *Las Vegas Gazette* of March 20, 1881, 354. And, Cole and Cole, "Charley Smith Still Wears His Six-Gun," 21. Brief sketches of the notorious Six-Shooter Smith may be found in both Metz, *Encyclopedia of Lawmen, Outlaws, and Gunfighters*, 227, and Thrapp, *Encyclopedia of Frontier Biography*, 1330.

639. Pioneer Foundation Interview. Wayne Whitehill. "And we went out and these fellas all had horses and here they was lined up out there, both gangs, the Santa Fe and S. P. And so we started out in this hack and Curly Bill and two or three got in the hack with us and we started out."

640. Alexander, *Dangerous Dan Tucker*, 73-4. Also, Gustafson, "Dan Tucker, Deming's Lethal Lawman," 8. And, Owen, *The Two Alberts*, 86-87.

641. Johnson, *John Ringo*, 148. And see Bell, "An Eye For An Eye," 52-3. Also, Tefertiller, *Wyatt Earp*, 85.

642. *The New Southwest & Grant County Herald*, July 30, 1881.

643. DeArment, "Deadly Deputy," 17.

644. Johnson, *John Ringo*, 121, quoting a Sept. 28, 1881, edition of *The New Southwest & Grant County Herald*, Oct. 1, 1881. And see Stanley, *The Deming, New Mexico, Story*, for "narrowed the dimensions," 3.

645. *Wichita Daily Eagle*, Oct. 10, 1884. And see DeArment, *Deadly Dozen*, 72. Alexander, *Dangerous Dan Tucker*, 87. Also, Gillett, *Six Years with the Texas Rangers*, 198.

646. *The New Southwest & Grant County Herald,* Oct. 15, 1881.

647. *El Paso Lone Star*, Nov. 11, 1881.

648. Muir, "Shakespeare Becomes a Ghost Town," 26. Also see Russell, "Russian Bill: The True Story of an Outlaw," 23. And Thrapp, *Encyclopedia of Frontier Biography*, 3:1411.

649. *El Paso Lone Star*, Nov.16, 1881. And see *The New Southwest & Grant County Herald*, Nov. 11, 1881. "On the night of Tuesday, the 8th inst., Russian Bill and Sandy King were taken from the jail at Shakespeare and lynched by the vigilance committee of that place.... On last Saturday Dep. Sheriff Tucker, at Deming, received a warrant for the arrest of Russian Bill on the same charge for which King was held. He was arrested at Separ on Monday last and taken to Shakespeare by Deputy Tucker."

650. Muir, "Shakespeare Becomes a Ghost Town," 26.

651. Hill, "The Sad Fate Of Russian Bill. Why Was He Hanged? A Series." This article, by far, is the most complete examination to date of the life, activities, and death of Russian Bill.

652. Ibid. Also see Williams, *Pioneer Surveyor—Frontier Lawyer*, 95. Williams, who at the time was a Silver City Post Office employee, writes: "...a letter came to that office from the Russian consul at New York City, stating that he had been asked by the mother of William Rogers Tettenborn to inquire as to the whereabouts of her son, from whom she had last heard in a letter written by that son under the postmark of Silver City. It fell to me to answer the consul's letter. Considering the feelings of the mother, I wrote the consul that Tettenborn had met with a serious accident sometime before at Shakespeare and thereafter died." And, Thrapp, *Encyclopedia of Frontier Biography*, 3:1411: "Again local gossip is the source for the report that the citizens, not wishing to distress her [Bill's mother] with the facts, replied that Bill had come to his end 'from a shortage of breath due to a sudden change in altitude,' and that ended the case of Russian Bill." Also Metz, *Encyclopedia of Lawmen, Outlaws, and Gunfighters*, 241: "Someone wrote back, sadly advising that her boy had

passed away from throat trouble."

653. Chase, *The Editor's Run*, 128. Also see Dike, "The Territorial Post Offices of New Mexico." The Deming Post Office was officially recognized on April 11, 1881; Charle H. Dane, Postmaster.

654. *The New Southwest & Grant County Herald*, March 12, 1881.

655. Calkins, *History of the Public Schools of Silver City*, 27.

656. Naegle, "History of Silver City," 133.

657. *The New Southwest & Grant County Herald*, April 16, 1881.

658. Ibid., April 23, 1881.

659. Calkins, *History of the Public Schools of Silver City*, 22.

660. Campbell and Hill, *Triumph and Tragedy*, 62.

661. *The New Southwest & Grant County Herald*, Feb. 12, 1881.

662. Campbell and Hill, *Triumph and Tragedy*, 63.

663. Hillard, *A Hundred Years Of Horse Tracks*, 10.

664. Gray, *When All Roads Led to Tombstone*, 48.

665. Lekson, *Nana's Raid*, 6.

666. Ibid., 7.

667. Ibid., 9-10.

668. Thrapp, *Conquest of Apacheria*, 212-3.

669. Lekson, *Nana's Raid*, 12. For additional data on Civilian Chief of Scouts Bennett, see Lummis, *Dateline Fort Bowie*, 155-9. And, Thrapp, *Encyclopedia of Frontier Biography*, 1:94 and 262, for profiles of Bennett and Chihuahua.

670. Ibid., 15.

671. Ibid., 16.

672. Michno, *Encyclopedia of Indian Wars*, 339. These deaths may be the ones cited by Lekson and referred to in the preceding sentence of this text.

673. Lekson, *Nana's Raid*, 19.

674. Michno, *Encyclopedia of Indian Wars*, 339.

675. Lekson, *Nana's Raid*, 22.

676. Billington, *New Mexico's Buffalo Soldiers*, 105. Also, O'Neal, *Fighting Men of the Indian Wars*. O'Neal places Shaw in Company K. 6th Cavalry rather than the 9th Cavalry. Also see Lekson, *Nana's Raid*, 22: "The Apaches showed every sign of pursuing, but one soldier, Sergeant Thomas Shaw, who had been born a slave in Covington, Kentucky, refused to abandon his position, even when the Apaches advanced to within 50 yards."

677. Ibid., 106.

678. Lekson, *Nana's Raid*. The author points out the Prussian-born Gustavus Valois' real name was not Valois but Haenel, 23.

679. Ibid.

680. O'Neal, *Fighting Men of the Indian Wars*, 33.

681. *The New Southwest & Grant County Herald*, August 27, 1881.

682. McKenna, *Black Range Tales*, 185.

683. Ibid. That McKenna was an early resident and pioneer is indisputable; the veracity of some of his remembrances, however, may rightly be arguable. In several instances his recollections do not square with historically documented truth.

684. *The New Southwest & Grant County Herald*. August 27, 1881.

685. Ibid. And see Michno, *Encyclopedia of Indian Wars*, 340. And, O'Neal, *Fighting Men of the Indian Wars*, 33.

686. Thrapp, *Conquest of Apacheria*, 215.

687. *The New Southwest & Grant County Herald*. August 27, 1881.

688. Ibid.

689. Worcester, *The Apaches*, 233.

690. Lekson, *Nana's Raid*, 32.

Chapter 11

691. *The New Southwest & Grant County Herald*, Jan. 7, 1882.

692. Ibid., Jan. 14, 1882.

693. Ibid.

694. Ibid., Feb. 25, 1882.

695. Berry and Russell, *Built to Last*, 22, quoting the *Grant County Herald*, Feb. 26, 1881.

696. Ibid., 23-4.

697. Naegle, "History of Silver City," 162-3.

698. *The New Southwest & Grant County Herald*, Jan. 14, 1882.

699. Calkins, "History of the Public Schools of Silver City," 27.

700. Ibid.

701. Ibid., 29. Classes at the newly completed public school building commenced on June 5, 1882.

702. Ball, *The United State Marshals of New Mexico & Arizona Territories*, 125. And see Bell, "The Dark Side of Wyatt Earp," 18-24: "He [Wyatt Earp] was indicted for murder in Arizona but he escaped as a fugitive from justice."

703. Marks, *And Die in the West*, 365.

704. Bartholomew, *Wyatt Earp*, 321-3: "The Earp gang could not take the rail coaches to the east or the west for officers all along the line were watching for them" and, "From a close study of numerous contemporary newspaper accounts, and from other archival material, it is seen that these fugitives were fleeing for their very lives, running from murder indictments, an outraged citizenry, and the realization that Territorial officials and other officers had decided that the time had come to clean house in southern Arizona." And see Thrapp, *Encyclopedia of Frontier Biography*, 3:1443: "In March 1882 the Earp crowd in their hasty exit from Tombstone toward Colorado, rather than take the train through Deming—Tucker's territory—went on horseback the long way around. Apparently they were reluctant to test Tucker's ability to make the arrests Arizona officials desired." Also see Alexander, *Dangerous Dan Tucker*, 86, 93-95.

705. Bailey and Chaput, *Cochise County Stalwarts*, 1:114: "There is considerable irony here. Wyatt Earp, due to literature, movies, and television, has become the 'leader' of the Earps, but only in the Twentieth Century, not in history.

706. Ibid. Absent ballistic conformation, when several people are firing at the same time, conclusively citing just who shot whom is a nebulous exercise at best, and darn near impossible to prove legally. Historians are yet looking for the time Wyatt and somebody shot it out, mano a mano.

707. *Deming Headlight*, March 25, 1882.

708. *The New Southwest & Grant County Herald*, April 22, 1882. And see Julyan, *New Mexico Place Names*, 245. And, Myrick, New Mexico's Railroads, 204: "When the Santa Fe built to Deming in 1881, the station of Nutt, named for H.C. Nutt, President of the A & P Railroad, was soon established to serve as the transfer point."

709. Thrapp, *Conquest of Apacheria*, 236. Worcester, *The Apaches*, 253, reports that in addition to Sterling and his Indian Police sergeant, nine others were killed.

710. Ibid. And see Thrapp, *Encyclopedia of Frontier Biography*, 3:1365.

711. Bailey, "John H. Jackson and the Arizona Rangers," 24.

712. Johnson, "The Redding Boys," 14 and 18: "Sometime after this they [Tom and Bill Redding] moved to Arizona, settling near Clifton. The brothers began working as freighters hauling ore to Lordsburg. The venture lasted less than a year. In early 1882 Tom Redding and four other teamsters were ambushed and killed by the Apaches. Bill Redding returned to Grant County and continued ranching."

713. Bailey, *The Valiants*, 34. Also see Julyan, *New Mexico Place Names*, 150.

714. Ibid.

715. Michno, *Encyclopedia of Indian Wars*, 342-343.

716. *The New Southwest & Grant County Herald*, May 27, 1882.

717. Berry and Russell, *Built to Last*, 24.

718. Ibid.

719. *The New Southwest & Grant County Herald*, May 27, 1882.

720. Dike, "The Territorial Post Offices of New Mexico." And see Julyan, *New Mexico Place Names*, 259.

721. Sherman and Sherman, *Ghost Towns and Mining Camps*, 169.

722. *The New Southwest & Grant County Herald*, Sept. 23, 1882. Also see 1880 United States Census, Brownwood, Brown County, Texas.

723. For the Silver City shooting affair involving Deputy James D. Burns, see DeArment, *Deadly Dozen*, 74-8, and Alexander, *Dangerous Dan Tucker*, 98-103. For biographical sketch of one of the players in the story, John Gilmo, see Alexander, *Lawmen, Outlaws, and S.O.Bs*, 152-168. And see Metz, *Encyclopedia of Lawmen, Outlaws, and Gunfighters*, 95-96.

724. Ibid. Also see *Silver City Enterprise*, Dec. 12, 1902.

725. Ibid. And see Territory vs. Glaudius W. Moore and William McClellan—Case Number 1175—District Court Civil and Criminal Cost Docket Book, SRC&A. Tucker was not listed, but was arrested and required to post a $2,000 bail bond.

726. *Silver City Enterprise*, Dec. 14, 1882.

727. Alexander, *Dangerous Dan Tucker*, 105-106. And, DeArment, *Deadly Dozen*, 78. Also see *Silver City Enterprise*, Dec. 21, 1882.

728. *The New Southwest & Grant County Herald*, Dec. 23, 1882.

729. Berry and Russell, *Built to Last*, 24.

730. Myrick, *New Mexico's Railroads*, 193.

731. *The New Southwest & Grant County Herald*, Oct. 7, 1882.

732. Ibid.

733. Ibid., Nov. 4, 1882.

734. *Silver City Enterprise*, Nov. 16, 1882.

735. Reynolds, *Trouble in New Mexico*, 196. For an additional incident during which Deputy United States Marshal Kennon drew ire from Grant County citizens, see Ball, *The United States Marshals*, 140-141. And see *Silver City Enterprise*, Dec. 21, 1882. For Florida Station, see Julyan, *New Mexico Place Names*, 132.

736. Ibid.

737. Berry and Russell, *Built to Last*, 24. And see Naegle, "History of Silver City," 134: "Then, in 1883, a new era was ushered in with the long awaited arrival of the railroad.... With the coming of the railroad, mining in Silver City settled down to an even tempo."

738. Neagle, "History of Silver City," 134.

739. Berry and Russell, *Built to Last*, 24.

740. Ibid. And see *El Paso Lone Star*, July 14, 1883. "The telephone line between Silver City and Georgetown will be rebuilt and put in first class order."

741. *Silver City Enterprise*, Jan. 11 and 18, 1883.

742. *Southwest Sentinel*, May 19, 1883.

743. Julyan, *New Mexico Place Names*, 132.

744. Sherman and Sherman, *Ghost Towns and Mining Camps*, 84-5. And see Dike, "The Territorial Post Offices of New Mexico." Also, Berry and Russell, *Built to Last*, 24.

745. Ibid. And, Julyan, *New Mexico Place Names*, 263.

746. *El Paso Lone Star*, July 14, 1883.

747. Reynolds, *Trouble in New Mexico*, Vol. 2, 135.

748. *Silver City Enterprise*, August 10, 1883.

749. Simmons, *When Six-Guns Ruled*, 93-6. And see Holben, "The Deaf Mute Witness of Silver City," 20-2 and 72-3.

750. Ibid. And see Reynolds, *Trouble in New Mexico*, 2:276: "Conway accidentally shot one of his gang in Trinidad, Colorado, while he was holding up a tenderfoot. From Trinidad he went to Wallace, New Mexico, where he was elected Justice of the Peace." Later he was imprisoned in Iowa.

751. Ibid., Jan. 25, 1883.

752. Gibson, *The Life and Death of Colonel Albert Jennings Fountain*, quoting the *El Paso Lone Star*, Feb. 10, 1883.

753. *Santa Fe New Mexican*, Feb. 18, 1883

754. Nolan, "The Life and Crimes of John Kinney," 13, quoting the *Albuquerque Journal*.

755. *Santa Fe New Mexican*, Feb. 17, 1883. Also see Rasch, "The Rustler War." And see Mullin, "Here Lies John Kinney."

756. *Silver City Enterprise*, Feb. 22, 1883.

757. Rasch, "The Rustler War," 259.

758. Ibid., quoting the *Santa Fe New Mexican*, Feb. 11, 1883.

759. Muir, "The First Militia," 45.

760. Nolan, "The Life and Crimes of John Kinney," 13, quoting the *El Paso Lone Star*.

761. Metz, *Encyclopedia of Lawmen, Outlaws, and Gunfighters*, 145: "A jury took eight minutes to find John Kinney guilty. It assessed a $500 fine and five years in prison." And, Mullin, "Here Lies John Kinney," 237. And, Alexander, *Dangerous Dan Tucker*, 118.

762. *Silver City Enterprise*, March 30, 1883. And see Simmons, *Massacre on the Lordsburg Road*, 88: "Thus even before leaving Sonora, Chato bore responsibility for five deaths." For Point of Mountains and the Total Wreck mine, see Barnes, *Arizona Place Names*, 340 and 450. Also for min-

ing activity in southeastern Arizona, see Varney, *Arizona Ghost Towns and Mining Camps.*

763. Simmons, *Massacre on the Lordsburg Road,* 96. For a brief biographical sketch of Chato, see Thrapp, *Encyclopedia of Frontier Biography, 1:259.*

764. *Silver City Enterprise,* March 30, 1883.

765. Simmons, *Massacre on the Lordsburg Road,* 100-1.

766. Pioneer Foundation Interview. Julius Caesar Brock. Brock regrettably thought it might have been his shot that attracted Apache to inspect the Silver City-Lordsburg road and their sighting of H. C. McComas and family.

767. Simmons, *Massacre on the Lordsburg Road.* The author's book-length treatment of this tragedy is far and away the most comprehensively researched and adroitly written account to date.

768. Semi-Centennial Celebration, Interview. Herbert E. Muse, SCM. An account in the March 30, 1883, edition of the *Silver City Enterprise* fails to mention Muse as being the first person to reach the murder scene. For additional data on H. E. Muse, see Metz, *Encyclopedia of Lawmen, Outlaws, and Gunfighters,* 178.

769. Pioneer Foundation Interview. Julius Caesar Brock.

770. Thrapp, *Conquest of Apacheria,* 271. Worcester, *The Apaches,* 267-269.

Chapter 12

771. Unger, *True Tales,* 165.

772. *Southwest Sentinel,* May 19, 1883.

773. Ibid.

774. Unger, *True Tales,* 167.

775. Ibid., 173.

776. *Southwest Sentinel,* April 7, 1883.

777. *Silver City Enterprise,* May 11, 1883.

778. *Southwest Sentinel,* April 7, 1883.

779. *Silver City Enterprise,* May 4, 1883. Also, Gilbreath, *Death on the Gallows,* 218.

780. *Southwest Sentinel,* March 28, 1883. "Within 24 hours after the Indians at San Carlos broke out the military at Fort Bayard were placed under orders to be ready to leave at a moment's notice." And see the edition of April 7, 1883.

781. Myrick, *New Mexico's Railroads,* 193-194.

782. Ibid.

783. Berry and Russell, *Built to Last,* 25. And see the *Silver City Enterprise,* May 18, 1883. "One building after another was decorated until it seemed to become contagious and the entire city was draped with evergreens and waving with flags."

784. *Southwest Sentinel,* May 19, 1883.

785. Ibid.

786. Calkins, *History of the Public Schools of Silver City,* 32.

787. Ibid.

788. Julyan, *New Mexico Place Names,* 142. And, Dike, "The Territorial Post Offices of New Mexico," 62. Also, Ungnade, *New Mexico Mountains,* 164.

789. Caldwell, "New Mexico's First Train Robbery." Certainly this 1883 robbery is credited as the first train robbery in New Mexico Territory; however, Winslowe's "Buscadero Outlaw," alleges a train robbery by Henry Blevens that predates the offense during which engineer Webster was murdered.

790. There are several more or less complete accounts highlighting the Gage train robbery: DeArment, "Sheriff Whitehill and the Kit Joy Gang"; Bryan, *Robbers, Rogues and Ruffians;* Alexander, *Dangerous Dan Tucker* and *Silver City Stalwart.* Perhaps one of the earliest secondary accounts may be fBronson, "The Evolution of a Train Robbery," 485-92.

791. *Southwest Sentinel,* Nov. 28, 1883.

792. *Silver City Enterprise,* Nov. 30, 1883.

793. Ibid.

794. Biographical data on both of these early-day criminal investigators may be easily located: Secrest, "Brave Len Harris Is Dead," and Dillon, *Wells, Fargo Detective.*

795. DeArment, "Sheriff Whitehill and the Kit Joy Gang," 14. Also see Alexander, *Dangerous Dan Tucker,* 124. In addition to the $8,000 put up by Wells, Fargo & Co. and the Southern Pacific Railroad, there was a $200 per man reward posted by the US Postal Service, bringing the total to $8,800.

796. Harvey Whitehill vs. Southern Pacific Railroad. Deposition of Len Harris. August 15, 1884. "We employed Mr. Frank Bennett a Scout from Fort Cummings." [SRC&A].

797. Kelly, *The Story of the Bisbee Massacre*, 8. Also see Bailey, *Bisbee—Queen of the Copper Camps*, 88. And, Metz, *Encyclopedia of Lawmen, Outlaws, and Gunfighters*, 25.

798. *Silver City Enterprise*, Dec. 14, 1883.

799. Dillon, *Wells, Fargo Detective*, 21-218. And Reward Poster: "The prevailing opinion based on Press Reports, etc., and the known bad reputation of the persons named, is that they were the parties who robbed train and murdered the Engineer, near Gage, on Nov. 24th, 1883. We have AN ABUNDANCE OF POSITIVE EVIDENCE, that at the VERY MOMENT of the Gage affair, the men named were at San Simon Station, 74 miles from Gage and en route for Bisbee" [SRC&A].

800. Alexander, *Dangerous Dan Tucker*, 128-9. And, Breakenridge, *Helldorado*, 324. Also, Dodge, *Under Cover for Wells Fargo*, 48. And, Kelly, *The Story of the Bisbee Massacre*, 12: After the massacre, "Kelly, rode to the San Simon station and boarded a train for the 'cooler' clime of Deming, New Mexico."

801. Kelly, *The Story of the Bisbee Massacre*, 23, 26.

802. *Silver City Enterprise*, Jan. 4, 1884. And, Register of Prisoners Confined in the County Jail of Grant County, New Mexico, SRC&A.

803. Harvey Whitehill vs. Southern Pacific Railroad. Deposition of Harvey Whitehill. August 14, 1884, SRC&A. Also see Holben, "Kit Joy's Gang," 61: "Cleveland's arrest and confession came on Jan. 4, 1884, more than six weeks after the robbery. His story made the subsequent arrests a little easier and the long hunt was finally coming to an end."

804. Ibid. Deposition of John W. Gilmo. August 15, 1884, SRC&A.

805. *Southwest Sentinel*, Jan. 26, 1884. Also see Harvey Whitehill vs. Southern Pacific Railroad. Deposition of Charles C. Perry. August 5, 1884, SRC&A. For more on the soon to be notorious Charley Perry, see Ball, "Lawman in Disgrace: Sheriff Charles C. Perry of Chaves County, New Mexico." And see DeArment, "The Fatal Defect of Charley Perry," 24-30. Also, Alexander, *Lawmen, Outlaws and S.O.B.s*, 73, 141-146, and 160. And, Larson, *Forgotten Frontier*, 82.

806. Berry and Russell, *Built to Last*, 27.

807. *Southwest Sentinel*, July 21, 1883. Also see *Silver City Enterprise*, Feb. 8, 1883.

808. Ibid.

809. Berry and Russell, *Built to Last*, 25.

810. Ibid. And see *Southwest Sentinel*, Nov. 31, 1883: "The Gem people will give an entertainment at the school house next Friday evening, the proceeds to be for the benefit of the Ladies Hospital Aid Society."

811. *Southwest Sentinel*, August 1, 1883.

812. Ibid., Jan. 2, 1884.

813. Ibid., Sept. 29, 1883. "There is talk of a sale of the Silver City, Deming & Pacific road to the Atchison, Topeka people. It is rumored that the trustees of our line made an offer in Boston to the Atchison, some time since, and that the same was taken under consideration." And, *Silver City Enterprise*, Oct. 5, 1883. "Nothing definite has been learned concerning the rumored sale of the Silver City, Deming and Pacific railroad to the Atchison, Topeka and Santa Fe Company."

814. Alexander, *Dangerous Dan Tucker*, 131. And, DeArment, "Sheriff Whitehill and the Kit Joy Gang," 16. Also, Bryan, Robbers, Rouges and Ruffians, 131. *Southwest Sentinel*, March 15, 1884 and *Silver City Enterprise*, March 14, 1884. And, Register Of Prisoners Confined In The County Jail of Grant County, New Mexico, SRC&A.

815. Harvey Whitehill vs. Southern Pacific Railroad. Deposition of Thomas M. Hall. August 23, 1884, SRC&A.

816. Nelson and Nelson, *Wild and Woolly Days*, 44. And see Pioneer Foundation Interview. Number 503. Wayne Whitehill. "And we run out there and when they got out there, out in the hills there, this nigger, they blamed him for the whole thing these other fellas did, that he's shot his head off [snitched.. So this Kit Joy shot this nigger right...right in the forehead."

817. Ibid. And see Alexander, *Lawmen, Outlaws and S.O.B.s*, 254: "This version implies Cleveland was killed by his cohorts for 'snitching.' Wayne Whitehill, who was a youngster at the time, told historian Lou Blachly that 'Kit' Joy shot Cleveland....Other versions and the newspaper story credit Ed Mayer with killing George Washington Cleveland."

818. Harvey Whitehill vs. Southern Pacific Railroad. Deposition of Daniel Coomer. August 12, 1884, SRC&A. And see *Southwest Sentinel*, March 15, 1884. "In this fight Coomer narrowly escaped being shot and it is almost certain that he wounded Chavez."

819. Simmons, *When Six-Guns Ruled*, 100.

820. *Southwest Sentinel*, March 15, 1884. And, Harvey Whitehill vs. Southern Pacific. Deposition of Coomer as previously cited.

821. Harvey Whitehill vs. Southern Pacific. Deposition of Thomas M. Hall, Grant County Deputy Sheriff. August 23, 1884, SRC&A.

822. Ailman, *Pioneering in Territorial Silver City*, 71 and 169. And, Bryan, *Robbers, Rouges and Ruffians*, 136.

823. *Silver City Enterprise*, March 14, 1882.

824. Ibid.

825. *Southwest Sentinel*, March 15, 1884.

826. Register of Prisoners Confined in the County Jail of Grant County, New Mexico. Notation by Kit Joy's entry: "Left on the 6th of Jan. 1885, for the Pen. At San. Fe." [SRC&A. Also see Bryan, *Robbers, Rouges and Ruffians*, 138-41. And, Alexander, *Dangerous Dan Tucker*, 132 and 135.

827. *Southwest Sentinel*, April 12, 1884.

828. *Silver City Enterprise*, July 25, 1884.

829. *Southwest Sentinel*, April 12, 1884. And see Berry and Russell, *Built to Last*, 25.

830. Ibid., May 17 and 31, 1884. "The ice trade is improving steadily. Black & Co. now deliver close on to 2,000 pounds per day."

Chapter 13

831. Ailman, *Pioneering in Territorial Silver City*, 157.

832. Ibid.

833. Berry and Russell, *Built to Last*, 35: "Hartford Meredith and Henry Ailman, whose bank was the sole survivor of the local crash of '83, would themselves fall victims to failure." And for more detailed data regarding this banking failure, see Ailman, *Pioneering in Territorial Silver City*, 96-102.

834. *Silver City Enterprise*, Oct. 16, 1885.

835. Berry and Russell, *Built to Last*, 35.

836. *Southwest Sentinel*, Feb. 21, 1885.

837. Ibid., April 4, 1885.

838. Kraft, *Gatewood and Geronimo*, 85. And, Worcester, *The Apaches*, 289: "Old Nana, who was especially irked by the ban on wife-beating, said something and then stalked out of the tent." Also see Betzinez, *I Fought with Geronimo*, 129: "In the spring of 1885 Geronimo, Chihuahua, Mangas (son of the chief Mangas Colorado), and a number of others got to making and drinking Indian beer in violation of orders from the authorities. This homemade brew made the Indians drunk and quarrelsome." And, Hatfield, *Chasing Shadows*, 71: "A tizwin drunk led to the 1885 Apache outbreak."

839. Ibid. And see Thrapp, *Conquest of Apacheria*, 315. Thrapp slightly downsizes the numbers: "Incorrigible old Nana also left, the total fleeing being thirty-four men, eight boys of fighting age, and ninety-two women and children."

840. Ibid., 88.

841. Ibid., 89. And, Faulk, *The Geronimo Campaign*, 58: "Later it was learned that the Indians had traveled 120 miles from San Carlos without pausing to rest or to eat."

842. Ibid., 90 and 236. Also see Davis, *The Truth About Geronimo*, 153: "The hostiles were now well mounted on horses stolen from American ranches in addition to the ponies they took with them."

843. Thrapp, *Conquest of Apacheria*, 316: "Chihuahua's people, meanwhile, had intended to hide out north of the Gila after Geronimo went south." And see Adams, *Geronimo*, 272: "Nachez and Chihuahua accused Geronimo and Mangas of lying and were so angry they even threatened Geronimo's life. Finally, they contented themselves by splitting from the rest of the band."

844. Michno, *Encyclopedia of Indian Wars*, 346-7.

845. Cook, *Fifty Years on the Old Frontier*, 143.

846. Thrapp, *Conquest of Apacheria*, 319.

847. Ibid.

848. Ibid., 319-20.

849. Cook, *Fifty Years on the Old Frontier*, 150.

850. Pioneer Foundation Interview. Number 501. Wayne Whitehill.

851. Reynolds, *Trouble in New Mexico,* quoting *Silver City Enterprise*, June 15, 1885.

852. Thrapp, *Conquest of Apacheria*, 319.

853. Pioneer Foundation Interview. Number 501. Wayne Whitehill.

854. Charles P. Elliot, "The Geronimo Campaign of 1885-1886," Journal of the United States Cavalry Association, September 1910. Reprinted by Cozzens, *Eyewitnesses to the Indian Wars, 1865-1890: The Struggle for Apacheria*, 427-446. Seemingly, there is validity to Elliot's assertion: "There are all kinds of absurd rumors in circulation regarding killings and fights which when sifted down amount to nothing; and it seems that the parties tell and concoct these stories knowing they are not true, simply to hear themselves talk, and with the knowledge that their stories will be found untrue, and themselves branded as liars." See Mullane, *Indian Raids*, 41-42.

855. Debo, *Geronimo*, 241.

856. *Southwest Sentinel*, July 4 and Aug. 1, 1885.

857. Ibid., and Aug. 25, 1885.

858. Thrapp, *Conquest of Apacheria*, 332.

859. *Silver City Enterprise*, Oct. 16, 1885. And see Simmons, *Ranchers, Ramblers and Renegades*, 65-68. Also, Mullane, *Indian Raids*, 41.

860. Ibid.

861. Simmons, *Rancher, Ramblers, and Renegades*, 66: "In spite of the hardships he [Jimmy] adapted to his new life well and came to enjoy the rough and tumble way of the Apache youngsters."

862. Thrapp, *Conquest of Apacheria*, 334.

863. Ibid. Although characterized as a fictional account, Schlesier effectively blends historical accuracy into his interesting piece highlighting this very formidable Apache in *Josanie's War*.

864. Alexander, *Dangerous Dan Tucker*, 141.

865. *Southwest Sentinel*, Nov. 17, 1885.

866. Michno, *Encyclopedia of Indian Wars*, 348. And see *Silver City Enterprise*, Dec. 25, 1885. "The mission of the party is to get the body of Dr. Maddox, who was killed in the ambuscade last Saturday morning by Indians....The body will be embalmed and sent east for burial."

867. Thrapp, *Conquest of Apacheria*, 337.

868. Worcester, *The Apaches*, 295. And see Thrapp, *Conquest of Apacheria*, 339, who adds: "...although twice dismounted and several times near capture [Josanie], he had escaped into Mexico with the loss of but one man."

869. Carm Sandoval, "Chinese In Silver City," *Excerpts From A Paper*, 16. Courtesy of the Silver City Public Library.

870. Metz, *Border*, 364: "The Chinese Exclusion Act of 1882 (which established the principle of denial by race) suspended the Orientals for 10 years. A similar prohibition followed a decade later. In 1902 the ban became permanent, not to be rescinded until the Immigration and Nationality Act of 1952."

871. Terry R. Koenig, "The Chinese of Silver City, 1870-1885," unpublished typescript. Courtesy of Western New Mexico University, Silver City.

872. Ibid., 6.

873. *Silver City Enterprise*, Nov. 20, 1885.

874. Ibid.

875. *Southwest Sentinel*, Nov. 24, 1885.

876. *Silver City Enterprise*, Nov. 27, 1885.

877. Ibid. The Committee of Ten was composed of Dr. W. M. Slough, H. H. Whitehill, John McDonald, Idus L. Fielder, David Gaul, Joseph Bell, A. C. Carwile, M G. Hardee and Albert Card. The newspaper edition, as noted, carries only the names of nine Committee of Ten members. Who the 10th man was is a question yet answered. Also see Koenig, "The Chinese of Silver City," 15. And see Sandoval, "Chinese in Silver City," 17: "Several well-known men were elected to different positions to lead this removal."

878. Ibid., Dec. 1, 1885.

879. Ibid., Dec. 11, 1885.

880. Koenig, "The Chinese of Silver City," 16. Additionally, the author reports that $148,000 in property damage occurred during the Wyoming anti-Chinese troubles.

881. *Silver City Enterprise*, Dec. 25, 1885, and *Southwest Sentinel*, Dec. 29, 1885.

882. Ibid. Dec. 18, 1885. For another account, see Pioneer Foundation Interview. Number 501. Wayne Whitehill. It is generally reported that this was the same band of Apache that had earlier attacked Lieutenant Sam Fountain's command above Silver City.

883. Ibid., Dec. 18, 1885.

884. *Southwest Sentinel*, Dec. 29, 1885.

885. *Silver City Enterprise*, Jan. 8, 1886.

886. Ibid.

887. Ibid., Sept. 17, 1886.

888. Alexander, *Dangerous Dan Tucker*, 142: "Without doubt, the crisis was bona fide, but there is no evidence that Grant County citizens actually rushed off into the hinterland with thoughts of ripping hair from bleeding skulls."

889. Lummis, *Dateline Fort Bowie*, 57-8.

890. Simmons, *Ranchers, Ramblers, and Renegades*, 68: "Later in life Jimmy McKinn grew a red beard, became a blacksmith, married and raised a family. In 1908 it is known that he was the smith for the W. A. Tenney Freight Company in Silver City. Afterward he moved to Phoenix where he died in the mid-1950s."

891. Meed, *They Never Surrendered*, 18. The author does a simply outstanding investigative piece of work researching and writing about the Apache who never surrendered. Well into the 20th century these outlaw Apache made cross-border raids into New Mexico and Arizona.

892. Ibid., 27. For another fine example of Apache raiding in the American Southwest—post Geronimo's incarceration—see Phyllis de la Garza's *The Apache Kid*.

893. Ibid., 55.

Chapter 14

894. *Silver City Enterprise*, March 11, 1887.

895. Ibid., March 19, 1986. In this account, Aguilar Santiago was killed while serving as a posse member chasing after the "Mexicans."

896. Bullis, *New Mexico's Finest*, 115-117. Also see Gilbreath, *Death on the Gallows*, 85.

897. Ibid.

898. Young, *Pete Spence*, 46. Also see *Silver City Enterprise*, May 7 and 14, 1886. And see Thrapp, *Encyclopedia of Frontier Biography*, 3:1345, for additional data about Spence.

899. *Silver City Enterprise*, March 19, 1886.

900. Ibid., June 24, 1887.

901. Ibid., Aug. 29, 1887.

902. Ibid., May 24, 1889; April 6, 1888; June 21, 1889; and Feb. 8, 1889. And see Berry and Russell, *Built to Last*, 43: "Most of the major and reported social events happened before the crash of silver: in 1892 a balloon ascension with a female parachutist enthralled the town, as did a steam merry-go-round a year later."

903. Bullis, *New Mexico's Finest*, 115-117. And, Gilbreath, *Death on the Gallows*, 86.

904. *Silver City Enterprise*, Sept. 7 and 14, 1888. From Sept. 14: "The 50 mile bicycle and horse race between this city and Deming was won by the horse Rattler in 3:46. The pinto horse covered the distance in 3:45, beating the world's record by nine minutes. The bicycle was beaten 1:08." Also, Campbell and Hill, *Triumph and Tragedy*, 35-41. Berry and Russell, *Built to Last*, 36, suggest the race was run from Mimbres to Deming. Also, Sonnichsen, *Billy King's Tombstone*, 142-160. And, *El Paso Herald-Post*, Dec. 3, 1960.

905. Berry and Russell, *Built to Last*, 33-34.

906. Ibid.

907. *Silver City Enterprise*, July 28, 1889.

908. Ibid., June 28, 1889.

909. Ibid., July 14, 1889.

910. Berry and Russell, *Built to Last*, 35.

911. *Silver City Enterprise*, Jan. 24 and Feb. 7, 1890. Grant County settlements having a public school were: Central, Lone Mountain, Cornell, Pinos Altos, Silver City, Coleman, Brockman, Lower Mimbres, San Isidro, San Lorenzo, San Juan, Georgetown, Upper Gila, Clark, Richmond, Deming, Mimbres Mill, Upper Mimbres, Malone, Cooke's Peak, Gold Hill, Blackhawk, Carlisle, Pine Cienega, Blue Creek, Mule Springs, Lordsburg and Middle Gila.

912. Ibid., Feb. 7, 1890.

913. Tanner, "Violence in New Mexico Territory: A Penitentiary Analysis," 32-44 and 55.

914. *Silver City Enterprise*, Jan. 10, 1890.

915. Ibid.

916. Ibid., May 30, 1890.

917. Ibid., March 7, 1890. Once again, an examination of the list of those pledging reward money is insightful. They were: the Lyons & Campbell Ranch, John W. Fleming, Sidney Lindauer,

Israel King, Richard Hudson, H. D. McKnight, Harvey H. Whitehill, John Brockman, W. H. Donaldson, Fleming Cattle Company, John H. Gillett, William Brahm, W. H. Taylor, T. W. Holson, H. G. Noel, C. M. Shannon and C. Castlic.

918. Ibid., March 21, 1890. Also, Julyan, *New Mexico Place Names*, 331.

919. Pioneer Foundation Interview. Number 501. Wayne Whitehill. And see Russell's excellently researched "A Young Lion of the Gila."

920. *Silver City Enterprise*, May 30, 1890. "The cause of the killing is well known to all of the citizens of this section and is of too painful a nature to be referred to now." Also see Berry and Russell, *Built to Last*, 41: "Lyons promptly shot and killed the suspected lover—an act for which he was fully acquitted in the courts." And, Campbell and Foster, *Triumph and Tragedy*, 57: "There was a preliminary hearing before Justice Givins who pronounced the murder as justifiable homicide and dismissed the case."

921. Ibid., August 1, 1890.

922. Berry and Russell, *Built to Last*, 35. Also see *Silver City Enterprise*, July 25, 1890.

923. For extensive coverage of the Grant County governmental scandal, see Mullane, *This Is Silver City*, 3:30-8. Also see Alexander, *Silver City Stalwart*.

924. Berry and Russell, *Built to Last*, 37.

925. Ungnade, *New Mexico Mountains*, 135-6. And see Sherman and Sherman, *Ghost Towns and Mining Camps*, 213: "...John E. Coleman, better known as 'Turquoise John,' rediscovered turquoise in some of the old pits and immediately staked a number of copper and turquoise claims. With interest revived in the area, considerable activity occurred and many properties were developed during the ensuing years."

926. Berry and Russell, *Built to Last*, 36.

927. *Silver City Enterprise*, Jan. 10, 1890. Also see Reynolds, T*rouble in New Mexico*, 190. And for a delightful look at this historic spot, see Hilliard, *Adios Hachita*, 2. After highlighting Apache troubles in the area, Hilliard says: "As well, there was danger from outlaws of every sort who disrupted the peace, attacking and robbing ordinary citizens, lawmen, and very frequently each other.... These were by no means unusual incidents and the town of Hachita itself was no safe refuge from violence."

928. Ibid., Oct. 24, 1890.

929. Cox, "Salty John Cox and Bronco Bill," 48. Also see Cole Railston to J. Evetts Haley and Hervey Chelsey, Feb. 26, 1945. Railston further describes Bronco Bill as being "about five, six or seven, and bony; no flesh and an awful crooked bony ugly face. Was crippled some way. Had been shot." Another who knew him, Walter Birchfield, told J. Evetts Haley on Nov. 2, 1939, that Bronco Bill was "a dead hard Hombre" and that he was "a thoroughbred outlaw." Courtesy of Nita Stewart Haley Memorial Library. Midland.

930. *Silver City Enterprise*, Oct. 24, 1890.

931. Harvey H. Whitehill to New Mexico Territorial Governor Prince, Oct. 2, 1890. "You will please send me the necessary papers to get him [Rosalio Hidalo. from the custody of J. H. White, Sheriff of El Paso County, Texas."

932. Reynolds, *Trouble in New Mexico*, 90. And, *Silver City Enterprise,* Oct. 24, 1890. It should be noted that the Enterprise edition of Aug. 1, 1890, mentions another individual identified as Frenchy and gives his name as Charles Russell. It is likely the two Frenchy characters were one in the same, though they've not been conclusively linked.

933. *Silver City Enterprise*, Nov. 7, 1890. And see *La Ventura Magazine*, July 27, 1968, "Under the name of 'Brick Bond' he [Harvey Whitehill] was one of the principal characters in Archibald Clavering Gunter's novel, *Miss Nobody of Nowhere*."

934. Ibid., Jan. 23, 1891.

935. Ibid., Nov. 29, 1889. "If the Methodists do not want a college here, why not turn the town lots over to some other denomination?"

936. Western New Mexico University 2004 Catalog. "University History," 17-18. Also, Berry and Russell, *Built to Last*, 37: "Fleming became a strong advocate of public education. A member of the Normal School's first Board of Regents, he donated 20 acres of his land at the west edge of town for the school site."

937. Cecilia Jensen Bell and Sharon Morgan Gonzalez and Michael Rock, A Centennial History: Western New Mexico University, 1893-1993, 2 and 8.

938. Berry and Russell, *Built to Last*, 37.

939. Metz, *Encyclopedia of Lawmen, Outlaws, and Gunfighters*, 37. Also see Reynolds, *Trouble in New Mexico*. Mistakenly the author has an entry [31] for Cantley under the name "Canfield," which he no doubt picked up from Joseph "Mack" Axford's garbled account in *Around Western Campfires*.

Reynolds has a subsequent entry, however, under the appropriate name, 34-37.

940. Pioneer Foundation Interview. Number 21. Robert Bell. "One thing I did see was Fielder had a cigar in his mouth and he just moved the cigar ever over on the other side. I guess Cantley did shoot first all right."

941. *Silver City Enterprise*, Oct. 11, 1895.

Chapter 15

942. Ball, *Desert Lawmen*, 55 and 71. And see Alexander, *Dangerous Dan Tucker*, 153: "It was more or less taken for granted that once the new county was surveyed and christened Logan, or by some accounts Florida, Harvey Whitehill would received appointment as the first sheriff."

943. *Silver City Enterprise*, Jan. 25, 1895.

944. Ibid., June 7, 1895.

945. Ibid., June 7 and 14, 1895.

946. Ibid., June 21 and July 5, 1895.

947. Ibid., July 26, 1895. Also quoted by Berry and Russell, *Built to Last*, 39.

948. Ibid.

949. Ibid.

950. Ibid. According to newspaper accounts the three floods dumped out 1,903,365,629,974 gallons of water.

951. Berry and Russell, *Built to Last*, 39.

952. Ibid., 59.

953. Ibid.

954. *Silver City Independent*, April 6, 1915.

955. Pioneer Foundation Interview. Number 23. Robert Bell.

956. *Silver City Independent*, April 6, 1915. "[Grant County cattle industry.... has practically grown since 1894, when the first shipments of cattle to eastern points were made." Interestingly, a blurb in the Feb. 7 [1885] edition of the *Southwest Sentinel* highlights an earlier delivery: "Thirteen car loads of beef cattle were shipped from Deming to Kansas City on the 2nd. They were from Corralitos, Mexico."

957. Ibid. For a synopsis of southwestern Grant County ranching see Hilliard's outstanding *A Hundred Years of Horse Tracks*. For the LCs, see Campbell and Hill, *Triumph and Tragedy*.

958. Hilliard, *A Hundred Years of Horse Tracks*, 61.

959. Pioneer Foundations Interview. Number 502. Wayne Whitehill.

960. *Silver City Enterprise*, Nov. 1, 1889.

961. Ibid.

962. For interesting reading regarding wildlife and early day hunting in southwestern New Mexico several works are fascinating as well as informative: Stevens, *Meet Mr. Grizzly*; Davis, *Mogollon Mountain Man*; Carmony, *Ben Lilly's Tales;* Campbell and Hill, *Triumph and Tragedy*, 233-244; and Pioneer Foundation Interview, Number 501, Wayne Whitehill.

963. Berry and Russell, *Built to Last*, 37. And see Julyan, *New Mexico Place Names*, 130. Also, Sherman and Sherman, *Ghost Towns and Mining Camps*, 82-83.

964. Allen, "Remember the Maine," 94 and 99.

965. Walker, *Rough Rider*, 117-118.

966. Rayburn, "The Rough Riders in San Antonio," 113. And see Berry and Russell, *Built to Last*, 44.

967. Paul O'Neil, *The End and the Myth*, 137.

968. *San Antonio News*, Oct. 20, 1965.

969. Rynning, *Gun Notches*, 144.

970. *San Antonio Daily Express*, May 30, 1898.

971. Walker, *Rough Rider*, 152.

972. Berry and Russell, *Built to Last*, 81.

973. *Silver City Enterprise*, Oct. 7, 1898. Also see Webb, "Arizonans In the Spanish-American War," 57: "That patriotic gentleman, Armour, is working a lot of 'salt horse' on the army that would make a dog sick, under the name of prime roast beef."

974. Berry and Russell, *Built to Last*, 44.

975. *Silver City Enterprise*, Jan. 20, 1899. "Ere another week rolls by the city will be lighted by electricity. The plant and everything connected therewith is first class in every particular."

976. Ibid., March 18, 1898

977. Ibid., Nov. 25, 2898.

978. Ibid., Aug. 17, 1900.

979. Berry and Russell, *Built to Last*, 44.

980. *Silver City Enterprise*, May 27, 1898.

981. Alexander, *Lawmen, Outlaws and S.O.Bs*, 50-68.

982. DeArment, *George Scarborough*, 229. Scarborough was actually ambushed in Arizona Territory but was removed to Deming where he resided with his wife and minor children.

983. Alexander, Lawmen, *Outlaws and S.O.Bs*, 53-55. For additional data on James Brooks' earlier crimes see Rasch, "The Las Cruces Bank Robbery," and Harold Edwards, "Sheriff Pat Garrett's Puzzle: A Blow by Blow Account of Solving a New Mexico Bank Robbery."

984. Ibid., 216. Also see *Silver City Independent*, Sept. 4, 1900, and *Silver City Enterprise*, Sept. 7 and 14, 1900. And, DeArment, *George Scarborough*, 247-250.

985. Henderson, *Wild Horses in My Blood*, 69.

986. Tyler, "Gringo Views of Governor Manuel Armijo," 41.

987. For additional data on the hell-town of Phenix, New Mexico Territory, see Devereaux, "Jagville," 3-19.

988. Gibson, *The Life and Death of Colonel Albert Jennings Fountain*, 188.

989. Ibid.

990. Ralph Twitchell, *The Leading Facts of New Mexico History*, 3:306: "The real cause for the creation of Luna county was the rivalry between Silver City and Deming and was largely political. The agitation for county division began in 1888 and much bitter feeling resulted."

991. Berry and Russell, *Built to Last*, 45. Hidalgo County [Lordsburg] would not be created until 1919, futher reducing the size of Grant County. Also see Julyan, *New Mexico Place Names*, 165.

992. Ibid. And see *Silver City Enterprise*, June 7, 1895, "Silver City—the World's Only Sanitarium."

993. Ibid., 46.

994. Ibid., 49.

995. Gilbreath, *Death on the Gallows*, 88-92. This would be the sixth, and last, legal hanging for Grant County's territorial period,

996. *Silver City Independent*, July 9, 1901.

997. Reynolds, *Trouble in New Mexico*, 28.

998. Alexander, Lawmen, *Outlaws and S.O.Bs*, 277-291. Also see Cline, "The Story of a Cowboy," and Turner, "New Mexico Shoot-Out." And see Territitory of New Mexico vs. Howard Chenowth, Cause Number 1111, SRC&A. And, *Silver City Independent*, Aug. 30, 1904.

999. Curry, *George Curry*, 252 and 262. And see Miller, *New Mexico: A Guide to the Colorful State*, 433.

BIBLIOGRAPHY

Non-published sources—manuscripts, typescripts, theses, dissertations, tape recordings, official documents, court records, tax rolls, petitions, correspondence, census records, interviews, etc.–are cited with specificity in chapter endnotes.

Museums, Libraries, and Collections

Arizona Historical Society, Tucson, Arizona.
Colorado Genealogical Society, Denver, Colorado.
Deming/Luna Mimbres Museum, Deming, New Mexico.
Denver Public Library, Denver, Colorado.
Lordsburg/Hidalgo Public Library, Lordsburg, New Mexico.
Miller Library, Western New Mexico University, Silver City, New Mexico.
Museum of New Mexico, Santa Fe, New Mexico.
New Mexico Records Center & Archives, Santa Fe, New Mexico.
New Mexico Vital Records and Health Statistics, Santa Fe, New Mexico.
The Nita Stewart Haley Library & History Center, Midland, Texas.
Silver City Masonic Lodge. Silver City, New Mexico.
Silver City Museum. Silver City, New Mexico.
Silver City Public Library. Silver City, New Mexico.
Texas State Library and Archives Commission, Austin, Texas.
United States Military Academy, West Point, New York.
U.S. National Archives and Records, College Park, Maryland.
Wells Fargo Historical Service, San Francisco.
Zimmerman Library, University of New Mexico, Albuquerque, New Mexico.

Primary and Secondary Books

Adams, Alexander B. *Geronimo: A Biography*. New York: Da Capo Press, 1971.

Ailman, H. B., with Helen J. Lundwall, ed. *Pioneering in Territorial Silver City, H. B. Ailman's Recollections of Silver City and the Southwest, 1871-1892*. Albuquerque, NM: University of New Mexico Press, 1983.

Aleshire, Peter. *The Fox and the Whirlwind: General George Crook and Geronimo—A Paired Biography*. New York: John Wiley and Sons, 2000.

Alexander, Bob. *Dangerous Dan Tucker: New Mexico's Deadly Lawman*. Silver City, NM: High-Lonesome Books, 2001.

———. *Lawmen, Outlaws, and S.O.B.s: Gunfighters of the Old Southwest*. Silver City, NM: High-Lonesome Books, 2004.

———. *Sheriff Harvey Whitehill: Silver City Stalwart—An Old West Lawman on the New Mexico Frontier*. Silver City, NM: High-Lonesome Books, 2005.

Austerman, Wayne R. *Sharps Rifles and Spanish Mules: The San Antonio-El Paso Mail, 1851-1881*. College Station, TX: Texas A & M University Press, 1985.

Averell, William Woods, with Edward K. Eckert and Nicholas J. Amato, eds. *Ten Years in the Saddle: The Memoir of William Woods Averell, 1851-1862*. San Rafael, CA: Presidio Press, 1978.

Axford, Joseph "Mack." *Around Western Campfires*. Tucson, AZ: University of Arizona Press, 1969.

Bailey, Lynn R., and Don Chaput. *Cochise County Stalwarts*. 2 vols. Tucson, AZ: Westernlore Press, 2000.

———. *The Valiants: The Tombstone Rangers and Apache War Frivolities*. Tucson, AZ: Westernlore Press, 1999.

Ball, Durwood. *Army Regulars on the Western Frontier, 1848-1861*. Norman, OK: University of Oklahoma Press, 2001.

Ball, Eve. *In the Days of Victorio: Recollections of a Warm Springs Apache*. Tucson, AZ: University of

Arizona Press, 1986.
Ball, Larry D. *Desert Lawmen: The High Sheriffs Of New Mexico & Arizona Territories 1846-1912*. Albuquerque, NM: University of New Mexico Press, 1992.
———. *The United States Marshals of New Mexico & Arizona Territories, 1846-1912*. Albuquerque, NM: University of New Mexico Press, 1978.
Barnes, Will C. *Arizona Place Names*. Tucson, AZ: University of Arizona Press, 1988.
Barrett, S. M., ed. *Geronimo's Story of His Life*. Oklahoma City: Harlow Publishing Corporation, 1938.
Bartholomew, Ed. *Western Hard-Cases or Gunfighters Named Smith*. Toyahvale, TX: Frontier Book Company, 1960.
———. *Wyatt Earp: The Man and the Myth*. Toyahvale, TX: Frontier Book Company, 1964.
Batman, Richard James. *Pattie's West: The Dream and the Reality*. Norman: University of Oklahoma Press, 1984.
Berry, Susan, and Sharman Apt Russell. *Built to Last: An Architectural History of Silver City, New Mexico*. Silver City, NM: Silver City Museum Society, 1995.
Betzinez, Jason, with Wilbur S. Nye. *I Fought with Geronimo*. Lincoln, NE: University of Nebraska Press, 1959.
Billington, Monroe Lee. *New Mexico's Buffalo Soldiers, 1866-1900*. Boulder, CO: University Press of Colorado, 1991.
Colorado Genealogical Society. *Colorado Families: A Territorial Heritage*. Denver: Colorado Genealogical Society, 1981.
Boardman, Mark, and Sharon Cunningham, eds. *Revenge! And Other True Tales of the Old West*. Lafayette, IN: Scarlet Mask Enterprises, 2004.
Bolton, Herbert E. *Coronado: Knight of Pueblos and Plains*. Albuquerque, NM: University of New Mexico Press, 1949.
Bourke, John G. *On the Border with Crook*. New York: Charles Scribner's Sons, 1891.
Breakenridge, William M. with Richard M. Brown, ed. *Helldorado: Bringing Law to the Mesquite*. Chicago: R. R. Donnelley & Sons, 1982.
Bryan, Howard. *Robbers, Rogues and Ruffians: True Tales of the Wild West in New Mexico*. Santa Fe, NM: Clear Light Publishing, 1991.
———. *True Tales of the American Southwest*. Santa Fe, NM: Clear Light Publishing, 1998.
———. *Wildest of the Wild West*. Santa Fe, NM: Clear Light Publishing, 1988.
Bullis, Don. *New Mexico's Finest: Peace Officers Killed in the Line of Duty, 1847-1999*. Santa Fe, NM: New Mexico Department of Public Safety, 2000.
Butler, Anne M. *Daughters of Joy, Sisters of Misery: Prostitutes in the American West, 1865-90*. Urbana, IL, and Chicago: University of Illinois Press, 1987.
Calkins, Helen M. *History of the Public Schools of Silver City, 1874 to 1928*.
Campbell, Ida Foster, and Alice Foster Hill. *Triumph and Tragedy—A History of Thomas Lyons And the LCs*.
Caperton, Thomas J., and Timothy Cohrs. *Fort Selden*. Santa Fe, NM: Museum of New Mexico, 1993.
Carmony, Neil B., ed. *Ben Lilly's Tales of Bears, Lions and Hounds*. Silver City, NM: High-Lonesome Books, 1998.
Casey, Robert J. *The Texas Border and Some Borderliners*. New York: Bobbs-Merrill Company, 1950.
Chase, C. M. *The Editor's Run in New Mexico and Colorado*. Fort Davis, TX: Frontier Book Company, 1968.
Clarke, Mary Whatley. *John Simpson Chisum: Jinglebob King of the Pecos*. Austin, TX: Eakin Press, 1984.
Cleland, Robert Glass. *This Reckless Breed of Men: The Trappers and Fur Traders of the Southwest*. Albuquerque, NM: University of New Mexico, 1950.
Clum, John, with Neil Carmony, ed. *Apache Days and Tombstone Nights: John Clum's Autobiography*. Silver City, NM: High-Lonesome Books, 1997.
Clum, Woodworth. *Apache Agent: The Story of John P. Clum*. Lincoln, NE: University of Nebraska Press, 1936.
Cook, James H. *Fifty Years on the Old Frontier*. Norman, OK: University of Oklahoma Press, 1980.
Cortes, Jose, with Elizabeth A. H. John, ed. *Views from the Apache Frontier: Report on the Northern Provinces of New Spain*. Norman, OK: University of Oklahoma Press, 1989.
Cozzens, Peter. *The Struggle for Apacheria: Eyewitnesses to the Indian Wars, 1865-1890*. Mechanicsburg, PA: Stackpole Books, 2001.
Cremony, John C. *Life Among the Apaches*. New York: A. Roman & Company, 1868.
Cruse, Thomas. *Apache Days and After*. Lincoln, NE: University of Nebraska Press, 1987.
Curry, George, with H. B. Hening, ed. *George Curry, 1864-1947: An Autobiography*. Albuquerque, NM: University of New Mexico Press, 1958.
Curry, W. Hubert. *Sun Rising on the West: The Saga of Henry Clay and Elizabeth Smith*. Crosbyton, TX:

Crosby County Pioneer Memorial, 1979.
Dary, David. *Seeking Pleasure in the West.* New York: Alfred A. Knopf, Inc., 1995.
Davis, Britton. *The Truth about Geronimo.* Lincoln, NE: University of Nebraska Press, 1976.
Davis, Carolyn O'Bagy. *Mogollon Mountain Man: Nat Straw, Grizzly Hunter & Trapper.* Tucson, AZ: Sanpete Publications, 2003.
DeArment, Robert K. *Deadly Dozen: Twelve Forgotten Gunfighters of the Old West.* Norman, OK: University of Oklahoma Press, 2003.
———. *Knights of the Green Cloth: The Saga of the Frontier Gamblers.* Norman, OK: University of Oklahoma Press, 1982.
———. *George Scarborough: The Life and Death of a Lawman on the Closing Frontier.* Norman, OK: University of Oklahoma Press, 1992.
Debo, Angie. Geronimo: *The Man, His Time, His Place.* Norman, OK: University of Oklahoma Press, 1976.
Dillon, Richard H. Wells, *Fargo Detective: A Biography of James B. Hume.* Reno, NV: University of Nevada Press, 1986.
Dodge, Fred, with Carolyn Lake, ed. *Under Cover for Wells Fargo: The Unvarnished Recollections of Fred Dodge.* Norman, OK: University of Oklahoma Press, 1969.
Dunlay, Thomas W. *Wolves for the Blue Soldiers:Indian Scouts and Auxiliaries with the United States Army, 1860-90.* Lincoln, NE: University of Nebraska Press, 1994.
Dunn, J. P. Jr. *Massacres of the Mountains: A History of the Indian Wars of the Far West, 1815-1875.* New York: Archer House, 1886.
Edwards, Harold. *Goodbye Billy the Kid.* College Station, TX: Creative Publishing, 1995.
Elliott, Richard Smith, with Mark L. Gardner and Marc Simmons, eds. *The Mexican War Correspondence of Richard Smith Elliott.* Norman, OK: University of Oklahoma Press, 1997.
Faulk, Odie B. *Destiny Road: The Gila Trail and the Opening of the Southwest.* New York: Oxford University Press, 1973.
———. The Geronimo Campaign. New York: Oxford University Press, 1969.
Ferris, Robert G., ed. *Soldier and Brave, Historical Places Associated with Indian Affairs and the Indian Wars of the Trans-Mississippi West.* Washington, DC: National Park Service, 1971.
Finch, L. Boyd. *A Southwestern Land Scam: The 1859 Report of the Mowry City Association.* Tucson, AZ: Friends of the Library, University of Arizona, 1990.
Forbes, Jack D. *Apache, Navaho, and Spaniard.* Norman, OK: University of Oklahoma Press, 1960.
Fradkin, Philip L. *Stagecoach: Wells Fargo and the American West.* New York: Simon & Schuster, 2002.
Frazer, Robert W. *Forts of the West—Military Forts and Presidios and Posts Commonly Called Forts West of the Mississippi River to 1898.* Norman, OK: University of Oklahoma Press, 1972.
Gatto, Steve. *Curly Bill—Tombstone's Most Famous Outlaw.* Lansing, MI: Protar House Press, 2003.
Giammattei, Victor M., and Nanci Greer Reichert. *Art of a Vanished Race.* Silver City, NM: High-Lonesome Books, 1975.
Gibson, A. M. *The Life and Death of Colonel Albert Jennings Fountain.* Norman, OK: University of Oklahoma Press, 1986.
Giese, Dale F. *Forts of New Mexico.* Silver City, NM: Phelps Dodge Corporation, 1995.
Gilbreath, West C. *Death on the Gallows, The Story of Legal Hangings in New Mexico 1847-1923.* Silver City, NM: High-Lonesome Books, 2002.
Gillett, James B. *Six Years with the Texas Rangers.* Lincoln, NE: University of Nebraska Press, 1976.
Gray, John Plesent, with W. Lane Rogers, ed. *When All Roads Led to Tombstone: A Memoir by John Plesent Gray.* Boise, ID: Tamarack Books, 1998.
Greer, James Kimmins. *Colonel Jack Hays: Texas Frontier Leader and California Builder.* College Station, TX: Texas A&M University Press, 1987.
Griffen, William B. *Apaches at War and Peace: The Janos Presidio, 1750-1858.* Norman, OK: University of Oklahoma Press, 1988.
Gunter, Archibald C. *Miss Nobody of Nowhere.* New York: The Home Publishing Company, 1890.
Harlan, John G.., Earl L. Mickelson, and Hurbert O. Robertson. *The Early Days of Silver City Lodge—A Century of Freemasonary at Silver City.* Silver City, NM.
Henderson, Eva P. *Wild Horses: A Turn-of-the-Century Prairie Girlhood.* Santa Fe, NM: Sunstone Press, 1983.
Hertzog, Peter. *Outlaws of New Mexico.* Santa Fe, NM: Sunstone Press, 1984.
Hill, Rita. *Then and Now, Here and Around Shakespeare.* Lordsburg, NM.
Hilliard, George. *A Hundred Years of Horse Tracks: The Story of the Gray Ranch.* Silver City, NM: High-Lonesome Books, 1996.
———. *Adios Hachita, Stories of a New Mexico Town.* Silver City, NM: High-Lonesome Books, 1998.
Holt, Willard E., ed. *Service Record Book of Men and Women of Hidalgo County. V. F. W. Post No. 3099.* Lordsburg, NM.

Horgan, Paul. *Great River: The Rio Grande in North American History*. New York: Rinehart & Company, 1954.

Horn, Calvin. *New Mexico's Troubled Years: The Story of the Early Territorial Governors*. Albuquerque, NM: Horn and Wallace, 1963.

Jacobsen, Joel. *Such Men as Billy the Kid*. Lincoln, NE: University of Nebraska Press, 1994.

John, Elizabeth A. H. *Storms Brewed in Other Men's Worlds: The Confrontation of Indians, Spanish, and French in the Southwest, 1540-1795*. College Station, TX: Texas A&M University Press, 1975.

Johnson, Dave. *John Ringo*. Stillwater, OK: Barbed Wire Press, 1996.

Julyan, Robert. *The Place Names of New Mexico*. Albuquerque, NM: University of New Mexico Press, 1996.

Kadlec, Robert F., ed. *They "Knew" Billy the Kid: Interviews with Old-Time New Mexicans*. Santa Fe, NM: Ancient City Press, 1987.

Keleher, William A. *The Fabulous Frontier: Twelve New Mexico Items*. Santa Fe, NM: Rydal Press, 1946.

———. *Violence in Lincoln County, 1869-1881: The New Mexico Feud that Became a Frontier War*. Albuquerque, NM: University of New Mexico Press, 1957.

Kelly, George H. *Arizona 1864-1912: A Legislative History*. Phoenix, AZ: The Manufacturing Stationers, 1926.

Kelley, Troy. *"I Don't Propose to Walk Into Anybody's Graveyard": The Story of the Bisbee Massacre*. Tombstone Travel Series. 2004.

Kenner, Charles L. *Buffalo Soldiers and Officers of the Ninth Cavalry, 1867-1898*. Norman, OK: University of Oklahoma Press, 1999.

Kraft, Louis. *Gatewood & Geronimo*. Albuquerque, NM: University of New Mexico Press, 2000.

Larson, Carol. *Forgotten Frontier—The Story of Southeastern New Mexico*. Albuquerque, NM: University of New Mexico Press, 1993.

Laumbach, Karl W. *Hembrillo—An Apache Battlefield of the Victorio War, the Archaeology and History of the Hembrillo Battlefield*. White Sands, NM: White Sands Missile Range, 2000.

Leckie, William H. *The Buffalo Soldiers: A Narrative of the Negro Cavalry in the West*. Norman, OK: University of Oklahoma Press, 1967.

Lekson, Stephen H. *Nana's Raid: Apache Warfare in Southern New Mexico, 1881*. El Paso, TX: Texas Western Press. 1987.

Lockwood, Frank. *The Apache Indians*. Lincoln, NE: University of Nebraska Press, 1966.

Lummis, Charles Fletcher, with Dan Thrapp, ed. *Dateline Fort Bowie, Charles Fletcher Lummis Reports on an Apache War*. Norman, OK: University of Oklahoma Press, 1979.

McCall, George Archibald, with Robert Frazer, ed. *New Mexico in 1850: A Military View*. Norman, OK: University of Oklahoma Press, 1968.

McDaniel, Ruel. *The Saga of Judge Roy Bean: "The Law West of the Pecos."* Kingsport, TN: Southern Publishers, 1936.

McFarland, Elizabeth F. *Wilderness of the Gila*. Albuquerque, NM: University of New Mexico Press, 1974.

McGaw, William C. *Savage Scene: The Life and Time of James Kirker—Frontier King*. New York: Hastings House, 1972.

McKenna, James A. *Black Range Tales*. Glorieta, NM: Rio Grande Press, 1936.

Marks, Paula Mitchell. *And Die in the West: The Story of the O. K. Corral Gunfight*. New York: William Morrow & Company, 1989.

———. *Precious Dust: The True Saga of the Western Gold Rushes*. San Francisco: HarperCollins, 1995.

Meadows, John P. , with John P. Wilson, ed. *Pat Garrett and Billy the Kid as I Knew Them: Reminiscences of John P. Meadows*. Albuquerque, NM: University of New Mexico Press, 2004.

Meed, Douglas V. *They Never Surrendered: Bronco Apache of the Sierra Madres, 1890-1935*. Tucson, AZ: Westernlore Press, 1993.

Metz, Leon C. *The Encyclopedia of Lawmen, Outlaws, and Gunfighters*. New York: Checkmark Books, 2003.

———. *Border, The U.S.-Mexico Line*. El Paso: Mangan Books, 1989.

Michno, Gregory F. *Encyclopedia of Indian Wars—Western Battles and Skirmishes, 1850-1890*. Missoula, MT: Mountain Press Publishing, 2003.

Miller, Darlis A. Soldiers and Settlers, Military Supply in the Southwest 1861-1885. Albuquerque, NM: University of New Mexico Press, 1989.

Miller, Joseph. *New Mexico, A Guide to the Colorful State*. New York: Hastings House, 1953.

Mitchell, Ena, contributor. *In the Shadow of the Pyramids*. Bicentennial History. Lordsburg, NM, 1976.

Moorhead, Max L. New Mexico's Royal Road—Trade and Travel on the Chihuahua Trail. Norman, OK: University of Oklahoma Press, 1958.

Moynahan, Jay. *Talkin' about Sportin' Women: A Dictionary of Terms Related to Prostitution on the American Frontier*. Spokane, WA: Chickadee Publishing, 2002.

———. *Fifty Years of Prostitute Photos, 1870-1920*. Spokane, WA: Chickadee Publishing, 2004.
Mullane, William H., ed. *Indian Raids as Reported in the* Silver City Enterprise. Silver City, NM: Silver City Enterprise, 1968.
———. *This is Silver City, Volume III, 1888-1890*. Silver City, NM: Silver City Enterprise, 1965.
Murray, John A. *The Gila Wilderness*. Albuquerque, NM: University of New Mexico Press, 1988.
Myrick, David F. *New Mexico's Railroads—A Historical Survey*. Albuquerque, NM: University of New Mexico Press, 1970.
Nelson, Susan, and David Nelson. *The Silver City Book I—"Wild and Woolly Days."* Silver City, NM: Silver Star Publications, 1978.
Nolan, Frederick. *The West of Billy the Kid*. Norman, OK: University of Oklahoma Press, 1998.
———. *The Lincoln County War: A Documentary History*. Norman, OK: University of Oklahoma Press, 1992.
O'Neal, Bill. *Fighting Men of the Indian Wars*. Stillwater, OK: Barbed Wire Press, 1991.
Owen, Gordon R. *The Two Alberts, Fountain and Fall*. Las Cruces, NM: Yucca Tree Press, 1996.
———. *Las Cruces, New Mexico 1849-1999: Multicultural Crossroads*. Las Cruces, NM: Red Sky Publishing Company, 1999.
Pike, David. *Roadside New Mexico—A Guide to Historic Markers*. Albuquerque, NM: University of New Mexico Press, 2004.
Price, Paxton P. *Pioneers of the Mesilla Valley*. Las Cruces, NM: Yucca Tree Press, 1995.
Rathbun, Daniel C. B., and David V. Alexander. *New Mexico Frontier Military Place Names*. Las Cruces, NM: Yucca Tree Press, 2003.
Reinhartz, Dennis, and Gerald D. Saxon. *The Mapping of the Entradas into the Greater Southwest*. Norman, OK: University of Oklahoma Press, 1998.
Reynolds, Bill. *Trouble In New Mexico: The Outlaws, Gunmen, Desperadoes, Murderers and Lawmen for Fifty Turbulent Years*. 3 vols. Bakersfield, CA, 1994.
Roberts, David. *Once They Moved Like the Wind: Cochise, Geronimo, and the Apache Wars*. New York: Simon & Schuster, 1993.
Rynning, Thomas. *Gun Notches*. San Diego, CA: Frontier Heritage Press, 1971.
Schlesier, Karl H. *Josanie's War*. Norman, OK: University of Oklahoma Press, 1998.
Seagraves, Anne. *Soiled Doves: Prostitution in the Early West*. Hayden, ID: Wesanne Publications, 1994.
Selcer, Richard. *Legendary Watering Holes: The Saloons That Made Texas Famous*. College Station, TX: Texas A&M University Press, 2004.
Sherman, Barb and James Sherman. *Ghost Towns and Mining Camps of New Mexico*. Albuquerque, NM: University of New Mexico Press, 1975.
Simmons, Marc. *Ranchers, Ramblers, and Renegades*. Santa Fe, NM: Ancient City Press, 1984.
———. *When Six-Guns Ruled*. Santa Fe, NM: Ancient City Press, 1990.
———. *Massacre on the Lordsburg Road*. College Station, TX: Texas A&M University Press, 1997.
Sladen, Joseph Alton with Edwin R. Sweeney, ed. *Making Peace with Cochise: The 1872 Journal of Captain Joseph Alton Sladen*. Norman, OK: University of Oklahoma Press, 1997.
Smith, Ralph Adam. *Borderlander—The Life of James Kirker, 1793-1852*. Norman, OK: University of Oklahoma Press, 1999.
Sonnichsen, Charles L. *The El Paso Salt War*. El Paso, TX: Carl Hertzog and the Texas Western Press, 1961.
———. *The Story of Roy Bean: Law West of the Pecos*. New York: Devin-Adair Company, 1958.
———. *Billy King's Tombstone*. Caldwell, ID: The Caxton Press, 1946.
Spicer, Edward H. *Cycles of Conquest*. Tucson, AZ: University of Arizona Press, 1962.
Stanley, Father (Stanley Crocchiola). *The Deming, New Mexico, Story*. Pantex, TX, 1962.
———. *The Shakespeare, New Mexico, Story*. Pantex, TX, 1961.
Stevens, Montague. *Meet Mr. Grizzly: A Saga on the Passing of the Grizzly Bear*. Silver City, NM: High-Lonesome Books, 2002.
Stout, Joseph A. *Apache Lightning: The Last Great Battles of the Ojo Calientes*. New York: Oxford University Press, 1974.
Sweeney, Edwin R. *Cochise, Chiricahua Apache Chief*. Norman, OK: University of Oklahoma Press, 1991.
———. *Mangas Coloradas, Chief of the Chiricahua Apaches*. Norman, OK: University of Oklahoma Press, 1998.
———. *Merejildo Grijalva, Apache Captive, Army Scout*. El Paso, TX: University of Texas Press, 1992.
Tefertiller, Casey. *Wyatt Earp: The Life Behind the Legend*. New York: John Wiley and Sons, 1997.
Tevis, James H. *Arizona in the '50s*. Albuquerque, NM: University of New Mexico Press, 1954.
Thrapp, Dan L. *The Encyclopedia of Frontier Biography*. 3 vols. Lincoln, NE: University of Nebraska Press, 1988.

———. *Victorio and the Mimbres Apaches*. Norman, OK: University of Oklahoma Press, 1980.
———. *The Conquest of Apacheria*. Norman, OK: University of Oklahoma Press, 1980.
———. *Juh: An Incredible Indian*. University of Texas at El Paso. El Paso. 1973.
Unger, Patti. *True Tales*. Silver City, NM: Sundog Publishing, 1991.
Ungnade, Herbert E. *New Mexico Mountains*. Albuquerque, NM: University of New Mexico Press, 1995.
Utley, Robert *High Noon In Lincoln: Violence on the Western Frontier*. Albuquerque, NM: University of New Mexico Press, 1987.
———. *Billy the Kid: A Short and Violent Life*. Lincoln, NE: University of Nebraska Press, 1989.
———. *Frontier Regulars: The United States Army and the Indian, 1866-1891*. Lincoln, NE: University of Nebraska Press, 1973.
Varney, Philip. *Arizona Ghost Towns and Mining Camps*. Phoenix, AZ: Arizona Highways Books, 1994.
Walker, Dale T. *Rough Rider: Buckey O'Neill of Arizona*. Lincoln, NE: University of Nebraska Press, 1997.
Weber, David J. *The Spanish Frontier in North America*. New Haven, CT, and London: Yale University Press, 1992.
Weedle, Jerry. *Antrim Is My Stepfather's Name: The Boyhood of Billy the Kid*. Tucson, AZ: The Arizona Historical Society, 1993.
Williams, O. W., with S. D. Myres, ed. *Pioneer Surveyor—Frontier Lawyer, The Personal Narrative of O. W. Williams, 1877-1902*. El Paso, TX: Texas Western College Press, 1966.
Wilson, R. Michael. *Encyclopedia of Stagecoach Robbery in Arizona*. Las Vegas, NV: RaMa Press, 2003.
Worcester, Don. *The Apaches: Eagles of the Southwest*. Norman, OK: University of Oklahoma Press, 1979.
Young, Roy B. *Pete Spence, "Audacious Artist In Crime."* Apache, OK: Young & Sons Publishing, 2002.

Periodicals

Alexander, Bob. "And We Say Well Done, Dan!" *National Association for Outlaw and Lawman History Quarterly*, January-March 2003.
Allen, R. S. "Pinos Altos, New Mexico." *New Mexico Historical Review*, October 1948.
Allen, Thomas B. "Remember the *Maine*." *National Geographic*, February 1998.
Anderson, Hattie. "Mining and Indian Fighting in Arizona and New Mexico, 1858: Memoirs Of Hank Smith." *Panhandle Plains Historical Review* 1, no. 1 (1928).
———. "With the Confederates in New Mexico During the Civil War: Memoirs Of Hank Smith." *Panhandle Plains Historical Review* 2, no. 2 (1929).
Aranda, Daniel. "An Episode from Victorio's War." *Real West*, February 1984.
Austerman, Wayne R. "The English Apache." *Real West*, February 1986.
Bailey. Lynn R. "John H. Jackson and the Arizona Rangers." *Western Outlaw-Lawman History Association Journal*, Summer/Fall 2004.
Ball, Larry D. "Lawman in Disgrace: Sheriff Charles C. Perry of Chaves County, New Mexico." *New Mexico Historical Review*, April 1986.
———. "Militia Posses: The Territorial Militia In Civil Law Enforcement in New Mexico Territory, 1877-1883." *New Mexico Historical Review*, January 1980.
Bell, Bob Boze. "An Eye for an Eye." *True West*, October 2003.
———. "The Dark Side of Wyatt Earp." *True West*, July 1998.
Bell, Olive W. "The Fabulous Frontier." *New Mexico Magazine*, November 1949.
Brand, Peter. "Sherman W. McMaster(s), The El Paso Salt War, Texas Rangers & Tombstone." *Western Outlaw-Lawman History Association Journal*, Winter 1999.
Bronson, Edgar Beecher. "Evolution of a Train Robber." *American Magazine*, September 1909.
Caldwell, George A. "New Mexico's First Train Robbery." *National Association for Outlaw and Lawman History Quarterly*, Winter 1989.
Cannon, Julia Brannin, with Ellen Lape. "Silver Boom Town." *New Mexico Magazine*, July 1951.
Clark, Neil M. "Wilderness Family." *Saturday Evening Post*, March 1948.
Cline, Ellen R. "Mowry City." *Silver City Enterprise*, March 2, 1978.
———. "Story Of A Cowboy." *Cochise County Historical Journal*, Fall/Winter 1997/1998.
Cole, Joe A., and Terry Cole. "Charley Smith Stills Wears His Six-Gun." *True West*, April 1978.
Cool, Paul. "Bob Martin: A Rustler in Paradise." *Western Outlaw-Lawman History Association Journal*, Winter 2003.
Cox, John. "Salty John Cox and Bronco Bill." *True West*, June 1977.
DeArment, Robert K. "Deadly Deputy." *True West*, November 1991.
———. "Sheriff Whitehill and the Kit Joy Gang." Old West, Winter 1994.
———. "The Fatal Defect of Charley Perry." Old West, Winter 1991.

Devereaux, Jan. "Jagville." *National Outlaw and Lawman History Association Quarterly*, January-March 2004.
Dike, Sheldon H. "The Territorial Post Offices of New Mexico." *New Mexico Historical Review*, nos. 33-34 (1958).
Dinges, Bruce J. "The Victorio Campaign of 1880: Cooperation and Conflict on the United States-Mexico Border." *New Mexico Historical Review*, January 1987.
Edwards, Harold. "Sheriff Pat Garrett's Puzzle: A Blow by Blow Account of Solving a New Mexico Bank Robbery." *National Tombstone Epitaph*, January 2003.
Greever, Wiliam S. "Railway Development in the Southwest." *New Mexico Historical Review* 32 (1937).
Gustafson, C. A. "Dan Tucker, Deming's Lethal Lawman." *Luna County Visitors Guide*, 1999.
Hill, Janaloo. "The Sad Fate of Russian Bill. Why Was He Hanged? A Series." *Silver City Enterprise*, October 1883.
Hill, Rita, and Janaloo Hill. "Alias Shakespeare—The Town Nobody Knew." *New Mexico Historical Review*, 1967.
Holben, Richard E. "The Deaf Mute Witness of Silver City." *Real West*, October 1969.
———. "Kit Joy's Gang." *Frontier Times*, September 1971.
Humble, Terrance M. "The Pinder-Slip Mining Claim Dispute of Santa Rita, New Mexico, 1821-1912." *Mining History Journal*, 1996.
Johnson, Dave. "The Redding Boys." *National Association for Outlaw and Lawman History Quarterly*, October-December 2004.
McGaw, Bill. "Billy the Kid's Teacher Saw Him as Sensitive, Effeminate, Fearful Youth." *El Paso Herald-Post*, Dec. 17, 1960.
Matson, Daniel S., and Albert H. Schroeder, eds. "Cordero's Description of the Apache—1796." *New Mexico Historical Review*, October 1957.
Muir, Emma M. "Bonanza Days at Shakespeare." *New Mexico Magazine*, September 1948.
———. "The First Militia." *New Mexico Magazine*, October 1952.
———. "Shakespeare Becomes a Ghost Town." *New Mexico Magazine*, October 1948.
Mullin, Robert N. "Here Lies John Kinney." *Journal of Arizona History*, Autumn 1973.
Myers, Lee. "Fort Webster on the Mimbres River." *New Mexico Historical Review*, January 1966.
———. "Military Establishments In Southwestern New Mexico: Stepping Stones to Settlement." *New Mexico Historical Review* 43, no. 1 (1968).
Naegle, Conrad. "The Rebellion of Grant County, New Mexico In 1876." *Arizona and the West*, Autumn 1968.
Nolan, Frederick. "Boss Rustler, The Life and Crimes of John Kinney." *True West*, September and October 1996.
———. "Saga of the San Augustine Ranch." *True West*, June 1999.
Nunn, Annie Dyer. "Boston Charlie's Last Stand." *Frontier Times*, December-January 1971.
Rasch, Philip J. "The Bonney Brothers." *Frontier Times*, December-January 1965.
———. "The Las Cruces Bank Robbery." *Frontier Times*, January 1981.
———. "The Rustler War." *New Mexico Historical Review*, October 1964.
———. "Six Shooter and Three Shooter Smith." *National Association for Outlaw and Lawman History Quarterly*, Spring 1985.
Rayburn, John C. "The Rough Riders in San Antonio, 1898." *Arizona and the West*, Summer 1961.
Reeve, Frank D., ed. "Frederick E. Phelps: A Soldier's Memoirs." *New Mexico Historical Review*, January and April 1950.
Russell, Sharman Apt. "Russian Bill: the True Story of an Outlaw." *Journal of the West*, April 1984.
———. "A Young Lion of the Gila." *True West*, July 1988.
Secrest, William B. "Brave Len Harris Is Dead." *True West*, December 1992.
Smith, Ralph A. "The Scalp Hunt In Chihuahua—1849." *New Mexico Historical Review*, April 1965.
Tanner, John D. "Violence in New Mexico—A Penitentiary Analysis." *Western Outlaw-Lawman History Association Journal*, Summer 2003.
Tittmann, Edward D. "The Last Legal Frontier." *New Mexico Historical Review* 2 no. 3 (July 1927).
Turner, Alton. "New Mexico Shoot-Out." *Frontier Times*, March 1969.
Tyler, Daniel. "Gringo Views of Governor Manuel Armijo." *New Mexico Historical Review* 45 no. 1 (1970).
Utley, Robert M. "The Buffalo Soldiers and Victorio." *New Mexico Magazine*, March 1984.
Wallace, William. Swilling "Short-Line Staging In New Mexico." *New Mexico Historical Review*, April 1951.
Webb, A. D. "Arizonans In The Spanish-American War." *Arizona Historical Review*, January 1929.
White, Marjorie. "Death Pass in the Peloncillos." *Frontier Times*, June-July 1966.

Winslowe, John R. "Buscadero Outlaw." *Westerner*, July-August 1970.

Newspapers

Arizona Miner
Deming (New Mexico) Headlight
El Paso (Texas) *Lone Star*
El Paso (Texas) Herald-Post
Galveston (Texas) *Daily News*
Grant County (New Mexico) *Herald*
Las Cruces (New Mexico) *Border*
Las Vegas Optic
Lordsburg (New Mexico) *Western Liberal*
Mesilla Valley (New Mexico) *Independent*
Mining Life
The New Southwest and Grant County (New Mexico) *Herald*
Santa Fe Daily New Mexican
Santa Fe Weekly New Mexican
Silver City (New Mexico) *Eagle*
Silver City (New Mexico) *Enterprise*
Silver City (New Mexico) *Independent*
Southwest Sentinel (Silver City, New Mexico)
Wichita (Kan.) *Daily Eagle*

INDEX

A

Abraham, David 59, *70*, 71, 77, 96, 125, 126
Abraham, Louis 84
Academy of Our Lady of Lourdes 205
Addis, A. S. 77, 140
Africo-Tubercular Sanatorium 260
Aguilar, Nicanor 158
Ailman, Henry "Harry" 72, 76, 176, *178*
Alamo Canyon 170
Albillar, Victoriano 171
Aleman's Well 147
Allen, E. L. 188
Allen, Frank 200
Allen, Hiram 10
Alma, New Mexico 204, 214, 215, 221
Alverez, Reyes 230, 231, 233
Anderson, Jessie 83
Andrews, Frank 208
Animas Mountains 122, 229, 237
Animas Valley 54, 169
Anthony, William 255
Antrim, Catherine [McCarty] *78*, 87, 91, 177
Antrim, Henry [Billy the Kid] 77, 78, 84, 88, 90, 91, *92*, 94, 119
Antrim, Joseph M. "Joe" 78, 84, 189
Antrim, William Henry Harrison 78, *79*, 84
Apache Pass 54, 55
Apache Tejo 28, 32
Aredia, Savero 22
Armijo, Jacinto 104, 137
Armijo, Jesus 47
Armstrong's Rooming House 241
Arnold, Philip 127, 128
Arroyo, Juan 54
Ashenfelter, S. M. 118, 132, 142, 145, 151
Ashton, Charles 196
Atkinson, James E. 47
Atkinson, John 120
Axtell, Samuel B. 114, 116

B

Baca, Cipriano 233
Bacthelder, Charles "Boston Charley" 137, 138
Bagsby, Charley 181
Bailey, George W. 76, 86, 141, 144, 250
Baine, Charles "Frenchy" *242*
Barela, Filoman 137
Barnes, Johnny 155
Barney's Station 26
Barragan, Nepomuseno 137
Barron, John C. 253
Bartlett, John Russell *21*, 22-24
Baxter, Jason 56
Bean, Petra 25
Bean, Roy 25, *30*
Bean, Sam 25, 30
Bear Creek 28,235
Beauford, Clay 105-108, 110
Bedonkohe Apache 11, 149
Bedrock Saloon 59
Bell, Verdie 144
Beltran, Pancho 137
Ben Moore Mountain 18
Benavides, Fray Alonso de 4, 5
Bencomo, Atanacio 115
Bennett, Cornelius 61, 76, 79, 86, 142, 145
Bennett, Cortie 84
Bennett, Frank P. 170, 202
Bennett, J. F. 86, 90, 95, 114
Bennett's News Depot 141
Best, Andrew J. "Jack" 204, 205
Beyer, Charles D. 131, 135
Big Ditch *251*
Big Hatchet Mountains 228
Big Jess 144
Billy the Kid [see Antrim, Henry]
Birch, James E. 26, 28
Birch, Thomas Henry
Birchville, New Mexico 28-33
Bisbee Massacre 202
Black & Company 143, 210
Black Range 11, 135, 146, 150, 153, 169, 171, 172, 213
Black, Pope 187
Black, Robert 82, 83, 117, 124, 134, 168, 177, 199, 210, 241, *254*
Black, Robert "Arkansas" 156
Bland-Allison Act 211
Blue Goose Saloon 76
Bolds, Jacob 48
Bonanza City, New Mexico 189
Bond, Jack 164
Bonito [Apache] 192, *214*
Borajo, Antonio120
Bottom, Charles F. 45
Bowe, Thomas "Tom" 116
Boyle, William G. 127,129
Boyne, Thomas 131, 132
Bradley, Newton 117
Bragaw, John 113
Branch, A. W. 14
Bremen, Martin W. 40, 51, 57, 82, 88, 117, 129, 199
Brewer, Alice 241
Bristol, Warren Henry 95, *96*, 135, 154
Brito, Frank 257
Brocius, "Curly Bill" 155, 164
Brock, Julius Caesar 193
Brockman, John 82, 173, 225
Brooks, Emory H. 141
Brown, William D. 45
Brownsville, Texas 15
Brush-Swan Electric Light Company 183, 188
Buffalo Soldiers 100, 103, 132, 135, 154, 170, 171, 174, 199
Buhlman, Joseph 117
Bullard Mining Company 46, 53, 58, 68
Bullard, James "Jim" 30, 41, 42, 44, 46, 48, 53, 54, 65, *74*, 184
Bullard, John 30, 41, 42, 44, 46, 48, 53, *56*, 57, 66, 68
Bullock, Earl Sprague 260
Buquor, J. A. 230
Burgess, John DeWitt 170
Burnett, George Ritter 172

Burnham, Parker 51, 68-70
Burns, James D. 185
Burrell, Roscoe 95
Burro Mines 44-46, 54, *128*
Burro Mountains 39, 44, 54, 62, 74, 133, 182, 184, 192, 193, 240, 241, 248
Burro Springs 119, 138
Burwell, Sterling 122
Butterfield Overland Trail 26, 39
Butterfield, John 26, 27

C

Caballo Mountains 146
Cabell, DeRosey C. 221
Cahill, Francis P. "Windy" 119
Caldwell, George 29, 30
Calhoun, James S. 20
Calhoun, R. N. 115
California Column 31, 69
Camp Grant 66, 111, 119, 213
Campbell, Angus 168, 226, 252
Campbell, Lee 76, 77
Cañada Alamosa 53, 66, 80, 81, 100, 101, 105, 150, 172
Canales, Bonito 263
Cantley, Charles L. 245, 246
Cantonment Dawson 21
Cardis, Louis 96, 120
Carey, Luther 190
Carlin, Samuel 117
Carpenter, S. P. 174
Carrasco, José Manuel 6, 7
Carrasco, Juan N. 47, 52
Carrillo, Felix 158
Carrizal, Mexico 158
Carrizo Canyon 172
Carroll, Henry 101, 146,149,150
Carroll, William 156
Carrolla, José M. "Portuguese Jo" 114
Carson, Christopher "Kit" *10*
Casas Grandes, Mexico 66
Casson, Myers H. 51, 69
Catholic 4, 76, 86, 120, 141, 197, 205
Centennial Saloon 117, 144, 154, *184*, 185 199
Central City, New Mexico 36, 38, 40, *85*, 89, 90, 190
Chacon, Juan 174
Chacon, Manuel 174
Chacon, Petronillo 174
Chamberlin, William 75
Chapman, George 207
Chase, C. M. 163
Chato [Apache] 182, 192, *195*
Chaves, Carlos "Charlie"190, 200, 207, 208
Chenowth, Howard Pickney 263, *264*
Cherry Creek 28
Cherrycows 11
Chicago White Stockings 255
Chick, Jack 150
Chie [Apache] 73, 74
Chihenne Apache 11, 12, 18, 24, 26, 28, 31-33, 41, 48, 50, 53, 57, 65, 73, 81, 100, 101, 106, 108, 109, 131, 132, 136, 137, 145, 149, 153, 158, 169, 174
Chihuahua [Apache] 170, 171, 182, *213*, 214, 215, 220
Chihuahua [state], Mexico 11, 19, 27, 60, 145, 159
Chihuahua City, Mexico 4, 7, 12, 66, 158, 170
Chihuahua Hill *60*, 61, 69, 72, 217
Chihuahuan Desert 36
Childers, T. N. 250
Chilson, George W. 80. 81
Chinese Exclusion Act 222
Chiricahua Apache 10-13, 22, 26, 27, 34, 54, 98, 102-104, 108, 109, 149, 152
Chiricahua Mountains 11, 54, 238
Chisum, John Simpson 95
Chloride Flat District 47, 52, 81, 129, 249
Chloride, New Mexico 169, 171, 172
Chocolate Pass, Mexico 66
Chokonen Apache 11, 31, 54, 57, 65, 73, 81, 149, 171
Chong, Wing 144
Christian, Jeff 235
Chung, Sam 93
Clark, Amos 56
Clark, John 116
Clark, P. J. 198
Clayton, Jeff W. 233
Cleveland, George Washington 203, 206-209
Cleveland, Grover 245
Cleveland, Ohio 183
Clifton, Arizona 96, 97, 182, 219, 241, 243
Clum, John Philip 104-106, *107*, 108-111, 113, 119, 130
Coahuila, Mexico 14
Cobb, Tom 226
Cochise [Apache] 31, 32, 54, 55, 57, 73, 81, 152
Cochise County, Arizona 180, 203
Cohen, Isaac *59*, 76, 177
Coleman, John "Turquoise John" 240
Collins, John 94
Colt, Samuel 63
Comerford, John 111
Committee of Ten 224
Compá, Juan Diego 11
Compá, Juan José 11
Conde, Alejo Garcia 23
Connely, Barney W. 59
Conway, Doc [aka O. L. Hale] 190
Conway, Thomas F. 95
Cook, James "Jim" 214, 216
Cooke's Peak 27, 31, 95
Cooke's Spring 26
Coomer, Dan 133, 208
Coomer, Jessie 82
Cooney, James 150
Cooper, F. H. 76
Cooper, Thomas F. 117
Copper Mine Apache 11
Corbin, James 47
Coronado, Francisco Vásquez de 3, 4
Cosgrove, Con 90
Cosgrove, Eugene *59*, 144, *247*

Cottage Saloon 250
Cottage Sanatorium 260
Cotton Saloon 173
Cradlebough, Samuel 52
Craig, Louis S. 22, 24
Crane, James "Slim Jim" 155, 164
Crawford House Hotel 127
Crawford, Ben 237
Crawford, C. P. 123, 177
Cremony, John Carey 22, *23*
Crittenden, James G. 79, 82
Crocker, Charles 162
Croenne, Lucy 242, 243
Crook, George 109, 170, 213, 217, 219, 220, 227, *228*
Croty, John 25
Crouch, John S. 62
Cuchillo Negro Creek 136, 172
Culberson, Vic 252
Currier, J. E. 166
Curtis, W. W. 141

D

Dallas, George 111
Daly, George 173, 174
Dane, Charles H. 166
Datil Mountains 11
Davis, Britton 212, 214, 219
Davis, Mary 84
Davis, Peter 111
Day, Matthias W. 135
Delard, Charles 65
DeLong, John 30
Deming, Mary Ann 163
Deming, New Mexico 162-164, *165*, 166, *167*, 170, 180, 181, 184-188, 197, 198, 201, 203, 210, 217-221, 225, 227, 233, 236, 248, 252, 260, 266
Denny, John 135
Denver, Colorado 46, 166, 184, 233
Derbyshire, Matt 86, 87, 117, 212
Diamond A Ranch *207*, *240*, 252, 263
Diamond, Ben 30
Dick, Bill 30
Doña Ana County 25, 30, 33, 36, 104, 114, 185
Dorsey, Frank 132
Dos Cabezas Mountains 11, 110, 192
Doubtful Canyon 27, 217
Dragoon Mountains 11
Duck Creek 111, 116
Dudley, Nathan A. M. 135
Dunn, Jack 102
Duran, Abel 190, 200
Dwenger, Dora 130, 159
Dwenger, Henry F. 130, 132, 159
Dwenger, William "Billy" 130, 159
Dyer, Alice 84
Dyer, Joseph D. 76, 77

E

Earp, Morgan 180
Earp, Virgil 180
Earp, Wyatt 180-182
Eckles, Isabel "Belle" 249
Eckles, Sam 56, 57, 86
El Camino Real [the Royal Road] 4
El Paso del Norte 12, 16-18, 20, 21, 46, 120
El Paso Salt War 120
Elephant Corral 181, 207, 250
Elguea, Francisco Manuel 6, 7, 22
Elias, José Maria 18
Elizabethtown, New Mexico 46
Elliott, Charles P. 217
Embry, Charles 115
Episcopal 141, 197, 235
Eureka, New Mexico 151, 174
Evensen, John N. "Uncle Johnny" 40, 166
Everett, Robert 77
Ewing, Thomas 19

F

Fambro, "Happy Bob" 156
Farrell, James K. 164
Fielder, James S. "Jim" 245
Findley, Tom 56
Flagstaff, Arizona 233
Flanagan, James P. 47
Fleming, Andrew 113
Fleming, John W. "Jack" 184, 189, 198, 207, *244*, 248
Fleming, New Mexico 189
Florida Mountains 11, 12, 39, 101, 103, 137, 161, 170, 220, 252
Florman, Robert 61, 76
Floyd, John B. 32
Flynn, Hugh 47, 56, 115
Foote and Booth Store 184
Forrer, Emil 116
Forsyth, George A. "Sandy" 182, 183, 194, 195
Fort Bayard 33, 36, 39, 42, 43, 54, 66, 73, 89, 90, 103, 105, 131, 149, 150, 154, 155, 183, 188, 190, 193, 199, 208, 213, 215, 216, 221, 237
Fort Bowie 54, 102, 156
Fort Craig 171
Fort Cummings 33, 39, 43, 85, 90, 104, 119, 156, 165, 169, 173, 174, 181, 182, 193, 202
Fort Floyd 32
Fort McLane 32
Fort Selden 80, 81, 101
Fort Thorn 26
Fort Webster *6*, 24-26
Foster, John R. 131
Fountain, Albert Jennings 135, 191, 192, 259
Fountain, Samuel Warren 221
Fourth Coinage Act 211
Fowler, Joel 204
Fowler, Ruby 144
French, James Hansell 146
Fresh, J. D. 46
Freudenthal, J. 96
Fuerte [see Mangas Coloradas]
Fuson, Henry M. 44, 46, 53, 68

G

G O S Ranch 252
Gadsden Purchase 25, 98, 161
Gage, New Mexico 200-203, 205, 207, 209
Gage, William 200, 201
Gaines, Louis 154, *155*
Gale, N. H. 118
Galeana, Mexico 66
Galindas, Manuel 237
Gallager, T. F. 200
Garcia, Cisto 104
Garcia, Juan 115
Garcia, New Mexico 172
Gasiner, Charles 200
Gatewood, Charles Bayer 152-154, 214, *215*
Gavilan Canyon 173
Gem Restaurant184
Georgetown, New Mexico 99, 103, 118, 127, 129, 141, 154, 177, 188, 190, 225, 231, 235-237, 262
Geronimo [Apache]101, 102, 105-108, *109*, 110, 113, 152, 182, 212-215, 218, 219, 226-228, 237
Gibbons, Mike 116, 117
Gila River 5, 0, 16, 20, 25, 36, 54, 104, 131, 254
Gileño Apache 4-6
Gilmo, John W., 203, 204
Givens, Isaac 85
Glanton, John Joel 17
Globe, Arizona 96, 98, 137, 182
Gold Dust, New Mexico 172
Gold Gulch, New Mexico182
Golding, Eugene 59
Golding, Robert "Bob" 96
Goldwater-Castaneda Store 202
Goodell's Corral 258
Gordon, Jack "Apache Jack" 17, 18
Grabe, Richard W. 245
Graham County, Arizona 237
Graham, Andrew R. 255
Graham, John 193
Graham, William 220
Grant Hotel 166
Gray, Dixie Lee "Dick" 168
Gray, John Pleasant 168
Gray, Michael 168
Grayson, C. F. 248
Greaves, Clifton [Clinton] 103
Green, S. 76
Greene, E. L. 141
Grounds, William "Billy the Kid" 155
Guilfoyle, John Francis 170-172
Gulf of Mexico 15, 21
Gunnels, Jesse B. 201
Gunter, Archibald Clavering 243

H

Hachita, New Mexico 241
Hackney, Aaron R. 47
Hall, Thomas 207, 230, 233
Hamilton Bill [statehood] 264
Hardie, Robert 238
Hardin, John Wesley 258
Harper, Bessie 141, 217
Harrington, George 29, 30
Harris, Ethel 225
Harris, Leonard "Len" 201, 202
Harshberger, H. M. 69
Harvey House Hotel 164, 233
Harvey, Fred 166
Harwood, Thomas 141
Hasford, C. D. 253
Haslett, Bill 156, 164
Haslett, Ike 156, 164
Hatch, Edward 99-101, 132, 134, *147*, 148, 151, 153
Hatch, New Mexico 26
Hatchet Mountains 39
Haynes, Francis 238
Hays, John Coffee "Jack" 16-20
Hearst, William Randolph 256
Hell's Forty Acres 130
Hembrillo Canyon 149, 150
Henry, Willis 81
Hepner, Gus 65
Herelda, Desiderio 174
Hickey, N. L. 137
Hidalgo, Rosalio 241, 242
Higbee, R. B. 125, 197
Hildreth, Peter 56
Hill, Frank 231
Hinds, J. B. 137
Hines, Pat 241
Hinman, O. C. 235, 239
Hodgkins, Thomas C. 201
Hoffman, Tess 263
Hoffman, William "Push" 263
Hold, George W. 76
Holliday, John H. "Doc" 180, 181
Holson, T. W. 252
Hoo Do War 129
Hooker, Ambrose E. 135
Horn, George 219
Horse Springs, New Mexico 169, 204
Houghton, Joab 38
Howard, Charles 120
Howard, J. J. 192
Howard, Oliver Otis 72-74
Howlett, Richard 47, 64, 116
Huachuca Mountains 11
Hubert, Joseph "Dutch Joe" 94, 99, 104
Hudson, Del 225
Hudson, Mary 76
Hudson, Richard "Dick" 31, *38*, 41, 43, 48, 49 51, 62, 66, 76, 79, 82, 86, 125, 126, 146, 167, *240*, 248, 255
Hudson's Hot Springs 38, *126*, 146, 167, 255
Hughes, James 102
Hughes, Jim "Sweetheart of the San Simon" 156
Hugo, Charley 164
Hull, Joe 138
Hume, James B. "Jim" 201, 202
Hunt, Zwing 155
Hurlburt, Andrew J. 31, 41-44, 46, 47, 53, 68
Hyatt, Tom 252

J

Jackson, J. C. 208, 210
James, S. E. 192
Jeffords, Thomas "Tom" Jonathan 72
Jenks, Ralph 259
Jewett Ranch 203
Jicarilla Apache 10
Johnson, John James 11
Johnson, John R. 44-47, 75, 250
Johnson, William D. "Keechi" *258*, 259
Jones, John 56
Jordan, Bill 116
Jordan, George 172
Jornada del Murerto 17
Josaine [Ulzana] [Apache] 220
Joy, Christopher Carson "Kit" 203, 204, 206-210
Juh [Apache] 101, 102, 137
Justice, Richard 84

K

Kaiser, Fred 95
Kane, W. H. 144, 154
Kansas State Penitentiary192
Kaytennae [Apache] 169, *170*
Keller Valley 151
Keller, James 151
Kelly, Daniel "York" 202
Kelly, William 54, 68
Kemp, Charles 12
Kendall, Thomas 189
Kennedy, H. J. 233
Kennedy, Martin "Mart" 263
Kennon, Jr., Louis 187
Kerber, Charles 120, 121
Kerns and Mitchell Stage Line 39, 90
Keystone Hotel 72, 82, 86
Kilburn, William H. 263, 264
King, Clarence 129
King, Israel 226
King, Sandy 155, 166
Kinney, John 120, *121*, *191*, 192, 196
Kiowa-Apache 10
Kirker, James 25
Kit Carson, Colorado 68
Kneeling Nun 6
Knox, David C. 46
Knox, Brag 248
Kuhne, A. 87
Kurl, Charles 46

L

La Ciénega de San Vicente 40-42, 44-46, 48, 49
Lacy, Jacob Melborne 129
Lacy, John Hancock 129
Ladies Educational Society 75
Ladies Hospital 225
Lafferr, Joseph N. 141, 208, 209
Laird, Andrew "Andy" 233
Laizure, William 245
Lake Valley Mining Company 173
Lang, William 190
Lara, Venceslao 137
Las Animas Creek 146
Las Cruces, New Mexico 18, 68, 80, 90 101, 120 149
Lawson, William 235
LCs Ranch 168, 226, 252
Le Beau, Alexander 156
Lee, A. Mitchell "Mitch" 203, 204, 206, 208, 209
Lee's Peak 127
Legal Tender Corral 46, 48-51, 53, 82, 130
Leggett, Benjamin 116
Leitendorf Hills 102
Leonard, Billy 155, 164
Lesinsky, Henry 59, 90, 96
Little Dry Creek 221
Lloyd's Ranch 136
Lohman, Henry 69
Lone Mountain, New Mexico 82, 116, 252
Loomis, A. J. 250
Loomis, Cyrus 126
Lopez, Fredrico 95
Lopez, Jesus 23
Lora, Aurilio 190, 200
Lord, Delbert 161
Lordsburg, New Mexico 158, 161, *162*, 192-194, 198, 200, 217, 234,-236, 238, 241, 243, 252, 258, 263, 266
Louisiana Purchase 14
Lowery, A. C. 127, 133
Lowthian, Thomas L. 52
Lucas, Belle118
Lucas, H. W. 140
Lucas, James A. 127
Luna County, New Mexico 260
Luse, Nat 215
Lyon, William B. 137
Lyons, Thomas "Tom" 85, 86, 97, 168, 276, *238*, 252, 253
Lytle, Leonidas S. 81

M

Madden, Dan 156
Madden, Emery S. 156
Maddox, Thomas J. C. 221
Maher, Martin 119, 125, 134
Maloney, J. D. [Mrs.] 188
Maney, James Allison 149, 150
Mangas Coloradas [Apache] 22, 23, 31, 32, 41, 57, 152
Mangas Creek 115
Mangas Valley 54
Mansfield, Joseph K. F. 26
Martin, John W. 183
Martin, Robert E. "Bob" 104, 156
Martin, William "Wild Bill" 114, 115
Mason County War 182
Mason County, Texas 129
Mason, Alva 46
Mason, John 68
Mason, W. J. 117
Massachusetts Mining Company 130, 142
Mathews, George 200
Maxwell, Lucien B. 52, 53, 85

May, Jacob "Jake" 72
Mayer, Ed 208
McBride, John 120
McClain, James 232
McClellan, Curwen Boyd 150
McClellan, William "Billy" 185
McComas, Charley 193, *194*, 196
McComas, Hamilton C. 193, *194*, 196
McComas, Juniata 193, *194*
McDonald, David N. 183
McGauhly, J. M. 141
McGeary, Bill 64
McGee, James 41
McGinnis, Mike 241
McGregor, Alex 104
McIntosh, Charles 79, 82, 88, 91
McKinn, Jimmy 219, *220*, 227
McKinn, John 219
McKinn, Martin 219
McLaughlin, James 231
McLaury, Frank 155
McLaury, Tom 155
McLeod, R. C.48
McMannigil, Johnny 238
Medal of Honor 72, 81, 103, 105, 132, 135, 136, 172, 174
Medill, William 16
Meeson and Marriage Stagecoaches 144, 168
Meredith, Hartford 176, *178*
Mescalero Agency/Reservation 132, 134, 135, 145, 149, 156, 170
Mescalero Apache 10, 137, 148, 149, 170, 172, 174
Mesilla Valley 26
Mesilla, New Mexico 26, 28, 30, 32, 33, 46, 68, 90, 95, 136, 170, 192
Metcalf, Robert "Bob" 96
Methodist 118, 141, 188, 197, 218, 224 244
Mexican Springs 128
Mexican War 15, 16, 20, 47
Mexico City, Mexico 4, 14
Mikesell, M. B. 189
Milby, William M. 41, 51
Miller, Ida 258
Miller, John A. 46, 177, 181
Mimbreño Apache 5, 24, 135, 146
Mimbres Apache 11, 134
Mimbres Hot Springs 87, 125, *126*
Mimbres Mountains 11, 173
Mimbres Reduction Works 104, 127
Mimbres River 25, 27, 36, 82, 113, 118, 127, 173, 197, 219, 220, 227 254
Mimbres River Station 26
Mineral Creek 150
Mississippi River 14, 16, 160
Mogollon Culture 2, 3
Mogollon Mountains 11, 56, 150, 151, 169, 213, 214, 221, 240, *254*, 259
Mogollon, Ignacio Flores [Governor] 5
Mohawk Minstrels 188
Mollitor, F. W. 156
Monticello, New Mexico 171
Moore, Alexander 39
Moore, George H. 132
Moore, Glaudius W. 185
Morehead, Alexander H 76.
Moreno, Manuel 47
Morrill, John B. 76, 96, 104, 232
Morris, James L. 81
Morrison, Sr., Alexander L. 187
Morrow, Albert P. *136*, 145, 146, 154
Mortimer, C. E. 120
Moses, J. A. 226
Moulton, Ed 51, 56, 57, 99
Mowry City, New Mexico 27, 252
Mule Springs 111
Munger, Nettie 235
Muñoz, Serapio 159
Murray, George 118
Murray, James 151
Muse, Herbert E. 194

N

Nachez 182
Nana 100, 135, 150, 152, 159, *169*, 170-175, 213, 221
National Mail and Transportation Company 39
National Restriction Act 222
Navaho 103, 131, 135
Nednhi Apache 11, 137, 149
Nelson, Bob "Nelson from the Gila" 114, 115
New Chicago, New Mexico 161, 162
New Mexico & Massachusetts Mining Company 130, 142, 168
Newsham, R. V. 168
Newsome, Robert 82
Nichols, J. R. 76
Noel, H. G. 239
Norris, Emma [Noyes] 89
North, Thomas 201
Nueces River 14
Nueva Galicia, Mexico 3
Nunn, Pat 263
Nutt, New Mexico 136, 181

O

O'Daugherty, Bernard 24
O'Grady, Mother Mary Paul 260
Ojo Alamo 39
Ojo Caliente 105-110, 131, 135, 145, 172
Ojo de Vaca [Cow Springs] 26
Olney, Joe [aka Joe Hill] 129, 156
O'Neil, Hugh 54
Organ Mountains 80, 86
Orleans Club Saloon 76
Orr, Edwin 47
Orr, John [aka John Donaldson] 114, 115
Orwig, Calvin215
O'Toole, Barney [aka Charles Williams] 154, *155*
Ott, Peter 82, 86, 144
Ownby, Bramble B. 195

P

Pacheco, Anselmo 99
Pacheco, Delesfero 99

Pacheco, Yrlneo 123
Padilla, Felipe 158
Palace Saloon *85*, 263
Parker, Charles 172
Parker, F. W. 262
Parker, Henry Kinney 153, 154
Parker, James 214
Parker, Leopold O. 156
Parker, Rhoda 28
Parks, George 193-195
Parks, T. E. 208
Parra, Citor 99
Paschal Hotel 184
Paschal, New Mexico 184, 185, 194
Pattie, James Ohio 10
Pattie, Sylvester 10
Peloncillo Mountains 11, 54, 121, 183
Penn, Delaware 131
Penrose, New Mexico 189
Percha Creek 146
Perez, Pilar 230, 231, 233, 237
Pern, Gasper 200
Perry, Charles 172, 204, 205
Perry, John 115
Philpin, Thomas 235
Picacho Peak 18
Pickett, H. L. 236
Pile, William A. 44, 65-67
Pines Sanatorium 260
Piños Altos Mountains 11, 28
Piños Altos, New Mexico 27, 30, 31, 33, 35, 40, 41, 43, 44, 45, 46, 50, 51, 57, 58, 62, 63
Piper, O. F. 66
Pleasanton, New Mexico 221
Polk, James K. 14
Pollock, Brady 219
Ponce [Apache] 23, 73, 74, 110
Pope, John 154
Porter, H. M. 76, 85, 95, 117, 119, 134
Posey, G. G. 226
Post Office Drug Store 144
Potten, George 143
Potter, Dell 250
Powers, G. W. 47
Pratte, Sylvester S. 10
Presbyterian 82, 141, 245
Price, Anthony "One-Arm" 164
Price, William 91
Provencia, Nicholas "Nick" 104
Provencio, Jose 171
Pulitzer, Joseph 256
Pyramid Mining and Milling Company 193
Pyramid Mountains 102, 127

R

Rafferty, Pat 103
Ralston, New Mexico 54, 62, 102, 121, 127, *128*, 129
Ralston, William C. 45
Ramblers Bicycle Club 233
Rattlesnake City, New Mexico 182
Raw Meat Creek 258, 259
Ray, Charles "Pony Diehl" *121*, 156
Red Canyon 171
Red Onion Saloon 76
Red Paint People 11
Redding, Thomas Searcy "Tom" 129, 182
Redding, William Zachariah "Bill" 129
Remine, Richard 103, 159
Richards, Mary Phillipa 90, 91-93
Richards, William "Dick" 122
Richardson, Israel Bush 24
Richmond, New Mexico 104, 11, 192, 193
Riding, M. 47
Ringo, John Peters 129, 156
Rio Grande River 4, 5, 11, 14, 15, 17, 18, 20, 24, 26, 32, 80, 81, 86, 119, 120, 131, 134, 146, 148, 171, 186, 190
Rio Mimbres, New Mexico 25, 44, 62, 66, 82, 163
Risque, J. P. 123
Riverside Park [San Antonio] 256
Robbins, C. 76
Roberts, Isaac 156
Roberts, Jim 151
Robidoux, Michel 10
Robinson, Tom 115
Rock Springs, Wyoming 224
Rodriguez, Enrique 95
Rodriquez, Perfecto 263
Rose, Dan 55, 84
Rose, Tom 84
Rosencranz, Al 84
Rosencranz, Charles 84
Rough & Ready 26
Rough Riders 256
Rubio, Luis 159
Rucker, John Anthony "Tony" 102, 103, 122
Rucker, Louis H. 146, 147
Ruellan, Father Oliver 86
Russell, Gerald "Jerry" 54
Russell, Samuel A. 134
Rynerson, William Logan 31, *35*, 36, 58

S

Sabinal, New Mexico 172
Sacramento Mountains 134
Safford, Anson P. K. 98, 99
Saint Vincent de Paul Catholic Church 141
Salvadora [Apache] 57
San Andres Mountains 808, 147, 149, 171
San Antonio, Texas 26, 41, 256
San Augustin Pass 80
San Carlos Reservation 104, 105, 107, 108, 110, 111, 113, 121, 130, 131, 134, 145, 148-150, 182, 198, 212, 237
San Diego, California 20, 21, 26, 46, 90
San Diego Crossing 18
San Diego Harbor 20
San Francisco, California 45, 90, 142, 162
San Francisco River 11, 56
San Jose, New Mexico 188
San Lorenzo, New Mexico 25, 113, 118, 219
San Luis Pass 229

San Mateo Mountains 146, 171
San Simon Valley 54
San Vicente Spring 45, 48
Sanaba [Apache] 4, 5
Sanches, Cleto 137
Sanchez [Apache] 100
Sanchez, José "Loco Joe" 262
Sanchez, Navarro 263
Santa Fe Depot 262
Santa Fe, New Mexico 1, 4, 23, 25, 35, 36, 38, 44, 46, 62, 66, 67, 75, 997, 98, 100, 114, 123, 141, 148, 210, 236, 244, 248
Santa Fe Railroad 161, 162, 181, 187, 206, 210
Santa Fe Ring 97, 99
Santa Fe Trail 9
Santa Rita del Cobre Copper Mine 6-10, 12, 17, 18, 21, 22, 24, 28, 32, 241
Santa Rita, New Mexico 27, 188 258, 262
Scarborough, George 258
Schaefer, George "Sombrero Jack" 93
Schell, Robert 54
Schutz, Aaron 144, 218
Schutz, Charles 120, 126
Schutz, Max 59, 143, 144
Scott, Owen L. 75, 77, 78, 88, 89
Scott, Thomas 201
Selman, John 258
Separ, New Mexico 238, 241, 242, 252
Shakespeare Gold and Silver Mining Co. 129
Shakespeare, New Mexico *128*, 129, 155, 156, 161, 165, 166
Shannon, Baylor 250
Shannon, Charles 75, 208
Shaw, C. A. 141
Shaw, Thomas 172
Shedd, Warren H. 80
Sheerin, John 81
Shelby, Valentine S. 85
Sheldon, Lionel A. 190
Sheridan, Jo E. 235
Sherry, H. W. 133
Sherry, Henry W. 142
Shields, Edmund G. 186, 199
Sierra Madre Mountains 36, 122, 170, 173, 198, 218, 228
Sigsbee, Charles D. 255
Silver City Beer and Ice Company 258
Silver City, Deming & Pacific Railroad 186, 187, 196, 206, 210
Silver City Dramatic Association 1140
Silver City Library Association 140
Silver City Normal School 244, 245, 248
Silver City Reduction Works 168
Silver City Waterworks 234
Silver Flat District 46, 47, 52, 69
Simon, Antoinette "Nettie" 144
Simpson, Charles 47, 68, 95
Sisters of Mercy 260
Skelly, L. A. 248
Slack, John 127, 128
Sladen, Joseph Alton 72-74
Slocum, John D. 46
Slocum's Ranch 137
Slough, John P. 35
Slough, W. M. 206, 239
Smith, Allen 214
Smith, "Bean Belly" 156
Smith, Erichus "Rackety" 209
Smith, George 127, 134
Smith, George Washington 173, 174
Smith, Henry Clay "Hank" *31*, 32
Smith, James "Jim" 94
Smith, John 181
Smith, O. K. 182
Smith, Pascal R. 184
Smith, "Six-Shooter" 163, 164
Snooks, Bill 181
Socorro, New Mexico 153, 156, 203, 204, 222
Socorro County, New Mexico 35, 116, 117
Soldier's Farewell 26
Sonora, Mexico 11, 22, 23, 27, 60, 100, 159, 182
Southern Apache Agency 105
Southern Hotel 197
Southern Pacific Railroad 98, 142, 161, 162, 180, 195, 201, 202, 209, 218, 238
Southwestern Stock Association 226, 238
Spaulding, A. J. 255
Spawn, George W. "Buffalo Bill" 104
Speck, J. M. 144
Spence, Pete 231
Spencer, Charles 207-209
St. Charles Hotel [El Paso]
St. Joseph Hospital/Sanitarium 260, *261*
St. Louis Canyon 240
Stangnon, John Baptist 141
Stanley, Henry M. 163
Stanselle's Miracle Works 232
Star Hotel 72, 86
Steelhammer, Charles 68
Steen, Enoch 17, 18
Stein's Peak 32, 121, 183
Stein's Peak Station 26, 27
Sterling, Albert D. 182
Stevens, Albert 84
Stevens, Charles E. 87, *88*
Stevens, Hiram S. 99
Stevens, Isaac James 52, 58, 75, 76, 84, 85, 88, 97, 141
Stevens, Isaac N. 46, 59, 81
Stevens, Olive Priscilla 61, *139*
Stevenson, George 258
Stewart, Kate 144
Stilwell, Frank 180
Stine, E. [Edmund] 227
Stock Exchange Corral 193
Stone, J. H. 74
Streeter, Zebina Nathaniel 72
Strong, George O. 46
Sullivan, Con P. 253
Sulphur Springs Valley 192
Sun, Charley 92, 93, 117
Sunderland, Thomas 65
Sunnyside Sanatorium 260
Swain, W. O. 201
Sweeney, M. A. 110, 111
Swilling, John "Jack" William 29

Swisshelm, John 31, 41, 42, 44, 46, 48, 53, 68, 86, 97, 184

T

Taft, William Howard 264
Taggart, Frank 203, 204, 206, 208, 209
Tait, B. W. 189
Tarbell, Homer 224, 225
Taylor, Will 30
Taylor, Zachary 14
Terrazas, Joaquín 158
Tettenborn, William Rogers "Russian Bill" 155, 165, 166
Tevis, James H. *27*, 28, 29
Thompson's Canyon 193, 194
Thorndykeson, C. M. 192
Thornton, Seth 14
Thurmond, Frank 188
Timmer House Hotel 205, 206, 226, 233, 250, 257
Timmer, Louis 86, 205
Tombstone, Arizona 168, 180, 265
Tower, George W. 47, 68
Treaty of Guadalupe Hidalgo 16, 21, 22
Tremont House Hotel 86, 144, 205, 248, 250, *253*
Tres Castillos 158
Tres Hermanas Mountains 11, 12
Treviño, Gerónimo 145
Trinfan, José 22
True, R. C. 76
Truesdell, Chauncey 84
Truesdell, Gideon 84, 86
Tucker, Dan 114, 115, 120, 124, 125, 133, 155, 159, 164-166, 180, 184-186, 201, 203, 220, 221
Tucson, Arizona 90, 145, 180, 201
Tularosa Basin 116, 147, 171

U

Upton, Lee 252
Upton, Tom 252
Utter, George H. 234, 239

V

Valverde Copper Company 184, 185
VanPatten, Eugene 136, 137
VanWagenen, G. S. 76, 118, 119
Veracruz, Mexico 15
Victorio [Apache] 11, 81, 100, 108-110, 131, 132, 134-138, 145, *146*, 147, 149-154, 158, 159, 169, 174, 200
Vienna Bakery 235
Virden, New Mexico 104

W

Wade, James Franklin 105, 108-110
Wade, Nicholas 25
Wall, Fred 92
Walley, Augusts 172
Walters, William "Bronco Bill" 24
Wardwell, K. K. 44
Warm Springs Apache 1, 3, 11, 12, 22, 53, 108, 109, 132, 136, 145, 146, 169
Warren, Elizabeth 206, 244
Warren, John A. 117
Washington [Victorio's son] 136, 154
Watts, William "Billy" 87
Webb, Abel L. 56, 59, 122
Webster, Daniel 24
Webster, J. [Professor] 83, 89
Webster, Theopholus C. 201, 209
Weeks, Elijah 31, 44, 45, 46, 53, 68
Welch, John [Thomas] 198
Wells, Fargo and Company 201, 231
West Point 15, 1146, 149, 152, 212
Western Apache 10
Western Associated Press 118
Western New Mexico University 244, 245
Wheelock, J. C. 76
White Sands 147, 171
Whitehill, Emma Sarah 84
Whitehill, Harriet "Hattie" 72, *139*
Whitehill, Harry Vance 84, 203, 225
Whitehill, Harvey Howard 46, 47, 51, 55-59, 61, 68, 75, 76, 79, *91*,92-94, 99, 103, 113, 114, 119, 130, 151, 155, 159, 164, 181, 185, 203, 224,241, 250, 252
Whitehill, Wayne 72, 75, 111, 216,225
Whitney, J. Parker 186
Wiley, W. H. 62
Willcox, Arizona 192
Williams, Bill 10
Williams, Font 43
Williams, George 133
Williams, Moses 172
Williams, Will T. 250
Wilson, Nellie 260
Wilson, Wayne 260
Wilson, Webb & Company 59
Wilson, William "Billy" 77
Winston, New Mexico 171
Winterburn, David 47
Wood, J. M. 190
Wood, Thomas Jefferson 56
Woods, Brent 174
Woods, James B. "Jim" 190, 224, 230
Woods, Ross 156
Worthington, Peter [see, Gordon, Jack] 17
Wright, Henry H. 103, 131, 132
W S Ranch 215

Y

Yankie, Joseph T. 31, 41, 44, 46, 48, 53, 56, 72, 118, 196
Yeamans, Richard 331, 41, 44, 46, 52, 53, 62, 99
Young, Ewing 10
Young, William "Parson" 130, 159
Yuma Bill 183